D1602682

NEVER CAUGHT TWICE

Jim,
I hope you
enjoy!

NEVER CAUGHT TWICE

HORSE STEALING IN
WESTERN NEBRASKA,
1850–1890

MATTHEW S. LUCKETT

University of Nebraska Press
Lincoln

Parts of this book were originally published as part of my PhD
dissertation, "Honor among Thieves: Horse Stealing, State
Building, and Culture in Lincoln County, Nebraska, 1850-1890,"
University of California, Los Angeles, 2014. Small sections were
originally published as "Cattle associations" in *Encyclopedia of Politics
of the American West* (SAGE Publications, Inc., 2013).

Publication of this volume was assisted by the Virginia Faulkner
Fund, established in memory of Virginia Faulkner, editor in chief of
the University of Nebraska Press.

Library of Congress Cataloging-in-Publication Data
Names: Luckett, Matthew S., author.
Title: Never caught twice: horse stealing in Western Nebraska,
1850–1890 / Matthew S. Luckett.
Description: Lincoln: University of Nebraska Press, [2020] |
Includes bibliographical references and index.
Identifiers: LCCN 2020007876
ISBN 9781496205148 (hardback)
ISBN 9781496223234 (epub)
ISBN 9781496223241 (mobi)
ISBN 9781496223258 (pdf)
Subjects: LCSH: Horse stealing—Nebraska—History—19th century. |
Indians of North America—Great Plains—History—19th century. |
Frontier and pioneer life—Nebraska—History—19th century.
Classification: LCC HV6661.N2 L83 2020 | DDC
364.16/2863610978290909034—dc23
LC record available at https://lccn.loc.gov/2020007876

Set in New Baskerville ITC Pro by Mikala R. Kolander.

For JoAnna,
Who always says more nice things

CONTENTS

ILLUSTRATIONS

MAPS

PREFACE

It is never a good idea to begin writing a history book without a central question in mind. Historical narratives, and scholarly monographs in particular, should answer some kind of salient query, even if it has never before been asked. Not only will the book then presumably (one hopes) answer that question, but the process of responding to it will also guide the author and their manuscript through the darkest parts of their journey. A single, coherent question can lend clarity when all the people and places and events start to blur and feel muddled. It is its own raison d'être and casus belli. The question is the signal in the noise.

This book does not have one. When my dissertation advisor suggested that I pivot from my study of rural anti–horse thief associations toward the history of horse stealing as a crime instead, I confess that no single overriding question came immediately to mind. In fact, I had a hard time keeping all the questions straight. There were just so many: Were horse thieves actually hanged? If so, why? Why do so many people today believe that horse thieves were hanged? Why were horses so important? But pinning down these questions was a challenge as well since, as I tumbled down the research rabbit hole, I began to realize that Americans intuitively understand horse stealing just as well today as they did one hundred years ago. But somehow we have collectively lost our *historical* understanding of the crime. And how does one construct a question around that?

By an "intuitive understanding," I mean that many Americans seem to have gained a latent understanding of horse stealing through popular culture. Western movies, television shows, books, and even video games like the *Red Dead Redemption* series have created a broader sense of awareness with respect to horse stealing and its severity. In addition, Americans can readily make the mental connection between horse ownership and vehicle ownership. In a nation of people who own personal automobiles or trucks, it is easy to associate a beloved twenty-first-century car with an equally admired and essential nineteenth-century horse. But these connections are not merely cultural and technological. Over the years, at conferences and workshops and even in my classrooms, several people have come up to me after learning what I am working on to say that their great-great-grandpa or uncle or some other ancestor was hanged for horse stealing. While I have no reason to doubt the veracity of any of their individual stories, the sheer number of times this has happened has made me wonder whether everyone in the western United States actually does have a horse thief hanging from their family tree or if some weird quirk of our collective historical memory causes us to believe such a thing. Even this question, however, is difficult to answer. The history of horse stealing is, in many ways, the story of ghosts, shadows, and rumors.

In an effort to dodge having to answer a single question, I have done the next best thing: I wrote a narrative that tells the history of horse stealing in western Nebraska. It is the story of a category of crime, the history of a means of exchange, and a powerful reminder of the durability of historical memory. Horse raiding among the Plains Indians quickly evolved into a critical adjunct to the nomadic lifestyle adopted by those tribes that fully embraced equestrian hunting, fighting, traveling, and acquiring wealth. It provided easy access to mounts, social mobility, and food security just as surely as it robbed those tribes on the losing end of subsistence and self-defense. Once whites began to travel through, and then later reside on, the Great Plains, large-herd managers began accumulating power and wealth more quickly than their less-well-off neighbors. As tensions between

Indians and whites mounted, the animals themselves became contested resources. Several plains conflicts started with the theft of a strayed horse or cow, and by the time the Great Sioux War broke out, both sides understood that healthy horse herds were their opponent's Achilles' heel on the plains. After the Plains Indians were sent to live in reservations, white horse-stealing gangs siphoned away reservation horses before turning their attention to their white neighbors. By 1890 fewer thieves were stealing horses as increasingly prosperous locals bought better, smaller, and more easily fenced items to steal. But those homesteaders and other small-herd managers continued to fear horse thieves—with good reason. Spoken myths became printed legends, and old fears about horse thieves continued to haunt Nebraskans even as passing Model Ts kicked up clouds of dust along Nebraska's desiccated, unpaved roadways.

As this narrative began to take shape, I started to better understand what horse stealing, in all its various and sundry forms, meant. And the emerging through line is grotesque: horse stealing was both inevitable and calamitous. Horse theft was to horses what climate change and drunk driving are to automobiles. It was the price humanity paid for the miracle of the horse, a creature that can liberate its riders from both the slow pace of walking and the linearity of steamboats and locomotives. Theft was an almost inevitable by-product of the horse's superior utility: horses and ponies can carry people, pull draft, and otherwise lend themselves to countless applications, and thus farmers, homesteaders, ranchers, freighters, nomadic hunters, and the U.S. Army alike all relied on them. But while pollution, traffic congestion, highway safety, and impaired or distracted driving are all understood today both as large-scale problems that stem from automobile usage and as separate issues that do not require the elimination of all cars to be solved, horse stealing is typically associated with bad (and perhaps disposable) humans, as opposed to eminently useful and necessary horses.

Horse stealing and horse thieves are often seen in the starkest terms and the dimmest light. In one recent study of horse stealing, perhaps the most extensive and summative history of the subject to date, author and criminologist John K. Burchill titled his fifth chapter "The Thieves," immediately followed by "The Good Guys," the section covering law enforcement. These labels state the obvious: even scholars often have difficulty resisting the urge to categorize horse thieves as "evil" (or at least as not "good"). However, one need only look at the bookshelves of a public library or museum gift shop to get a sense of how western criminals are portrayed—either as characters in a fast-moving, action-packed story or as sinister villains in a frontier tableau. The titles tell the story: *Outlaw Tales of Nebraska; Lynchings, Legends, and Lawlessness* (about Sidney, Nebraska); and *Bullets, Badges, and Bridles* (by Burchill) all suggest an emphasis on sensationalized frontier history.[1] Perhaps this book's own title does as well. But while each book listed is both factual and fun to read, they all fail to explain why horse thieves stole horses. When reading popular histories of frontier crime, one comes away with a sense that little seems to have changed since the late nineteenth century: horse thieves continue to be desperadoes, outlaws, brigands, and rascals. These brands require no elaboration.

Yet nothing is quite that simple. What makes a rascal a "rascal?" Is it in their DNA? Did they play violent games as children or skip school a lot? Fortunately, while horse thieves remain elusive, the rationale behind their crimes is not: horse stealing lay at the confluence of a variety of social, economic, cultural, and even moral factors that made having horses stolen more likely while mitigating, if not justifying, their seizure. Seasonal unemployment, high prices, large remudas on major ranches, a total lack of alternative transportation options, pervasive alcoholism, emotional immaturity among those living on the range, and jealousy were just some of the reasons that drove Nebraskans to steal horses. Some horse thieves believed they were justified in taking mounts. A few probably were. Most thieves were not members of formally constituted gangs, with secret ciphers, hidden hideouts, and horse relay stations, although local bosses could persuade or compel less powerful associates to steal or cover for other thieves. For a crime whose historical reputation is as egregious as that of horse stealing, it is essential to try to get at the whole story before simply subscribing to puffed-up anecdotes and blustery newspaper articles and to try to learn the reasons why anyone would literally risk their neck to take someone else's animal.

The baggage behind the horse thief label also forces historians into contortions when dealing with the subject of Plains Indian horse raiding. Surely the Lakotas and Cheyennes were not all "outlaws" for stealing horses, right? Of course not. Yet by walling off the two categories of stealing from one another, or by vigorously explaining away one over the other, we do little justice to the overall problem of horse theft across the plains and even less to those victims of horse stealing and raiding within indigenous communities who experienced and suffered the crime's consequences even more acutely than homesteading whites. We lose sight of the complexity of horse raiding, which was as much a source of tribal wealth, pride, and folklore as it was a critical if flawed mechanism for protecting, growing, and replenishing horse herds. Just as violence became, according to historian Ned Blackhawk, "a necessary form of social, economic, and political survival [among Indian peoples], a practice that beleaguered as much as benefited," in time horse raiding offered mixed blessings to Plains Indian nations as well.[2]

Overall, horse stealing was not a problem because it was evil or because horses were important. It was a problem because horse theft destabilized communities, institutions, nations, diplomatic relationships, and cross-cultural exchange throughout the plains. Thieves stole thousands of horses across western Nebraska between 1850 and 1890, but that was just the beginning. Horse jealousies within Indian bands created new and novel conflicts over private property that sometimes culminated in homicide. Horse raiding added higher stakes to and increased violence within intertribal conflict. Horse and animal theft from emigrants deepened suspicions between the United States Army and the Plains Indians and in a few cases sparked much larger confrontations.[3] Horse seizures came to dominate much of the tactical action and strategic thinking of the Plains Indian

Wars. White horse-stealing gangs taxed frontier law enforcement and disrupted local economies in which the horse was both the means of production and the greatest source of local capital. In time Nebraskans and other horse owners throughout the Great Plains desperately turned to literal and rhetorical violence in hopes of eliminating the threat. Horse stealing might not have brought Plains Indians and whites together, but it did force them to contend with many of the same problems.

This project began in the summer of 2010, when the Autry Museum of the American West awarded me a summer research grant to explore the John Bratt Ranching Collection. Bratt's extensive notes and tabulations chronicled several years of horse and livestock purchases, sales, trades, births, deaths, brands, and of course thefts. This data, plus his autobiography and his voluminous written correspondence stored at the Nebraska State Historical Society, became in many ways the nucleus for this book. It is rare to find a ranch (particularly a large one) with such a rich combination of meticulous record keeping and, later, self-mythologizing. This focus on Bratt soon grew to include Lincoln County, and my task in that regard was aided tremendously by Mark Ellis's masterful *Law and Order in Buffalo Bill's County* (and Mark Ellis himself), which lays out Lincoln County's legal and criminal history. To some degree I retraced his steps, traveling to the Lincoln County Courthouse in North Platte and to the Nebraska State Historical Society in order to review the district and county court records, respectively. But Fort McPherson's location near North Platte gave me the ability to extend my horse-stealing investigation even further back in time by investigating the extent and impact of horse raiding in Lincoln County and the Platte Valley in general, while Bratt and his wider ranching world helped me move beyond the legal interplay between horse thieves, sheriffs, and judges and take a broader, cross-cultural, and decidedly more transactional view of the horse-stealing phenomenon for my dissertation.

For this book I decided to cast a wider net and reframe my original thematic discussion as an intercultural narrative of horse stealing. Since "western Nebraska" is much larger than Lincoln County, I attempted to capture this vast expanse by selecting several places for specific analysis: Fort McPherson and Lincoln County, Sidney Barracks and Cheyenne County, Camp Sheridan and Dawes County (Camp Sheridan is technically outside of Dawes County limits but, for reasons that will be later discussed, provides a more compelling pairing), Grant County, and the Overland Trail from Fort Kearny to Scotts Bluff. This approach allows me to replicate the strategy I used in my dissertation by focusing on specific forts (and the many records they generated) as well as the civilian jurisdictions that grew up around them. Together they offer geographic and chronological diversity, allowing the narrative to jump from horses stolen from emigrants camping underneath the stars near Chimney Rock to criminal ranchers in the Sandhills seizing their neighbor's animals to Lakota raiders seeking shelter within the Pine Ridge after a successful horse-stealing expedition.

Yet I have tried not to hew too closely to this design. I include several stories that fall outside these designated zones, not merely because they are illuminating and interesting but also because this aspires to be a story about western Nebraska writ large and not a heavily parameterized social science study. This is particularly important with respect to any credible discussion of horse raiding across the region. For instance, Northern Cheyenne warrior and horse raider Wooden Leg (who, like John Bratt and Doc Middleton, is one of the principal characters in the pages that follow) spent most of his time outside of Nebraska. However, he did visit the area frequently, and in 1877 he and several companions surrendered themselves to United States authorities at Fort Robinson, near Crawford. What emerges, I hope, is a curated yet representative history of a crime whose true extent and impact is almost impossible to fathom, let alone quantify. This book merely scratches the surface.

The chapters are organized in a narrative fashion. The introduction maps Nebraska's historical geography by breaking it into several distinct regions. It explains how the region's aridity and environment affect human habitation, hunting, ranching, and agriculture. It also summarizes the importance of horses, both generally and with specific reference to western Nebraska's unique challenges for nomads and settlers alike. The first chapter covers the origins and history of intertribal raiding as well as the effects of horse theft on Indian-white relations along the Overland Trail. Chapter 2 explores the wider conflicts that broke out along the Overland and Bozeman Trails following the Sand Creek Massacre in 1864. It also examines white participation in the regional theft culture. The third chapter tells the story of how horse raiding continued to fracture and complicate relations between Indians, soldiers, and officers. These tensions culminated in the Great Sioux War, which itself hinged on the degree to which both sides were able to keep their horse herds intact while also seizing their enemy's horse reserves. Chapter 4 takes a closer look at white horse-stealing and cattle-rustling gangs, including Doc Middleton's, and their unique and powerful impact on regional legal and community development. Chapter 5 explores horse stealing as a crime in settler communities such as North Platte, Sidney, and Chadron and compares its effects on farms and ranches. It also illustrates some of the problems western Nebraskans faced when investigating, apprehending, and prosecuting horse thieves, which led to a variety of extralegal efforts to curb the practice. Chapter 6 chronicles how western Nebraskans responded to horse stealing with vigilante violence and rhetoric, before describing how horse stealing ceased to be an important crime. The rest of the chapter shows how twentieth-century historians, writers, producers, and surviving pioneers made horse thieves into anonymous bogeymen starring in a modern-day parable—anonymous, of course, with the notable exception of any given reader's great-great-grandfather.

On a final note, there are few templates for how scholars should write the history of a statutory crime. The twentieth and twenty-first centuries offer a few analogues, such as the war on drugs and recent legal struggles over domestic and global intellectual property protection in an increasingly digital world. But marijuana and Metallica bootlegs both lack the horse's singular cultural, economic, and even interpersonal importance. Moreover, it is easier to visualize the fault lines surrounding these crimes because they are part of our lived reality. Nowadays, most people enjoy horses from afar: they watch them on television, admire the animals while passing them on a drive or bike ride, or place bets on them while sipping mint juleps at the Kentucky Derby. Therefore, this book will do three things: illustrate how crimes themselves can become important historical subjects in their own right, show that an understanding of both horse stealing and its destabilizing effects are essential to a broader understanding of the history of the American West, and help articulate a better sense of why modern Americans struggle trying to reconcile their appreciation of and support for law enforcement with their own intuitive understanding of its inherent limitations. Perhaps a stronger understanding of horse stealing will not only help us understand why our great-great-grandparents were hanged but also why that fact does not seem to bother many of us.

Maybe I had a question in mind all along.

ACKNOWLEDGMENTS

Historians are not in the habit of putting half a dozen names or more on the cover of a paper or manuscript, but that does not mean history writing is not a collaborative enterprise. From the archivists and teachers who show us the way to the colleagues and students who show us the error of our ways, many people touch, influence, and at critical moments rescue book manuscripts. Each monograph is in so many ways the product of a team effort, even though any and all mistakes in this book are mine alone. I would like to start this section by giving props to my students at the University of California–Los Angeles; California State University, Dominguez Hills; California State University, Sacramento; and Sierra College. Thank you for listening to me drone on about horse cultures over the years and for always motivating me to be better. Special thanks go out to my Humanities External Master's Degree program students over the years. I learned a great deal from you all.

I can't thank my students without also thanking the many teachers and professors who challenged and inspired me, from high school to grad school. This list includes, but is not limited to, Judy Rethwisch, John Pessina, Cheryl Forbes Horst Ward, David Cameron, Dalton Curtis, Frank Nickell, James Marten, Kristen Foster, Steven Avella, Michael Meranze, Kelly Lytle Hernandez, Ben Madley, and Bill Deverell. Thank you for everything and for putting up with me!

I wish to express my deep gratitude to all the people who have read and commented on this manuscript. Chuck Rankin at the University of Oklahoma Press was kind enough to send my unrevised dissertation out for review in 2014 while the ink was still drying on the signature page. Although I was not yet able to commit to the vast amount of work it would ultimately take to recast and reframe my manuscript, my reader reports (while sobering) provided me with an invaluable roadmap for turning my last student paper into my first book. I greatly appreciate both of them. Emily Bowles, Elizabeth Gratch, Erik Greenberg, Carl Hanson, Molly Holz, and Randall Williams all read this manuscript at different points during its development, and I appreciate their thoughtful comments and suggestions. The same goes for my reading group buddies, Xochitl Flores-Marcial and Citlali Sosa, who always pushed me in the right direction. Many thanks go out to the docents at the Autry Museum of the American West, who read my manuscript for their October 2018 meeting and invited me down to Los Angeles to talk about it. Their comments were incredibly helpful. I am also indebted to Will Bagley, Mark Ellis, and Mark Scherer for their trenchant and thorough readings as well as their thoughtful feedback and to Bridget Barry, Joeth Zucco, and everyone else at the University of Nebraska Press for their tireless support and assistance. Joan Waugh has been a champion for both me and my work since the beginning, and her encouragement and wisdom over the years has helped keep me going. And words cannot even begin to express my deep appreciation and thanks for Stephen Aron's continued guidance, support, and sage advice.

I am very grateful for the research support I have received over the past several years. The College of Arts and Humanities, the College of Extended and International Education, and the Provost's Office at California State University, Dominguez Hills, all awarded me critical travel grants for ongoing research in Nebraska and Washington DC. Furthermore, this project simply would not have been possible without the help I received from Mitch Avila, Tim Caron, Kim McNutt, and Lynda Wilson. Danielle Ireland in Washington DC made my always-too-short visits to the National Archives more productive and much more fun, and Andrea Faling never hesitated to help me navigate the Nebraska State Historical Society's voluminous and wide-ranging archives. Also, this project would not have been possible without the accommodation and hospitality provided by the hardworking county and district court clerks in Cheyenne, Dawes, Grant, and Lincoln Counties. Many thanks to all of you.

Special thanks go to Paris Fisher of Paris Fisher Auto Sales in Chadron, Nebraska, for coming to unlock my rental car at the Chadron Airport when I visited the city in October 2018. I had accidentally locked my luggage inside the trunk after arriving about forty-five minutes before my flight back to Denver, which was unfortunately scheduled for 7:05 a.m. Paris jumped out of bed and sped over to the airport in time to bail me out. Paris Fisher Auto Sales is the place to call if you ever decide to fly to northwestern Nebraska (it is worth the trip and is only an hour south of—and often cheaper than flying directly to—Rapid City, South Dakota) and need a rental car. Just be sure to remember to take your keys when you exit the vehicle.

Last but not least, I have to thank my friends and family for their support over the past several years as I've lurched my way toward finishing this book. Special shout-outs go to Steve and Phyllis Luckett, for never doubting me for a minute; Richard and Catherine Luckett, for all of your help; Elmer Luckett and Lettie Smith, who are no longer here to read this but are both responsible for inspiring me to become a historian; Madeline Thompson, David Luckett, Helen Wall, Margaret Bowles, Michael Wall, and Ron Dicken, for everything that you do; Ricardo Garcia, who knows how to mix academic conversations with beers and karaoke; and Jeremy Wolfe, for always making my trips to the plains memorable. And to JoAnna and Clementine, I can only express my gratitude to you both for your constant encouragement, patience, and support. And now that it's done . . . we're going to Disneyland!

NEVER CAUGHT TWICE

Introduction

Maps, Meridians, and Mounts in Western Nebraska

There are many false ideas prevalent relative to the state of Nebraska
in general, and especially with reference to the Western part of
the state. To correct these mistaken ideas, we have given proof and
testimony sufficient to convince the unprejudiced mind that
Western Nebraska is, at least, not a desert.

—*Description of the Bay State Livestock Co.'s*
Lands in Cheyenne County, Nebraska

Nothing does more for the inside of a man
than the outside of a horse.

—WILL ROGERS

Nebraska is probably one of the least understood and most geographically mischaracterized states in the Union. Americans from other parts of the country often imagine it as the location for some of Alexander Payne's most acclaimed movies or as an interminably long and boring stretch of driving between the Rocky Mountains and the Missouri River. While people are certainly entitled to decide for themselves whether they prefer the plains to mountains, forests, swamps, or a sun-soaked beach, it is unfortunate that for so many travelers their only exposure to Nebraska is gained while traveling on a four-lane divided highway that follows perhaps the flattest, least-interesting watercourse on the continent. Few venture more than a few minutes north or south of I-80. If they did, they would find rich, riparian habitats and topographical variety. Even fewer travel far enough to see the ravines, forests, and buttes that split, checker, and crumple the landscape closer to the South Dakota border. And only a handful of visitors realize how it is precisely the Platte River valley's flatness and torpidity that made it the easiest, most economical, and most heavily traveled route from east to west throughout the nineteenth century.

If any group is in a position to confound geographical expectations of Nebraska, it would be the Western Nebraska Tourism Coalition. In an effort to highlight this ostensibly obscure and difficult-to-reach area, the Coalition maintains a well-developed website and offers a free guidebook to potential visitors. The group has also divided western Nebraska into four distinct subregions, each with a different set of attractions to offer tourists, in order to help interested persons prioritize their travel and make sense of this vast space. These subregional definitions are divided along historical-geographic lines, and the logics underlying each region's name and formation lend themselves readily to our discussion. In the interest of describing the region's natural landscape while also drawing attention to its geographical and historical drama, we will borrow from the Coalition's *Journey to Western Nebraska* guide when describing the four subregions, which are (from south to north) the Wild West, Trails West, Sandhills and Scenic Rivers, and Pine Ridge (map 1).[1]

The first of these regions, the Wild West, refers to the aforementioned Platte River valley. The term itself—though it justifiably draws attention to the popular historical interest of a region that may otherwise be seen as forgettable by today's travelers en route to the Rockies, the Black Hills, or eastern cities—is both the most amorphous and the most misleading. On the one hand, the Wild West region (which primarily encompasses Lincoln, Keith, Cheyenne, Perkins, Deuel, and Kimball Counties today) has a visible historical memory of frontier violence.[2] There are "Boot Hill" monuments in Sidney and Ogallala, referring to the burial grounds of gunfighters who "died with their boots on"; the Union Pacific Railroad tracks and their

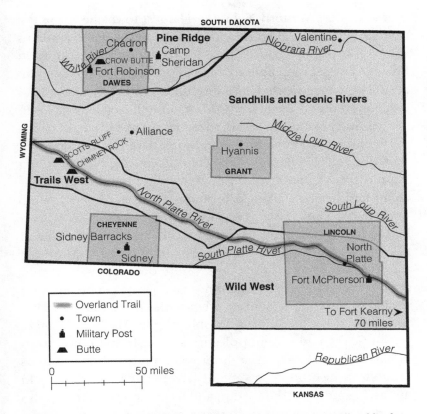

Map 1. Map of western Nebraska, including the four regions outlined by the Western Nebraska Travel Coalition, the four counties of emphasis, and major landmarks and towns. Map created by the author.

legacy of railroad worker crime and violence; and a historical park established in the memory of Brigadier General William S. Harney's 1855 massacre of eighty-six Brulé men, women, and children near Ash Hollow. Frontier violence also pervades much of the region's local historical literature and lore, adding a morbid psychological dimension to a mostly level physical landscape. On the other hand, although Sidney and Ogallala had a few "wild and wooly" years, these cities (as well as North Platte) along the Platte River valley settled down fairly quickly after the Union Pacific Railroad opened to transcontinental traffic in 1869. Western Nebraska's largest towns lie along the railroad, to which I-80 is roughly parallel today. It also contains the largest primary source base for data and information on horse stealing, owing both to the region's relative (and comparatively well-documented) urbanization and the presence of all three ingredients necessary for horse theft: horses, folks who owned horses, and thieves who wanted to take them.

When English immigrant John Bratt arrived in this region in 1866, the still-wild nature of the country appealed to the young man. After completing a seven-year apprenticeship as a merchant and briefly starting a business, Bratt resolved to immigrate to the United States in 1864 in spite of the Civil War. "I had made up my mind to close out my business as soon as I reached the age of twenty-one and go to America, that land of the free and home of the brave, where one man was as good as any other and where I would not be obliged to bow and doff my hat to the country squire and give him three fourths of the road," Bratt recalled in his autobiography, *Trails of Yesterday*. "[America's] large, red apples that came to my home town in barrels had made a great impression on my child mind, its republican institutions, its mighty rivers, broad prairies, gold mines, its undiscovered wealth, and its great possibilities! Who would not want to emigrate to such a great and glorious country and get out of the ruts trodden by my forefathers generations ago?"[3] Bratt's journey to Nebraska was eventful: after attending President Abraham Lincoln's funeral, he lost almost all of his possessions during a terrible storm while at sea, en route to New Orleans, and later began inching his way northward up the Mississippi River while working as a laborer. After arriving in the Platte Valley, his enthusiasm, maturity, and business training served him well. He soon found work as a freighter in the region and went on to start multiple businesses, build a home, and raise a family on his sprawling 125,000-acre ranch in western Lincoln County.

Although Bratt decided to stay in the Platte Valley, thousands of others continued moving west through the region while on their way to California, Oregon, Colorado, and Montana. The

4

Trails West area diverges from the Wild West near Ogallala, following and enveloping the North Platte River valley west from Kingsley Dam and up to the Wyoming border. The Overland Trail followed this route, veering away from the Union Pacific Railroad near the city of North Platte and following its namesake river northwestward, while the railroad continued along the South Platte until it reached Julesburg. Trails West is perhaps best known for its physical landmarks, especially Chimney Rock. This geographic signpost, familiar to anyone who has played the *Oregon Trail* computer game, was also well known to emigrants. The North Platte cut a dramatic relief through the area, producing Chimney Rock, Courthouse Rock, Scotts Bluff, and a long series of cliffs along the south side of the river. Though several large towns exist along the route today (including the Panhandle's largest community, Scottsbluff), before 1890 the area was most important as either a highway for westbound emigrants or, less charitably, as a physical hindrance to northbound military traffic moving toward Fort Robinson and miner caravans scurrying toward the Black Hills. Most of the horses stolen in this region prior to 1890 were taken from migrants traveling along the trail, from army detachments, or from Plains Indian herds. The North Platte Valley was a favored camping and hunting ground among the Oglala Lakota through the mid-1870s, but Scotts Bluff County was not established until 1888 (late in the period of this study), and the differently spelled city of Scottsbluff filed for incorporation in 1900.[4] Some homesteaders established farms along the river, but the bluffs and escarpments on either side of the stream are uninviting settings for agriculture.

Unlike the Trails West region, the Sandhills and Scenic Rivers area had more settlers, many more horses, and quite a few thieves. This subregional area conflates two ecologically, geographically, and culturally dissimilar environments that nonetheless were both conducive to horse theft. For one, the Sandhills do not require a marketing term or slogan to set them apart: Plains Indians, the military, ranchers, homesteaders, and other residents of western Nebraska understood them to be a separate region because of their topography. Even today, curious visitors to North Platte or Ogallala need only drive north for thirty minutes before they find themselves in the midst of seemingly endless sandy hills, some of which are over one hundred feet in height. The topsoil throughout this biome is so thin that only grasses can reliably grow in many places. This verticality, uncharacteristic of the Great Plains and more reminiscent of a much drier Ozarks or Appalachian foothills environment, contributed to the Sandhills area's historically terrible compatibility to unaided agriculture.

After a half-century of failed agricultural experiments, the 1904 Kinkaid Act attempted to rectify the problem by making 640-acre sections available for public entry—quadruple the amount available under the provisions of the original 1862 Homestead Act. However, even these large tracts were not enough to reestablish the Sandhills zone as a breadbasket or cornbelt. Instead, ranchers claimed additional lands for themselves, further entrenching the region's reputation for grazing. Of course, the lack of rainfall and arable land in the Sandhills never dampened the spirits, at least initially, of those who tried plowing fields there. Many homesteaders tried and failed to carve out homes and businesses from the land. Those who succeeded—like Mari Sandoz's father in *Old Jules* or the fictional Bergman clan in Willa Cather's *O Pioneers!*—fought an uphill battle in more ways than one against the sand dunes' unforgiving environment and prospered only after surviving long enough to buy out their less-successful neighbors who abandoned their stakes and relocated.

Nestled amid and between the Sandhills are the "scenic rivers" formed by a handful of west-to-east-running rivers north of the Platte Valley. With mostly year-round water flow, these streams attracted ranchers and homesteaders. The primary rivers fitting this description, and thus attracting the most settlement, are (from north to south) the White, Niobrara, North Loup, Middle Loup, Dismal, and South Loup Rivers. The Platte River lies to the south of these waterways. South of the Platte, the Republican River cut a large swath of settlement through southeastern Nebraska and northern Kansas. Although excluded from the

Coalition's service area and more often historically associated with Kansas, through which most of its length is located, the Republican River region mirrors many of the historical trend lines found farther north. Although few large towns lie along these streams, those that do include Valentine (on the Niobrara) and McCook (along the Republican).

Horse thieves thrived in both the Sandhills region and the river valleys. The latter contained many farms and ranches with horses, and the former offered many places to hide. During the winter of 1878–79, Little Wolf's escaped band of Northern Cheyenne encamped in the Sandhills, safe from view of the United States Army, whose men frantically scoured western Nebraska and the northern plains in an attempt to find them. Not surprisingly, the topographically challenging landscape that made their escape possible also helped shelter horse thieves and army deserters over the years. "Law [in the region] was remote," Sandoz wrote while describing the region in *Old Jules,* and "the broken hills or the Sioux blanket offered safe retreat for horse thief, road agent, and killer." Along the "scenic" rivers, thick stands of cottonwoods, ash, elms, and other riparian trees may be why some of the state's largest vigilante organizations were established in the surrounding valleys. The Niobrara River valley alone harbored at least three organized vigilante outfits.[5]

The most severe—and dangerous—horse stealing and raiding occurred in the Pine Ridge area. This northernmost subregion hugs the state's northern border with South Dakota and is closest to the Pine Ridge and Rosebud Reservations. Its namesake geographic feature, Pine Ridge, is a hilly, one hundred–mile–long escarpment between the Niobrara and White River basins. Ponderosa pines carpet these bluffs and buttes, offering a preview of the Black Hills for those traveling north toward Rapid City and a welcome refuge for horse thieves and wildlife alike. Camps Robinson and Sheridan were both located in the Pine Ridge region, as were the towns of Chadron and Crawford. The Brulé Lakota frequently visited this country, and the Red Cloud and Spotted Tail Agencies would later be located in the area. Because of this, the Pine Ridge was a no-man's-land for

Fig. 1. Farm located in the Platte Valley near Maxwell, Nebraska, 2011. The eastern half of Lincoln County has more farms and more productive agriculture. Photo by the author.

horse owners: raiding parties from the north traveled south to cut horses from white and Pawnee herds, while rustling gangs and ranchers from the south often slipped into the reservation to steal Lakota ponies. The hills themselves offered cover and concealment, with lots of nooks for hiding stolen animals. Camp Sheridan's officers and soldiers—often overlooked by historians because the Brulés who were encamped at the nearby Spotted Tail Agency were mostly friendly with the whites during the Great Sioux War, thus making the outpost peripheral to that conflict—dealt constantly with horse thieves, trespassing whites, Lakota raiding parties, and other transgressors in the region.

With all these differences, it is easy to underestimate the characteristics that these regions have in common. Perhaps the most significant shared trait, and one whose presence itself has been cited endlessly by contemporaries and historians alike, is western Nebraska's aridity. The 100th meridian, which parallels the twenty-inch annual precipitation isohyet line made famous by John Wesley Powell in 1878, slices northward across Nebraska just east of Lincoln County, through Cozad. Powell pointed out that the meridian effectively and more or less accurately segregated the drier western third of the state from the remainder, which was at least wet enough to sustain unirrigated agriculture. Given that the lands west of the meridian were too dry for traditional homesteading, this climatological shift profoundly shaped the history of western Nebraska.[6] Although the existence of the line was not always clear to those who crossed it, a careful observer following the Wild West tourist itinerary along Interstate 80 today will notice the stark geographic and ecological differences between the eastern part of Lincoln County—which contains farms, large stands of cottonwood and box elder trees, and fields full of crops—and the western half, which has fewer trees, more tallgrass prairie, and much less agriculture (figs. 1 and 2).

These geographical and environmental differences affected how people lived their lives. For instance, they influenced how American Indians on either side of the 100th meridian lived. Pawnees, like those tribes farther to the east, had better access to water than groups on the high plains to the west. However, since the Pawnees straddled this line, their system of subsistence evolved to encompass the advantages of each region, namely reliable agriculture and mounted bison hunting. The Brulés, by contrast, spurned agriculture in favor of hunting game in the Sandhills. While the eastern prairies offered different subsistence opportunities to the Pawnees, who chose to utilize both wild game and agriculture, the plains promised freedom, mobility, strength, and a new way of life for the Lakota, who had lived farther east only a few generations earlier.[7] Horses made this change possible since the Lakota used the vast grasslands on the plains as biofuel for horses.[8]

The 100th meridian also influenced agriculture and ranching. East of the isohyet, land values were usually prohibitively high for raising livestock, which require vast acreage or large quantities of feed to be profitable. In effect the meridian repre-

Fig. 2. Cattle grazing on a sandhill in northwestern Lincoln County, 2011. Compared to the eastern half of the county, this section is mostly treeless. Photo by the author.

sented the border between the fourth and fifth zones in Johann Heinrich Von Thünen's model of land use, in which the farther one went from the city, the more diffuse land use became.[9] But since the line between successful and calamitous homesteading was hardly clear to those whose optimism compelled them to accept cheap land on either side of the meridian, prospective farmers paid little heed. Some believed that rain would "follow the plow," and countless booster pamphlets explained the "science" behind the reasoning. Other real estate and railroad companies, which always had land to sell, trumped up the success of early efforts to farm the region. The Bay State Livestock Company informed readers that the country west of Kearney was "rich; their farmers are prosperous and happy; their towns are growing into cities; their agricultural products are bursting the cars on their march eastward to feed the hungry poor— [yet] no system of irrigation has yet been adopted."[10]

The meridian represented something more palpable than an imaginary line. By signifying the point at which water ceased to be a reliable resource, both the line and the arid zone it demarcated on the map had dramatic consequences on the region's development.[11] Laborers, for instance, had fewer options as they went west. In eastern Nebraska young men had more opportunities for employment than they did in places like North Platte. Ranch work was seasonal—there was little demand for cowboy labor during the winter, when most activities on the stockyard ground to a halt. The year-round jobs that did exist in ranching areas were primarily in service industries that existed to serve the cowboys themselves. As a result, ranch hands had to make their wages last throughout the year. When they could not, some turned to stealing.[12] Homesteaders faced even longer odds. Although prospective farmers fared better in the eastern and central thirds of the state, western Nebraska homesteaders contended with intermittent rainfall, unscrupulous ranchers, frontier warfare with American Indians, locust invasions, harsh winters, exorbitant freight prices, sandy soil, poor drainage, and severe isolation. It is no wonder that Mari Sandoz's father in *Old Jules* appears, at first glance, to be such a brutal figure. He did not survive on the plains because he was persistent; he survived because he was stubborn.

The meridian's tangibility caused other lines to blur. One was the line that separated fairness from unfairness—in other words, where is the "line" when one goes "over the line?" Fairness as a historical subject requires that historians proceed with an overabundance of caution. A presentist bias may be unavoidable, especially when questions of property "fairness" in the settlement of the West address the decidedly unfair process of American Indian land dispossession. It is important to try to reconstruct the thought processes that justified land seizures while also demanding that private property be protected. The same moral, legal, and economic apparatus that wrested control of the land and other forms of property from American Indians not only legitimized the subsequent ownership of that land by Euro-American parties; it also helped negotiate tort claims, disputes over fresh water supplies, probate actions, and other conflicts in a "civil" manner. These structures were all too important on the plains, where failure did not mean what it meant in Illinois or Ohio but something far worse.

These perceptions of unfairness are well documented. In his landmark study of property along the Overland Trail, historian John Philip Reid argued that legal behaviorism—norms of conduct dictated by adherence to the law—prompted emigrants to adhere to eastern protocols governing the ownership and exchange of private property, even in the face of starvation, dehydration, and other mortal perils for want of necessary provisions. When addressing horse raiding by American Indians along the trail, however, Reid refused to use the word *stealing* when describing the appropriation of Euro-American-owned livestock by American Indians. He pointed out that just as raiders felt justified in culling horses from emigrant herds, the migrants similarly justified their own "right" to graze their horses on prairie grass, lead them to drink fresh water from non-alkali sources, and hunt animals along the trail, in spite of the raiders' simultaneous reliance on these things.[13] Each group was depriving the other of essential resources while yet viewing their own actions, as well as those of others, through the lens of fairness. Reid's thesis about property ownership along the Overland Trail is significant because the Overland Trail represents the farthest point for most migrants away from "the law." Migrants left well-established law areas in the East, and upon reaching Utah, Oregon, or California, they joined communities with nascent but functional law enforcement authorities of their own. The Overland Trail thus represented the migrants' best opportunity to rob, cheat, and steal with impunity. But most migrants continued to obey the law in spite of its absence.

More broadly, cultural misunderstandings over property rights profoundly shaped how Euro-Americans responded to American Indian hegemony on the plains and beyond. Specifically, whites did not understand how and why Plains Indians used and claimed land, horses, and property. But there were similarities as well, especially with regard to hunting and water rights.

Homesteaders, cowboys, and other Euro-Americans who did not own vast tracts of land often agreed with American Indians that wildlife and water on undeveloped lands should be fair game throughout the West.[14]

This confusion, as well as the ecological and cultural constraints imposed on persons on either side of the meridian, made it nearly impossible to build a functioning state apparatus in western Nebraska. To be sure, the state of Nebraska and its constituent county and municipal governments were all created in relative peace. Outside of those areas controlled by the Lakota or the Northern Cheyenne, there were no competing governments or disputes over who had civilian authority. However, the lines we have described made western Nebraska at least partially ungovernable for the first decade of its existence, and its residents continued to undermine law enforcement into the 1880s and beyond. In addition to representing the point at which equestrian American Indian resistance against white hegemony threatened to stop westward expansion in its tracks, the line marked the tipping point for both ranchers and farmers in the region.

Ranchers and farmers sought different things from the state. Ranchers needed to protect the massive amounts of land and animal capital required for their businesses, and they wanted the state to mediate the many conflicts that arose over water and grazing rights. They also had the money and the influence to bend the state toward its own prerogative. Farmers, on the other hand, demanded egalitarian governance. They did not have as much as the ranchers in terms of property and influence, so they needed to protect all of what they had, including their land and their livestock. But those county jurisdictions that straddled the margins of both prairies and plains could only accommodate the demands of one of these groups. That conflict of interest is why John Bratt and other local cattlemen moved to establish a rancher-centered government around several of their ranches once the area around North Platte began filling up with farmers in 1872. Calling their new stock-raising protectorate "Frontier County," they even named their one-horse county seat "Stockville" in hopes of dissuading home-steaders from claiming land there. With no consensus on the issue of fairness vis-à-vis property rights until the 1880s, it is no wonder that so many people west of the meridian took actions that blurred the line between theft and legitimate acquisition.

It may come as little surprise that horses were especially subject to these ambiguities. Horses were the most valuable possessions on the plains, apart from the land itself—and even then, only some of the time. Horses transcended culture—whites and natives, ranchers and farmers, travelers and settlers, itinerant preachers and confidence men, all needed them to get where they were going. But for a few major towns connected by a far-flung transportation network of trails and railroads, geographically vast and sparsely populated western Nebraska posed a special set of challenges for anyone who needed to cross the region's deceptively difficult terrain, treacherous streams, and long distances. Horses gave humans the ability to travel farther and faster, plow their fields more efficiently, generate power, and make war. They were often worth more than stocks and were much easier to sell. In a pinch they could even be used as food. In short, horses were indispensable, and the horse economy connected the fortunes of the cattle king and the Brulé hunter on the high plains with those of the homesteader. Horse theft's ubiquity in this time and place is as much a reflection of the nineteenth-century Nebraskan's dependence on horses as it is of any cultural permissiveness toward stealing.

The horse's importance in these arid spaces began with the humans who first imported them for use in the region. Historians and anthropologists who study the Plains Indians have long been interested in American Indians' rich and often complicated relationship to horses. These scholars pioneered a variety of approaches to the study of horses and their economic, social, cultural, and military value within Plains Indian communities.[15] This overall equine value, also known as "horse wealth," has been used to explore and evaluate the role that horses played within these societies. But while horse wealth is a versatile index for studying equestrian societies, its applicability is not limited to Native Americans. Historians of the American West can use the concept in myriad situations and contexts, as evidenced by its ability to illuminate the problems posed by horse theft on both ranches and farms.

The term *horse wealth* refers to the economic, utility, and monetary value of a horse relative to an individual or family's overall wealth and to the relative scarcity of horses within a community. This idea provides insight into the overall value of horses in a specific time and place. Horse wealth measures how successful Plains Indians were at appropriating the horse to conduct military operations, provide transportation, and facilitate hunting. It is also essential for investigating how horses and other forms of property were integrated into each community's economy, society, and culture. Anthropologists and scholars of American Indian history have employed the concept of horse wealth for decades to describe equestrian wealth within and between different post-contact American Indian tribes, especially those on the Great Plains. According to anthropologist John C. Ewers, horse wealth is defined in terms of how well an individual or a family is able to utilize horses for their private economic, social, and political needs. "A man who owned merely enough horses to perform the necessary tasks required for his subsistence . . . might live well," argued Ewers, "but he was not wealthy." Conversely, "to be rich in horses a man had to own a considerable number of animals over and above those required for subsistence." The term can be applied to a community or tribe as well, however, and as Ewers argues in one essay, the Blackfeet were "horse poor" compared to neighboring tribes.[16]

This concept is also useful for understanding the horse raid as a tactical, strategic, and economic tool for bands to use against one another. Anthropologist Frank Roe wrote that American Indians raided horses to acquire them as a means of "self-aggrandizement." However, whites seldom interpreted horse stealing by Plains Indians as being motivated by honor but, rather, viewed it as a criminal matter or an act of war. As a result, once the U.S. Army successfully ended horse raiding throughout most of the plains in the late 1870s, young Plains

Indian men lost a crucial means of gaining social capital within their tribe since no corresponding activity sanctioned by whites offered the valor and respect gained from bravery in the face of adversity during a horse raid.[17] Horses were an important military target for other reasons as well since the loss of a horse herd for an enemy tribe would expedite their defeat. In this sense the destruction of horse wealth became a military imperative. Horse raiding and other depredations by the Lakota challenged Pawnee subsistence and sovereignty by the 1860s since the Lakota sought to expand their hunting lands in the face of white encroachment at the expense of neighboring tribes. On the southern plains horse raids by the Comanches and Kiowas took a massive toll on northern Mexico in the 1830s.[18]

Horses would not have been such a highly valued prize if they were not materially valuable. Many scholars have highlighted the myriad ecological and economic benefits that horses offered their owners. In the southern plains the Comanches gained their horse wealth through predatory raids on neighboring tribes and settler communities in Mexico, but then the stolen horses were subsequently converted into foodstuffs and other commodities in Taos and other markets. The Comanches' ability to turn the hitherto unused grasses of the southern plains into bioenergy for their horses further augmented their horse herds, thus changing a wealth of grass into horse wealth.[19] Individuals benefited from horse wealth as well. Leaders of successful raiding parties also gave horses away, which brought prestige to the giver. According to Lakota author Delphine Red Shirt's mother, Lone Woman, horses were "currency." "My grandfather's worth was established by his own prowess in obtaining the things he valued," Lone Woman told her daughter. "A horse could 'buy' a wife. A swift horse helped him in times of war. He liked a fast horse. Perhaps to run from the wives he left behind."[20]

In light of these examples, one may assume that all Plains Indians valued the horse as an important part of their community and culture. However, some tribes eschewed or limited their use of horses, and those tribes that fully incorporated horses into their way of life did not all adopt them in the same manner. A diverse array of horse cultures existed among the Plains Indians, reflecting a range of climactic, social-economic, and ecological conditions across the entire vertical span of the Plains. Ultimately, American Indian equestrianism responded not only to the economic and strategic benefits provided by the adoption of the horse but also to the hazards of overdependence. The diversity of horse cultures on the plains almost matched the assortment of dangers that they faced.[21]

When the Spanish brought horses to the Americas in the sixteenth century, they did not foresee the changes their animals would bring to American Indian life in the West. On the Great Plains horses revolutionized hunting, warfare, and commerce. More bison and other game could be hunted on horseback than on foot and more quickly. The infusion of both horses and game extended and capitalized the American Indian's trading economy, and when combined with guns and other commodities, they waged war with much greater force and effectiveness.[22] As a result, horses quickly began to occupy a central place in Plains Indian culture. This cultural importance was manifest in many different ways. For instance, the Apaches and the Cheyenne both had horse worship societies.[23] Elsewhere, American Indian folklore often dramatized and celebrated the companionship that many people felt for their horses. According to Lone Woman, the Lakota called their ponies "holy dogs." "When the horses took over the work of the dogs, we relied on the horses for much more," she recalled. "They became a part of us, like an arm or leg, and it was hard to think we could ever live without them. So it was, they were sacred or holy to us, like the turtle. Their spirits sometimes came to us in ceremonies and spoke to us." One Lakota legend, as told by Luther Standing Bear, describes how during a particular raid only one warrior lost his horse. During the celebrations following the conclusion of the raid, the warrior was sad over losing his horse, which he had left to die on the battlefield. The camp was shocked, however, when later that night the horse wandered into the camp, having miraculously found his way home, and his owner was overjoyed.[24]

Lone Woman has also discussed how her mother, Turtle Lung Woman, remembered and described the rituals her husband, Paints His Face with Clay, performed with his horse before a hunt or a battle. "He painted his horse right before he rode it into the [buffalo] herd . . . he took certain precautions to make sure the horse didn't panic at the strong smell of the [buffalo]. He made it wear a strip of buffalo hide as a halter to get used to the smell." Moreover, he would use the same clay for himself as he would use for his horse. "He revered [the horse], particularly the one he rode into battle or into a herd of buffalo. He painted it to signify that it was a sacred animal, a messenger of Wakįyą, the thunder being. It was believed then that the horse came from the west, where the dreaded thunder being dwells. The power of Wakįyą resided in it." Horses "came to kill, the way the thunder being has the power to destroy." Therefore, horses gave "man the ability to slaughter [buffalo] for the good of all. In times of war, it allowed him to count coup, then slay his enemy."[25]

Women as well as men were attached to their horses. Women cared for the herds while the men were away hunting or making war and used horses frequently to move camp, transport goods, travel, and even carry the pole used for the Sun Dance to its ceremonial location. Like their male counterparts, women learned how to ride horses at an early age, and they valued their mounts as cherished friends and companions. Women also took the lead in designing horse masks, saddles, and halters, which they covered with sacred quilling or beadwork. In particular, the role that masks played in physically and spiritually protecting the horses made this an important step in preparing a horse for battle or for other functions.[26]

The value of companionship among equestrian American Indians is evident in several ways. Among the Comanches and the Kiowas, horse wealth represented freedom, prestige, upward mobility, and the ability to marry. But their favorite horses meant more to them than just their individual values as bargaining chips. One Comanche even claimed in an interview that "some men loved their horses more than their wives." If ponies represented currency that could be used to acquire brides, then per-haps for some men that objectification of marriage ultimately reduced the connection they felt toward their spouses. A horse stolen in a raid may have held a different place in a man's mind than a wife he acquired in trade.[27] In any event horse compan-ionship at best facilitated human relationships and at worst supplanted them.

Some of this uncertainty arises from the fact that the Ameri-can Indian equestrian's relationship to their horse is often seen through the lens of Euro-American assumptions. It is exoti-cized as evidence of the American Indians' special relation-ship with nature, and horses are seen as a natural extension of the American Indian. This assumption is false—as noted ear-lier, the Plains Indians evolved several distinct horse cultures, which with varying degrees of success attempted to capitalize on the benefits of using and accumulating horses relative to climactic and ecological restrictions on horse and bison pop-ulations.[28] It also precludes the existence of a similar kind of relationship between Euro-Americans and their horses. These bonds transcended race.

While the historical and anthropological understanding of American Indian equestrianism has taken an exciting turn toward greater complexity, many historians still assume that Euro-Americans shared a single, unitary horse culture. Much like the Plains Indian horse cultures, American pastoralists, ranchers, and farmers all had different strategies for horse usage and herd management—the economics and culture of ranch life dictated that horses be accumulated, bred, and used in a way that promoted the large operation's ability to conduct bian-nual roundups, whereas the horse economy on a yeoman farm functioned on a much smaller scale and in a much smaller geo-graphic area.[29] In this context the concept of horse wealth is a powerful tool for understanding how horses were used, where they were concentrated, who owned them, and how difficult it was to procure, train, or care for them. In ranching communi-ties horse wealth was more heavily concentrated and easier to acquire. A stable horse was worth about fifty dollars, and a mustang could be acquired at no cost. Since vast herds of horses were bred for use and sale in the West, and given the availability of forage and pastureland, it was much cheaper to own and take care of a horse in a rural ranching community. However, a large percentage of the total number of horses was concentrated in the hands of a few ranchers, who maintained large herds for sale, for moving cattle, and for the use of their cowboys. On the other end of the social ladder, aspiring cowboys hoped to save enough money to buy an entire team of horses, which they could then use to transport people and goods or to start a small ranching operation of their own. Ranching communities, therefore, may be considered to be horse rich.

This distribution of horse wealth broke down in farming communities, where horse ownership was much more widely distributed among farmers and townspeople. Each family or individual might have owned or mortgaged a few horses for their own personal use. Horses were an essential tool for many people in these communities since they were needed to traverse the long distances between different points in a mostly rural area as well as for a variety of farming tasks. According to a prominent handbook for prospective farmers, "One horse is almost a necessity, even on a small farm, for use in travel, and it might be that some farmers would be so circumstanced that it would be more profitable for them to keep an extra horse to complete the farm-team than to keep in addition a pair of oxen."[30] Horses were indispensable enough to farmers that the demand for good draft animals was inelastic. But since demand was even higher in the cities, prices for horses went up in these areas, making them an expensive commodity. The value of a horse in proportion to the rest of a farmer's assets was higher as well since late-nineteenth-century agriculture was beset by several major economic dilemmas: a depreciating currency, the concentration of capital in the East, rising rates for rail freight, and the overproduction of food crops and other commodities. This combination of factors added fuel to the fire of industrial development since producers in the East benefited from increased railroad competition and falling prices for crops. It was a major problem for farmers in the South and the Midwest, however, who grew more indebted to moneylenders and banks to cover their losses, impoverishing them and their families.[31]

Other problems piled on top of the farmer's mounting debts. The eastern freight market was extremely competitive, and companies built parallel railroads and engaged in price wars in an effort to boost their business over that of their rivals. The marketing logics changed as one moved to the West, however, where single lines often monopolized entire sections of a state. These lines were longer and thus more expensive to build than in the East. Consequently, railroad companies profited from the operation of these rural rail lines, which were noncompetitive and therefore free to set prices as high as they liked. Farmers complained bitterly about these fare hikes, which cut deep into their own profit margins at harvest time.[32]

The midwestern yeoman farming economy was much less romantic, individualistic, and profitable than it has been depicted in popular culture. Farmers were stuck between increasing costs of production, falling commodity prices, and the rising value of both capital and money itself, all of which threatened their very economic existence. Yet while these problems radicalized the rural producers of the midwestern states, a very different economic story unfolded in the West. On the Great Plains following the Civil War, a beef bonanza in eastern markets combined with an explosion in the supply of Texas longhorn cattle and the availability of millions of square miles of government-owned grass, creating a massive boom for meat production that spanned from San Antonio to the Dakotas and west toward the Great Basin. New railroad construction facilitated the movement of cattle to eastern markets, and by 1889 three railroad systems connected the Nebraska Panhandle with Omaha, Chicago, San Francisco, and other cities throughout the continental United States.

The Great Plains cattle industry was a classic example of a boom-and-bust economy. Ranchers invaded the range, brought up millions of cattle from Texas and elsewhere, overgrazed the region's seemingly limitless supply of grass, and then left when meat prices collapsed in the late 1880s following a massive livestock die-off during the winter of 1886–87.[33] In the meantime ranchers built towns, established state and county governments, defended their turf from sheepherders and homesteaders through violence and barbed wire fencing, and etched the iconic image of the horse-riding cowboy into the annals of American history. Unlike the economic conditions bedeviling farmers in older agricultural areas farther east, ranchers capitalized on the high price of beef, the extended reach of the railroad to eastern markets, and the comparatively small production cost of simply turning cattle loose to graze before rounding them up and shipping them to market. Some of the northern plains' most venerable and memorable ranchers and outfits, including John Bratt in North Platte and James Cook in Agate Springs, found success in western Nebraska. However, the ranching industry would have not been possible without the use and availability of horses on the range.[34]

These comparative differences in horse wealth add a new layer of complexity to the socioeconomic and cultural landscape of late-nineteenth-century America since both the horse market and the economic utility of horses in a given area can affect that community in a variety of ways. A farmer whose access to capital is limited and whose profit margins are low due to falling commodity prices and rising production costs will pay a much higher opportunity cost for a single horse than a rancher, who usually has more capital and who can buy horses for less money. In the cash-poor Midwest and Great Plains, horses could also be traded for other goods or sold for cash, though since they netted more money in more populated markets, sellers often took their livestock to towns or cities. But fluctuations in the supply of horses had serious repercussions on the economics of a given community.

In spite of the horse's economic importance on both farm and range, the western hero as embodied by dime novels and movies seemed to have a strictly utilitarian relationship with his mount. Horses are in the background in most Western movies, and the wonders of Gilded Age technology have long overshadowed the horse in the celebration of the frontier myth.[35] However, a close reading of western memoirs, travelogues, and autobiographies proves that horses were very much a part of the story of western conquest. The hard-boiled bounty-hunter-turned-detective Charlie Siringo, whose exploits as a Pinkerton agent, cowboy, and reporter were as dubious as they were daring, frequently spoke of his horse in his autobiography *A Texas Cowboy*. He spoke wistfully of his adventures with his horse and of the last time he saw him: "Leaving Whisky-Peet behind was almost as severe on me as having sixteen jawteeth pulled. I left him, in Horace Yeamans' care, so that I could come back by rail the coming fall. I failed to come back though that fall as I expected, therefore never got to see the faithful animal again; he died the following spring."[36] When recalling their roles in the "civilizing" of the West, some western "heroes" waxed nostalgic about their horses more often than they did about lost comrades or the long-dead frontier.

The names that ranchers and cowboys gave to their horses tell us a great deal about the relationships humans had with them and the owners themselves. On his ranch in Lincoln County, Nebraska, owner John Bratt recorded every name he gave to the hundreds of horses he owned between 1875 and 1883. Bratt, likely with a lot of help from his foremen and ranch hands, chose these names for a variety of reasons. Some of the horses were named after their personality quirks, such as Rowdy, Nip, Reliable, Stump Sucker, Gentle, and Alert. Others were named after famous or otherwise notable persons, especially military leaders, such as Ben Butler, General Carr, and Joe Hooker. He also called one of his stallions "Buffalo Bill," which says as much about what he thought of the stud horse as it does about popular opinion of the world-renowned showman. But while these names are interesting, many of Bratt's horses did not have names at all and were identified in his records by number and by brand. Not all names were complimentary either. "One horse that I broke . . . had an exceptionally mean disposition. He would bite, strike or kick," recalled Arthur McCoy, a cowhand in northwestern Nebraska. "The only name we ever found for this horse was 'Old Son of a Bitch.'" Horse naming was not arbitrary or random. It was an organic process made possible by the idiosyncratic relationships ranchers and cowboys shared with each individual horse.[37]

Owners reserved the right to name their horses, but everyone else was free to exchange opinions and gossip. Horses were a frequent topic of conversation in late-nineteenth-century Nebraska, and owners often shared social billing with their ponies. Standout horses were the talk of the town, and residents often traded news about other people's mounts. An 1878 issue of the *North Platte Republican* in Nebraska declared that "many fine horses were on the street" the previous Thursday but that A. J. Miller's horse, Tib, was "the admiration of all eyes."[38] Traits such as color, tack, and behavior, reflecting the quality of its training, were particularly prized among horses, much like they are today. Sympathy was also given to well-known individuals whose horses were known to have died, particularly if those individuals had been frequently seen on their horses while in town conducting business. The *Western Nebraskian* noted that it was "sorry to learn" that North Platte lawyer William Neville's horse had died unexpectedly, and in 1891 the *Grant County Tribune* announced that John O'Neill "was so unfortunate as to lose one of his best horses Tuesday night to colic."[39] Frequent chatter about horses and their owners illustrated the powerful hold a horse could have on a community, which in turn would admire the owner for their excellent steed.

Unfortunately, admiration seldom led to acquisition, at least through legal means. A horse owner was often reticent to forfeit the love and friendship of an animal that he or she trusted by selling or trading it, which created a curious paradox in the horse market: the more loved a horse was, and by extension the more desirable the animal was, the less likely it was to be for sale. One of the last living old-time cowboys, Bob Kennon, told Ramon Adams about a favorite horse he refused to ever sell: "I had a [beautiful black horse], a single-footer named Peacock. He could travel like the wind and had the best endurance I ever saw in a horse. Everybody was trying to make a deal to get a hold of him. They even tried to win him as a stake in a gambling game. [But] I couldn't part with him, for we had been pals so long."[40] In many cases the best horses available were those that were not for sale.

Despite the influence that the value of companionship had on transfers of horse wealth, it had a much greater effect on involuntary transfers. Unlike the economic, criminal, and social consequences of horse theft, the psychological and interpersonal ramifications are often forgotten. Yet it is these personal, individualized consequences that dictated how individual persons responded to the stealing of their horses. John Bratt would have probably reacted less harshly to the stealing of a half-dozen unnamed horses than would have Charlie Siringo at the loss of Whiskey-Peet or Theodore Roosevelt upon discovering that his precious Manitou had been stolen. It was this range of reactions that clouded and complicated the array of punishments for horse theft throughout the West. The emotional, mnemonic geography of western Nebraska, while certainly variable depending on the person and their experiences there, and thus impossible to historically replicate, was deeply furrowed by the hoofprints of horses once loved and later lost. Those memories, thoughts, and passions drove individuals to make more emotionally based decisions than the theft of a car would in the present day.

Another way to think about the impact of horse stealing is to compare horse theft with another crime: cattle rustling. Cattle rustlers and horse thieves are synonymous in the popular imagination: both are prominent villains who incur the wrath of homesteaders and cattlemen alike in popular Westerns. Both are unconsciously linked to the pastoral, even though horse theft was a frequent occurrence in cities. Neither crime is believed to be modern, even though both cattle and horses are still frequently stolen from unsuspecting owners. Most important, our assumptions about cattle rustlers and horse thieves derive from what we think we know about the perpetrators. For example, we believe that horse thieves were more likely to be hanged and cattle rustlers were more likely to be involved in organized gangs. That is why the term *cattle rustlers* almost always appears as a plural noun.

The real difference between cattle rustlers and horse thieves lies not in the individuals stealing the animals or in the nature of their organization but in the animals themselves. While cattle and horses were both highly valuable commodities, they were reckoned differently in western Nebraska. Cattle were bred, raised, and sold with one goal in mind: producing meat, dairy products, leather, and other goods. Of course, many farmers and ranchers, especially small operators who only had a few milk cows or oxen, loved and named their livestock.[41] But on large farms and ranches, whether the product was beef or milk, most cows and cattle were only kept for their ability to create food. Horses, on the other hand, were seldom eaten in the English-speaking world. The subject is borderline taboo, like the eating of cats and dogs, because Americans associate all three creatures with feelings of love, family, and companionship. But horses were not just pets. They were partners.

Horses served a variety of different functions on the Great Plains: they produced power, provided transportation, conferred status, represented wealth, and epitomized grace and beauty. It was much easier to love a creature that was valued for its strength, beauty, and brawn, rather than one destined to end up on a dinner table. Perhaps this is why the Western Nebraska Travel Coalition's travel guide, entitled *Journey to Western Nebraska*, does not feature a stockyard or a grazing calf on the cover of the 2018 edition but, instead, shows two women sitting astride a pair of horses in front of a forested bluff. In the bottom-left corner the brochure urges readers to "find your next adventure." Nebraska history, much like its geography, is best traversed while in the saddle.

1

You Must Watch Your Horses

Crow Indian
you must watch your horses
a horse thief
often
am I

—Lakota Sioux song

When the federal government and representatives from over half a dozen different Plains tribal nations signed the Fort Laramie Treaty of 1851, superintendent of Indian affairs David Mitchell believed that the document would recast and reshape indigenous geopolitics and laws along Euro-American lines. When introducing the treaty to a gathering of chiefs at Fort Laramie, Mitchell declared that each of their nations would be "divided into geographical districts," which in turn could "show what country each nation claims and where they are located." Mitchell added that "in doing this it is not intended to take any of your lands away from you, or to destroy your rights to hunt, or fish, or pass over the country, as heretofore. But it will be expected that each nation will be held responsible for depredations committed within its territory." After years of increasing travel by whites along the Overland Trail, which had culminated in the recent swell of emigrants en route to California's gold fields, the government sought to protect these travelers from violent intertribal raiding and, coincident with the whites' own safety, keep the Plains tribes happy enough to not prey upon them.[1]

The Fort Laramie Treaty's practical underpinnings overshadowed its more intrusive and systematic attempt to destroy the logics of horse raiding. During the 1840s a wave of Lakota attacks upon the Pawnee, Otoe, Omaha, and other tribes seemed to imperil the parade of whites moving west along the Platte as well as a smaller but growing number of settlers along the Missouri. In an attempt to undermine the Plains Indian raiding cultures, commissioners David Mitchell and Thomas Fitzpatrick inserted into the document language designating a single "chief" to act as a point person for each tribe. In theory this would have diminished the importance of attaining influence through gift giving and counting coups, which were acts of bravery that included horse stealing. The districts drawn by the treaty were to function as hunting grounds and legal jurisdictions simultaneously. Yet as Mitchell himself put it when explaining the treaty's benefits to the Indians, these legal boundaries were also meant to force their inhabitants to adopt white law-ways and conceptualizations of private property that necessarily precluded horse theft and other types of raiding. "Your Great Father only desires to punish the guilty and reward the good," Mitchell explained. "When a horse is stolen, or a scalp taken, or a woman or child carried off, or any other wrong done, he wants to find out who did it, and punish the bad men or nation; and the nation will be held responsible for the acts of its people." Now elevated to the same level of social and cultural taboo as murder and kidnapping, officials hoped that the Plains Indians would delegitimize horse raiding and eventually define pony ownership the way whites defined their possession of horses, cows, and oxen.[2]

Mitchell's optimism proved to be shortsighted and naive. The Lakota, Cheyenne, and Arapaho continued to raid the Pawnee, Crow, and other tribes, augmenting their horse herds in the process. Some of the most successful warriors were just getting started. From about 1841 through the early 1870s, Big Turkey, a Brulé warrior, joined or led at least twenty different horse

raids against Shoshones and Pawnees. His autobiography cataloged his horse raids and other coups: "The next winter I stayed
awake all night in a Pawnee camp, and when the sun was up
I captured many horses. I robbed again many Pawnee horses.
Again in nearby territory I took many of the Pawnee horses." At
least one of these thefts occurred near the Forks of the Platte,
where in 1866 or 1867 Big Turkey pilfered several ponies from
visiting Shoshones. In addition to Big Turkey, other men "the
likes of [him]" stole hundreds of horses over several decades.
Finally, in 1871, two decades after the first Fort Laramie Treaty
was signed and three years after its 1868 replacement took effect,
the aging warrior was ready to "[stop] the fighting" because
"the President took pity on all the foreign tribes."[3] Meanwhile,
the Northern Cheyennes also raided western Nebraska and the
surrounding frontier. A boy named Wooden Leg, following in
his father's and brother's footsteps, joined the Elk Warrior society after his fourteenth birthday in 1872. During the next few
years he learned the art of horse raiding, having joined several
war parties in search of Crow ponies throughout the region,
though he later gained notoriety for publicly discussing his participation in the Battle of Little Bighorn.[4]

As Big Turkey, Wooden Leg, and many other Plains Indians
continued—and in some places amplified—their horse-raiding
efforts, whites kept bringing more animals to steal. Throughout
the 1840s and 1850s the Overland Trail migration represented
not only the movement of white travelers to Utah, Oregon, and
California but also the journeys made by countless thousands
of horses, cows, oxen, dogs, and other creatures who accompanied their owners on the road west. This steady procession of
humans and beasts required federal protection, and the Fort
Laramie Treaty was written in part to help guarantee the migration's safety. However, the many migrating animals along the
route offered tempting targets for theft, not just among the
Plains Indians but also among many whites. Only three years
after the treaty was signed, stolen and missing animals would
break Mitchell's peace and plunge the region into war.

Throughout the mid-nineteenth century the Lakota Sioux were the most powerful tribal nation on the northern plains. The Brulé and Oglala Lakota presence in western Nebraska dates back to the eighteenth century, when bands began moving west from the Missouri River, across the plains and toward the Black Hills. Claimed by the Pawnees, Crows, Comanches, and other Plains tribes, the Lakota conquered this broad swath of land, which stretched roughly east from the Powder River watershed in Wyoming and the plains adjacent to Fort Laramie into Nebraska and Kansas toward the Republican River. Emboldened by their conquest of the White River valley in Dakota and their seizure of prime hunting grounds from the Missouri River tribes, the Lakota sought new sources of bison as their own numbers grew during the first half of the nineteenth century. While smallpox and a host of other illnesses weakened other tribes, the Lakota Sioux, who moved in small groups and were divided into seven *oyáte*, or tribes, were flourishing on the Great Plains by the 1850s.[5] In addition to the Brulé and Oglala Lakota *oyáte*, other tribes included the Sans Arcs, Hunkpapas, Two Kettles, Sihasapas, and Miniconjous.

The stories of Lakota expansionism and the wide-scale horse raiding that took place between Plains tribes are chronicled within an array of winter counts, calendrical records created and maintained by tribal record keepers. Each year was represented with images depicting a key or memorable event in that band's history. One of the earliest extant Lakota winter counts began in 1700. Battiste Good, a Brulé, copied the original counts into a sketchbook in 1880 at the Rosebud Reservation. The original counts coincided with a critically important era in Lakota history: the tribe's acquisition of horses and the equestrian revolution that followed. In 1709 the count depicted a horse with a cropped head, indicating that the Lakotas had seized many Omaha horses that winter. The following year another horse with the Assiniboine sign marked the winter when the Sioux captured many horses from that tribe as well. While these were years of bounty, the next two years were remembered differently: in 1711 three Lakotas died in a skirmish with the Assiniboine, and in 1712 four lodges drowned during a spring flood. Over the next several decades, horses feature prominently in the tribe's recorded history: seven additional years before 1750 refer to winter horse raids and acquisitions. The count also hints at the start of the Lakotas' multigenerational war with the Pawnees by recalling how the winter of 1718–19 was characterized by the bringing home of many of their horses.[6] However, the Pawnees at the time could more than hold their own against the Sioux. The following year a combined Pawnee-Otoe war party defeated a Spanish expeditionary force in eastern Nebraska, led by Pedro de Villasur, killing forty-six and nearly wiping out the entire group.

Growing horse wealth helped the Lakotas claim larger bison hunting ranges, and pony herds required careful management. Great Plains winters were not kind to open-air pony herds, and a certain critical mass of horseflesh had to be maintained to equip war parties, group hunts, and their own internal economy of horse redistribution. In the 1840s, as white traffic to Oregon began to disturb the bison population and siphon off game from the surrounding range, the Lakotas decided to expand even farther to the west. Because of these pressures, the Lakotas stole horses to maintain their equine and bison economy. As a result, they fought a long war against the Crows, who occupied the Powder River country in Wyoming, and continued their struggle against the Pawnees to the east. Lakota winter counts from this period tell the stories of these wars through each tribe's acquisition of enemy horses.

One of the most memorable battles in this long-running conflict occurred in the northwestern corner of the Nebraska Panhandle. In 1846 James Bordeaux opened a trading post near Chadron in hopes of extending his operation at Fort Laramie (which the American Fur Company owned until the United States purchased it in 1849) farther east and capitalizing on the growing Overland Trail caravan traffic by investing in Indian ponies. His wife, a Brulé Lakota, facilitated these trade connections. A Crow war party discovered their herd in 1849 and stole over eighty horses after burning down Bordeaux's family's ranch. The Brulés set off in pursuit and soon caught up with the now horse-heavy Crow expedition. Some of the fleeing warriors scrambled up a tall butte near present-day Crawford for safety. The Brulés besieged the butte, and the Crows fought back, taunting and throwing rocks at the Lakotas below. Later that night the Crows repelled down the cliff and escaped. When the Brulés finally ascended the cliff, after waiting for four days, they discovered three dead Crows who had succumbed to their battle wounds. Today Crow Butte, as the promontory came to be called, dominates the horizon southeast of Crawford, Nebraska. A historical marker off of Highway 20 commemorates the site and the battle that took place there, and several Lakota winter counts took note of it as well. As for Bordeaux, he soon decided to move back to Fort Laramie, and another forty years would pass before a new settlement, Chadron, was founded at that site, in 1886.[7]

Although Indians had access to wide trade networks that included ponies and horses, war parties also seized ponies to replenish their tribes' horse stocks. The Pawnees played the middleman role within Nebraska's indigenous horse economy, trading guns and other American and French goods west to the more isolated Utes in exchange for mounts and then trading many of these horses to the Omaha and white travelers within the region. The Spaniards also traded horses to the Pawnees. Americans soon got in on the act, capturing wild mustangs and buying additional animals from the Wichitas and Comanches in order to supply markets in St. Louis and New Orleans. Many of these trade horses were stolen as well, and without pony brands, it was difficult to tell the difference between recently pilfered and recently broken horses.[8]

Horse stealing was a corrective to low social standing. Lakotas used horses to gain status, ensure social mobility, and accumulate wealth, and ponies were among the few possessions acquired by the Lakotas that were not subject to gifting by the chiefs. Horses represented a different form of capital—the more

YOU MUST WATCH YOUR HORSES

horses that a Lakota or Cheyenne had access to, the more power he had. Conversely, families with fewer horses lacked the status that those with more horses claimed.[9] As a result, new generations of Plains Indians led or joined raids to acquire leadership roles. Intertribal warfare soon evolved into a complex web of horse raids since military prowess began to reward individual courage over the ability to hunt buffalo. Individual risks, however, led not only to community gains but also to collective sorrow. Winter counts memorialized horse raid–related deaths and celebrated the fallen. During the winter of 1786–87 multiple counts each commemorated a different hero who had died fighting, including Broken-Leg-Duck, who perished while trying to steal horses from a Crow village.[10]

Scalps, wounds, acts of bravery, and stolen horses were all valuable returns on a successful raid or battle, but only one of the these forms of coup was redistributable. According to Oglala chief Red Cloud, warriors "must have horses, stolen or captured, which he must give away to the old, the poor, the weak, the sick, and the cowards, any of which circumstances may be mentioned by the warrior with impunity upon presentation" (fig. 3). Although horses were not as highly respected as scalps won in battle or wounds, "this very material proof [of bravery could not] be dispensed with for any length of time without seriously affecting the brave's reputation." Over time the benefits of war honors carried through society—women preferred to marry war-honored men with horses, and horses were used as status markers during a time when tribal relations were being destabilized from disease. Other warriors and tribes placed a more direct emphasis on horse raiding for individual gain. In his memoir Wooden Leg compares Cheyenne expectations with those of the Crow. "I have been told that when a Crow stole a horse or found an article it was expected of him that he give it away," he stated. "It was considered not right for him to keep it. A Cheyenne might present a stolen horse or found article to a relative or friend, but it was regarded as entirely fair and proper for him to keep it for himself . . . Ordinarily he kept it."[11]

Occasionally, the material benefits of horse raids caused prob-

Fig. 3. Multiple Lakota winter counts, including those by Flame (*left*) and Swan (*right*), recall the murder of dozens of Miniconjou chief Swan's horses by other tribesmen out of jealousy in 1824 or 1825. National Anthropological Archives, Smithsonian Institution, INV 08633800 and INV 08633900.

lems. Three different winter counts cite 1824–25 as the year when one or more jealous Indians killed all of Miniconjou chief Swan's horses. The number of dead ponies ranged between twenty and thirty-nine. In the early 1860s, according to Hunk-papa chief Long Soldier's winter count, the Sihasapa Lakotas murdered each other's racehorses out of jealousy.[12] Worse yet, Cheyenne men on a few occasions murdered their fellow tribes-people over disputed horses. As murderers were banished from the tribe for at least four or five years, killing another Cheyenne was not a decision to be made lightly. Nonetheless, Wooden Leg recalled multiple examples of men committing homicide over a horse. In one case Wooden Leg's aunt decided to leave her husband and move in with another man, Chief of Many Buf-falo. Her husband, Rolling Wheel, appealed to the chiefs and demanded that Chief of Many Buffalo forfeit his fastest racing horse. The chiefs agreed to these terms. When Chief of Many Buffalo kicked his wife out in hopes of keeping the pony, the chiefs insisted that the transaction was final and that the horse must still be delivered to Rolling Wheel. When the spurned hus-

YOU MUST WATCH YOUR HORSES

band arrived to claim the animal, however, Chief of Many Buffalo shot and killed him. The chiefs banished the murderer for four years, and his lover moved in with her father.

In a separate incident Hawk and Sharp Nose returned from a raid with a fresh span of ponies. The two warriors argued over which of them would keep the best horse of the lot. Although Sharp Nose had a stronger claim to the animal, Hawk took it anyway. When Sharp Nose and his father attempted to reclaim the horse, Hawk shot an arrow at Sharp Nose, killing him. Then Hawk's father hurried over and, upon hearing Sharp Nose's father's angered shouts, shot him. The chiefs immediately banished both Hawk and his father from the tribe. Years later Sharp Nose moved in with Wooden Leg's band, whereupon Wooden Leg heard the story.[13] Stories such as these may have caused the chiefs to discuss the potential for theft, murder, and other conflicts over horses. Cheyenne military societies prohibited the lending and borrowing of horses after one man "borrowed" a pony from another and did not return it for over a year. Chiefs soon began to take more proactive roles in mediating horse and other property-related conflicts.[14]

Reciprocity and revenge also motivated American Indians to steal horses. Lakotas, Cheyennes, and Arapahos often covered the dead by killing representatives of bands that had murdered one or more of their own, and they stole horses from those who originally stole from them. But Plains Indians sometimes paid blood debts with horses rather than scalps. When Oglala chief American Horse's father killed a Crow dressed as a woman on the prairie, the Crow responded by stealing nearly eight hundred Lakota horses. The Lakotas later recovered most of them, but the two nations continued to engage in tit-for-tat horse raiding. Later, after Crows murdered eight Miniconjous, Lakotas stole three hundred Crow horses in retaliation. "It seemed like a vicious cycle," Lone Woman noted. "They came to kill and we went to strike back. Sometimes they came to take horses and we went to take them back." The Plains Indians later expected similar transfers of horse wealth, voluntary or otherwise, whenever whites killed one of their own. No Flesh and his followers decided to seek payment for Oglala chief Whistler's murder in 1872, presumably at the hand of a settler, by petitioning the commander at Fort McPherson for fifty horses. No Flesh repeatedly threatened war if the United States did not hand over the animals, but he preferred to receive the extra mounts.[15]

Other bands and victimized owners insisted on exacting blood for horseflesh. This made horse stealing inestimably dangerous in most cases, regardless of the tribes' own embrace of horse stealing as a materially beneficial yet eminently dangerous means of counting coup. On a certain level the risks involved in carrying out a horse raid helped legitimize the activity as something deserving of plaudits and laurels. Successful thieves proved their bravery, obtained wealth, rewarded their family, secured their subsistence, and gained influence. Those who failed and were captured in the act faced swift and brutal retribution. Wooden Leg recounted an instance during the winter of 1867–68 when two Crows stole most of his band's horses from their camp along the Tongue River. The warriors mounted the few remaining animals and followed the thieves' tracks in the snow. The Crows abandoned the herd and took shelter in a cave. When the Cheyennes discovered their location, they set a fire at the cave's entrance and smoked the two men out. One Crow was immediately captured and clubbed to death, while his companion leaped astride a horse and tried to escape. He had inadvertently picked a slower pony, however, and was soon overtaken, beaten, scalped, and beheaded.[16]

Wooden Leg described another unsuccessful enemy raid along the Tongue River seven years later, when a larger group of nine Crows stole several Cheyenne horses. This time Wooden Leg was old enough to help hunt down the thieves, but he and three companions had to turn back when their horses tired. While camping one night on the return journey, the sound of a cantering horse woke one of his friends. When the friend demanded that the intruder identify himself, the horse galloped away, prompting him to fire his rifle in the pony's direction. The party later learned that someone had discovered a dead Crow who had been shot in the back near their campsite.

YOU MUST WATCH YOUR HORSES

As for the rest of the pursuers, the Cheyennes discovered their herd grazing near the Bighorn River and noticed that the Crow thieves were out bathing in the stream. After resting their horses for a few minutes, the war party splashed into the Bighorn and attacked the surprised thieves, killing three.[17]

Sometimes a single horse raid sparked a larger confrontation, especially if the tribes involved already had a contentious relationship. In 1873 a small Shoshone party stole several horses from Wooden Leg's camp, a theft that was reported to the rest of the band. The other Cheyennes suspected that it was the beginning of a larger attack and demanded revenge against the aggressors. "All were for immediate war against the Shoshone tribe," Wooden Leg recalled. That night, as the band prepared to go to war, Cheyenne sentinels discovered thirty-two Shoshones en route to attack the main camp. Their suspicions thus confirmed, the band decided to attack that night and engaged the Shoshone war party along a canyon near the Powder River. The battle lasted all night and extended well into the day, killing thirty Shoshones and seven Cheyennes. Although Wooden Leg's camp recovered their four stolen horses, they paid a heavy price.[18]

Just as horse raids sometimes led to war, horse gifts had the opposite effect: they could pave the way for peace agreements and lead to new friendships and alliances. In 1846 the Kiowas and the Comanches, both flush with horses from their raids throughout Texas and northern Mexico, invited the Cheyennes to end the fighting between their nations. The Comanches told the Cheyennes that they had many horses and wanted to give some to their people—not just to the Cheyenne chiefs, they said, but to everyone, including the children. In exchange, the Comanches indicated that they would accept other gifts—just not horses. When the three tribes met, the Comanches gave the Cheyennes so many horses that, according to George Bird Grinnell, they ran out of ropes to herd them. The Cheyennes reciprocated by offering guns, calico fabric, brass kettles, and other items. "The peace then made," remarked Grinnell, "was never broken."[19]

While individual leaders or small groups organized and orchestrated most raiding parties, the cultural, economic, and legal legitimacy of horse raiding as a means of accumulating horse wealth influenced the decision-making process made by each member of every raid. Participants weighed whether to risk their time, energy, and possibly their lives for the reward of stolen horseflesh, and over time the danger of horse stealing rose with the convergence of soldiers, settlers, and railroads. Whenever Oglala Lakota warrior Paints His Face with Clay prepared for a raid, he would "choose his best horse," pack the herb *thícanicanu* "to keep [the horse] going on a long journey," and bring some pemmican. He and the other raiders would then leave at daybreak, and during the journey they "listened for 'wanáǧi,' for ghosts . . . [they] returned to our world to hover near us, sometimes to warn us of bad things." Depending on whether the songs they heard were celebratory or mournful, they could anticipate the results of their expedition. Ultimately, Paints His Face with Clay "did not consider it an honor to be asked to join the war party. He felt that the honor would be in coming home victorious."[20]

There was no such thing as a "typical" horse raid. Red Cloud's autobiography, in which the legendary Oglala chief recounts the stories of several memorable raids, illustrates a variety of strategies, targets, motives, and outcomes. Red Cloud's first raid, which he joined at the age of sixteen against his mother's wishes, descended upon a Pawnee village north of the Platte in present-day Kearney County. The expedition's leaders conducted the attack to avenge the death of Red Cloud's cousin during an earlier battle. In the ensuing engagement the Oglala lost the element of surprise when they discovered that some of the Pawnees had scouted earlier, decamped, and moved across the river, from whence they engaged the visitors. The two groups fought a brief battle, in which the Pawnees killed two of their opponents, and the Lakotas took four scalps and captured fifty horses. Red Cloud claimed one of the dead, and his exploit burnished his growing reputation as a skilled, fearless warrior. But

YOU MUST WATCH YOUR HORSES

since two Oglalas died in the battle, the raid was only a qualified success as several families mourned their losses.[21]

A more successful raid, albeit one that did not go according
to plan, occurred later, when Red Cloud joined a party sent
to steal horses from the Crows. He and a trusted friend broke
away from the group after disagreeing with the party's leaders on whether or not the Crow village was nearby. Believing
that the Crows were closer than his companions thought, the
two snuck away in the middle of the night. They moved about
ten miles, and at dawn they spotted a lone Crow attending to a
herd of fifty horses. Red Cloud attacked and scalped the herder,
and the two men secured the horses. Both expected to be dis-
ciplined when the raiding party's leaders caught up to them
since Lakotas on horse-stealing expeditions were supposed to
stay close to the party unless ordered otherwise. But instead of
being whipped, the expedition's leaders, Old Man Afraid of
His Horse and Brave Bear, celebrated the coup and deduced
that a large, undefended Crow village with even more horses
was nearby. The party found the village shortly thereafter and
surrounded it, threatening to make war with the horses' owners while small groups of Lakotas secretly rounded up the herd
during the distraction. The expedition returned with over three
hundred horses. Since no members of the party had died on the
trip, the band celebrated the party's success when Red Cloud
and the rest of the group arrived home.[22]

Ceremonial practice was essential to guaranteeing one's safety,
the security of their family and tribe, and their success as raiders. Among the Cheyennes, Great Medicine could both punish
and protect against horse thieves. Wooden Leg described one
(likely apocryphal) story in which a Sioux warrior approached
a Cheyenne medicine man in hopes of killing another Sioux
who owned a horse that he believed was his. The medicine man
directed the Sioux to draw a picture of a man outside of the
targeted warrior's tipi and then stab it in the heart. The warrior did this, and according to the story, the victim died that
night. "I do not like that kind of medicine actions," Wooden
Leg recalled. "Such use of the powers makes bad Indians." A

more positive action occurred when Wooden Leg was making medicine alone in a dark lodge for several days. Cut off from communication with the outside world and unable to see outside, he grew concerned when at one point the sound of galloping horses approached the lodge, followed by women and children running past as if fleeing some disaster. Hours after the scene quieted down, a medicine man came into the tent and informed Wooden Leg that they had repelled several Crows on a horse raid. Although one Cheyenne died in the ensuing battle, the medicine man assured Wooden Leg that the skirmish proved "the Crows can never hurt us."[23]

Regardless of whether the medicine successfully protected the Cheyennes from Crows and other enemies, the plains raiding culture continued to eat away at intertribal and interpersonal relationships. The immense and incalculable value of ceremonial and ritual items notwithstanding, horse ownership enabled not only new modes of subsistence, trading, and warfare but also new understandings of personal property and wealth accumulation. Ponies quickly became the most essential, productive, and economically valuable type of property one could own, mainly because they promised many positive returns to their owners, including mobility, wealth, and power. But with the horse's growing importance in Plains Indian cultures came an equally important and opposite condition: the fundamental disadvantage of not having many horses, having older or weaker ponies, or not owning any horses at all. Horse raiding helped correct some of these disparities, but it also exacerbated them as well. Before long, for some people the value of a horse began to outweigh the value of another person's life.

Unhappy Trails

In a region where horse power translated into political, military, and economic hegemony, Plains Indians looked on as the slow, mostly oxen-bound stream of whites and wagons marched up the Platte River toward the mountains. Only a handful made the journey in 1841, but by 1843 the number could be measured by the thousands. Every year seemed to bring more of them, especially during the spring months, when a snow-free passage across the Sierras was mostly assured. Traffic along the Overland Route increased dramatically in 1849 as migrants hurried west toward the golden fields and streams of California. The route through Nebraska followed both sides of the Platte, creating a trunk line connecting the various Missouri River trail entry points in the east with the divergent California, Oregon, and Mormon Trails to the west.

Soon America's most important transportation corridor was also one of its most hotly contested. The United States Army and Plains Indians fought several wars along the span of the route—including conflicts in 1854, 1857, 1864, and 1865 in Nebraska Territory alone—and at times war parties threatened to shut down traffic along the Overland Route altogether. As it passed through several vital hunting grounds, intertribal raiding often threatened to consume the road. And tensions among the emigrants themselves frequently jeopardized the movement of caravan trains across the continent. While the pioneers' dramatic and physically taxing transcontinental journeys are celebrated and remembered for bringing out the best in people, their vulnerability and distance from protective communities also brought out the worst. Horse theft and appropriation lay at the heart of many of these conflicts.[24]

Plains Indians recognized, celebrated, and worked to obtain horses as private property, even while sanctioning intertribal horse stealing as a means of both gaining plunder and proving one's courage. Horses were thus carefully, and sometimes jealously, guarded from covetous neighbors, other Indians, and whites. This cultural respect for horse property did not extend to cattle, oxen, or other domesticated livestock, which Plains Indians saw not as a means of production or investments but as food. In contrast, livestock and wagons represented the only property of significant value among the emigrants, who did not own land along the trail and could not even legally settle near the Platte until the passage of the Kansas-Nebraska Act in 1854. Being so far removed from both eastern laws and established western communities meant that emigrants remained vulnerable to theft throughout the journey unless vigilant, proactive measures were taken to secure their property. Unfortunately, these measures did not dampen pioneers' suspicions or anxieties; if anything, the necessity of protecting their animals amplified their fear of losing them. The only institution that stood between the Indians and emigrants was the United States Army's frontier units, whose own horse supply was chronically hobbled by theft, stampedes, inexperienced soldiers, haughty officers, and administrators in St. Louis and Washington DC who remained unconvinced by field reports suggesting that the army's frontier policies were failing.

Early Overland Trail emigrants feared for the security of their livestock. These included some of the route's first travelers and popularizers. While journeying up what would become the Oregon Trail in 1832, Nathaniel Jarvis Wyeth repeatedly ran into traveling parties who complained of losing their horses to theft and rightfully feared losing their other livestock. On July 31, 1832, according to Wyeth's journal, he "found a party of 4 whites who have lost their horses and one of them wounded in the head with a Ball and in the body with an arrow . . . they suppose the Snakes did it but I think not." The next day he encountered Benjamin Bonneville, who would later command Fort Kearny in 1849. Bonneville confirmed that Snakes stole seven of the party's horses: "On farther inquiry I changed my opinion expressed above in regard to the Indians who stole the horses[.] I think they were 15 Snakes who left our camp at Green river a few days before we left." Reverend Jason Lee, the Methodist preacher whose efforts to convince Americans back east to come to Oregon and support his missionary work helped popularize the newly blazed Oregon Trail, lost some of his horses on his 1834 trip to Oregon. "Last night did not stake the horses," Lee wrote in his diary. "About 1 o'clock they took fright and nearly all ran with all speed with their hobbles on. The guard and others pursued them and soon came back with two-thirds of them but ours were nearly all gone still." Lee eventually recovered most of the stock, but he began to believe that the animals had been taken from their camp. "Three of the Otto [Otoe] Indians came into camp this morning—were very friendly but we strongly suspect that they stole the horses that were lost."[25]

The United States Army established Fort Kearny in 1848 to lend military and logistical support to the overland migration. It replaced a short-lived post, also named after the recently deceased General Stephen Kearny, whose location on Table Creek near the Missouri River offered little practical support to emigrants. The army placed the new military reserve on the south side of the Platte River near present-day Kearney, Nebraska, not far from the point where several different feeder trails from various Missouri River towns converged to form the Overland Route. Beyond its proximity to the trails and to the Pawnee camps along the Platte and Loup Rivers, the reserve offered little in terms of forage, lumber, trade, and entertainment. Nonetheless, it represented for travelers the first true frontier fort after leaving Kansas, Missouri, or Iowa, and it grew into an important troubleshooting location for emigrants hoping to fix their equipment, unload unnecessary weight, procure supplies, and collect or send mail.

Fort Kearny's primary role was to protect emigrants. But while the post prevented some depredations upon migrants through its very presence near the Overland Route, it was not always effective in doing so, nor was it capable through the first decade of its existence of quickly and effectively punishing thieves. Poor strategic decision-making by the War Department, which often garrisoned the fort with infantry units that could only chase mounted war parties on foot, caused many problems for its commanders. Soldiers stationed at the fort were often fresh recruits with little combat experience and no prior knowledge of life on the plains. Some of the dragoons, or cavalrymen, could not even ride horses upon joining their mounted companies. This lack of seasoning contributed to an incident on October 29, 1849, when twenty dragoons under the command of Lieutenant Charles H. Ogle skirmished with a small group of Pawnees whom they believed to be responsible for harassing emigrants and forcing a small mail party to return to Fort

Leavenworth. When the Pawnees used hand signs to try to surrender, one of the soldiers misread their intention and fired at the group. In the ensuing fracas three Pawnees died and six soldiers, including Ogle, were injured. Ogle was subsequently court-martialed, but the post commander defended his actions, blaming the incident on inexperience and asserting that, overall, the fight would deter further molestations by the Pawnees. In later years commanders blamed the fort's shortcomings on insufficient forage, tired horses, and the strenuous demands of supplying a remote post without ample timber reserves with necessary lumber.[26]

Fortunately for the emigrants, it was mostly smooth sailing for each successive fleet of prairie schooners. While a dramatic increase in Overland Trail traffic during and immediately following the gold rush further stretched the resources of those who guarded and supplied the annual caravans, the number of depredations along the road between the Big Blue River and Chimney Rock did not rise. Between 1849 and 1854 emigrants reported several depredations to the garrison at Fort Kearny, and in due diligence the officers attempted to investigate as many as it could. In most cases, however, the command found nothing to support these allegations. Additionally, there was little evidence to connect the few substantiated reports with any Indian culprits. "Although several horses have been stolen from the emigrants at night," reported Major Bonneville in 1849, "no Indians have been seen on the road." In 1850 Captain Robert Chilton went so far as to compliment the Pawnees on their conduct: "The Indians when met treat [the emigrants] very civilly and have never been better disposed than at present."[27] Post commander Henry A. Wharton expressed a similar level of confidence while enumerating the number of depredations to occur each season along the route. In June 1852 he announced that no "annoyances from Indians have been reported," with the exception of one alleged raid that turned out to have been committed by whites. By 1854, once the cholera epidemic within the region had subsided, Wharton could paint an even rosier picture to his commanders: "The emigration is advancing very well thus far, no depredations from Indians have been reported and there is little sickness."[28]

The most audacious raids along the trail during the early 1850s targeted the Pawnees, rather than the emigrant trains. Believing that the raids against the Pawnees were coming dangerously close to the road, the command at Fort Kearny tried to broker an informal peace between the Pawnees and their aggressors. These efforts ended in disappointment. In one instance, immediately after Captain Henry Wharton managed to convince several Cheyenne and Pawnee chiefs to shake hands and leave one another in peace, "[the Cheyennes] went out a few miles from the post, found a party of Pawnees hunting, and killed and scalped several of them." Sometimes war parties possessed the temerity to directly ask the soldiers at the post to share information about the Pawnees and their whereabouts. "I will add the Cheyennes came to the post on a friendly visit . . . and had then their usual talk, receiving a small supply of provisions," First Lieutenant Henry Heth reported. "During the talk the Cheyennes asked me if they saw any Pawnee Indians coming to the post [and indicated] they might attack them, I replied that they knew very well that such a request would not be granted." An even larger group attempted to slip past the post in June 1860 in order to attack the Pawnees. According to Major Charles May, "During the last three days I have been visited by four bands of Sioux and Cheyenne Indians, numbering in all about 250 warriors. These Indians are on a war party after the Pawnees and have left all their women and children between this [post] and [Fort] Laramie."[29]

Among the few confirmed cases of Indian horse raiding against emigrants during those years, responsibility fell upon a handful of Otoe, Arapaho, and Cheyenne war parties. A band of Otoes struck several trains in 1849, and the emigrants' lack of familiarity with that tribe led them to blame the depredations on the Pawnees. During the fall of 1849 Otoe war parties carried off at least eleven mules and horses from Fort Kearny and robbed the post's Pawnee interpreter of three more. Captain Robert Chilton lambasted John Barron, the Otoe agent at Council Bluffs, for the thefts and demanded that the animal losses be reimbursed out of the Otoe's annuities. He further alleged that the Otoes were not simply converting government horses for their own use but were trading them to settlers along the Missouri River for a profit. Similar motives might have driven several Arapaho and Cheyenne war parties to plunder emigrant trains in 1851. "It appears they have attempted and, in some instances, succeeded in stealing animals and provisions from the emigrants," Wharton speculated in his report, "but [they] have not . . . evidenced any violent intentions, their sole purpose is to steal."[30]

Identifying exactly who was responsible for these thefts was often difficult. Most emigrants were unable to distinguish between different Indian languages, let alone differentiate between the myriad bands and councils that wove in and out of the region. Nonetheless, travelers quickly learned how to stereotype them, and these assumptions often filtered into their reports. For instance, many whites believed that the Pawnees were an especially villainous and troublesome tribe. "Being now in the Pawnee Indian country," complained Reverend Wyllis Alden, who was making his way to Oregon in 1851, "we were obliged to stand guard every night, to keep our horses from being stampeded, and it was not the most agreeable thing in that mud and rain." Members of neighboring tribes, most of whom were at one time or another at war with the much-loathed Pawnees, often spread rumors among the emigrants about Pawnee misdeeds. According to Joseph Williams, "The Caws (or Kauzas) told me that the Pawnees were a bad nation, and that they had a battle with them; that they had their women and children hide in a thicket, whom they (the Pawnees) slaughtered in a barbarous manner."[31]

There was some truth to the stereotype. In 1855 several parties from the Kit-ke-hahk'-I band of Pawnees stole horses and mules from several emigrant trains. This band, which lived and acted separately from the remaining Pawnee councils, was "one of the smallest [yet also] one of the most troublesome" groups in the tribe. Later they stole several horses belonging

YOU MUST WATCH YOUR HORSES

to dragoons traveling from Fort Leavenworth to New Mexico. "There have been other depredations committed by the same band which have accidentally come to my knowledge," wrote First Lieutenant Henry Heth, "[and] their disposition at present is anything but friendly." Later still, Captain Alfred Sully blamed the Pawnee's constant state of being at war with most of its neighbors on the tribe's complicity in horse raiding. "The Pawnees are the greatest horse thieves I have ever seen," he claimed, "and as long as they are plundering other Indians, it cannot be expected that they can live in peace."[32]

Pawnees were also more likely than other tribes to approach emigrants along the route and ask for food, a tendency that often alienated and offended travelers, who believed that beggars were inherently more likely to steal. For some Pawnees, however, migrants provided their only source of subsistence when wars with the Sioux and Otoes prevented them from leaving their territory to hunt and occasionally kept them from returning to their territory to harvest their corn, squash, beans, and other crops along the Loup forks. The Pawnees' proximity to the Overland Trail also meant that they were the usual suspects whenever emigrants lost cattle or horses. In some cases thefts by Omahas and Otoes were attributed to the Pawnees by emigrants who simply did not know any better. "Unfortunately," noted Chilton in a letter to the Adjutant General's Office, "depredations committed by that most rascally and thieving tribe, the Otoes, have been attributed to the Pawnees who from former misconduct [are] made scapegoats," and as a result, "the sins of the Comanches, Kaws, and Otoes are placed [upon the Pawnees] by immigrants moving upon this or the Santa Fe Road."[33]

Like the Pawnees, the Crows enjoyed friendly relations with white soldiers, officers, and officials. However, while many emigrants believed that the Pawnees were inveterate thieves and murderers, travelers seemed to think that the Crows were glad-handing tricksters. Instead of stealing horses, the Crows "swapped" them. Emigrant Charles Ferguson recalled one instance when a Fort Laramie deserter escaped with his commander's horse, only to run into a band of Crows the following night. They "came down on him and took his provisions, every stitch of his clothing, and his horse, saddle and bridle, [and in exchange] gave him the buffalo rug, some jerked buffalo meat and the poorest pony they had and told him to go back." According to Ferguson, this kind of trading "is not deemed robbing or stealing, but a pure business transaction, not unlike . . . a modern Wall street operation, though in the latter instance, the winning party rarely contributes even a blanket to cover the nakedness of the party fleeced. The Crows call it swapping." By "swapping" instead of stealing, the Crows could grow their herds while protecting their alliance with the whites. "They said the Sioux are mean and will steal—but Crows, 'they good Indian, they swap.' When they swap, [however,] they are pretty sure to get the best of the bargain." Forty-niner William G. Johnson remembered a similar event that occurred when a friend of his strayed too far from their camp, whereupon "a band of Crows . . . relieved him of various incumbrances [sic], including [his horse], the clothes he wore, watch, pocketbook, gun, etc., and setting him upon an old, worn out, limping nag, [and] with a wild whoop which he mistook for his death knell, they sent him back to his friends, who received him with shouts of laughter."[34]

Emigrants did not only stereotype Indians as probable thieves. As thousands of Latter-day Saints trekked westward to escape persecution back east, many of the same stereotypes that had chased them out of Missouri and Illinois still stalked them. Beginning in 1847, members of the Church of Jesus Christ of Latter-day Saints followed the Overland Route across the plains and over the mountains toward their new home in Utah. In his autobiography California migrant William Manly described meeting a half-dozen Latter-day Saints near Court House Rock in 1849. "They were dressed in buckskin and mocassins [sic]," Manly wrote, "with long spurs jingling at their heels, the rowels fully four inches long, and each one carried a gun, a pistol and a big knife. They were rough looking fellows with long, matted hair, long beards, old slouch hats and a generally back woods get-up air in every way." Manly also noticed that the party carried with them "an extra pack mule, but the baggage and provisions were very light." This led Manly to conclude that the mule was stolen: "I had heard much about the Mormons, both at Nauvoo and Salt Lake, and some way or other I could not separate the idea of horse thieves from this party, and I am sure I would not like to meet them if I had a desirable mule that they wanted, or any money, or a good looking wife."[35]

Several tales of alleged thievery also circulated among the church's critics. One popular anecdote, attributed to "Reverend Mr. Slater" in California and popularized by several authors, recounted an instance when a traveler purchased a horse from a passing Latter-day Saint for one hundred dollars, only to lose that horse a couple days later. Another migrant then purchased the same horse for one hundred dollars. The former owner discovered the missing animal in the other traveler's possession sometime later, and the pair realized that the same man had sold the same horse to both individuals. When they complained to the local magistrate, who happened to be a Latter-day Saint, the judge stated that there was no way to know for sure whose horse it was and then declared that the horse would be sold at auction to pay the costs of the trial. One anti-Mormon author, William Kirby, used the story to introduce what he believed was the "Mormon theory and practice in relation to the rights of property," which ultimately concluded that "the Mormons are the real owners of all the property on Earth, and therefore have a perfect right to take possession of the same, whenever they have power to do so, and can do it with safety to themselves."[36] Both Kirby and Manly cited horse-stealing anecdotes as evidence of Latter-day Saints lawlessness, but Manly's glib remark about "a good looking wife" suggests a more patriarchal reason to question congregants' attitudes toward private property: a fear among emigrants that Utah-bound polygamists would steal Gentile women, perhaps even their own spouses.

Many emigrants feared white horse thieves more than they did Indian raiders. White thieves deserved their poor reputation in part because they enjoyed more opportunities to steal from other whites than the Plains Indians did. War parties, while often well armed and experts in the art of stealing horses, were often deterred by and subject to the U.S. Army's punishment. Conversely, white horse thief gangs along the route operated outside of most state and local jurisdictions and on some parts of the trail could rob passing wagon trains with impunity. Sarah Sutton reported that the area around Devil's Gate in Wyoming was "infested with thieves and robbers, watching for a good opportunity to take emigrant cattle and horses . . . The Indians are better than the whites in my estimation." Other emigrants shared Sutton's sentiment. "'Did the Indians steal [those horses] from you, Peter?'" Alonzo Delano remembered asking a recently victimized friend. "'No,' he replied, with some energy; 'it was the cursed whites. Indians will steal sometimes . . . but these white men are robbers, and they have so much bad law that they can cheat the scalp off your head, and you can't help yourself . . . I can trust an Indian further than I can a white man.'"[37]

Other emigrants complained about company leaders and guards stealing animals, supplies, and cash from their charges and then moving up or down the line to join or lead a different train. "[May] 19th . . . A man had three horses and $500 stolen last night by his own guard," one man reported, "who left him with his wife and two other women without a team." Zenas Leonard described a similar crime within his own outfit. "One morning when the roll was called it was discovered that two of the company had stolen two of the best horses and started back to the state of Missouri. This had a bad effect—it impaired that full confidence which had heretofore existed between the members of the company." Company leaders and guards robbing and then abandoning their own trains became such a problem that in June 1850 the Fort Kearny post commander urged the Adjutant General's Office in St. Louis to offer a solution. "Numerous applications are almost daily being made to me for protection by emigrants who have been cast off by their companions and deprived of their property," he wrote. "If practical something should be done to meet such cases, not only with the view to justice but also on the grounds of economy as all those thus left destitute . . . [are] necessarily supplied stores at the post until enabled to reach the states."[38]

YOU MUST WATCH YOUR HORSES

False alarms were common on the trail and could be caused by something as innocuous as loose livestock. Horses often strayed away from emigrant campsites in search of food and water while their owners slept. When they awoke, many of them panicked and assumed that a thief had carried the horses off. California emigrant Willard A. Burnap received such a fright while camping on the plains. He immediately assumed an Indian had taken his missing pony, Beauty. "One night I was suddenly awakened. Something had happened; I could not hear Beauty. I reached for the lariat and pulled in about twenty feet of it. I found it broken; my pony was gone . . . an Indian had raided us." After taking stock of his situation, Burnap began to look for the missing animal. He made circles around the camp, putting his ear to the ground in hopes of hearing Beauty. As he searched, he imagined how his encounter with the thief would go. "I had no fear of the Indian should I run across him," he wrote. "He would probably meet with a 'How,' I should likely get my ponies back if he still had them, and we should most likely part friends." But Burnap never got the chance. After several hours he "heard, away off, the crop, crop, crop of some animal feeding, I carefully worked up nearer, then I softly whistled and called, 'Beauty!' A whinny answered me." Emigrants who lost other people's horses while on guard duty sometimes claimed that the animals had been stolen by Indians. J. M. Stewart lost horses under his charge when he fell asleep on guard duty. Noticing that the horses were gone, he returned to his camp and told his company members that Indians had stolen their horses. Fortunately, his peers suggested that they search for the horses anyway, which "they did [locate] in a half hour's time, where they had found better feed."[39]

Lost horses occasionally wandered far enough that Pawnees or other Plains Indians picked them up as strays, claimed ownership, and brought them back to their camps. Worried emigrants then reported these missing animals as being stolen, thus prompting the army to follow up. Once the detail sent to investigate reached the suspects' camp and saw the reportedly stolen animals in their herd, the commander then had to decide whether or not the horses had been stolen or simply picked up on the range. Fortunately, most Fort Kearny commanders were savvy enough to know when to give the chiefs the benefit of the doubt, and the Pawnee chiefs themselves began to voluntarily surrender strayed horses whenever the command came looking for them. In July 1850 Chilton wrote that the Pawnees had surrendered several emigrant strays "without application on my part" after a spate of reported depredations along the trail. However, it seems unlikely that local bands returned these missing animals without some inducement. "Many animals have been lost," Wharton reported in an 1852 letter, "but the probability seems to be that they have strayed off and may eventually be taken by the Indians."[40]

Sometimes the appearance of a strange or unexpected remuda was enough to cause a scare. In these cases overzealous lookouts and bleary-eyed emigrants on guard duty would mistake a few horses on the horizon for an Indian war party. Sarah Cummins recalled the bedlam that followed when one of her company's guards screamed, "Indians! Indians!" while camping along the Platte in 1845. "The entire company seemed almost wild with excitement," Cummins later wrote in her autobiography. "Children crying, mothers screaming or praying, men running wildly about, not knowing what to do . . . [soon] the opinions of the more calm and judicious finally prevailed, and an effort was made to arrange the company in order for defense. About this time I saw a woman assisting her husband in making bullets from bars of lead which were carried for that purpose." Not long after preparations for their mutual defense had begun, however, the emigrants realized that the approaching men on horseback were U.S. cavalry soldiers. Soon Cummins and the rest of her group met and shook hands with Captain Stephen Kearny, who went on to play an important role in the Mexican War.[41]

Scares and occasional raids aside, the vast majority of the thousands of travelers along the Overland Trail route did not lose any livestock to the Plains Indians. Indeed, for many people Nebraska was uneventful. Diarists, letter writers, and future chroniclers remembered the wide, shallow, and languid Platte

YOU MUST WATCH YOUR HORSES

River; Chimney Rock's prominent and decaying spire; and the swarms of annoying insects that arrived uninvited at campsites in the evening. Like many others, Zenas Leonard complained of the lack of scenery and forage along the route. "We continued to travel up the river Platte for several days—passing through extensive barren prairies, the soil being too poor even to produce grass; and game exceedingly scarce." Others were even less impressed. "I would not have given a dime for all of Nebraska west of Fort Kearney," J. E. Miller later wrote.[42] For the vast majority of emigrants who made the trip, the plains were a prelude to the spectacular mountain ranges to come farther west. On some of the hills along the North Platte near Scotts Bluff, travelers could clamber up the ridge on a clear day and grab their first glimpse of Laramie Peak nearly one hundred miles to the west.

To the degree that emigrants complained of horse stealing, Indian raids, and other misdeeds, however, the region's reputation was exaggerated. "On this portion of the road [along the Platte] we had great difficulty also with the Indians," claimed J. Watt Gibson, "that is we continually feared trouble. We were not attacked at any time nor did we lose any of our horses or cattle, but we lived in continual fear both of our lives and of our property." Gibson went on to describe the Crows and Lakotas as "war-like and troublesome savages. Scarcely a man in the company dared go to sleep during the whole journey from Fort Laramie to the point where we reached Platte River again, opposite the mouth of Sweetwater." Some of Gibson's biases clearly originated from personal experience: "It was in this very country . . . that these Indians tried to kill and rob my brothers and myself in '51, and in '55, while my brother James and my youngest brother Robert were bringing a drove of cattle across, my brother Robert, only seventeen years old, was killed." However, Gibson believed that this fear, if not his own lived reality, pervaded the thoughts of most overland emigrants. "I think all the early travelers across the plains dreaded the Indians on this portion of the road more than any other obstacle to be found on the entire journey," he argued, "not excepting the alkali deserts of Utah and Nevada."[43] Gibson's worries about the Platte section of the route were comparatively extreme, but many other travelers echoed these anxieties before, during, and after their journeys.

While most traveler impressions of Nebraska vacillated between admiration and apathy, writers took firmer stances on other, later parts of the Overland Route. The Humboldt River basin in Nevada quickly emerged as the California Trail's most hazardous segment for horse stealing. Ute raiders and white horse thief gangs plagued this stretch of road, in some cases shadowing trains for miles before striking. "August 1 had been a long and sultry day," wrote J. W. Thissell, when describing his train's descent into the Humboldt Valley. "The train had been traveling down the river. The banks were lined with willows. For miles they had seen Indians lurking in the brush." The next day, according to Thissell, a large war party struck a nearby train and escaped with fifteen head of horses and mules. One group of emigrants who lost their horses to the Utes in the Sierra Nevada approached Alonzo Delano's company on foot and asked to buy some flour. "They had pursued the Indians twenty-five miles into the country north, where they came to a large lake of fresh water in the mountains," he recalled, probably in reference to Lake Tahoe, "but here they lost all traces of the marauders, and were compelled to relinquish the pursuit." J. Watt Gibson's company lost some cattle to a raiding party. "One night just before we reached Big Meadow, while we were camped alongside the Humboldt River," wrote Gibson, "a band of Digger Indians slipped into our herd and drove two of the cattle away." Historian David M. Potter later gave a more general account of the Humboldt Valley's many reported depredations: "The emigrants approached the Humboldt Valley, which was inhabited by as diligent and skillful a tribe of cattle thieves as the continent could produce, namely the Utes, whom the emigrants called Diggers . . . The Indians promptly inaugurated the practice of approaching the camps at night by stealth, putting an arrow into the guard if there happened to be one, and driving off the mules or cattle."[44]

YOU MUST WATCH YOUR HORSES

For the most part, however, these reports and rumors were overblown. Horses were a cost-prohibitive option for many emigrants—only about 20 percent of Overland Trail migrants used horses for the journey. The dry, overgrazed grasses along the Platte provided poor sustenance for the large draft horses preferred by Americans and Europeans, unlike the smaller and ecologically better-adapted Spanish ponies favored by the Plains Indians. Moreover, feed was too heavy and cumbersome to haul in large amounts. Those emigrants who did bring horses were much more likely to lose them in a stampede or to a host of trailside maladies, ranging from exhaustion and malnutrition to broken legs and rattlesnake bites.[45] But none of these other dangers caused quite as much anxiety or suspicion as the specter of horse stealing. Soon, as traffic along the Overland Trail continued to swell and as relations with regional tribes continued to sour, the growing sense of fear and loathing began to cause problems.

The War of the Mormon Cow and the Fight over Little Wolf's Horse

Raids and thefts on emigrant trains during the early 1850s were intermittent and infrequent, but the 1854 Grattan fight changed the dynamic. It exposed some of the central tensions that had festered in the region during the previous fifteen years of increasing Overland migration to Oregon, Utah, and California (map 2). Emigrant horses, cows, and oxen consumed vast amounts of grass and pasture along the trails, forcing Indian ponies, bison herds, and game to graze elsewhere. Overhunting jeopardized wildlife populations in the region, as did the trash and diseases the emigrants spread along the route. Forced into a peacekeeping role, the United States Army frenetically tried to prevent Indian bands from raiding each other and passing emigrants while also scurrying to protect those bands from food scarcity and trigger-happy whites. But while environmental, diplomatic, and humanitarian concerns caused conditions along the trail—and relations between the tribes and the whites—to deteriorate, private property disputes provided the spark that ignited a powder keg of violence on the trail. The Grattan fight, which some historians believe was the precipitating event in the ensuing quarter-century of warfare between the Plains Indians and whites, resulted from a misunderstanding over livestock.[46]

On August 18 a Latter-day Saint migrant en route to Utah complained to Lieutenant Hugh Fleming that High Forehead, a Miniconjou Lakota whose lodge had been camping with Conquering Bear's Brulés, had killed one of his oxen. Although Conquering Bear reported the incident to Fleming and even offered to help bring High Forehead to the fort, Fleming determined that troops would ultimately be necessary to apprehend the suspect. For this purpose the commander detailed Second Lieutenant John Grattan, twenty-nine infantrymen, and two twelve-pound mountain howitzers to the village. When Conquering Bear and other Brulé chiefs came to meet the arriving party, they were expecting an agent, not an infantry company. Man Afraid of His Horses, who had accompanied Grattan to the village, entered High Forehead's lodge in hopes of coaxing the man out. Instead, he and several other Miniconjous told Man Afraid of His Horses that their chief, Little Brave, had been killed the previous year by whites and that they were prepared to die. High Forehead added that he "did not think the whites wanted to kill him for a poor, lame cow."[47]

Conquering Bear urged Grattan to "go back to the Fort and tell the chief [Fleming] to think the matter over," going so far as to offer a mule in hopes of calming the situation until the Indian agent arrived. The young officer, however, flanked his men around the two cannons, which were pointed directly at the Miniconjous. At that critical moment, according to Brulé chief Big Partisan, "[The] soldiers, one of them a tall man, fired and shot an Indian in the mouth and another in the hand. After that two others fired, and then all the small arms." The situation quickly ignited, and not long after the Miniconjous and Brulés returned fire, the infantrymen tried to retreat. But it was too late. At the end of the day Grattan and his entire party succumbed to the onslaught. Conquering Bear lost his life as well, and within just a few hours the United States had lost a longtime and valuable ally. The battle, referred to in the press as

YOU MUST WATCH YOUR HORSES

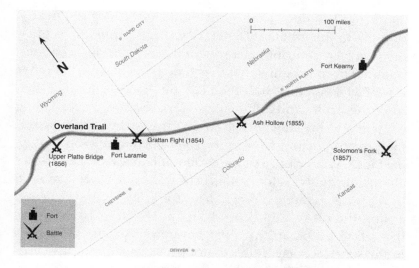

Map 2. Forts and battles along the Overland Trail, 1854–57.
Map created by the author.

the "Grattan Massacre," started a domino effect on the plains: the following year an army unit under Brigadier General William S. Harney assaulted a peaceful village of Brulés near Ash Hollow in revenge, killing eighty-six people, capturing another seventy, and taking at least fifty horses.[48]

Raiding and fighting during the war spilled eastward. During the fall that followed the Grattan fight, a Lakota war party struck Fort Kearny and succeeded in running off twenty-nine horses from the government herd. Eleven days later three Lakotas stole "a number of mules" from U.S. mail contractors in the middle of the day within one mile of the post. Offended by the flagrancy of the attacks, Henry Heth complained that war parties would not respect Fort Kearny so long as it was garrisoned by infantry companies. The following year Heth tried to convince his superiors that a more general Lakota war was underway across the region after several contractors were attacked on a nearby island and robbed of their horses. "The [victim] informs me that the Indian recognized was an Ogallala Sioux, this is the band that have denied being implicated in any former act of hostility," Heth noted in a letter to Major Oscar F. Winship in the Adjutant General's Office. "From the fact that the Ogallalas contributed a part of the present depredations, is it not fair to presume that they have been engaged in other acts of aggression?" Heth then laid out his case, arguing that since the Brulés and Miniconjous were responsible for killing Grattan and his men and given that the parties that attacked the post and mail service in 1854 were believed to be Yankto-nai Sioux, it was clear that the "guilty and incessant Sioux—are all equally guilty!" Heth's concerns were soon overshadowed by his pleas a couple of weeks later for Winship to take action against the Kit-ke-hahk'-I band, and in March he issued a similar call to action against the Cheyennes. But the press back in the states echoed Heth's dystopian assessment of the situation, with newspapers such as the *Missouri Republican* hysterically crying wolf even though virtually no raiding was occurring along the trail.[49] Migrants, while undeterred by the reports, read them in earnest.

The Grattan fight and the Harney massacre at Ash Hollow each represent deadly watershed moments in the military and diplomatic history of the central plains, but the less well-known Cheyenne War of 1857 had a much more pronounced—and devastating—effect on horse raiding along the route. A litany of factors contributed to the Northern Cheyennes' growing frustration with the whites, including dissatisfaction over John W. Gunnison's 1853 transcontinental railroad survey through Northern Cheyenne and Arapaho hunting lands, growing wariness over the Platte Road's seemingly endless caravan traffic, the death of trusted Indian agent Thomas Fitzpatrick, and the beginning of civilian white settlement in the mid-1850s following the passage of the Kansas-Nebraska Act in 1854. However, the Harney expedition against the Brulés in Ash Hollow was a turning point. The army's brutal slaughter of eighty-six Lakotas sent a stinging message to the Cheyennes and other regional tribes: that they could be next if they ran afoul of United States military authority. It also embittered them to the prospect of permanent white occupation of their lands. Rather than simply traveling across the plains and over the mountains, a new reality dawned on the region's native inhabitants: the whites intended to stay.[50]

Once again, stock theft accusations ignited smoldering tensions. In April 1856 the Upper Platte Bridge near present-day Casper, Wyoming, provided a vital river crossing for emigrants on their journey west. A small army detachment protected the passing travelers, and Indians often camped nearby to trade with the whites. One day a white visitor to a Cheyenne trading camp complained to the detachment commander that four horses belonging to a white man were grazing with the Indian ponies. Two Tails (later known as Little Wolf) and two of his companions claimed to have picked them up earlier as strays, but the original owner furnished a claim matching the horses' descriptions. The officer urged the Cheyennes to turn over the four horses and promised rewards once the owner reclaimed his animals.

Two of the men complied and returned three of the horses, but Two Tails (later known as Little Wolf) refused to give up the fourth, arguing that he had picked up the horse he now claimed at a different time and location. In response the commander ordered the arrest of the three men with the intent of holding them hostage pending the return of the fourth horse. However, the Cheyennes, who feared they would be killed rather than merely detained, jumped on their horses and fled for their lives. The troops killed one, captured and imprisoned another, and wounded Two Tails as he escaped. When Two Tails reached the rest of his people and told his story, the band feared for its safety. Remembering what had happened at Ash Hollow, they immediately broke camp and moved north toward the Black Hills. Their haste may have spared them, as troops from Fort Laramie soon arrived and burned all of the abandoned tipis. In the days and weeks that followed, news of the incident traveled fast. The remaining Cheyenne bands moved south toward the Republican River, and their young men clamored for war against the whites. Although the chiefs tried to counsel them against attacking the whites, there was little they could do.[51]

Stolen horses continued to fan the flames. This time a

mounted Fort Kearny detachment seized thirteen Cheyenne ponies while attempting to locate Big Head and three companions who had recently escaped the post. Arrested on suspicion of murdering an emigrant near the Little Blue River, Big Head's war party managed to break free from custody and escape. Big Head was severely wounded during the struggle, but he made it to a nearby rendezvous point with several Cheyennes. They took him back to the main camp. Before mounting a waiting horse and fleeing with his men, he tossed his bloodstained coat onto the ground. Soon after Big Head's "breakout," post commander Captain Henry Wharton sent several men on horseback to track down and apprehend the escapees. Instead of finding the prisoners, they settled for taking back Big Head's discarded coat and a small pony herd that they found near a Cheyenne camp. Wharton sent the animals to graze within the company herd. A second Cheyenne war party soon approached Fort Kearny, where they found two items of interest: Big Head's bloody jacket and thirteen Cheyenne ponies in the company herd. The infuriated party stampeded the horses and carried the Cheyenne animals back to the main camp.

The theft and subsequent recapture of this pony herd added yet another argument to the Cheyenne council fire in favor of war with the whites and also moved Wharton a step closer toward exacting summary punishment. The final straw came on August 24, when a war party fired on a mail wagon that was heading west. No one was killed in the attack (one contractor was shot in the arm with an arrow), nor were any horses stolen. But when the contractors reported the event to Wharton, he ordered Captain George H. Stewart to pursue with his cavalry, which had arrived at the post the previous month. Had Stewart's First Cavalry Company K been present at the post in June, it is possible that they would have responded more forcefully and in greater numbers to the Big Head affair. Now that Wharton had his chance to answer with a show of strength, he dispatched Stewart with fifty-seven mounted men to track down the marauders responsible for attacking the mail coach. The following morning they caught the village by surprise and

YOU MUST WATCH YOUR HORSES

attacked, killing ten Cheyennes and capturing nearly two dozen horses. This extraordinary and disproportionate response to the injuring of a single mail carrier motivated many more Northern Cheyennes to join the growing chorus for open war with the whites.[52]

From June through September 1856 these assembled Cheyenne Dog Soldiers continued to wage war on the Overland Trail and its posts. The majority of attacks occurred in Nebraska Territory; the Dog Soldiers evaded detection by avoiding the reinforced Fort Kearny and focusing their depredatory activities on travelers who veered off the main trail or away from larger groups. In the meantime there was little that the garrison could do in response with only four infantry companies, until August 24, when Captain Henry W. Wharton arrived with a company of cavalry. But by then it was too late: that same day a war party attacked a mail contractor, wounding one; the next day they struck a small train north of the Platte, killing two men, a child, and a woman (after kidnapping her); on August 29 they killed four Latter-day Saints in a train along the North Platte; and on August 30 one man died when another small train was attacked. Several additional hits occurred during the first week of September, including one in which Almon W. Babbitt, who served as secretary and treasurer for Utah Territory, was killed along with two other men in a raid that occurred only eight days after he had survived another attack on a larger train (determined to get himself and his government papers to Salt Lake City, he had ignored Wharton's advice after the first attack and proceeded west with an even smaller and less-well-defended party than before). Obviously, the mounting death toll was paramount in the actions and thoughts of both the passing emigrants and the army, but most of the victims' animals were run off as well. Fortunately for both the emigrants and the officers, once autumn began, the Cheyennes withdrew south into Kansas Territory. Indian agent Thomas Twiss believed that peace was at hand, and by October the Cheyennes agreed to end their attacks on the white caravans.[53]

The calm was short-lived, as Cheyenne attacks began again

the following spring. And just as the weather and the overall tensions along the trail were beginning to heat up, the Second Dragoons departed Fort Kearny on June 6, 1857, once again leaving the only army installation between Fort Leavenworth and Fort Laramie on the Overland Route without any mounted troops. "Allow me again to state that an infantry post in this country is entirely useless," complained new post commander Elisha G. Marshall, "[and] that depredations are continually perpetrated by hostile Indians near this garrison without our being able to even assist those who are so unfortunate as to be attacked by them." On August 2 nearly 150 Cheyennes attacked two herds of beef cattle en route to Salt Lake City to support the Utah Expedition. They killed and mutilated one man, William Sam Byrne, and ran off 824 head of cattle plus 20 horses and mules. Although a small detachment soon located most of the cattle, the audaciousness of the attack prompted Marshall to post a general warning to all travelers on the Platte Road: "All persons down the road are informed that they are liable to be attacked by the Cheyenne Indians at any moment, and there-fore it is necessary that they should be cautious, and always on the alert, having their arms always ready for use."[54] Coinciden-tally, Marshall issued his urgent warning to the emigrants only days after Edwin V. Sumner and five hundred men skirmished with and defeated the Cheyenne Dog Soldiers at the Battle of Solomon's Fork in Graham County, Kansas, killing nine Indian warriors and capturing thirty Cheyenne ponies.[55]

For the second time in three years, a dispute over a single miss-ing white-owned animal had started a war on the Overland Trail. Although myriad factors on both sides fueled hostility and ani-mosity between the Plains Indians and the whites, the central role played by stolen stock in both conflicts was not happen-stance. In both the Grattan fight and the Platte Bridge incident, the missing animals and subsequent accusations of Indian theft set off chain reactions that led to larger conflicts. Whites did not believe that strayed livestock ceased to become their prop-erty, and many held out hope for months that their animals would be recovered. For the Lakota and Cheyenne, however, possession was more than nine-tenths of the law. Stray horses were fair game for Plains Indians, who could then acquire and integrate them into their own herds.

Over the course of the 1850s, the commanders at Fort Kearny asked the Pawnees and other tribes to turn over livestock that matched the descriptions furnished by their original owners, but as was the case with Two Tails and High Forehead, these efforts were not always successful. On the one hand, Plains Indians often refused to submit themselves to arrest or otherwise accede to military authority. On the other hand, whites were nothing if not persistent at their attempts to reclaim missing property, particularly when the property was both mobile and valuable. After all, the Fugitive Slave Act of 1850 exercised nationwide federal authority over escaped southern chattel slaves, regardless of whether or not they were found in slave states. In this context horse stealing—and even accusations of horse theft—was especially dangerous to the peace.

These conflicts over stolen horses and cows illustrate the radically different perspectives held by natives and whites over the future of the plains. The Lakotas, Cheyennes, and Pawnees tenaciously defended their hunting grounds and their horses from their enemies and envisioned a future in which they could continue to pursue buffalo and be free. Meanwhile, whites looked west toward the plains and began to see the potential both within and beyond them. Long believed to be a "Great American Desert," the Great Plains would soon be quickly and enthusiastically carved up into farms, orchards, ranches, and homes. The region would cease to be something "in the way," an obstacle to cross between the Missouri and the mountains. Historian Elliot West eloquently described the fundamental differences between how whites and natives imagined the region in his seminal study on the subject, *The Contested Plains*: "Indian peoples discovered the horse . . . A bit later Euro-Americans found gold in the Rocky Mountains. As they had for thousands of years, horses and gold triggered fresh imaginings and set loose quests for power. People heard a summons to new lives. They were called out to greatness."[56]

Although their differences were palpable, these encounters also reveal how much the whites and Plains Indians had in common, especially with respect to their horse herds. Both groups relied on their animals, valued them, named them, loved them, and tried their best to protect them. Both inhabited the world of the horse. It is no wonder these incredible animals were the source of so much trouble on the trail: neither the Indians nor the emigrants carried anything of greater value. Additionally, both groups sought to increase their horse wealth through raiding, theft, and appropriation. This was certainly truer for Plains Indians than it was for whites, at least in the sense that the former evolved a number of raiding cultures that incentivized horse theft and redistributed its returns. Whites also took other people's horses; within a cultural and religious milieu that prohibited outright theft, they found other ways to go about it. Yet the white theft culture went far beyond horses, as they stole other things as well: grass, water, wildlife, buffalo, and of course the land itself. And while horse stealing's negative consequences could fall harshly on Indians and whites alike, the overall legacy of white theft fell most severely and disproportionately on the Plains Indians themselves. After all, the Ten Commandments prohibited horse stealing, but the Old Testament was less clear about the morality of land cessions and the wholesale butchering of entire buffalo herds.

2

Theft Cultures

When plunder becomes a way of life for a group of men in a society,
over the course of time they create for themselves a legal system that
authorizes it and a moral code that glorifies it.

—FRÉDÉRIC BASTIAT, *Economic Sophisms; and,*
What Is Seen and What Is Not Seen

Compared to the previous decade, the 1860s were a much more turbulent time in western Nebraska. Many new things arrived in the region: a railroad, a telegraph line, new military posts, and several new towns. Dots and lines and proper nouns began filling in the blank spaces on the territorial maps. The Colorado gold rush pulled migrants along the Overland Trail like a magnet, and as Denver grew, so did westbound traffic. Conflict throughout western Nebraska intensified, spurred by local events but increasingly, and more urgently, by developments further afield, in Colorado, Wyoming, and Washington DC. For the Lakotas and Cheyennes horse raiding was an important component of this warfare—it sent a critical message to their enemies while dispossessing them of important animals. But for some whites the movement of so many Indian, migrant, and army horses through this domain created irresistible opportunities for graft and theft.

Horse thievery further destabilized the region from the 1860s through the 1870s. Plains Indian horse raids and other depredations threatened ranchers' and migrants' lives, Overland Trail traffic, railroad construction, telegraph operation, transcontinental mails and freighting, and of course the all-important horse herds upon which everyone depended in one way or another. Sometimes the situation deteriorated to the point that the trail would shut down, effectively closing overland access to Denver and points west. But Plains Indians were not the only ones stealing horses. White thieves targeted Plains Indian bands, harassed migrants, and even pilfered animals from military posts, stretching army resources to the limit as cavalry detachments often could not tell at first, when responding to reports of a raid, whether they should be chasing Indians or Euro-Americans. Ranchers got in on the act by skimming animals off the range, filing fraudulent reports for stolen animals, and occasionally stealing directly from migrants and settlers themselves. Some soldiers snuck off with horses as well.

All this wanton stealing created a regional theft culture, one that encouraged, incentivized, and failed to adequately enforce laws and mores against horse appropriation. In this environment civilian authorities were utterly incapable of helping migrants protect their property and could only respond after the fact, which was usually too late. The army by default was the most effective, and on occasion the only meaningful, arbiter that could pursue or stop a white gang of horse raiders, but both military and civilian laws limited what they could do. Since no single institution effectively held a monopoly on violence, there was little to prevent people from stealing or skimming on the side. The fact is that many people in western Nebraska during the 1860s and much of the 1870s were simply more than willing to steal horses, cattle, and other things to get what they wanted. Western Nebraska was a horse thief's paradise.

Raiding along the Platte

Throughout the decade following the fight over Little Wolf's horse and the subsequent Battle of Solomon's Fork in 1857, horse raiding along the Overland Trail increased as tensions rose between American Indians and Euro-Americans. The 1858

THEFT CULTURES

Colorado gold rush ushered travelers along the South Platte, which led to more emigrant traffic through valuable bison hunting grounds. This prompted several bands of Lakotas, particularly the Oglalas, to retaliate against intruding whites by stealing horses, killing cattle, and attacking wagon trains and ranches. Trails in the western half of Nebraska Territory were especially vulnerable to attack since Forts Kearny and Laramie were located several hundred miles apart. In 1858, for instance, a raiding party attacked a wagon train near the confluence of the North and South Platte Rivers, killed several settlers, and stole most of their horses.[1]

Plains Indians were not the only ones responsible for stealing more horses along the Overland Trail. Charles M. Clark noted the presence of organized, hidden gangs of stock thieves when describing a journey he took across the plains to Pike's Peak in 1861. The country around the forks of the Platte was "infested with bands of thieves and robbers," he wrote, "whose sole business [was] to stampede and secure the emigrants' stock." While on the lookout for villains, Clark remembered seeing "suspicious looking characters . . . lurking around the camp at night" who were allegedly "in the endeavor to secure the horses or mules lariated out." As a result, "constant vigilance was exercised" to mitigate the threat since fears of horse and cattle theft on the trail were a matter to be taken seriously. "There is perhaps no point wherein the emigrant is more sensitive than that regarding the safety of his stock," Clark wrote, "and he anxiously watches them."[2]

In spite of the threat posed by white horse thieves, the war along the Bozeman Trail, together with the establishment of the pony express and the construction of the first transcontinental telegraph line, made protecting the Platte Valley a national priority. As a result, the army established Cottonwood Post, renamed Fort McPherson after the Civil War, to protect settlers, migrants, and freighters along the Overland Trails from sporadic raiding (map 3). The army began construction of the post in 1863 at Cottonwood Springs, near the intersection of the Overland Trail and Cottonwood Canyon, which led south

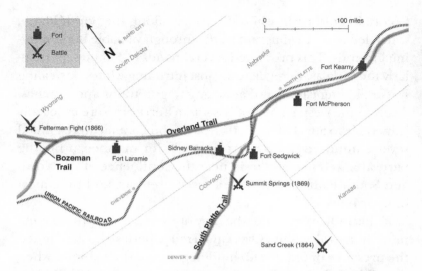

Map 3. Forts and battles in and around western Nebraska, 1860–69. Map created by the author.

to the Republican River valley. The Cottonwood Springs post quickly became the front line of defense against raids in the surrounding area; the army's presence briefly prevented further violence in the region, and in 1864 General Robert B. Mitchell forged a nonaggression pact with the Brulé and Oglala bands at the post.[3] Per the agreement, the Lakotas would not interfere during the Colorado War in exchange for several protections and accommodations, including a promise to allow the Lakota into the Platte Valley for trade.[4] Problems along the South Platte, however, quickly cast a shadow over southwestern Nebraska as tensions between the whites and the Plains Indians rose in Colorado.

Apart from the usual intertribal raiding, Nebraska's trails were quiet from 1862 through early 1864. But the dangers along the South Platte began to mount during the summer of 1864, due largely to the efforts of Colorado territorial governor John Evans and U.S. army colonel John Chivington. Ominously, both men sought to remove the Cheyenne from eastern Colorado and began looking for excuses to take action against them. In April,

Chivington found his opening, when a rancher reported that a band had run off his mules. Chivington dispatched Lieutenant Scott Dunn with forty men to chase down the suspected culprits. The soldiers, upon catching up with the Cheyennes, fired on the party. Two cavalrymen died in the skirmish. The following week another alleged attack prompted a second expedition. This time the troopers killed two dozen innocent Cheyennes who happened to be in the way. One after another, horse-stealing reports gave Evans and Chivington the cover they needed to aggressively seek out and destroy Cheyennes throughout Colorado Territory.[5]

Provoked by these aggressive acts, Cheyenne chief Black Kettle and other leaders could no longer keep their younger and brasher warriors in line. Cheyenne war parties began attacking stagecoaches, emigrant trains, and road ranches along the Platte, Smokey Hill, and Arkansas Rivers. Horse raiding in the region intensified as Brulé, Oglala, and Arapaho bands soon followed suit, motivated in part by the rich rewards the Cheyennes were returning back to their camps. Later that summer, from August 7 to 9, several bands of Northern Cheyenne swept through southern Nebraska, striking ranches, military outposts, and wagon trains. Farmers along the Little Blue River suffered the worst violence as Cheyenne war parties scalped, killed, wounded, and took captive dozens of whites in the region. In Lincoln County raiding parties killed three men at the Gillette Ranch, another three men at Gilman's Ranch, and one settler near Cottonwood Springs. By the end of the summer hundreds of horses, mules, and cattle had been stolen.[6]

Both violent attacks and horse raids continued to multiply across the region. Of the approximately forty instances of horse stealing reported to authorities at Cottonwood Post between 1864 and 1880, twelve occurred between May 1864 and September 1865. The army blamed Plains Indian horse thieves for eight of those cases. This massive outbreak of violence in the region during the Platte Valley War prompted one local historian to claim that "the year 1865 was the most troublesome for Lincoln County."[7] And raiding reports did not need to be true to cause panic, as rumors of additional Lakota and Cheyenne raiding in southwestern Nebraska circulated ominously throughout the Platte Valley. One officer reported seeing at least twenty-five hundred raiders near the Platte Road near Julesburg and warned "everyone with property" along the river to be vigilant, while Brigadier General Robert B. Mitchell implored emigrants to stop where they were on the trail and prepare to fight for their own protection. Major George M. O'Brien rode east to rally citizens to their own defense.[8]

As rumors frightened migrants, ranchers, and soldiers alike, fears that the conflict in Colorado would spread toward Nebraska intensified during the summer of 1864. Scout Alfred Gay warned authorities that the Cheyennes intended to sweep through the Platte Valley and kill every white person they came across. Cottonwood Post's geographic isolation raised fears among the troops and their commanders that they could not fight off the impending onslaught. Military leaders warned the Brulés, many of whom were caught between the warring Oglalas and Cheyennes on one side and an anxious U.S. military presence on the other, to report "foolish and bad white men" to military authorities while also refraining from committing "depredations" and other acts of "crime." On June 8, after a second round of peace negotiations had failed, General Mitchell closed the Platte Road, effectively shutting down travel throughout the region. He posted additional escorts and guards along the trail and sent an order of mules to Fort Laramie under heavy guard. In spite of Mitchell's orders, some migrants, freighters, and travelers continued to use the road anyway.[9]

Mitchell was also powerless to stop Evans and Chivington's war against the Cheyennes in Colorado. Hostilities spiraled out of control after November 29, 1864, when eight hundred Colorado militiamen under Chivington launched a brutal and unprovoked assault on an Arapaho and Southern Cheyenne encampment on Sand Creek. They slaughtered over one hundred peaceful Cheyenne men, women, and children; mutilated their bodies; and stole their tipis and horses. George Bird Grinnell's unsparing account of the tragedy describes the extent of the atrocity and the depravity of the troops who committed it: "Women and children who asked the soldiers for pity and protection were killed. Lieutenant Olney . . . swore at the investigation in 1865 that he saw Lieutenant Richmond, of the Third Colorado Cavalry, shoot and scalp three women and five children . . . [who] screamed for mercy, while Richmond coolly shot one after another." Chivington arrived at the camp with one goal in mind: mass murder.[10]

As news of the massacre spread, nearly all of the Lakota, Cheyenne, and Arapaho chiefs in the central plains agreed that Chivington's actions amounted to a declaration of war. While most of the raids the previous summer had been unsanctioned acts by young warriors, the response to Sand Creek demanded coordination and swift punishment. On January 7, 1865, nearly one thousand Lakota and Cheyenne warriors retaliated by attacking Julesburg, Colorado, and nearby Fort Riley. They killed fourteen soldiers and made off with hundreds of animals. In the following weeks other Indian war parties hammered ranches, caravans, and posts along the South Platte and Overland Trails as well as the telegraph line. They wreaked havoc along the way: according to one historian, for over a month not a single telegram or stagecoach successfully made it through the Platte Valley to Denver. War parties killed at least fifty whites and stole as many as fifteen hundred head of cattle. Meanwhile, General Mitchell could only watch helplessly as winter snows, spring floods, and troop shortages prevented him from casting a wider net. Only after several weeks of raiding did most of the allied bands decide to move northwest toward the Powder River Valley. Meanwhile, the Brulés returned to the North Platte. Not wanting to compete with the Oglala for bison and grass, Spotted Tail and Little Thunder surrendered their lodges at Fort Laramie in April 1865.[11]

Scattered war parties continued to steal horses and attack whites throughout western Nebraska that spring, although the level of mayhem was nowhere near what the region had experienced in August 1864 or January 1865. On May 13 raiders struck Dan Smith's ranch. When a detachment of soldiers guarding the ranch attempted to prevent the attackers from running off Smith's cattle, a battle ensued. Several Cheyennes and one U.S. sergeant died during the late-morning engagement 20 miles southeast of Cottonwood Post. Several horses also perished in the fray, although none were stolen. In spite of the Platte running high, the survivors managed to ford the river and pursue the band northward. Soon after the attack on the Smith Ranch, on July 13, a band stole ten horses from a train 7 miles south of the post. A week later they stole two horses from a civilian and another nine horses from a wagon train near O'Fallon's Bluff. Another party attacked a unit near Box Elder Creek, about 175 miles southwest of Cottonwood Post, killing ten soldiers and running off their entire horse herd. Later that summer a separate group stole ten more horses from Captain John Wilcox's command.[12]

The raiding in western Nebraska largely had subsided by late 1865, when most of the Lakota and Northern Cheyenne combatants moved north into the Powder River region, but the perceived threat of horse raiding by Plains Indians still preoccupied white ranchers, soldiers, migrants, and businesses. By 1867 the region included another important target for raiders: the transcontinental railroad. The Union Pacific entered Lincoln County in the summer of 1866, and by November it had reached the forks of the Platte. Threats of imminent raiding overshadowed the construction, and wary crews and planners prepared to defend themselves. According to General Grenville Dodge, Lakota and Northern Cheyenne raiding parties threatened the construction crews and company property throughout Nebraska and Wyoming, ensuring that the entire line would have to be built under the guard of an armed camp. One local writer claimed that the Union Pacific proactively employed veteran soldiers to build the track so that they could line up at a moment's notice and repel a possible attack.

Although virtually none of the potential hazards they faced along the rail line could compare with the horrors of Antietam or Petersburg, workers feared the worst. "A report came that [Chief] Red Cloud was coming near Rawling with three thousand hostiles," one employee working near North Platte recalled. "We got a consignment of breech-loading rifles, the first I ever saw . . . with these guns, I hoped the Reds would keep away. We had only fifty to their thousands. Glad they didn't come." Corporal Lauren Aldrich believed the show of strength succeeded. "Owing to our force of arms hostile Indians usually kept at a respectful distance," he wrote, "but occasionally would venture within a danger zone and our men neglected no opportunity to exchange compliments with them." While there is little evidence that the railroad was attacked during its construction in western Nebraska, raiding parties targeted the railroad after its completion, forcing the military to send engines with patrol cars up and down the road in search of possible damage. At one point the railroad authorities ordered civilian trains not to use the line at night.[13] Once the Union and Central Pacific Railroads connected at Promontory Point, Utah, on May 10, 1869, the U.S. Army established Sidney Barracks the following fall to provide additional support and protection to the line.

The completed transcontinental railroad dramatically alleviated the pressure placed on the army's horses and mules to carry supplies across the plains, reducing the number of horses needed at the forts while also making it easier for quartermasters to supply remounts by train. Although western Nebraska, lacking navigable waterways, could only be reached by foot or by hoof during the Civil War, the forts themselves were more or less accessible by rail soon after it ended. The Union Pacific connected Fort McPherson to Fort Kearny, ninety miles east, by 1867. Within another year the line reached Sidney after briefly dipping down into Colorado Territory to connect Julesburg. Once it was finished, the army could quickly reinforce and resupply herds along the Platte Valley (at least in theory) using animals from verdant horse pastures of the East, whose herds were restocked and repopulated after the war.[14]

Yet trains, unlike horses, could only travel as far as their tracks could take them. In northeastern Wyoming, beyond the railroad's reach, Oglala chief Red Cloud successfully shut down the Bozeman Trail between 1866 and 1868 by attacking caravans, patrols, and even military posts. The U.S. Army built three forts along the road to protect gold seekers, freighters, and migrants, but Red Cloud repeatedly harassed the new installations and stopped virtually all traffic along the road. He and his followers lured Captain William J. Fetterman and a detachment of eighty troops out of Fort Phil Kearny in December 1866, drew them onto a ridge, and annihilated the entire force. The Fetterman fight was an unmitigated victory for Red Cloud and his allies, but it was not without human cost. Although the final Indian death toll is not known, Strong Wind Blowing, Wooden Leg's oldest brother, was killed in the fighting.[15] Nonetheless, the defeat rattled political and military leaders in Washington. The Johnson administration, which already had its hands full with Reconstruction and an openly hostile Congress, agreed to settle the matter with the Lakotas. In 1868 a second Fort Laramie Treaty established the Great Sioux Reservation as a permanent reserve for the Lakotas. The military abandoned Fort Phil Kearny and the rest of its forts near the Powder River, and Red Cloud accomplished what General Robert E. Lee never could: he forced the United States government to the peace table.

Brulé chief Spotted Tail signed the 1868 Fort Laramie Treaty, and in 1869 he and his people relocated to the Whetstone Agency in Dakota Territory. But while they were supposed to abandon bison hunting and begin farming, Spotted Tail secured the right of his people to hunt south of the Republican River via a meeting with President Ulysses S. Grant in 1870. By the next year Spotted Tail had also succeeded in moving the agency farther south, onto the White River in Nebraska just north of Pine Ridge.[16] During the next several years Spotted Tail and the Brulés worked closely with the officers at Camp Sheridan and Fort McPherson, the posts serving as gatekeepers to the new Spotted Tail Agency and to the Republican River valley, respectively. However, the Brulés' frequent and unrestricted access to the Republican River hunting grounds placed them in a prime position to continue waging war upon the Pawnees, whose villages suffered the loss of lives as well as horses in wake of the Lakotas' unrelenting attacks.

Despite the peace established by the 1868 treaty, the region's stockmen suffered from frequent thefts. In his autobiography cattle rancher John Bratt described one event that occurred as he was constructing his ranch. "The many little thieving bands of Sioux and Cheyenne Indians kept us busy before we finished our ranch, corrals and pasture. They would take a sneak on us and drive off a few horses every chance they got," he claimed. Over the next few months, according to Bratt, the attackers became even more brazen: "About forty Sioux Indians stole up on us one dark night and took seventy-five head of horses out of a herd of one hundred twenty-five in spite of the fact that some twelve herders were sleeping around them with saddle horses tied to their arms, legs or bodies." These were not isolated incidents. According to the Fort McPherson post returns, raiding parties attacked the surrounding country six times between 1868 and 1874. Three of the raids targeted local ranches. One Northern Cheyenne raiding party struck the Greenwood Ranch, located on the North Platte near Bridgeport, and ran off twenty-one horses as the cowboys sat nearby playing poker. Elsewhere, Kansas rancher Nelson Story, well aware of the raiding problem plaguing the northern range in 1866, hired twenty-seven armed men to accompany one thousand head of cattle from Baxter Springs to the Montana mining camps via the Platte and the Bozeman Trail. Only twenty-four of these men made it alive and uninjured to the goldfields, with Indians killing one and wounding two during the drive, but remarkably all the cattle arrived unscathed.[17]

This constant raiding instilled a siege mentality among western Nebraskan ranchers. Not only did they run the risk of losing their entire horse or cattle herds to a hostile party; they also feared losing their lives. "Up to 1880," Bratt claimed in his autobiography, "each employee carried his gun or revolver with plenty of ammunition if going on long trips, also bowie knife and field glasses, as a protection against roving bands of thieving Indians and wolves, and to supply the camps with game." Bratt's cowhands were apparently safe while carrying out their duties, but not all ranchers and ranch hands were so lucky.

A raiding party killed two men on August 9, 1864, as they ate breakfast at the Gilman Ranch, located only about thirteen miles east of Cottonwood Post. The group took a large percentage of the Gilman brothers' stock, and a second raid that afternoon resulted in even more losses. Although the Gilmans kept their ranch running throughout the rest of the Platte Valley War, the losses they suffered during the conflict (notwithstanding the human cost) contributed to their decision to end their partnership after the war and enter new lines of business.[18]

Raiding decreased after the army's 1865 campaign against Red Cloud and the Lakota and Cheyenne bands; later raiding parties would only strike the fort or the area surrounding the Fort McPherson reservation five times after the Battle of Summit Springs. In the spring of 1872 a party stole 7 horses from the post, and three unidentified Plains Indians died during the subsequent pursuit. A more serious incident occurred about a year later, on the morning of April 4, 1873, when a raiding party tried to run off the post quartermaster's herd of 171 horses from a grazing pasture near the fort. This loss hobbled the Third Cavalry since that many horses would have been used to outfit two or three of the five companies stationed at the post that month. However, Company I, whose horses were safe and ready to deploy, dashed off in pursuit and recovered the stolen mounts after a twenty-mile chase.[19]

Whites contributed to this siege mentality by frequently breaking the peace. Some stole Indian ponies for profit or out of desperation, while others falsely reported raids in progress to an overstretched frontier army. A few whites took matters into their own hands by pursuing suspected horse thieves themselves—an extraordinarily foolish and potentially catastrophic thing to do, however well-intentioned. In one case near Plum Creek, a wood hauler witnessed a single Pawnee gallop by with three horses in tow. The rider was moving northeastward, away from nearby Fort Kearny and presumably toward the Pawnee reservation. Perhaps suspecting that these horses belonged to the army or to local residents, the man charged after the escaping thief and began firing his gun at him. Stunned at this turn of events, the

THEFT CULTURES

rider halted and relinquished the ponies before escaping across the Platte. The Good Samaritan then returned to the fort with the three ponies, which upon closer inspection turned out to be Brulé horses that had recently been stolen from Spotted Tail's camp near the Platte forks. According to Corporal Lauren Aldrich, however, the wood hauler was quickly arrested at the fort "for shooting at a friendly Pawnee with intent to kill. He was also informed [that] the entire Pawnee tribe would be after his scalp as soon as this affair was reported to them, so the teamster begged to be set at liberty that he might disappear." The commander complied, and when the Pawnee Scouts arrived the next day to take both the ponies and the shooter into custody, they found only the ponies.[20]

While Fort McPherson responded vigorously to reports of raids, Camp Robinson sent fewer details after fugitive thieves. Located in the far northwestern corner of the state, the army established Camp Robinson in 1873 as the primary military gatekeeper to, defender against, and protector of the Red Cloud Agency. In light of the post's role, Camp Robinson's garrison had a much larger infantry population and was therefore unable to spare its cavalry as frequently for scouts and pursuits. Nevertheless, the men stationed there occasionally responded to reports of theft throughout Nebraska as well as the Wyoming and Dakota Territories. In June 1875 cavalry detachments from Fort Robinson responded to reported horse raids on the Laramie Plains in Wyoming and on the Pawnee Reservation in eastern Nebraska, and in December another detachment chased after an Indian band reported to have stolen forty-seven ponies from Cedar Canyon near the Union Pacific Railroad's Antelope Station.[21]

Camp Sheridan's location was even less hospitable to its troops than Camp Robinson's. Located on Beaver Creek about thirteen miles east of Chadron and ten miles south of the Dakota Territory border, the army established Camp Sheridan in March 1874 for the purpose of protecting and servicing the nearby Spotted Tail Agency. Beaver Creek provided a small, though intermittent, source of water, and just two miles to the south, Pine

Ridge contained numerous stands of ponderosa pines and cottonwoods for construction and fuel. But winters were bitterly cold, with low temperatures averaging about 15 degrees Fahrenheit between the months of December and February. Summers were equally extreme, with high temperatures averaging almost 90 degrees in July and August. Other factors, including punishing prairie winds, surprise snowstorms, low rainfall, and unobstructed sunshine, made Camp Sheridan an uninviting destination for the soldiers stationed there. In addition, the outpost did not have any permanent buildings at first, prompting the camp surgeon to request permission to issue earmuffs to his soldiers on April 14, 1875, writing that they were "absolutely necessary in this climate."[22]

By the end of the 1860s the Fort McPherson garrison had received some additional help. The army founded Sidney Barracks in 1867 as a satellite station for Fort Sedgwick. Located at the Union Pacific Railroad's intersection with the Sidney–Black Hills Trail in the Panhandle, the outpost served two vital functions: it offered additional protection to the transcontinental railroad, and more important, it serviced the trail north toward Dakota Territory. This route assumed greater prominence a few years later, following the construction of Camps Robinson and Sheridan, the establishment of Oglala and Brulé Agencies along the White River, and the 1874 Black Hills gold rush. Despite its location at a critical junction point in the Nebraska Panhandle, the garrison at Sidney Barracks had little to do. This inactivity was partly due to the Department of the Platte's decision to station infantry companies at the post, as opposed to cavalry units. The decision made strategic sense in light of the post's proximity to the railroad, but trains were hardly useful when chasing down a Lakota raiding party in the Sandhills. Once the army abandoned Fort Sedgwick in 1871, Sidney Barracks immediately inherited its role as the principal military station defending southwestern Nebraska and northeastern Colorado.

The Sidney garrison was less inured to combat when compared to their counterparts at Sedgwick and McPherson, but reports of local depredations did reach the post on occasion. Many of these incidents occurred along the now-undefended South Platte River in Colorado. Post commander Captain Charles O. Wood sent a list of sightings and attacks to the Department of the Plate headquarters in Omaha in early 1870. "On the night of the 24th day of March two lodges of Indians were camped . . . on the South Platte," he recalled in his letter. "On the 26th day of March, 50 Indians crossed the railroad between Potter and Antelope Stations . . . on [April] 11th, a party of fifteen Indians coming from the north . . . [drove] in a herder who they [had] badly wounded by shooting with an arrow." Other reports filtered in over the next several years. In November 1874 Amos Miller, of Julesburg, reported that two Sioux Indians had stolen a horse from him. The following year settlers along the South Platte reported two more horse thefts.[23]

Even infrequent raids took their toll on local ranches. James A. Moore, one of western Nebraska's earliest and most immediately successful stockmen, established his range west of Sidney along Lodgepole Creek. Moore had earned his frontier bona fides as a pony express rider between Scottsbluff and Julesburg, and by 1869 he owned the second-largest ranch in the region. But in December 1871 Moore reported to Captain Gilbert S. Carpenter that a Cheyenne band had stolen five mules and three horses from his outfit. The missing animals included a bay horse, a light bay horse with a white stripe on his forehead, and a four-year-old sorrel with white hind feet. Eight other Sidneyites reported losing a total of fifteen horses, including another four sorrels. Carpenter listened to the reports with a sympathetic ear. However, he refused to send his foot soldiers into a potential combat zone over a few missing horses, blaming "inclement" winter weather for keeping his troops close to their post. Instead, he tabulated the missing animals, their descriptions, and their rightful owners and then sent the information to Fort Laramie in hopes that troops there would be able to locate the missing stock.[24]

The specificity within these citizen reports was the exception and certainly not the rule. Vague, nervous tales of Indian sightings oftentimes forced the post garrison to chase shadows and wild geese. The region's geography further compounded the problem, as Sidney was flanked on the north and south by a series of low bluffs and treeless hills that obscured, but did not completely hide, anyone peering down on the town. First Lieutenant James Hardenbergh lamented both problems when requesting additional horses in 1870. "There are but three animals at this post that can be ridden," he complained. "I would respectfully ask that there be sent to this post six cavalry horses . . . It is a frequent occurrence for citizens to report seeing Indians on the bluffs, being unable to see them from the post and being without horses I cannot send out a mounted party and ascertain if it is a true or false report."[25]

The lieutenant's wisdom would soon appear prescient. On May 17, only two weeks after Lieutenant Hardenbergh wrote his letter, an uncorroborated Indian sighting by a nervous picketer threw Sidney into a panic. The soldier thought he had seen as many as twenty mounted Indians on top of the bluffs and had fired his rifle to sound the alarm. The party then retreated upon hearing the report. Having no horses to spare, Hardenbergh mounted a few of his men on mules and brought along several armed (and better mounted) civilians on a scout to find the offending parties. Later that afternoon a man arrived in town with news that Indians were fighting railroad section workers west of town. This report further spooked the residents, many of whom began to fear the worst. "The excitement was great," recalled Hardenbergh. "All the citizens that had arms were on the street, [and] the majority of the females took refuge in a railroad roundhouse." After investigating the latest rumor, however, the commander discovered the true culprit behind the scare: a cavalry detachment whose unexpected arrival had appeared from a distance to be a raiding band of Indians. The lieutenant suspected shenanigans by the intruding cavalrymen: "It was their intention in my opinion to get up an Indian scare and they were successful."[26]

Once Spotted Tail agreed to move his people to the agency north of Camp Robinson, only the Dog Soldiers of the Northern Cheyenne remained within a hundred miles of either Sidney Barracks or Fort McPherson. By this time the Plains Indians south of the Platte were in a precarious spot. Dwindling bison herds, railroad construction along the Platte and Smokey Hill Rivers, a rising white population, growing ranches, and millions of newly claimed acres threatened to transform northern Kansas and southern Nebraska into "civilized" districts. As always, Euro-Americans exacted a heavy toll on the native inhabitants of these lands. Whites hunted bison and other game, depleting the amount of protein available for consumption on the plains, while their horses and cattle chewed up countless pastures' worth of valuable grass. These pressures strangled the Northern Cheyennes' food supply, forcing them to steal crops, cattle, and horses to survive. Throughout 1868 and the first half of 1869, Chief Tall Bull's band of Cheyenne raided farms, ranches, military posts, and stage stations across the Republican River valley in Nebraska and Kansas.

As during the Platte Valley War, this conflict soon threatened to engulf the newly formed state. This time the raiders attacked settlements and forts along the Platte as their reprisals against Euro-American abuses ranged farther north. The trouble began in 1867, when on May 6 Fort Laramie wired the commanders at McPherson that four Cheyenne war parties were en route to "plunder" the Platte Road between Plum Creek and O'Fallon's Bluff. Local citizens took the reports seriously: although prominent road rancher Jack Morrow and several other settlers ventured off to search for a band rumored to be in the area, by the end of month settlers had "abandoned" all of the ranches between Fort McPherson and Fort Kearny, and those who remained were alarmed "hourly." The discovery of a scalped corpse two miles west of the fort did not help matters either. Intermittent attacks continued into 1868, when Fort McPherson's commanding officer reported three major raids in his monthly post returns, including one on the Hinman Ranch in which raiders killed six civilians. In one particularly dramatic incursion on a U.S. military installation, Chief Yellow Hand stole twenty-six ponies from Fort McPherson itself. Raids by non-Cheyenne bands of stock stealing Plains Indians likely exacerbated the situation, as John Bratt recalled in his autobiography that "many raids were made by bands of thieving Sioux" during this time. One of these raids, which destroyed John Burke's ranch near North Platte, nearly claimed the lives of Bratt's future bride and her family.[27]

In response the army organized a punitive campaign at Fort McPherson. The Republican River Expedition was a slow, bitter, and deadly slog for its combatants. However, the campaign, led by Colonel Eugene Carr, succeeded in defeating Tall Bull at the Battle of Summit Springs in northeastern Colorado on July 11, 1869. Of the more than four hundred Cheyenne combatants involved, about thirty-five were killed in the assault. The victorious troops took seventeen Indian women and children prisoner and rescued one white woman who had been previously captured. The most economically crippling loss for the Cheyennes was the seizure of their horse herd. The army carried off 274 horses and 144 mules, destroying the band's ability to hunt bison and organize war parties. This defeat at the hands of the Fifth Cavalry put an end to most of the raiding in the region and encouraged further white settlement.[28]

Nebraska's settlers, migrants, and indigenous inhabitants continued to suffer raids for nearly another decade, but the Republican River campaign represented a watershed moment. From that point forward, many of the raiding parties would emerge from, and most of the fighting would occur, outside of the state's borders. As the theater of operations continued to lurch toward the north and west during the 1870s, more settlers and ranchers began trying their luck in western Nebraska. Still, even as the conflict seemed to move beyond the horizon, western Nebraska was a region in transition between two very different types of horse herd management: large and small. As more homesteaders brought their small herds into the Platte and Republican Valleys, large-herd owners continued to predate on one another. Ranchers, officers, and soldiers stole, appropriated, and swindled horses from Indians as well as from other whites. While the raiding frontier slowly began to fade

THEFT CULTURES

away in Nebraska, in many ways the region's theft culture was more pervasive than ever.

Hustling on the Side

The Battle of Summit Springs ended one wave of horse theft and started another. After Tall Bull and his supporters were killed or driven off, army officers distributed the captured horses to soldiers and themselves. The recipients raced them to see which were the fastest. Although the army eventually owned the vast majority of these animals, sometimes soldiers cherry-picked the horses they wanted for themselves. Buffalo Bill Cody, who fought at Summit Springs as a scout in the Fifth Cavalry, later claimed that he had captured two prize horses during the fight. After seeing Tall Bull, the Dog Soldiers' war chief, ride in on an "extremely fleet" bay, Cody decided to "capture the horse if possible." Cody coveted the horse so much that he claimed to have hidden himself in a ravine so that he could assassinate Tall Bull at close range; he feared that shooting the chief at a safer distance would endanger the animal. Another soldier rounded up the riderless mount once the fighting ended, and Cody used his growing celebrity status to claim it. Cody took another horse, Powder Face, after the battle; it later won several high-stakes horse races across the plains as its owner's fame grew. Cody went so far as to call Powder Face the "fastest horse west of the Missouri," and the pony became a celebrity in its own right after appearing in a series of Ned Buntline dime novels chronicling Buffalo Bill's adventures on the high plains.[29]

After the army seized these Cheyenne herds, citizens placed claims on those mounts that they believed had been stolen from them during previous raids. The victory at Summit Springs invited a flurry of demands from local farmers and ranchers who insisted that some of their own horses were among the recently acquired animals, and boards of survey heard claims from several local citizens. Some, though not all, of these claims were legitimate. The board granted as many as 50 mules to James A. Moore. Moore's claim was that a total of 150 mules had been stolen, yet the army only recovered a third of them following the battle. There is no way to tell if these ponies were dead, traded elsewhere, or if Moore was again "adding iron to his hay shipment." The board also rejected a portion of road ranch owner Jack Morrow's claim, mainly because 6 of the horses he identified had government brands on them. The board sometimes heard multiple cases from the same claimant, as when John Burke, after being granted 6 mules and a horse by the government, decided to claim 3 additional mules. The board awarded these to Burke as well. In spite of the locals' tendency to over-claim seized horses, many of the stolen animals recovered by the army after Summit Springs remained in the army's custody. The army added these horses to the post's "Indian herd." Rancher Jacob Schnell informed authorities at the post in 1870 that he saw 3 of his stolen horses in the fort's corral, but the commanders ignored his claims.[30]

Summit Springs mitigated, but did not end, the danger posed by Plains Indian horse raiding in western Nebraska. Thieves still struck local residents, especially ranchers. A band of eight Winnebagos allegedly stole thirteen horses from M. C. Keith and his neighbors on March 21, 1871. The Fifth Cavalry chased them from Fort McPherson, but the raiding party escaped once snowfall covered its trail. In 1874 several dozen suspected thieves had run off a herd of horses near Brady Station. To prevent additional depredations, John Bratt established a new ranch thirty-four miles north of the Platte, in the Sandhills, to serve as a buffer from future attacks. Bratt outfitted this diversionary ranch with a token herd of livestock in hopes that raiding parties would target it before reaching his much larger herds along the Birdwood and North Platte Rivers. At the same time, raiding parties targeted Fort McPherson as well. In an 1873 letter addressed to "Mrs. Barnes," E. B. Fowler claimed that a raiding party had recently "made a run at the herd" and escaped with several horses. The horses were recaptured after an eighteen-mile chase.[31]

Intertribal raiding did not slow down, either. The Lakotas regularly stole horses from the Pawnees and other regional tribes, and nations from outside of the region often stole horses from

THEFT CULTURES

the Lakotas and Cheyennes. In November 1874 a band of Utes stole hundreds of horses from the Lakotas and Cheyennes in a single raid. The Lakotas were not equipped to stop them, but after the military repeatedly forced them to relinquish captured horses, they demanded that the military grant them the right to give chase and recover them. Post commander Nathan A. M. Dudley urged his superiors at the Department of the Platte to force the Utes to return the stock since the Lakotas needed them for hunting. Meanwhile, the *Western Nebraskian* reported that the Sioux "were in a starving condition due to [the] theft [of their horses] . . . now they lack meat." The Lakotas also recorded the significance of the event, which is depicted on three different winter counts.[32]

Army officers also continued stealing, or claiming, horses seized from surrendering bands. In 1871 a detachment from Fort McPherson seized sixty horses believed to have been stolen near Birdwood Creek. There is very little information on what happened to these sixty horses, but some evidence suggests that the Fifth Cavalry added some of the animals into its herd and sold a dozen others in North Platte. According to the post returns, the Fifth Cavalry companies at Fort McPherson received thirty-one horses in June 1871 and claimed that an additional twelve animals were unserviceable. On June 12 Major Eugene Carr convened a special board of survey that discussed whether or not to sell some army horses, and on July 6 the Department of the Platte authorized the sale. By the end of July the fort had eleven fewer unserviceable horses. Later, on August 24, the post commander issued instructions for working with the many "untrained" horses at the fort, which suggests that the new horses it had recently acquired were unprepared for cavalry drills.[33] The following year Fort McPherson's command prepared to sell a "lot" of recently seized "ponies." But just before one of the garrison units, Company E of the Second Cavalry, transferred to Fort Laramie on February 2, the post commander, Captain James Curtis from the Third Cavalry, asked the department for permission to allow each officer to "select one or two ponies each out of the lot to be sold here."

The officers would then pay the average price garnered for the auctioned horses per head. Although there is no evidence that the sale went ahead as planned, at least one officer criticized the transfer because it might deprive the Pawnee Scouts of mounts in the event of a spring campaign.[34] The officer did not mention whether he believed that Pawnee soldiers should only be given "Indian ponies" or that the army did not wish to purchase new ones for its American Indian troops. But either way, the animals were to be redistributed.

Even in the midst of war, migrants, visitors, and other whites in the area did not stop stealing from other Euro-Americans. J. C. Foster claimed that one of his ranch hands had stolen a horse from him while traveling up the Overland Trail in September 1865, just two weeks before a war party ran off four horses from a migrant train in the same area. Four months later soldiers from Fort McPherson seized a horse and a mule from two citizens who allegedly had stolen the animals from the post herd. The men were arrested for horse theft. As a result of the crime, the commander ordered his men to ensure that no horses be taken from the post herd without a pass, except during water calls. In another incident the door to the corral was found broken and the corner of the stockade dug up on the morning of February 9, 1866. Thirty-six mules were missing. The commanding officer, Lieutenant Colonel R. E. Fleming, was not sure if the theft was committed by raiders or thieving citizens. However, the Northern Cheyennes did not often break into corrals since they preferred to count coup in the open.[35]

Perhaps the boldest white horse thieves were the ranchers themselves. Many stockmen padded their profits by "skimming the ranges." Most cattlemen north of the Platte River in the early 1870s earned lucrative government contracts to provide beef for Indian reservations and agencies. Although some ranches furnished this meat by honest means, less-reputable firms underbid their competitors to secure the contracts, sold the best beef to whites, and then weighed down the scales. This practice, common at the time, was not only morally questionable—often other people's herds got caught up in the beef suppliers' efforts to quickly round up as many strays as possible on the range in order to have enough beef to provide to the Indians—but also led to one public call for "the stockmen . . . To band together and start Judge Lynch out on important business."[36]

While most ranchers who skimmed and hustled on the side tried to keep a low profile, others could not help but develop infamous reputations. One of the most disreputable men on the trail, Jack Morrow, owned a road ranch near the forks of the Platte. Morrow allegedly stole stock from migrants heading west and then sold "replacement stock" to the migrants once they passed through his road ranch that looked suspiciously like the stock that was stolen. Morrow may have also used that stock to fulfill government livestock contracts, and in 1870 Nebraska senator John M. Thayer advised the secretary of interior to send "incorruptible" special inspectors to ensure that Morrow was not delivering emaciated cattle to the Upper Missouri reservations.[37] The state of Nebraska never indicted Morrow for any wrongdoing, but several witnesses later wrote about his shady dealings. John Bratt claimed that Morrow wore a $1,000 diamond "in his yellow and badly soiled shirt bosom" and that "scarcely a train passed [his ranch]" that did not lose stock. Also, while Captain Eugene Ware did not explicitly call Morrow a thief in his memoir of the Platte Valley War, he did recall a scene in which he and a small group of officers visited Morrow's ranch, ate dinner, and played faro afterward. Morrow used the opportunity to lobby for a government corn-shelling contract. Before speaking to Ware directly, Morrow secretly talked up the proposed contract to every other member of the party. "This whole proceeding was so raw," wrote Ware, "that none of us every made any visit again to Jack Morrow."[38]

Morrow's relationship with Spotted Tail and other Lakotas might have caused some of this suspicion. These bands frequently visited Morrow, and in 1864 the Brulés asked to receive their annuities from the government near his ranch. Morrow had also married an American Indian woman. Unfortunately, local whites did not approve of Morrow's choice of friends. "Thieving bands of Sioux never bothered [Morrow]," Bratt claimed, because he was "usually the beneficiary of these raids; so much so, the commander at Fort McPherson gave Jack a hint to leave and he did. This broke up a bad nest of hard characters, both whites and Indians." While there is no evidence that this "hint" was given, Morrow frequently clashed with the commanders at Fort McPherson up until the point he left Lincoln County in 1868 or 1869. He also knew when to turn on the charm. After meeting Morrow at his ranch while en route to Fort Laramie, Colonel Henry B. Carrington's wife, Margaret, gushed over the encounter, calling Jack Morrow "the prince of ranchmen, and the king of good fellows. *He* is a ranchman indeed!" When well-behaved, Morrow's business was very good—he amassed over $100,000 in assets, stock, and improvements in 1864, and his road ranch was important enough that army garrisons and escorts from Cottonwood Post regularly visited and protected the facility.[39]

Whenever ranchers targeted the herd at the post, which, according to one commander, resembled an "extensive stock ranch," they did so indirectly. In one instance a pair of thieves stole a horse and four mules from the fort and a nearby ranch in 1866. When soldiers tracked the suspects to Dan Smith's ranch, they appeared to be completely destitute and "without means of support." The two men attempted to sell the animals with Smith's help, perhaps in exchange for the rancher's financial assistance or a share of the profit, but after the two suspects were arrested, Smith denied any wrongdoing. Another man submitted a claim to the Quartermaster General's Office in Washington DC, alleging that a detachment from Fort McPherson had illegally seized two horses from his ranch in 1866. The quartermaster general ruled against the rancher, however, when it discovered that the horses bore the United States Army's official brand. In a separate case an army officer accused rancher John Burke of having swapped two broken-down ponies for fresh draft horses (or remounts) from the government stable after he was commissioned to repair the road between the post and the Union Pacific. Justice of the Peace William F. Cody heard the case, and after reading two sworn depositions from the soldiers

THEFT CULTURES

in charge of the corral testifying to Burke's innocence, Cody declared that the accusation was meritless. Burke was exonerated, but it was not inconceivable that he might swindle a couple of fresh horses from the military.[40]

When they were not busy fighting, drilling, or cleaning the stables, soldiers stationed at the post found time to steal horses. According to one report in 1865, "The troops stationed along the line at the different stage stations are in the habit of taking horses, mules, and cattle belonging to citizens and hiding them until they can sell them or extort a large sum for their trouble." Not only does this letter implicate the soldiers at Cottonwood Post in stealing from migrants passing by on the trail, but it also raises the possibility that one of the stations referred to in the report was Jack Morrow's. In another incident a soldier shot "a friendly Indian" on Medicine Creek in 1867 and stole his horse. Randall requested that the horse be returned to "quiet" the aggrieved parties.[41] Soldiers stole from local herds as well. In early 1866 an army private stole a horse from the Union Pacific Railroad and traded it to a friend at Cottonwood Post. Later that year a cavalry sergeant stole a company horse and sold it to the Overland Stage Company. The post commander informed the stage company agent that the United States Army would reclaim its rightful property, but when another officer arrived to receive the stolen horse, he discovered that it had been sold to a third party. Instances such as these suggest that thieving officers found civilian herd managers who were more than willing to purchase ill-gotten animals from the army. Since the discovery of the stolen horse sold by the stage company was an accident, it is possible that soldiers at the fort stole and sold more animals in a similar manner.[42]

Deserters also stole horses to escape Fort McPherson. They posed a major threat to the garrison's security and mobility once the Platte Valley War ended and the tedium of peacetime began to set in. Between 1864 and 1867 escaping soldiers stole at least thirty horses while deserting the fort. In June and July 1866 alone, soldiers absconded with at least a dozen cavalry horses.[43] One of the most notorious incidents of horse theft to befall the post came at the hands of three soldiers who stole several ponies and then deserted. One of the soldiers, John Ryan, had had a previous run-in with Captain Eugene Ware, who called Ryan and his two companions "three of about the worst men I ever saw." By 1867 desertions were so common and conditions at the fort were so burdensome that Captain John Mizner complained to Adjutant General Edward D. Townsend about the problem, arguing that the cost of making the soldiers' lives better would be far cheaper than the expense incurred by pursuing and apprehending missing soldiers.[44] Part of that cost included the loss of dozens of valuable horses. In fairness to the soldiers, horses were necessary to expedite as quickly as possible their getaway from what would almost certainly already be a harsh punishment for having left their post. Deserters were often lashed with a rawhide whip, or their heads were shaved and branded with a *D*. Technically, deserters could be shot as well, though this seldom happened. In any case, taking a horse in the process of escaping did not seem to be as big a risk as the decision to escape itself, which alone speaks volumes about the unhappiness many soldiers experienced in these encampments.[45]

By late 1867 deserters did not need to steal horses to get away from Fort McPherson. The newly constructed Union Pacific Railroad was located only a few miles north of the post, giving soldiers an even faster route out of the area. Soldiers also risked capture when stealing horses since cavalry animals were well guarded, and the post commanders only telegraphed deserters' descriptions to other military authorities when soldiers left the fort on stolen ponies. The railroad's opening explains the sudden rise in desertions: while 83 men deserted in 1866 and 57 men escaped in 1867, another 107 left in 1868, and 187 ran away in 1869. In April 1869 alone, 54 deserters left the post, or about one half of an entire company of infantry. While the additional heat that came from having to steal a horse in order to get away from the post probably disincentivized desertion, train hopping made it possible for soldiers to flee anywhere.[46]

Unfortunately for troops stationed at Camps Robinson and Sheridan, the Union Pacific was over two hundred miles distant.

The Red Cloud and Spotted Tail Agencies lay to the north, Pine Ridge and the largely unexplored Sandhills inhibited escape to the south, and both Fort Laramie to the west and the Missouri River to the east were several days of travel away. The isolation of these posts did not prevent those who were desperate to leave from stealing horses to do so, however. One Camp Sheridan soldier, Private Charles E. Lathrope, wrote a letter to the post commander explaining his reasons for deserting with a company horse. "I thought I would write you and tell you all about this little crime," he began, "and ask you hurry up the Tryal [*sic*] as soon as possible." Lathrope wished to get back to his father, who had announced his intention to move to Nova Scotia. But since he "knew that it was impossible to get" a discharge, he decided to make his move on his next overnight guard shift. After 11:00 p.m. the soldier called his horse, which he had already saddled, and dashed away from the post. During his getaway, however, he ran into several Indians. Fearing an ambush, he took out his gun and started firing. After several minutes of shooting, the Indians called out to him and invited him to come over. Unbeknownst to him, the Indians had been heading in the opposite direction, toward the post, when they encountered the frightened soldier. He met his pursuers, who understood that he was deserting and promised not to tell his commander. Once they arrived at the post, however, they informed the officers about their encounter. Although Lathorpe likely foiled his own escape attempt when he engaged with the passing Indians, he probably believed that his desire to see his father before the older man moved abroad would elicit some sympathy at his court-martial.[47]

Posse Comitatus

The army spared no effort attempting to apprehend deserters, especially those who stole public horses, but after 1868 its approach toward thieving regional tribes was more muted. Keeping the peace between American Indians and Euro-Americans was a matter of paramount importance as well as growing confusion. President Grant's "peace policy" subordinated the frontier army to the Bureau of Indian Affairs (BIA) and its constituent agencies across the plains. The policy simultaneously tasked the military with guarding and protecting agency tribes from settlers and from each other while also protecting settlers from raiding and frontier violence. The Grant administration began staffing agencies and other posts within the Department of Interior and the BIA with Christian missionaries, as opposed to political appointees, on the assumption that missionaries would protect the Indians' best interests while simultaneously educating them about farming and Christian morality.[48] Local army commanders, however, continued to exercise influence over their posts and regional diplomatic outreach. One way of doing this was by reaching out to local friendly Plains Indians. Spotted Tail became one of the United States' greatest military and diplomatic allies in the early 1860s, after realizing during his imprisonment at Fort Leavenworth, from 1855 through 1856, that the Lakotas did not have the logistical means or manpower necessary to defeat the whites in a protracted war. For their part, commanders in western Nebraska recognized that the Brulés should be protected whenever possible. When several bands of Northern Cheyenne encamped in the Republican River valley threatened to attack Spotted Tail's people, the fort offered shelter and provisions to the Brulés.[49]

Wishing to avoid engaging peaceful bands who traveled through or hunted in restricted areas (or near places colonized by whites), the command at Fort McPherson also interpreted treaties, orders from the War Department, and other mandates from Washington in such a way as to maximize the American Indians' freedom of movement whenever possible. Colonel Henry Carrington sent an unsolicited letter to General George Custer in 1867, advising him that while American Indians had "no business being on the road" within a day's march of either Fort McPherson or Julesburg, Morrow's Ranch was close enough to the fort that Plains Indians could cross the river safely there. Soon enough, Lakota bands were crossing south of the Platte to visit Morrow's so often that the Fort McPherson post commander had to revisit this policy, ordering that "if possible" Lakotas must be stopped from crossing so as to prevent "serious collision with the whites" who settled or traveled along the Platte Road.[50] But he did not force the issue.

Later, the treaty of 1868 prohibited Plains Indians from making camp south of the Platte. In practice, though, there was some wiggle room. Officers at the fort continued to host Spotted Tail and Swift Bear from time to time, and post commanders had given permission to the Brulés, Otoes, Pawnees, and Omahas to hunt on the Republican as late as the winter of 1872–73. The commanders also forwarded requests for ponies and provisions from Spotted Tail to their commanders. Not everyone was pleased with these kindnesses, however. Annoyed at the fort's hospitality, General Philip Sheridan reprimanded the commander of the Department of the Platte, General Edward Ord, stating that he "was exceedingly sorry to hear" about these visits and reminded Ord that no American Indians were to set foot near any of the forts between the Platte and the Arkansas.[51]

The army sometimes extended similar kindnesses to civilians as well. Until the 1878 Posse Comitatus Act prohibited the United States Army from participating in local law enforcement, Fort McPherson and its satellite post in North Platte were important allies in Lincoln County's efforts to control crime. Before the county constructed its first jail, in 1868, the sheriff often sent suspects to the fort's stockade for imprisonment. Officials also brought the accused to the jail for their own protection when necessary, such as when the sheriff sent murder suspect Peter Manning to the fort to prevent a vigilante mob from lynching him. Local authorities also requested the garrison's services for manhunts. On at least one occasion, in 1873, the deputy sheriff of Lincoln County requested the use of five officers to help him pursue and capture a gang of horse thieves and recover the stolen horses. Evidence shows that the post commander had obliged since on September 15 five soldiers received a special commendation from the post commander for helping the Lincoln County sheriff pursue and apprehend two horse thieves in Fort Hayes, Kansas. The joint expedition also recovered five stolen horses.[52]

Sheriffs, officials, and even lawyers from other counties solicited help from the post in law enforcement matters. They sometimes sent descriptions of suspected horse thieves to the fort, where the garrison was ready to detain the suspects and investigate the claims when possible. Daniel Freeman, a lawyer in Plum Creek, sought the post commander's help in March 1872, when he sent a letter to the fort that included descriptions of two alleged thieves and the brands of the horses supposedly taken. When both suspects appeared at the fort, the commander examined their horses and concluded that the horses were not the ones previously stolen. The commander notified the Plum Creek resident that the two men would be at the fort for a week in case the lawyer wanted to further investigate the matter. A few days later Freeman, dissatisfied with this outcome, wrote to General Ord requesting that troops be sent to his area. A citizen from Dawson County sent a plea for help to the governor the following year.[53]

The success of the military's efforts often impressed the locals. Settlers were sometimes so enamored by the army's ability to track down and eliminate horse-raiding parties that they wanted to enlist its resources when protecting their own stock. Prominent rancher William Plummer reported a horse theft to Fort McPherson in 1874, claiming that a party of raiders was responsible. Although the incident occurred only a month after a much larger raiding party had killed several settlers on a local ranch and ran off its stock, post commander Nathan A. M. Dudley, skeptical of Plummer's report, asked if the rancher was sure that the theft was not the work of whites. Plummer later admitted that some of his men found the horses, which had strayed off. He sarcastically told Dudley that he did not need to forward his personal thanks to the department. Other ranchers appealed to the commanders' sympathies. Reuben Wood argued that he had little choice but to solicit the army's help when he asked that an escort from Fort McPherson be detailed to help him find some missing cattle. If the army refused to help, he claimed, he would be "powerless to move" and that he could "ill-afford [the] serious loss."[54]

Requests such as these were common enough that the army had to clarify its rules of engagement. In a 1874 letter to his lieutenant, Major Dudley alluded to an earlier General Order that prohibited the army from chasing down white horse thieves. He agreed with the order, noting that it was more appropriate for these crimes to be handled by civil authorities. This was a major policy shift from a year earlier, when the post commander had sent several men to accompany the Lincoln County sheriff in search of two suspected horse thieves. However, post commanders enjoyed a small amount of flexibility when following orders from the War Department. The assistance rendered by the fort a year earlier may have been illegal at the time, and if so, then Dudley made a conscious decision not to offer any additional help to the sheriff in the future.[55]

In time these demands on the fort subsided as its influence began to wane. In an 1874 inspection report on the condition of the post, George Woodward argued that Fort McPherson, which was located in the eastern part of the county, should be abandoned and its resources located farther west. "Its period of usefulness [has] passed," argued Woodward. "The country both north and south of the post is so far settled and so rapidly filling up that it is really self-protective." Saturated by a wave of homesteaders that moved up along the Union Pacific Railroad, eastern Lincoln County was in some respects beginning to resemble the mostly agricultural counties that lay east of the 100th meridian. This wave seemed to crash and break at North Platte, however. As Woodward noted, the lands west of the county seat land were and would continue to be used primarily for livestock raising, which consequently left those areas prone to the "ravage of raiding Indians." The writer recommended that the fort be abandoned, that the North Platte post be maintained and reinforced, and that Sidney Barracks receive more troops in an effort to protect the pastoral range country.[56] Fort McPherson had outlived its usefulness.

Yet Sidney Barracks had problems of its own. White villains and horse thieves continued to cause more problems than Indian raiders for the command there. In March 1872 Major Nathan Dudley reported that James A. Moore had recently traded two revolvers and a rifle to an Indian for his pony, but when Moore's pony was stolen shortly thereafter, he immediately returned to find the Indian and demanded he turn over his arms to Moore. Not surprisingly, the Indian had not taken the pony. That dubious honor belonged to Henry Newman, a local thief who in 1871 had nearly been arraigned by a grand jury in Cheyenne County for stealing thirty head of cattle. After this discovery Major Dudley explained in his report to department headquarters that the incident was symptomatic of a larger problem within the town. "I'm not a favorite with the ring which rules Sidney," he humbly bragged to his superiors. He accused the locals of stealing wood, nails, rations, and "almost all kinds supplies required by the people [in town]."[57] But the scheming locals did not limit themselves to petty thievery. The post commanders encountered frequent difficulties finding dependable contractors as well. Moore, once furnished with a hay contract for the post, was caught weighing his loads with iron so that he could charge more money. Later Dudley quietly investigated the post's beef subcontractor, Carrigan, and his "business qualifications." Not only was Carrigan "lazy" and "indolent," but he did not own any stock and thus relied on whatever cattle he could acquire locally. Major Dudley had his suspicions about where those animals were coming from as well. Carrigan listed Newman, the recently accused rustler, as one of his guarantors. Dudley must have suspected that Newman fenced stolen cattle with Carrigan, who then readily converted the carcasses into beef rations for hungry soldiers.[58]

Fort McPherson's commanders also grew increasingly concerned about civilian horse theft, which caused them to ratchet up the pressure on civilians, contractors, and uninvited guests over time. As early as 1871, "to prevent the repetition of thefts and to place responsibility where it belongs," the post commander declared that all citizens found "about the stables" would be arrested. He also prohibited the post laundresses from washing civilians' clothes or harboring them, perhaps believing that the women in camp and at the fort were liable to being taken advantage of by potential thieves seeking admission into the reservation. Earlier, in 1869, the War Department had issued an order to its frontier posts that required all civilian employees and people passing through military reservations to apply for and carry a pass at all times. All those found without a pass were to be arrested and escorted off of government property. This sweeping policy intended to keep "horse thieves" out of the forts, even though commanders generally knew who their civilian contractors were and had their own ideas of whether or not to trust them. In any event, it became increasingly difficult to tell who had designs on army horses and who did not, regardless of whether or not they were white or American Indian, civilian or military. Thieves lurked everywhere, and telling them apart from everyone else was quickly becoming a challenging full-time job.[59]

The Lakotas and the commanders at Cottonwood Post remembered the Platte Valley War in very different ways, but they often described it in less dangerous and more routine terms than either the settlers or later chroniclers. According to Big Turkey, 1864 was the year when he "captured the Pawnees's [*sic*] horses. Again, I robbed many horses on this side of their territory . . . the following summer, I killed one of the Pawnees and I killed a second one. I killed one that was his wife. In the border area, I again robbed the Pawnee horses. I captured many." In contrast, Captain Eugene Ware later wrote that by November 1864 a temporary lull in the fighting, just before Sand Creek and the Cheyennes' siege at Julesburg, gave the soldiers time to catch their breath. "Confidence along the road seemed to be restored," Ware recalled, but he also noted that even when "one Indian raid followed the other, the tide [of traffic along the road] moved on between-times." Officers started comparing Lakota and Cheyenne depredations to "bad spell[s] of weather," while the migrants themselves "rather enjoyed the prospect of having a little skirmish with the Indians, at some point, so as to enliven the trip and something to tell when they got back to the 'States.'" Although protecting the road ranches, the telegraph line, the Overland Trail, and other important assets was "hard work" for the soldiers and officers at Cottonwood Post, in hindsight Ware did not believe that he or his men were in mortal peril.[60]

Those migrants who were scalped or who lost all of their live-stock likely would have disagreed with Ware's characterization of war parties and horse raids as being comparable to inclement weather, but most Nebraskans understood horse stealing as an ongoing, almost routine phenomenon. During the Platte Valley War, when Oglala and Northern Cheyenne bands attacked the region dozens of times, stole hundreds of head of stock, and killed multiple citizens and soldiers, cultural and practical undercurrents that legitimized certain kinds of horse stealing lent the period a strange sort of normalcy that was less visible to outsiders, who had to contend with more raiding (and a lot more killing) than usual. While one might imagine a "theft culture" as one in which people steal from one another regularly, with impunity, and out of habit, western Nebraska did not always resemble a scene of bedlam where no pocket was safe and where no safe's contents could not be pocketed. To be sure, Nebraska during the 1860s and 1870s was rough around the edges, but many thousands of people also lived in or passed through the region without incident and with their property intact. Rather, the term *theft culture* describes a region where the legal, political, military, and even moral logics of property, possession, and theft are in flux; where the appropriation of essential chattel is legitimized by situational circumstances; and where there is a lack of clear consensus on the parameters of personal property rights. The Platte Valley War and later conflicts in western Nebraska intensified the expression of this culture through increased horse stealing, but these conflicts themselves were not mandates on the legitimacy of horse theft itself.

Participants in western Nebraska's theft culture did not passively accept the legitimacy of stealing horses. Rather, they seized the opportunity to better adapt to rapidly changing ecological, economic, political, and demographic circumstances. The Lakotas stole from other tribes to grow herds, punish their enemies, demonstrate bravery and courage, secure new hunting grounds, provide an important avenue for self-actualization, and ensure social mobility and resource distribution within the band. The U.S. military adapted to the plains by flexibly enforcing eastern rules protecting private property; they later embraced the logics of theft as a means of guaranteeing the self-sufficiency of their horse supply while also depriving the enemy of theirs. Road ranchers and other whites in the region lived an economically and militarily precarious existence, and horse theft provided a means of acquiring plenty in a land of almost perpetual want. Even soldiers who wanted to desert the army adapted to the massive and pedestrian-unfriendly plains surrounding Fort McPherson by stealing horses to escape. In this sense it was a shared need for horses, rather than a proclivity for stealing, that created the basis for a theft culture in southwestern Nebraska.

Perhaps a tacit recognition of this state of affairs played a part in shaping the 1868 Fort Laramie Treaty. Written seventeen years after the 1851 original, new terms were presented in light of a renewed truce between the Lakotas, Cheyennes, and Arapahos, on the one hand, and the United States government, on the other. Gone were the idealized and geoculturally misplaced nations along the Missouri and Loup Rivers; Lakota control remained mostly uncontested in those areas hereto unoccupied by whites. Absent were any illusions about the government's ability to recast tribal nations in ways that made sense to whites; although the second Fort Laramie Treaty attempted to incentivize farming, it also ostensibly granted sovereignty to the Great Sioux Reservation, extended hunting rights to the plains north of the Platte, and promised the closure of the Bozeman Trail to Montana. Rather than imposing American legal strictures on indigenous lands, the treaty instead promised to prosecute "bad men" among the whites who trespassed upon native lands while notably refusing to grant the same privilege to indigenous criminal suspects by handing them over to the native justice system. Finally, the government attempted to protect settlers and emigrants by explicitly prohibiting raiding and coup counting against whites: "And they, the said Indians, further expressly agree . . . 3rd. That they will not attack any persons at home, or travelling, nor molest or disturb any wagon trains, coaches, mules, or cattle belonging to the people of the

United States, or to persons friendly therewith. 4th. They will never capture, or carry off from the settlements, white women or children. 5th. They will never kill or scalp white men, nor attempt to do them harm."[61]

The omission of horse theft from the list of raiding activities might have been a mistake, perhaps due to forgetfulness or to the authors not understanding the difference between a pack mule and a Percheron. It might have also represented a realistic concession to its signatory parties and a sincere desire to avoid another war over a stolen horse. Either way, though, it would not have made much of a difference. Even if horses were mentioned, it is almost certain that Plains Indians, along with their "bad" counterparts among the whites, would have continued stealing horses with near impunity until the late 1870s. It would take a lot more than a piece of paper to end the region's theft culture.

3

The Horse Wars

One does not sell the land people walk on.

—CRAZY HORSE

When describing conditions in the Department of the Platte for the secretary of war's 1872 annual report, General Edward Ord did not exude optimism. "Along up the Republican and Loup Fork, and on the streams near the North Platte, heading in the Black Hills," he explained, "the settlement's nearest neighbor is sometimes eight, ten, or twenty miles distant, and every man plows and mows with his rifle in his hand or at his back. Stock to be safe have to have armed herders with them, and with such an extensive district and series of almost helpless frontiers, and such a severe winter to stimulate the hunger of the Indians, the wonder is that so little harm was done by them."[1] In 1872 war clouds had not yet appeared on the horizon: the 1868 Fort Laramie Treaty continued to broker an uneasy peace between the whites and the Natives; the Black Hills gold deposits remained undiscovered; and western Nebraska was safe enough in January 1872 to host a bison hunt for the visiting grand duke Alexis of Russia, led by the regionally if not yet globally famous Buffalo Bill Cody. But like prairie grasses after a prolonged drought, the stage was set for a larger conflagration.

Ord's words were prescient. In November 1872 Whistler, an Oglala chief, was found murdered on the Nebraska frontier.

He was well-known to whites, having joined the Russian duke's bison hunt earlier that year. Brulé chief Spotted Tail led the Plains Indian delegation, which in turn led the hunt. Like Spotted Tail, Whistler sought to make peace with the whites, and since his band frequently camped in the Republican, Platte, and Loup River valleys in western Nebraska, regional military officials were already comfortable working with him. Buffalo Bill in particular vouched for Whistler and understood his intentions. Otherwise, they would not have invited him to join the highly choreographed hunt and endanger their royal guest's safety.[2] Though Whistler did not possess Spotted Tail's diplomatic acumen, he was a formidable and well-respected leader of several dozen Oglalas who frequently camped and hunted in the Republican River region. The United States government classified Whistler's group as a "cut-off band" that lay outside of Red Cloud's influence and authority. Whistler fought against the army for most of the 1860s and refused to sign the 1868 Fort Laramie Treaty. Nevertheless, he and his war parties primarily raided the Pawnees. Colonel Henry Carrington also endorsed Whistler and praised his intentions in a letter to General George Custer, asking the famously impetuous commander at the outset of his 1869 Republican River campaign to allow Whistler some time to lead his people north of the Platte to avoid hostilities.[3]

In spite of Whistler's separation from Red Cloud and the main *oyáte* of Oglala Lakotas, his murder, along with the death of two companions, Fat Badger and Handsmeller, unleashed a torrent of resentment. This tragedy threatened to implode the carefully constructed, albeit informal, alliance between local military officials in western Nebraska and the friendly Brulés and Oglala Lakotas. The killing, originally believed to have been carried out by Pawnees on a horse-raiding mission, was blamed on white settlers upon further investigation. With the situation spiraling out of control, Whistler's compatriot, No Flesh, demanded that the military compensate them with fifty ponies for Whistler's death, which the cut-off Oglalas believed was an acceptable alternative to violent retaliation. Post commander Joseph J. Reynolds understood this and forwarded the request to the Department of the

Platte headquarters in Omaha.[4] But during the spring months of 1873, both the Lakotas and the post commanders anxiously awaited word from the authorities in Washington as to whether or not to requisition the horses. At that critical moment no one who had participated in the hunt with the grand duke thought it worthwhile to memorialize their former companion and ally, let alone honor his loss with a pittance of ponies. Whistler's murder jeopardized the peace in western Nebraska for several months, but the worst was yet to come as white and Indian outrages against and among one another began piling up throughout the region. Over the next five years war blazed across the plains like a grass fire on a hot, windy day. And Whistler, of course, was not on hand to help extinguish the flames.

Many authors have written about the Plains Indian Wars and, in particular, the sequence of events preceding, during, and following the climactic battle at Little Bighorn. And most authorities on the subject seem to agree on a few things—namely, that the Lakotas fought to protect their treaty-guaranteed claims to the Black Hills and that the United States government reneged on its obligations in order to appease thousands of civilians, officers, and government officials who wanted to open that territory up for exploration (and exploitation). However, far less attention is paid to the tens of thousands of horses on whose backs this war was fought and to how important the give-and-take of reciprocal horse raiding was to the war effort on both sides. Successful herd management—maintaining a sufficient population of fresh, healthy mounts; supporting those horses by ensuring proper amounts of grass, feed, and water; and safeguarding those horses from appropriation or murder by the enemy—was absolutely critical for both the Plains Indians and the United States Army. These considerations, in turn, helped transform the plains theft culture into a theft crisis. Once the outcomes of horse raiding became existentially linked to the future success of a tribe or an army, reciprocal action began to transcend mere exchange. It became a matter of survival.

Meanwhile, the herds themselves multiplied across Nebraska during this period as more and more emigrants began settling there, as opposed to just passing through. Numerous small homesteads and a growing number of ranches exponentially increased the number of individual stakeholders responsible for their own herds, to say nothing of the safety and welfare of their families, employees, and selves. More stakeholders meant more target opportunities for horse raids, thus leading to more complaints to post commanders, more angry letters to newspapers and representatives, and more friction in general. Some settlers began arming themselves, as General Ord noted in his 1872 report, while others started banding together to create their own ad hoc militias. As a swelling population of emigrants began claiming Nebraska lands and building new lives in the state, its members also inadvertently interjected themselves into a long-running conflict over stolen horses and butchered livestock without fully understanding the terms of engagement. Many struggled to survive the repercussions.

The flip side to this growing horse-raiding crisis was that success was measured, at least in part, in terms of horse capture. Dispossessing the enemy of its horses became as much a function of offensive action as it was of self-preservation. Plains Indian cultures, as shown in the previous chapter, already possessed the cultural, economic, and legal architecture to lionize raiding as an especially powerful form of coup counting. But increasingly, as the conflict raged on, American military planners also began to conceptualize and imagine victory in terms of horse confiscation. Indian reservations would be meaningless, many officials believed, if they were populated by a defeated yet armed and fully mounted foe. In some cases horse appropriation from the Plains Indians became its own means to an end. Some officers used confiscated ponies to mount previously horseless cavalry units, while others appropriated horses at auction and then ostensibly spent the proceeds purchasing reservation oxen. Many whites desired to own the more ecologically adaptive ponies as well, a point that was proved time and time again when horse thieves began chipping away at the already diminished reservation horse herds toward the end of the decade. This spate of white-on-Indian horse stealing continued to produce crisis moments years after the war had ended since the United States Army had to evolve from being the region's most successful wartime horse-raiding gang into a peacetime law enforcement agency responsible for policing reservations and their surroundings against thieving civilians. More important, the horse-stealing crisis years coincided with a stark reality: pony thefts and captures led to a massive and unprecedented transfer of wealth from American Indians to whites, one that rivaled only the concurrent land cessions in terms of scale, value, and sheer audacity.

A Wary Peace

In the years immediately following Whistler's death, a growing sense of unease descended upon western Nebraska as Plains Indians, army officials, and seasoned settlers began noticing a drop in the region's barometric pressure. Even before gold was discovered in the Black Hills, tensions rose throughout western Nebraska as ranchers and homesteaders competed for land claims in the Platte and Republican Valleys, while Lakotas, Cheyennes, and Pawnees competed for buffalo wherever they could find them. There seemed to be less of everything than there had been before, except for people. An increasingly privatized landscape meant more domesticated livestock, and both of those trends meant less grass for grazing. Growing animal herds also meant larger amounts of personal property. This combination of more people, more livestock, more property, less available land, and less available game ensured that the Great Plains would face its own unique tragedy of the commons. Civil lawsuits skyrocketed as property owners stuffed themselves into tiny courthouses with tort claims against their neighbors and as banks and lenders sued their borrowers for betting against the region's aridity.

As whites duked it out in courtrooms, Pawnees, Lakotas, Cheyennes, and other tribes in the region struggled to feed themselves. The great bison herds that had once roamed the plains were now only a few straggling bands in a crowded land. The fact that there were fewer buffalo and, because of constant raiding, fewer horses compounded the subsistence struggle that the

Pawnees and other Missouri River tribes already faced in the wake of multiple land cessions to the whites. The Pawnees in particular had experienced a catastrophic loss in horses during the mid-nineteenth century: in the 1820s, they had possessed between six thousand and eight thousand ponies, but by 1860 this number had been reduced to twelve hundred.[5] As large as the plains were, they were too small to sustain farmers, ranchers, and multiple competing Indian nations. For the Lakotas these pressures made holding onto the Black Hills, their winter hunting reserve, even more essential to their long-term survival. Sitting Bull, Crazy Horse, and other Lakota leaders were not prepared to forfeit their claim without a fight.

Horse raiding existed at the center of this simmering conflict as both a means of proxy warfare without resorting to large-scale bloodshed and as a dangerous assault that threatened to destabilize and infuriate its victims. And Plains Indians were not the only ones to commit to this strategy. Whites often attacked American Indians, regardless of whether they were "friendly" or not and usually without any cause or justification apart from stealing horses. A herder who worked for Major Walker shot and seriously wounded an unidentified American Indian near North Platte in April 1873 before taking the injured man's mule, while elsewhere soldiers often stole ponies while out on patrol or leave.[6] Unfortunately, the army could not deal with white thieves militarily but could only treat them as criminal suspects and turn them over to civilian law enforcement, assuming that they were ever caught. From the American Indians' perspective, white antagonists were representatives of the United States government. Whenever they demanded recompense, they expected the government to grant it. According to the Fort Laramie Treaty of 1868, American Indian victims could only seek justice for crimes committed against them through whites; they could not apprehend or search for white horse thieves themselves. Information on white thieves and murderers was to be given to reservation agents or military representatives.[7] This put the American Indians at a major disadvantage whenever they attempted to curb horse theft by settlers. But while military officers acknowledged the disparity and even empathized on occasion with the Plains Indians, there was little they could do without also riling up the citizens they were charged with protecting. The military received their marching orders from Washington DC, but ultimately the people giving those orders had to answer to voters in Nebraska and elsewhere.

Conversely, white settlers felt entitled to civilian law enforcement, self-defense, and army mediation whenever they believed—with or without evidence—their horses had been stolen by Indians. This was certainly the case whenever raiding parties swept through defenseless settlements, just as it was whenever citizens made specious or undocumented claims on horses belonging to friendly American Indians. Lieutenant Colonel Henry Wessells wrote to the adjutant general of the Department of the Platte in 1867 seeking instructions on how to deal with these claims while preserving the peace. "Every party of friendly Indians passing [Fort McPherson] has mules or other animals claimed by citizens," Wessells stated. However, he also emphasized the fragility of the peace, noting that although "it [is] proper and just to take by force all stolen property proven to be such," he was reluctant to "compel restitution" for fear of causing "unfriendly collisions" with friendly bands.[8]

Avoiding unnecessary conflict was difficult enough when officers were not always able to distinguish those responsible for the raids from members of other hunting parties. In 1867 both of these considerations led to an emergency dispatch from General Christopher Augur in Omaha. Augur directed the command at Fort McPherson to track down Colonel John Mix, who was on an expedition to apprehend a renegade band of Brulés who had allegedly stolen several head of horses from rancher J. A. Moore. Spotted Tail and Swift Bear both warned Augur that some other American Indians who were not under their control were stealing horses in the area. Fearing his men would accidentally attack an innocent band, Augur immediately tried to contact Mix with orders to withdraw. After Auger sent a runner to intercept Mix, the colonel received the message in time, averting what could have been a bloody encounter.[9]

Insufficient army resources, including personnel and horses, also limited the army's ability to prevent and chase thieves. Along the trails each post commander had to garrison his fort while also reserving enough manpower for detachments to engage with possible Indian threats. While the establishment of Fort McPherson in 1863 alleviated some of the pressure on Fort Kearny and other nearby installations, scouts and patrols still had to police a vast area that stretched from Dan Smith's Ranch in the east to Alkali in the west and from the Republican River in the south to the Niobrara River in the north. This jurisdiction contained about twenty thousand square miles, an area roughly the size of Maryland and New Jersey combined. At its greatest strength in February 1867, the fort garrison had 678 troops, which gave the post a total operational distribution of about one soldier per thirty square miles. Defenses were spread so thin that in some cases the garrison could only chase one or two bands of horse raiders at a time. When horse raiders struck Brady Station in September 1874, stealing several horses from citizens, the dispatch of a squad in pursuit weakened the fort's garrison to such a degree that they had to borrow men from the North Platte Post to shore up the fort's manpower. Captain Dudley warned his superiors that if any other raids were to occur during his detachment's absence, he would not be able to make pursuit.[10] In general, however, the garrison at McPherson was evidently large enough to send detachments of soldiers off to pursue thieves, protect key assets, or investigate reports of depredations. When raiders ran off nearly two hundred horses from the corral in 1873, a company of cavalry stationed at the fort successfully tracked and recaptured the stolen ponies.[11]

The army responded swiftly to reports of raids and worked assiduously to prevent them, which made the placement of its resources a critical factor in determining the success of its mission to keep the peace. Post commanders regularly sent detachments or special duty details to chase raiding parties and recover lost stock. The units in pursuit were armed, usually well provisioned, and prepared to remain in the field for weeks at a time. Although most of these detachments returned without finding

THE HORSE WARS

any signs of the guilty parties, on occasion the pursuers engaged them and even recovered some of the stolen horses. When raiders ran off over one hundred horses from the public herd in April 1873, the cavalry company sent in pursuit returned with the stolen horses on the same day, after chasing the band of thieves over twenty miles.[12] The army also worked proactively to prevent raids. Since the army could not efficiently patrol the entire inhabited area of southwestern Nebraskan, the fort sent scouting parties into the surrounding area on a regular basis. The command also acted on information provided by friendly Lakotas or by their agents. These military parties searched for American Indians and evidence of their movement, investigated possible depredations, and conducted reconnaissance. Whenever a scouting party returned, the officer in charge filed a report, which described the path taken, the length of the journey, the kinds of things the soldiers saw—particularly trees, wildlife, settlers, and signs of Plains Indian activity—and whether or not the troops had engaged with the American Indians.[13]

As massive horse raids, depleted game populations, growing numbers of white settlers, and new conflicts over land brought the region to a crisis point once again, Plains Indian tribes had to decide whether to fight the whites or seek the best possible terms. Fortunately for the army, thousands of American Indians chose the latter, playing an integral role in helping the military accomplish its mission. It is hard to overstate the impact that American Indians had on the success of the army's operations on the plains. The Pawnees and the Brulés in particular were valuable, though not always valued, allies to the United States. Although they were longtime enemies, both groups found compelling reasons to support the United States military.

After decades of warfare against neighboring tribes, many Pawnees welcomed the opportunity to join the army's campaign to quell American Indian opposition to federal policy. But rather than simply informing on rival groups, the Pawnees enlisted as United States soldiers. These men pursued, captured, and fought hostile Lakota and Northern Cheyenne bands. The Pawnee Scouts were tremendously effective and earned a sterling reputation among military officials. General Augur in particular praised their equestrian ability and dedication.[14] Formed in 1864 by First Lieutenant Frank North, the Pawnee Scouts played a vital role in keeping the peace and, when necessary, combating the Lakotas and Cheyennes. Unlike white soldiers and officers, the Pawnees had both the wherewithal and the skill sets needed to effectively combat Plains Indian resistance—they were long beleaguered by Lakota and Cheyenne horse and scalp raids, and they sought to even the score against their old foes. Affiliation with the United States Army gave them access to arms, logistics, and support that tipped the balance in their favor. As a result, they were especially valuable in tracking down horse raiders and recovering stolen horses. When the Union Pacific laid tracks across western Nebraska, for example, the army ordered the Pawnee Scouts to protect company horses and other property. One railroad worker marveled at the manner in which the scouts responded to the presence of a raiding party in July 1867. After noticing "a large drove of horses resting nearby," a keen-eyed scout yelled, "Sioux!" and the Pawnees mounted their ponies in varying states of dress before taking off. Some were completely naked. However, the scouts returned later that day with ninety stolen horses.[15]

The enforcement role played by the Pawnee Scouts was important, especially during the army's operations against the Lakotas and Northern Cheyennes. But some bands of the Lakota were also critical allies of the frontier military. The Brulés, in particular, were valuable sources of enemy intelligence. They informed the command at Fort McPherson whenever they received news of a horse raid being planned or carried out, and the army trusted them enough to act on their information. In September 1868 Spotted Tail reported that a band of Cheyennes were preparing to steal horses near the South Platte River, so the commander at Fort McPherson deployed scouts to find them. No sign of the Cheyennes was found, but after the scouts returned, another band attacked a separate detachment in the Republican River valley.[16] Anxiety motivated the Brulés, who were caught between two groups that generally hated one

another: the whites, on the one hand, and the Northern Cheyennes and most of the remaining Lakotas, on the other. In a
letter to Fort McPherson's commanders, an unsigned correspondent from Swift Bear's band admitted that they provided
information to the whites on the "northern Indian" movements
because they were "just as afraid of [them] as the whites were."
In addition to the "trouble" those American Indians made for
the Brulés, the correspondent feared that whites would mistake
him for the thieves. If the Brulés failed to report the raid, the
letter writer noted, the whites would "blame it on us."[17] These
countervailing pressures put Spotted Tail and his followers in
an impossible position.

The Brulés also recognized the diplomatic benefits of collab-
oration. Spotted Tail never lost sight of his goal, which was to
secure his people's right to hunt, camp, trade, travel, and live
freely. He leveraged his cooperation with the whites and his relationships with numerous officers, bureaucrats, and ranchers to
secure favorable treaty terms and successfully persuaded officials to give him what he wanted. When his people were relocated to the Whetstone Agency in 1868, for instance, he believed
they would be allowed to hunt on the Republican, in spite of
the Fort Laramie Treaty's prohibition of hunting south of the
Platte. His agent, Stanley Poole, insisted that this was not possible. Through a combination of deft negotiation and visible anger
by the Brulés, however, Poole received permission from officials
in Washington to grant the Brulés hunting rights south of the
Platte.[18] Even though his band had officially become attached
to the agency, few people in the military or the government
wanted Spotted Tail as an enemy. Spotted Tail's assistance was
a bargaining chip through which he won favorable treatment
from the Indian Bureau, the army, and the federal government.

Though both the Brulés and the Pawnees were effectively
United States allies through the 1870s, they remained at odds
with one another. They fought over the prized hunting grounds
in southwestern Nebraska as white settlement and the rapid
decline of the bison population pushed each tribe farther west.
As nearly constant horse raiding and coup counting between the

two tribes jeopardized settlement and travel through the area, the U.S. government attempted to mediate the conflict by granting hunting rights north of the Niobrara River to the Lakotas and rights south of the Niobrara to the Pawnees. Agency officials believed this arrangement would mitigate conflict between these groups.[19] However, the boundary did little to end Lakota hunting expeditions into Pawnee hunting territory and horse raids on Pawnee herds. As the bison population began to decline even along the Platte, the Lakotas defended their claim to the region.

Spotted Tail pressed the United States government for hunting rights south of the Platte, but by 1873 the Lakotas decided to protect their grounds with force. On August 5 a large group of Brulé, Oglala, and Isanti Dakota raiders attacked a hunting party of seven hundred Pawnees, sixty-nine of whom were killed in what would be the last large intertribal engagement in southwestern Nebraska. Adding insult to injury, the Lakotas stole seven hundred ponies from the group, forcing the Pawnees to retreat to Plum Creek Station on foot. The Battle of Massacre Canyon played a key role in the Pawnees' decision to vacate their reservation near Genoa, Nebraska, and relocate to the Indian Territory. But while the death toll from the battle alone was more than enough to justify their move, the material loss of seven hundred ponies—approximately half of their remaining horse herd—was also a significant factor. Even for a semi-agricultural tribe such as the Pawnees, horses were necessary for a successful bison hunt, and the loss of so many crippled the Pawnees' ability to carry out future hunts. Spotted Tail successfully evicted the Pawnees from not just their hunting grounds but also their own home.[20]

By 1874 even some Lakota bands began to grow increasingly anxious about horse herd loss. Oglala chief Fire Lightning expressed such concerns while writing a letter to the commander at Fort McPherson, in which he pleaded that no one in his band was responsible for killing cattle along the South Platte. He had heard rumors that raiders were destroying livestock in that area and that local settlers had asked the army to intervene. Fire Lightning also informed the commander that whites had destroyed numerous bison in the area and implored anyone who killed one to take all of the meat and "not to let the wolves eat it." But almost as an aside, the author mentioned that the Lakotas along the Platte were "starving" and that they could not hunt or return to the reservation because their horses had been stolen. Not only were the Lakotas in this region not killing cattle up and down the river, but they no longer possessed the means to do so. Fire Lightning de-emphasized the latter point, concluding his letter by telling the commander that "you may believe me that we shall not do anything wrong."[21]

One-sided, unanswered horse raiding inflicted either by whites or American Indians on a single tribe or group would paralyze its victims by denying them their means of hunting, fighting, traveling, herding domestic livestock, or trading. But on a family or individual level, it further destabilized relations between the victims and the rest of their tribe or group by depriving the former of one of their primary sources of wealth and means of production and pressuring the latter to help the victims find food and new mounts. In addition, this process of systematically thinning out a tribe's aggregated pony herd contributed to the increasing domination of the plains by the U.S. Army and the destruction of the region's bison population. As the Pawnees, Lakotas, and Cheyennes contemplated their respective removals to reservation lands, each faced rapid declines in herd size. They also continued to defend themselves against raiders from other tribes, overzealous military commanders, unscrupulous ranchers, and bandit gangs. Losses from enemy horse raids and surrenders to the army alone resulted in the loss of hundreds of horses at a time. Once the United States government moved them to reservations, the American Indians were ill equipped to prevent or respond to horse theft and relied on the government to pursue their cases for them. For all of the fears of horse raiding among Euro-American settlers, ranchers, and military men, few whites understood that they posed a greater threat to American Indian herds than American Indians posed to their own.

A Contest for Ponies

As Fire Lightning and his band of Oglalas gave, and intended
to keep, their word, whites elsewhere were in the process of
breaking theirs. In flagrant violation of the 1868 Fort Laramie
Treaty, General Sheridan dispatched General George Custer
and nearly a thousand men, including sixty-one Arikara scouts
and two "practical miners," to scout a location for a new fort in
Ȟe Sápa, or the Black Hills. Custer's illegal expedition departed
from Fort Abraham Lincoln on July 2, 1874, and a nation suf-
fering from the ill effects of the Panic of 1873 eagerly awaited
the expedition's report on the region and its gold deposits.
Of course, Ȟe Sápa was not open to mining. The Lakotas had
conquered the area generations earlier, and it provided them
with an important game preserve. However, since the Lakotas
did not maintain a year-round presence within the Black Hills,
Custer and his men were able to visit unmolested. When the
general's two miners discovered small amounts of gold in the
area, word quickly reached American newspapers that a new
bonanza awaited prospectors in the Black Hills (Custer himself
was more guarded in his assessment of the region's gold supply). The reports energized a new wave of westward-bound gold
seekers, who ignored official warnings that whites were not welcome in the Ȟe Sápa region. It also enraged both agency and
non-treaty Lakotas, who viewed the incursion as a step too far.[22]

Authorities at Camp Sheridan, charged with preventing
non-natives from entering the Black Hills and with protecting
the agency Lakotas and Nebraska settlers from one another,
struggled to intercept the trespassing whites. On April 15, 1875,
thirty-eight mounted cavalry troops left the post with ten days of
supplies in search of a dozen whites en route to the Hills to prospect for gold. First Lieutenant William W. Rogers commanded
the detachment. In his report he recounted following the group
into the Hills, whereupon he "followed their trail through the
pass and followed it to their camp, which was located about 20
miles south-west of Harney's Peak." Before Rogers arrived, however, one of the miners noticed the coming troops and raced

back to the camp to warn his companions. The group scattered, and the soldiers were only able to apprehend five of the twelve men. After eleven days the thirty-eight cavalrymen and their five prisoners arrived back at Camp Sheridan, but as they made their way back, hundreds of others began their own hastily arranged trips to the gold diggings. Despite their best efforts, the agency post garrisons and the Third Cavalry were not able to stop them all. The following month Camp Sheridan issued two additional detachments after incoming miner parties. Only one of the two succeeded in capturing anyone, and for that effort it took fifty cavalrymen to find and arrest eight adults and a child. Yet the large detachments were warranted, perhaps out of concern that a party of overly enthusiastic and well-armed whites who were already flouting the law and disregarding military directives would make trouble. In one especially revealing post return, Second Lieutenant William Abbot reported that in June 1875 the post sent out two detachments: one group of sixty-six men to capture "a large party of miners" (they eventually arrested five of them) and another of thirty-five men to search for a party of Plains Indians who had raided Pawnee horses and escaped north to the Niobrara. Not only did the former group anticipate more trouble by bringing almost twice as many soldiers along for the trip, but they also took a Gatling gun.[23]

Despite the army's exertions, Custer's expedition had opened a Pandora's box that could not be easily closed. As the emigrants and natives moved inexorably toward war, the frontier army was stuck in the middle. On one side the miners persistently caused trouble before their arrival and even after their expulsion, as one party of argonauts reportedly killed two Indians at the headwaters of Wolf Creek in 1875.[24] Not long afterward, Spotted Tail complained of miners stealing four horses from his camp. On the other side, Lakota bands began attacking emigrants and ranches more frequently, thus incurring the wrath of the army's brass. When Brigadier General Edward Ord learned in October 1874 that someone had killed ten head of cattle near the Spotted Tail Agency, he called for swift and immediate punishment: "If [these parties] belong to Agency,

Agent will be called on to recommend proper prompt action to punish depredators." But if they did not, they were ordered to "follow [their] trail to their village, so that (a) proper force may . . . Attack it."[25]

Ultimately, most Americans believed that the surest and fairest way to prevent future conflict was to simply cede the contested lands to the United States government. As the U.S. government attempted to renegotiate its 1868 treaty with the Lakotas, General William T. Sherman tried to reassure his officers that the Grant administration was not simply trying to protect the Plains Indians by sending the frontier cavalry after whites. "All expeditions into . . . The Black Hills must be prevented as long as the present treaty exists," Sherman wrote in a telegram to his commanders. However, he then explained that "efforts are now being made to arrange for the extinguishment of the Indian title and all proper means will be used to accomplish that end."[26] Those efforts were spearheaded by Iowa senator William Allison, who led a commission to Dakota Territory to negotiate either a mining lease worth $400,000 per year or the cession of the Black Hills for $6 million. The Lakotas responded with several demands of their own: seven years of total support by the United States government, continued access to the region, the replacement of all Episcopal missionaries with Catholic priests, and a prohibition on all additional road and trail construction. Believing that these terms were too steep, the Allison commission withdrew. So, too, did the U.S. cavalry, which the War Department ordered to leave, thus leaving the Black Hills undefended from further infiltration and exploitation. As gold seekers continued pouring into the region, conflict between the Lakotas and the trespassers became inevitable. The government soon gave the Lakotas an ultimatum: they must vacate the Black Hills and return to their agencies by January 31, 1876, or face the consequences (map 4).[27]

When the Lakotas refused, the army sent three large columns into the plains to compel Crazy Horse, Sitting Bull, and their bands to relocate to federal reservations. Unfortunately for the United States, the conflict did not begin well. General

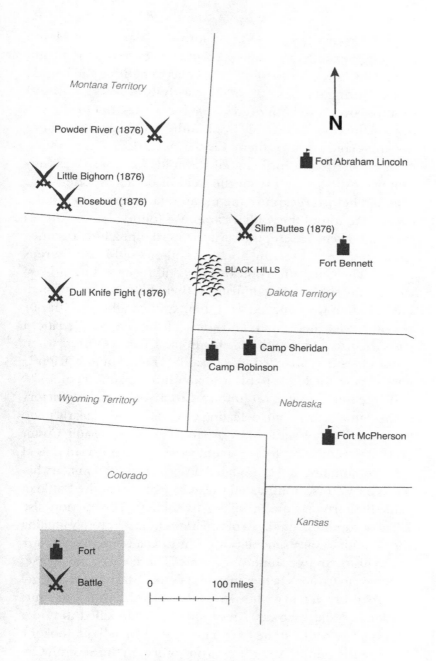

Map 4. Major battles and forts during the Great Sioux War, 1876–77.
Map created by the author.

George Crook's first expedition into the Bighorns in March accomplished little, although the Battle of Powder River encouraged the Cheyennes to join the Lakotas in fighting the United States. During the battle Captain Joseph Reynolds's command captured over seven hundred Cheyenne ponies, but the following day the Cheyennes stole five hundred of them back before Reynolds could destroy them. Livid over the loss of the ponies, General Sheridan reprimanded Reynolds for not successfully removing the animals from the field of battle. Wooden Leg, who had helped recapture the mounts, later remembered the event: "We found the soldier camp. We found also our horses they had taken. We crept toward the herd, out a little distance from the camp. 'I see my horse.' Another would say, 'there is mine.'" The Cheyennes quickly moved to recover their horses, though the soldiers began firing at them before they finished. Later, "when we returned with them and caught up with our people we let the women and some of the old people ride. I gave then to Chief Old Bear his horse I had captured when the soldiers first attacked us. He said, 'Thank you, my friend,' and he gave the horse to his woman while he kept on afoot."[28]

Three months later, on June 17, Crook won a pyrrhic victory at the Battle of Rosebud, defeating Crazy Horse and nearly 1,800 men. While Crook survived Crazy Horse's surprise assault, Custer and his Seventh Cavalry Regiment were not so lucky. In one of the most stunning and thorough defeats in American military history, Crazy Horse annihilated Custer's regiment at the Battle of Little Bighorn on June 25, killing 212 soldiers. The warriors also killed or captured hundreds of American horses, severely limiting the Seventh Cavalry's mobility over the next few months. According to historian Josephine Waggoner: "There were many horses captured in Custer's battle. Íŋkpadúta's son, Makȟánaówaza, got a sorrel horse, it had a white stripe down its face with four white stockings. Makȟánaówaza, or Sounding Earth, killed the rider of this horse with a stone tomahawk and, as he fell off, took the horse to the camp." According to one officer in the Seventh Cavalry, the horse belonged to Captain Myles Keogh.[29] The loss of so many soldiers and horses notwithstanding, the crushing defeat came just days before the nation's grand centennial celebrations were to begin, and Little Bighorn quickly cast an ominous pall over the conflict. Angered into action, Congress soon authorized the army to raise twenty-five hundred additional troops and prohibited the government from sending food or money to the Lakotas until they came to terms to sell their land.

In spite of Little Bighorn's terrible if galvanizing fallout, the disasters did not end there. Crook led his column northward along the Powder River on August 24, after separating from General Alfred Terry, but two days later he turned east and then south toward Fort Robinson. The meandering expedition did not pass any settlements or encounter any supply trains along the way. By the second week of September the soldiers were so starved that they began eating their horses and mules. On the seventh Crook sent a detachment ahead to Deadwood to find food for the men; it accidentally came upon Miniconjou chief American Horse's camp near Slim Buttes. Crook's main body rejoined the expedition, and the combined forces attacked the village. Briefly sated after defeating and then ransacking the abandoned camp, the emaciated troops continued on to Deadwood. If the expedition had a silver lining, it was Crook's capture of four hundred Indian ponies at Slim Buttes.[30]

The war soon revolved not around capturing land or even annihilating the enemy but on the need to capture the foes' horses. Little Bighorn was not only a human disaster for the Seventh Cavalry; the loss of hundreds of valuable horses during the battle had severely depleted the entire regiment's ability to function that summer. While this did not necessarily factor into any kind of grand strategy for the Lakotas and Cheyennes, horse dispossession did become an important tactical consideration. Wanting to avoid a critical battle with the soldiers during the spring of 1876, Cheyenne chiefs Spotted Wolf, Medicine Wolf, and Twin agreed that they and their people should stay encamped by the Powder River and avoid going to the agency. But if white soldiers come, the chiefs decided, "we shall steal their horses. Then they cannot fight us." Later Wooden Leg and his brother approached an abandoned soldier camp with the intent of stealing horses: "Our [ponies] were gone, and we needed mounts."[31]

The army, however, did conceive horse seizures as part of a larger strategy. This played out during and after a handful of battles, such as Slim Buttes, where the victorious soldiers seized as many ponies as they could. The army captured thousands of horses this way, although in some cases the Indians managed to steal them back. But Terry, Crook, and Sheridan also implemented this strategy in several other significant ways. For one, surrendering Indians were to give up their firearms as well as their ponies. When Dull Knife's village surrendered the following spring, they gave up over seven hundred mounts. More insidiously, the army moved proactively to preempt any further trouble by seizing agency horses as well. In October 1876 the army confiscated ponies from the Sihasapas, Hunkpapas, Miniconjous, and Oglalas. Over thirty-eight hundred horses were seized at the Cheyenne River, Standing Rock, and Red Cloud Agencies. Crook disregarded Sheridan's orders upon arriving at the Spotted Tail Agency, however, believing that the Brulés' cooperation with the army should be rewarded. Sheridan fumed at Crook's decision, but the Brulés got to keep their horses. As a last resort, the army destroyed ponies that it could not carry away for whatever reason since the army's main priority was to deprive the Indians of their mounts and thus impede their war-making ability. During the "Starvation March," concerned that his men and their horses would be overtaken by the Plains Indians, Crook ordered Captain Anson Mills to shoot worn-out horses. He killed seventy that day.[32]

By 1877, after nearly a year of relentless military pressure, the half-starved and demoralized Lakotas began to consider surrendering. Merely returning to the reservations, however, was no longer an option. The army, in a policy that would become known as the "Rule of 76," forced surrendering bands to give up their guns and horses. Unfortunately, the Plains Indians' love for and reliance upon their horses ensured that the mass seizure of animals from surrendering bands during the Great Sioux War would transcend the mere loss of property. Lieutenant Colonel George P. Buell issued such terms to a peace envoy from Crazy Horse's camp in early 1877, requiring that the famous war chief of the Oglalas and his people give up their ponies. As a result, the desire to protect Lakota pony herds became one of the key sticking points that prevented some of Crazy Horse's followers, such as Spotted Elk and Roman Nose, from readily agreeing to the army's surrender terms.[33] But as starvation, United States military might, and low morale devastated Plains Indian camps, Crazy Horse, Dull Knife, and other surrendering bands eventually gave up thousands of horses in exchange for peace and provisions. The army's horse herd seizures produced the intended result: they depleted the Plains Indians' stock and prevented them from raiding or attacking whites after the tribes were confined to reservations.

Though successful, these mass seizures created a major logistical problem: the sudden appearance of thousands of horses under U.S. Army supervision that needed care, feed, and shelter. The army had no real plan for these animals, and the officers tasked with caring for the thousands of captured animals wrote to the quartermaster general, asking if the government intended to do anything with them.[34] But while having thousands of extra ponies was perhaps a good problem to have, the government faced a moral and legal conundrum when deciding how to dispose of them: on the one hand, officials believed they could not simply hand the war horses back to their recently defeated owners. Although General Grant trusted Robert E. Lee and his men to leave Appomattox with their horses, General Crook and most of the frontier military feared that if they were to remount the enemy bands, the Indians would eventually renew their attack. Besides, "if the Indians are to be kept at the agencies and fed and cared for by the government," reasoned one frontier commander, "they do not need horses. A Sioux without his horse is, comparatively, a very harmless being."[35] On the other hand, the ponies represented real, tangible Indian property. In spite of the fundamental intent of legal land cessions, officials seemed to respect—and, in fact, sought to augment among the vanquished tribes—individually owned private property. Unlike the

Black Hills or any other territory ceded from tribal sovereignty, ponies were generally treated by policy planners as private property. Disposing of them without reimbursing the original owners was anathema to the legal logic that justified taking Indian land in exchange for nominal compensation.

One possible solution was to retroactively impress the horses into service, either as mounts or, in some cases, as food. Brevet General Nelson A. Miles supplied four companies of the Fifth Infantry with horses he had captured from Lame Deer during the 1876 winter campaign, allowing his unit not only to bypass the busy quartermaster's office but also to employ the far better suited ponies for expended plains warfare. During the Nez Perce War, Miles and the Fifth Infantry used many of these horses while hunting Chief Joseph and his followers on their ill-fated escape to Canada. In some cases enlisted men ate captured horses once their provisions began to run low. Horseflesh was on the menu for many soldiers serving in the 1876 winter campaign in Dakota Territory.[36] But even these functional demands were unable to make a dent in the captured horse supply, whose numbers far exceeded what was needed to satisfy the army's various appetites.

The army eventually tried to resolve this dilemma in a bureaucratically elegant if decidedly unfair, inefficient, and infantilizing manner. Reconciling the military's desire to avoid remounting the surrendered bands with the Bureau of Indian Affairs' intention to turn the Lakotas into farmers, the army decided to sell off the captured ponies and then use the money to purchase livestock for their owners. Secretary of War George McCrary's 1878 annual report to President Rutherford B. Hayes provides an overview of this process. His statement, which compiled reports from across the field on the outcome of the recently concluded war against the Lakota, enumerated the number of ponies taken into custody upon the surrender of "hostile" bands and explained what had happened to them. Lieutenant Colonel William P. Carlin, of the Seventeenth Infantry and commander of the post at Standing Rock, reported "disposing" of 1,963 seized Indian animals under his command. Over half of them (1,124) were delivered to Fort Lincoln, located just north of Standing Rock. However, 44 of them were sold at the post, and another 107 were sold at three separate public auctions in Bismarck, North Dakota, in June 1877. Overall, the United States Army seized about 5,000 horses from these bands.[37]

At the Dakota Territory Cheyenne Agency, Lieutenant Colonel William Wood reported that "since the close of the campaign of last year, 589 Indians have come in from the hostile camps and delivered themselves up to the military at the post . . . surrendering 1,040 ponies and mules and 266 fire-arms of various kinds. Of the horses, 974 were sent to Yankton, Dak., for sale by the Quartermaster's Department." The quartermaster then applied the proceeds of that sale toward the purchase of 450 cows for the agency Lakotas. Wood believed that the army was acting magnanimously, and proactively, in swapping Indian ponies for cows: "At that agency they were permitted to retain, when the dismounting took place, some 400 horses—about one for every able-bodied warrior . . . for the purpose of assisting them in tilling the soil, and in carrying their rations from the agency to their villages." One horse per "able-bodied warrior" was sufficient for farming but not for raiding—and certainly not for an extended campaign requiring several remounts per rider. Ultimately, Wood believed these transfers were successful and cited the Yankton Agency's successful transition to agriculture as a cause for optimism: "It is reported that the Indians at the Yankton agency raised last year some 800 bushels of wheat, 2,000 bushels of corn, and 1,200 bushels of vegetables, and cut some 2,700 tons of hay, and that this year the crops at that agency will be threefold greater than those of last year."[38]

Like the previous land cessions that not only grabbed land but forced Indians to legally permit those handovers by signing treaties, the pony-to-cow exchange was similarly formalized through the execution of signed contracts. In exchange for receiving "the number of cows and calves set opposite our respective names, furnished us by the government from the proceeds of the sale of our ponies," the Indians were expected to "protect and care for" the cattle and their "increase." The contractual language also enjoined the recipients from trading their new animals and strongly discouraged the recipients from butchering them for beef. Violations of this agreement were to be punished with reduced rations, which would disincentivize the owners from killing them in hopes of increasing their food supply. Second Lieutenant George Brown, commander of the Eleventh Infantry's Company E, stationed at the Cheyenne River Agency's Fort Bennett in South Dakota, delivered the livestock to their new owners and supervised the signing of the contracts. At the Cheyenne River Agency he turned over 231 cows and 27 calves to 130 different families and 60 individual chiefs representing the Miniconjous, Sans Arcs, and Two Kettle Lakotas. Spotted Elk, whose village would later be savagely attacked by the army at Wounded Knee, acknowledged receiving one cow. The Sihasapas received a separate distribution of 18 cows, with similar terms attached to the transfer.[39]

Most of the seized ponies were never returned to or converted into cattle for their owners. Crook sold hundreds of Red Cloud Agency horses at Fort Laramie, Sidney, and the Cheyenne Depot. He gifted the remainder to the Pawnee Scouts. Meanwhile, of the nearly five thousand ponies sent from Standing Rock and Cheyenne River, only one in ten survived the trip to Minnesota. A gauntlet of factors siphoned away the captured Lakota herd on its journey eastward: winter weather, careless herding, gifting and selling animals to civilians along the way, and of course, rustling. The army also sold many of the surrendered bands' horses throughout the West. Later the Lakotas fought to recover damages for their "pony claims" in court. Congress responded by allocating $28,000 in section 27 of the Sioux Act of 1889 for Lakotas who had surrendered their horses to the army in 1876. It offered forty dollars for each stolen horse. With these terms set by Congress, in 1876 other Lakota tribes succeeded in petitioning the government for and receiving compensation for surrendered ponies. In 1890, after Wounded Knee, Congress increased the amount to five thousand horses and extended the offer to the Standing River and Cheyenne River tribes as well. Eventually, Lakota pony claims amounted to over $320,000 for approximately eight thousand missing, stolen, or otherwise misappropriated Indian horses.[40]

Break-Ins and Breakouts

Perhaps the army deserves some credit for not simply shooting surrendered Indian horses and setting fire to their corpses, as General Custer did to hundreds of animals following the Battle of Washita in 1868.[41] However, its unilateral and involuntary conversion of Indian horse wealth to cattle in the first place helped encourage more brazen forms of thievery. Soon the Lakotas and Cheyennes began to understand firsthand just how devastating the loss of mounts was toward preventing the theft of their remaining horses. Like the Pawnees a few years earlier, the vanquished tribes were left largely defenseless against outsiders raiding their livestock. Whites could now steal with impunity from the Lakotas and Cheyennes, who lacked both permission and the necessary horse power to pursue the criminals. Red Cloud complained during an 1877 meeting with President Hayes that whites stole "horses from us every day, sometimes forty, sixty, and eighty head, and that has made us very poor . . . because I am not a white man I can count very easily the number of horses." Spotted Tail accused Frank North of stealing forty horses from his agency, claiming that other whites stole about one thousand horses a year. Although North denied the charges, he believed Spotted Tail did not exaggerate the volume of horses whites stole from the reservation.[42]

The epidemic of white raiding and trading from the reservations soon began to rival that of the Comanches years earlier, as thieves grew more powerful and fat with stolen bounty. In June 1877 the scale of this thievery was apparent when General Crook informed the Third Cavalry that approximately 150 stolen ponies were spread out along the Kearny Trail between the Loup and the Niobrara. Crook learned that the thieves were taking the horses in small groups down to Grand Island to avoid capture. Hoping to avoid a violent confrontation between the thieves and the natives, Crook's assistant, Lieutenant Colonel L. P. Bradley, ordered the men at Camp Sheridan to discreetly look into the matter and round up as many of the animals as they could without detection. "Be careful not to let anything get out as to the route or object of the party," Bradley warned, "and send out some sensible Indians who will be likely to know stolen stock." However, Bradley noted, "one difficulty" was already unavoidable: "The [surrendered] ponies sold last year are scattered throughout the country, and we have got to rely on the Indians to distinguish between them and the ones stolen." The effects of this illicit trade rippled all the way down to and across the Platte, where rancher John Bratt recalled in his autobiography that gangs of thieves often sold stolen ponies to cattlemen, stole the same ponies back from the cattlemen, and then traded them back to the American Indians. Bratt was so concerned about the possibility of a "war" between the reservation Lakotas and the cattlemen that he requested a list of brands from Nebraska and Dakota reservations, disseminated the list to "every stock grower in the Platte Valleys," and encouraged anyone who found stray Lakota mounts during their roundups to send them back to the reservation. Not even the Republican Valley settlements farther south were immune. The "citizens" of Indianola, a town located near the Kansas-Nebraska border south of North Platte, mailed a letter to the fort in March 1875 complaining of "white devils," including "hunters, trapers [sic], and desperados such as you will always find on the frontier," stealing Plains Indian horses during the winter. Worried that the victimized Plains Indians would take their "revenge" out on the local farms and ranches, they implored the army to send troops to Indianola to "protect us from the revenge of the Indians" and, if possible, return the stolen ponies.[43]

Abhorring the law enforcement vacuum in and around the reservations, officers at Camp Sheridan dealt with both indigenous and white horse thieves. In late 1879 a United States marshal based in Omaha informed Captain Ernst Crawford, the Camp Sheridan post commander, that rancher J. McCann held three U.S.-branded government mules at his ranch on the Missouri River, near Running Water. Crawford believed that the mules had been "lost or stolen from a detachment of troops" a year earlier and had previously suspected McCann's involvement in their disappearance. Once the marshal confirmed the mules' location, Crawford dispatched Lieutenant F. H. French with several men to recover the government property. Although he noted that "it has been almost impossible heretofore to find these mules at the ranch as McCann or his foreman are in the habit of running [the mules] off upon the approach of troops," he expressed optimism that "Lt. French will be able to recover them." As the commander set out to finally take back his mules from McCann, he was also "tak[ing] steps to secure" three government mules reported to be at the Rosebud Agency.[44]

By the fall of 1878 the situation in the Pine Ridge region had deteriorated to such a point that no existing institution could effectively or legally contend with the horse thieves. In a letter to General Crook, Captain Deane Monahan complained that "the country [surrounding Camp Sheridan] is at the present time literally swarmed with horse thieves, who are ready to depredate upon white men or Indians as opportunity would allow." Enforcement was elusive if not impossible: "There is no civil officer to take cognizance of offenses committed by this class, even if found in the act of stealing, and the few honest citizens, who are scattered through this country, cannot protect themselves." He further warned that "these horse thieves are particularly dangerous in the vicinity of the Indian Reservation and may at any time cause serious trouble" by jeopardizing the peace. In closing, Monahan urged that "vigorous means should be used by the proper authority to rid the country of such a dangerous element." However, Crook himself was not a "proper authority" on this matter, as the Posse Comitatus Act tied his hands and proscribed him from intervening.[45]

Making matters worse, the Indian police on the reservations had little power to stop the thefts. In late 1878 Indian inspector James H. Hammond complained that the Red Cloud police force was unorganized and low on ammunition. Seeking assistance from the army to recover a band of stolen Indian horses from thieves holed up about thirty miles north of the agency,

Hammond insisted that the army would be helping to train the Indian police to solve similar problems in the future on their own. "In your judgement," he wrote, "will it be well to send a few soldiers with that Indian Police can be got together here? For the purpose of capturing the horses which belong here and to hold the Indian Police to their duty and encourage them?"[46] The following year Red Cloud and other Lakota chiefs at Pine Ridge circulated a petition urging the agency to make good on several missed payments and other promised support, including a $25,000 payment to the Oglalas in exchange for their right to hunt along the Republican. The petition also included a plea for the government to take urgent steps to end white horse stealing on Indian reservations.[47]

Military authorities could arrest citizens for stealing horses, but detaining them was legally problematic. Camp Sheridan's post commander, Captain Daniel W. Burke, for want of evidence, immediately released a group of government-contracted mail carriers who had been arrested for stealing agency horses upon their arrival at the post. While he was legally obligated to let the men go, he minced no words about their alleged guilt. "There is no doubt but that a number of the employees at the Kearney and Deadwood mail route have been engaged in running off ponies from this agency," he wrote. Burke then sounded a conspiratorial note in reference to the recent death of Gilbert Fosdick, a Kearney and Deadwood Stage Line driver who had been supposedly murdered and scalped by Indians. "It is also believed by some that Fosdick was killed by these parties," he claimed, "fearing he would expose them." Despite the great exertions of the alleged thieves to commit and cover up their crimes, Burke offered some unsolicited advice to the Brulés. "The Indians here have been instructed [to] be more careful in guarding their stock," recalled Burke, "which with frequent scouts that will be made from this Point, will prevent in the future the wholesale stealing of ponies."[48]

Racial ambiguities and post-Reconstruction politics complicated military efforts to control horse thievery. In one instance General Crook pointedly asked the Camp Sheridan post commander in October 1878 if several stolen mules recovered during a recent expedition belonged to the government or to a private party. And if claimed by the latter, then "by what authority [did] the C.O. Camp Sheridan use troops to recover the property of white men, stolen from them by white men in the state of Nebraska?" The Posse Comitatus Act, which had taken effect only three months earlier as Reconstruction ended in the South, compelled Crook to respond forcefully to reports of army interference in civilian policing. In his reply Captain Monahan responded that the mules did belong to L. N. Sawyer, a white man from Sidney. However, the identity of the thief was less clear and subject to interpretation: "I was informed that these mules were on the Red Cloud Indian Reservation, in the possession of one Todd Randall who has lived among the Indians for many years and is one of the class known as 'Squaw men.'" It is not clear if Monahan would have moved on Randall had he lived outside the reservation and married a non-native woman, but these circumstances provided the commander with some cover as he defended his decision to use army personnel and resources to recover civilian mules.[49]

Settlers who lost stock were less willing to see the distinction between marital and civilian law enforcement. Many citizens who had lost animals submitted their reports directly to the army. Theorizing that the recently surrendered Indians still held their teams within the agencies, a rancher named M. Burton informed the Black Hills district commander that he believed several of his stolen horses had been taken to the Spotted Tail Agency after Crazy Horse's surrender there on May 5. Upon reviewing Burton's claim and his brand book, the commander endorsed the rancher's claim, and on May 7 he ordered the Camp Sheridan commander to investigate the matter.[50]

For their part many Lakotas and Cheyennes suspected white law enforcement motives—both civilian and military. On September 18, 1877, Sam Bass and his Black Hills Bandits gang held up a Union Pacific locomotive near Big Springs, Nebraska, and successfully pulled off one of the most lucrative train heists in American history. They escaped with over $60,000 in gold (worth over $1.45 million in 2020), and local, state, federal, and corporate authorities, as well as would-be vigilantes, set out in pursuit of the robbers. This kicked the hornet's nest, so to speak, stirring up enforcement activity throughout western Nebraska as the gutsiness of the theft—and the massive $10,000 reward offered by the Union Pacific for information leading to the thieves' arrest and capture—compelled Nebraskans to act. The following day General Crook ordered cavalry and Indian scouts from Camp Robinson to scour the surrounding country and "arrest the robbers at all hazards." In response the post sent four dozen men, who blazed a ninety-mile-long trail around the region before returning three days later.[51]

While an army of pursuers combed the Pine Ridge and Sandhills regions for the fugitives, agency Indians grew increasingly concerned about what was happening. Later that month about seventy Lakota and Cheyenne lodges left the Spotted Tail Agency to investigate the trouble and to protect their herds and homes from possible intruders. Indian agent Lieutenant Jesse M. Lee, after learning of their escape, sent five chiefs to intercept the lodges. Lee then asked the army to be patient while he waited for a report, arguing that "the cause of their starting was the sending out of the cavalry and Indians after the Train Robbers, they supposing that the movement was against them and that other troops were coming from Camp Robinson to take their ponies." In a later letter Lee promised that he would "severely chasten" the escaped Indians while simultaneously urging the army to steer clear of the agency to prevent further excursions.[52]

The frontier army as a whole was unprepared for the much larger breakout that occurred a year later in Indian Territory (map 5). This crisis began in September 1878, when Dull Knife and approximately three hundred sick and starving followers left the Darlington Agency in Oklahoma without leave and trekked north toward the Pine Ridge reservation in Dakota Territory. Refusing to stay at the agency any longer, Dull Knife, Little Wolf, and many other members of their band escaped on the morning of September 9, 1878, and began a long, cold, and perilous journey across Indian Territory, Kansas, and Nebraska.

The group repeatedly fought off the U.S. military, which stalked them for weeks. But some members also raided several communities in Kansas, murdering over forty civilians and destroying a large amount of property. Many of these murdered families had only recently emigrated from Czechoslovakia.[53] By October the group reached the Platte River, but after fording the stream, the escapees split into two separate parties: the larger group, led by Dull Knife, headed northwest toward Fort Robinson, while Little Wolf's band made winter camp in the Sandhills.

Desperate to apprehend and return Dull Knife and his band to the Darlington Agency, some officials advocated horse raiding as a possible tactic to halt their advance. Having already started the process of moving federal resources out of the Great Plains and toward the outposts farther west, the frontier army scrambled to intercept the escapees as they marched northward through newly settled counties in Kansas and Nebraska. At a conference with Red Cloud and other Lakota leaders, several officers floated an idea of soliciting the recently vanquished tribes' help with apprehending the fugitive natives. One officer proposed offering an extra issue amounting to "50 lbs. tobacco, 50 lbs. hard bread, 37½ lbs. bacon, 7½ lbs. sugar, and 5 lbs. coffee" in hopes of "making the Indians feel as friendly as possible and to aid in procuring information concerning Cheyenne Indians supposed to be in their camp." But when it became clear that a few extra pounds of food was not going to be enough to help turn the Lakota against their friends and kin, who had already risked so much to join them in Montana and Dakota Territory, the army tried to sweeten the deal by "requesting that Red Cloud and the Sioux be informed that they can retain all arms and ponies captured from Cheyennes." By encouraging other tribes to strike the Cheyenne encampment and steal their horses, which they could then keep, the army had weaponized intertribal raiding.[54]

This communication relayed an extraordinary, and perhaps even desperate, offer, given how only a year earlier the army had insisted on dismounting and disarming entire Lakota bands before accepting their surrender. In many ways, however, it was yet another iteration in the horse-stealing cycle. On Sep-

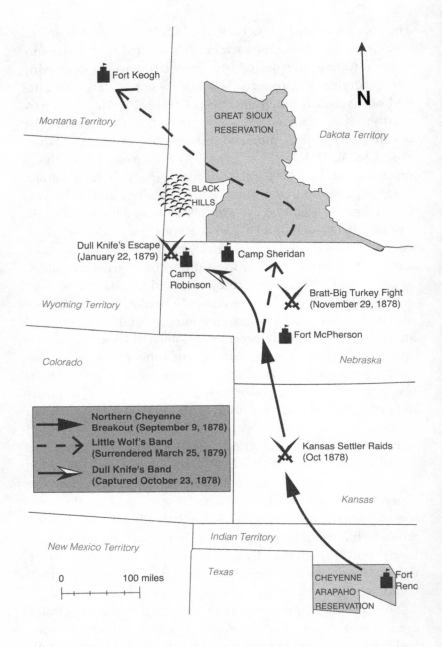

Map 5. The Northern Cheyenne Breakout and other raids, September 1878–March 1879. Map created by the author, inspired by Peter Cozzen's map of the Cheyenne Breakout in *Earth Is Weeping*, 287.

tember 27 the Fourth Cavalry succeeded in seizing or destroying most of the Cheyenne pony herd, therefore forcing many to escape on foot. Now in dire need of new animals, the Cheyennes focused on taking them from settlers in Kansas, many of whom attempted to engage the incoming raiders. This resulted in the Cheyennes killing dozens of Kansas farmers in short, frenzied gun battles over their stolen animals. Dull Knife's lodges emerged from Kansas with over two hundred fresh mounts, and word of their depredations spread quickly to a frightened Nebraska. Mounting fears of horse theft among residents and civilian reprisals among officers created both strategic and logistical dilemmas that reverberated across the region. When the Bureau of Indian Affairs arranged to send fifty wagons full of supplies from the railroad depot at Sidney Barracks to the Pine Ridge Agency, inspector J. H. Hammond notified the army, on December 3, 1878, that he planned on sending fifty Lakotas and two hundred horses south to Sidney to "form a train for transportation of supplies." Hammond, echoing "fears [that] have been expressed," claimed that "rough characters [could] attack the Indians on account of late Indian excitement and trouble about horse stealing."[55]

The two chiefs met very different fates. Dull Knife's party, which included a majority of the band's women and children, ran out of food as it traveled over the cold, desolate landscape of western Nebraska. In December, Dull Knife surrendered his hungry and freezing group to the commander at Fort Robinson. He believed that the military would send the Northern Cheyennes to live with their Lakota cousins in Dakota Territory. However, by early January, Dull Knife realized that the military intended to send the band back to the Darlington Agency instead. In protest he and his people refused to eat, and on January 9, 1879, Dull Knife and his party attempted another daring escape. This time, however, the army wasted no time firing on the escaping captives as they fled into the moonlit prairie. Soldiers captured most of the survivors and shot at least 24 escapees in a battle two weeks later. Meanwhile, Little Wolf and 114 of his followers decided to camp for the winter and live off of the land. They moved into the northern Nebraska Sandhills and camped in the vicinity of Lost Chokecherry Creek, near present-day Valentine. The band remained hidden, hunting for game and staying away from the whites, before resuming their march northward. By March 1879 they had reached Montana, where they surrendered to Lieutenant William P. Clark near Fort Keogh. In spite of their defeat, Little Wolf and his band joined the army as scouts, and a few years later they received a reservation in Montana.

Although the Northern Cheyenne Breakout left whites in western Nebraska mostly unscathed, it exacerbated worries throughout the region over attacks from the north. On September 5 Brulé raiders stole twenty-two horses from retired major Frank North, who cofounded a ranch with showman and former scout Buffalo Bill Cody on the Dismal River. Over the next two months Lakota parties from the Rosebud and Pine Ridge Reservations committed increasingly "bold and frequent" depredations throughout the Platte Valley. The climate in Lincoln County worsened by late November, when one of M. C. Keith's ranch hands, Ben Case, was murdered along the North Platte on the twenty-second. A local newspaper reported that "the killing was done after the Indian fashion." Two days later "Cheyennes" stole three horses (Nelly, Henry, and XL) from the Bratt ranch and another eight horses from North's ranch. Although one cavalry detachment pursued the raiding party, it did not pick up the trail.[56] However, the largest raid occurred on December 20, when Brulé bands swept through the northwestern section of the county, stealing horses from retired major Leicester Walker; Helen Randall, a widowed rancher; and John Bratt. Sheriff Con Groner telegraphed the fort, saying, "Indians have stolen nine horses ten miles North of here. There is sixteen of them, can catch them if can go soon. Ten men will go from here." Major Eugene Carr, who was in command at McPherson, responded that his garrison was too "absurdly small" to chase and apprehend the thieves. Meanwhile, Bratt pursued the war party the following morning with his local civilian militia, the North Platte Guards. After a day's ride the group caught up with the group and began exchanging fire with them. One raider died in the ensuing gun battle between the two parties, and the Guards took the survivors' horses and the rest of their property. The next day Bratt telegraphed news of the battle to the command at Fort McPherson. Rather than admonishing him, Carr was pleased at the result. "I hope that this will show those Indians that they can not raid with impunity on the people of this neighborhood," he wrote.[57]

Further investigation revealed that these raids were not unprovoked. According to North, who sent two representatives to speak with Spotted Tail after the first raiding party targeted his ranch on September 5, the thieves followed a group of cowboys carrying some of their own stolen horses south to North's ranch. They later returned and stole North's horses in retaliation and to replenish their decimated herds. Although North denied any involvement, he recalled having seen a party of cowboys on September 4 heading south past his ranch. He assumed the men rightfully possessed the animals they brought. Spotted Tail also claimed that whites had stolen over one thousand Brulé horses during the previous year, drastically reducing the tribe's ability to hunt and travel.[58] Decades later Bratt expressed similar views in his autobiography, *Trails of Yesterday*, adding that he asked the agents at Pine Ridge and Rosebud to furnish him with information on Lakota horse and cattle brands. He also directed local ranchers to collect stray Lakota horses during the annual roundups and send the mavericks back to the reservations. But the rancher confronted Spotted Tail over the fall raiding outbreak when he traveled to Rosebud to visit the famous leader the following spring. Unlike North, however, who hinted that Spotted Tail had authorized the raids, Bratt argued that the longtime United States ally had denounced the attacks; he remarked that the North Platte Guards' bloody retribution "served [the raiders] right"; and asserted that the leader of the raiding party, Big Turkey, had no authority to go out stealing horses. The chief warned Bratt to watch out for Big Turkey, who wanted revenge after losing his horses, provisions, and one of his men to Bratt's militia company the previous November.[59]

Big Turkey's appearance in this drama may come as a surprise, considering how the renowned raider of Shoshone horses claimed in his autobiography to have disavowed horse stealing after moving to the Spotted Tail Agency in the early 1870s. Apart from how incredibly skilled Big Turkey must have been in his craft to have mostly eluded both military and civilian authorities while raiding Nebraskan ranches in the 1870s, his ongoing career highlights an important truth: the decline of Plains Indian horse raiding did not negate the place it held in Plains Indian culture or society. Although Big Turkey was by then a member of the agency police and a military scout, these positions did not accord the same privileges or even warrant the same amount of self-respect as one gained by counting coup. Overall, the loss of raiding as a ladder for socially and economically mobile Indians to move up the ranks in their society, a means of gaining influence through gifting, and a surefire strategy for augmenting remudas and curbing herd loss created a vacuum that could not be easily filled. Recidivism among the reservation's once-retired horse thieves suggested not a rejection of horses as personal property or a rebellion against white law ways but something far more personal: an embrace of honor, bravery, and tradition before it threatened to disappear forever.

On that cold November morning north of the Birdwood Creek, two universes of horse wealth collided with one another: the growing mass of ranchers and settlers in western Nebraska, who despaired over losing expensive animals essential to their own plans for survival; and the vanishing equestrian empire of the Lakotas, who fought to hold on to horses as well as tradition. Viewed in that light, Bratt's attack on Big Turkey's party was a dramatic, unjustified, and violent assault on what was supposed to be a horse-stealing raid. Big Turkey's anger was justified on that score, as Bratt took the less-honorable course and condemned not only the raiding party but the leader's reputation as well since Big Turkey had returned home without one of his warriors. As Red Cloud once observed, this was the true mark of a failed raid. It may well have been Big Turkey's last.

Small raiding parties like Big Turkey's continued to stoke fears of another breakout, despite the reservation herds' exposure to white horse thieves who did not have to fear the military's ever-watchful gaze. One letter, dated May 14, from an apparent informant at Pine Ridge, Women's Dress, claimed that the Lakota were planning a sun dance for June 1 and that "some of the Rosebud Indians contemplate a visit to the Platte . . . those Indians who are speaking of the Sun Dance say they are making arrows for [the] war path which they will take when [the Dance is] over." He also alleged that an Indian from the Rosebud Agency had recently shot and killed a white man for his two horses. Fortunately, the post commander doubted the letter's veracity and "suppos[ed] 'Women's Dress,' who is in Fort service as a scout, dictated its contents to some white person at the agency." Like most reports of Indian horse raiding in Nebraska from that point onward, there was little truth to the story. While intertribal raiding and sporadic, scattered raids on white-owned horses would continue for the next several years, mostly in the Dakotas and in Montana, Nebraska lay almost entirely outside of the raiding zones. Yet Nebraska's whites continued to steal reservation horses for as long as Fort Robinson and Camp Sheridan stood guard over the Pine Ridge, and one fact would remain clear: whites could pass through the military's protective cordon like water through a sieve, but reservation Indians could not, at least not without potentially risking their lives and freedom.[60]

By the end of the 1870s remounts and captured ponies flooded the forts in Nebraska and elsewhere, and for once the army had more horses than it needed. With the removal of the Lakotas, Cheyennes, and Arapahos to reservations outside of Nebraska, Fort McPherson ceased to be on the forefront of the military's vanishing defensive perimeter. In time the fort assumed a different function, one that lasted for the remainder of its existence: it evolved into a very large and well-guarded stable for unused horses. Just three months after Crazy Horse's surrender at Fort Robinson, the post commander at Fort McPherson asked for additional help taking care of the 225 unassigned horses living on his reservation. Since these horses belonged "to the Department [of the Platte]," and not to a specific unit, it was difficult to delegate their care to companies who already had to tend their own horses. In September 1878, just before Dull Knife's escape from the Darlington Agency in Oklahoma prompted army units across the region to give chase, the number of unassigned cavalry horses at the fort had dropped to 130. By March 1880 only 14 unassigned horses lived at the post.[61] That year the army abandoned Fort McPherson and several other installations as part of the War Department's decision to concentrate its resources in a select number of frontier posts. As a result, the stables were disassembled, and the remaining horses were removed to outposts and units elsewhere. The Fort McPherson Military Reservation land later became Fort McPherson National Cemetery.

The decommissioning of Fort McPherson and the dispersion of its horse population provided the United States Army, perhaps out of a spirit of postwar generosity and goodwill, with an excellent opportunity to square an old account: gifting fifty ponies, ones that No Flesh believed that he and his band would receive as compensation for Whistler's death years earlier, to the newly horse-poor Oglalas. Needless to say, the army never offered any horses. In fact, at the time United States officials granted no favors to No Flesh and other Oglala subchiefs, who petitioned Reynolds for the fifty horses reserved for them as retribution for Whistler's murder. Instead, military leaders in Omaha and Washington DC considered preemptively destroying the remnants of Whistler's band rather than simply giving the ponies as a peace offering. Later that spring a hundred Oglalas appeared outside of Fort McPherson. Captain Reynolds had already left on a trip to Washington DC, leaving Captain Joseph DuBois in command. When the party's representatives informed DuBois that they had not received the fifty ponies they "expected" as recompense four months earlier, the commander claimed that Reynolds was presumably trying to acquire the mounts in Washington DC. He then promised the Oglalas that he would look into the matter and wrote an urgent dispatch to Omaha requesting instructions. DuBois warned the officials that the Oglalas were intent on receiving their horses, and if the visiting bands could not have them, then there "might be trouble this summer."[62]

Twelve days later General Philip Sheridan rejected the request in an angry missive directed at the fort's leadership. He criticized the command's history of working with Spotted Tail and other bands in the region and questioned why such a gift was necessary. "If it is entirely certain that these Indians intend to massacre the settlers . . . because Whistler was attacked by unknown persons," he asked, "would it not be best to jump them first?" Sheridan then claimed that "there has been too much talk with these Indians about Fort McPherson," arguing that he had "repeatedly advised and ordered that the commanding officers at Fort McPherson attend to his legitimate business and let the Indian Department attend to theirs." In other words, if the Oglalas requested horses, it was the Bureau of Indian Affairs' problem, not the military's. Sheridan's letter killed Reynolds's peace offering, but it did not settle the matter. That summer Reynolds, after returning from Washington DC, pointedly requested that the War Department change its published description of Fort McPherson to note that Miniconjous were frequently raiding the area. Whistler's band, it seemed, had stopped providing information as to the whereabouts of the raiding parties from the north.[63]

Contemporaries and historians alike have debated the identity of Whistler's murderer for over 140 years. One writer suggested that Dr. W. F. Carver, the "Wizard Rifle Shot" of the plains, killed Whistler and his two companions in self-defense when they intruded upon Carver and his partner in their tent. Other historians have claimed that it might have been Wild Bill Hickok. Perhaps the most convincing account, however, comes from Bayard H. Paine, who corresponded with Luther North on the subject. According to Paine, North told him that in spite of Carver's claims, he was "certain" that Newt Moreland, a local settler, had committed the crime. North recalled seeing Moreland on "a nice looking spotted horse" while on a trip to Kearney in 1873. When asked where he got it, Moreland claimed the horse had belonged to Spotted Tail. If that is true, then the career of a once notorious horse raider ended at the hands of a white horse thief.[64]

In some ways Whistler's murder—and the Oglalas' demands for justice—marked a turning point in relations between the Lakotas and the United States. As homesteaders invaded western Nebraska, the military increasingly restricted, and then prohibited, American Indians from hunting or even entering the region.[65] By the time the war started, Lakota and Cheyenne frontiers had already receded to north of Nebraska's Pine Ridge and beyond its western border with Wyoming. Officers out on scouting missions reported fewer signs of Lakota or Northern Cheyenne activity, greater numbers of communities and farms, and a declining amount of wildlife and forage. By the summer of 1876 scouting missions deployed in response to rumors of possible raiding came back with reports of no Plains Indian activity whatsoever, instead finding a growing homesteader population that dismissed the threat. Many of the new settlers arrived after the last cluster of raids ended in 1874, and few understood why the U.S. Cavalry gallivanted around the plains, hunting Plains Indians who were fighting a war hundreds of miles to the northwest in Wyoming.

This new sense of peacetime normalcy was confirmed by a scouting party that visited Big Spring, a small community about ten miles west of Ogallala, after rumors of depredations near the village reached the fort. The party, led by Captain Henry Wessels, arrived there about a week before the Battle of Little Bighorn broke out four hundred miles to the northwest. "Wherever I went," reported Wessels, "I met unarmed men and loose horses." At one homestead "there were 14 horses running at large, the sole occupant of the ranche being a negro who said that he did not even own a pistol."[66] In a few years the scouting parties themselves would become difficult to organize as cavalry detachments encountered an increasingly crowded landscape. There were more people than before as well as more horses. More survey lines stretched across maps of the region, creating a checkerboard tapestry of homesteads, ranch houses, roads, and rails. There seemed to be more of everything. But there were far fewer Indians.

Fig. 4. Brulé war party, ca. 1907. Cropped from original.
Photo by Edward S. Curtis, Library of Congress, LC-USZ62–46958.

Fig. 5. North face of Crow Butte, near Crawford, Nebraska, 2018. A skirmish occurred here in 1849 between the Crows and the Brulé Lakota after a failed horse raid, giving this feature its name. Photo by the author.

Fig. 6. Red Cloud in 1880 during his visit to Washington DC.
Photo by C. M. (Charles Milton) Bell, Photographs of Indian Delegates,
Beinecke Rare Book and Manuscript Library, Yale University.

Fig. 7. Brulé chief Spotted Tail worked informally with officers at Fort McPherson to maintain peace in the Platte Valley during the early 1870s. This included passing information along about known and rumored horse raids to the army. William R. Cross, Sentegaleska—Spotted Tail, carte de visite, Carl Mautz Collection of Cartes-de-Visite Photographs of Indians of North America, Yale Collection of Western Americana, Beinecke Rare Book Collection and Manuscript Library, Yale University.

Fig. 8. Photograph of Lakota warrior Big Turkey, 1912. Big Turkey cut horses from Plains Indians as well as whites, including John Bratt. Photo by F. W. Glasier & Co., Beinecke Rare Book and Manuscript Library, Yale University.

THE EUQITABLE

FARM & STOCK
Improvememt Co.

Of the State of Nebraska, Limited

Being the firm of

John Bratt & Co.
INCORPORATED.

Offices:
Room 9, Creighton Block, Omaha, Neb.
Room 1, Bratt Building, North Platte.

Officers:
ISAAC COE, Pres't, Nebraska City, Neb.
LEVI CARTER, Vice Pres't, Omaha, Neb.
JOHN BRATT, Sec'y and Treas., North
Platte Neb.

P. O. Address, North Platte, Nebraska.

Range, North and West of Birdwood
Creek, north of the North Platte river.

Some cattle branded OO left hip, same loin
brand and earmark as cut.
Also own right side and hip, T

right jaw. Earmark

Horse baand O on left shoulder.

REWARD!

$100.00 reward will be paid for the
arrest and conviction of any person or
persons, for stealing, unlawfully killing,
or defacing, or altering the brands of
cattle or horses owned by us.

Fig. 9. Advertisement in the *Grant County Tribune* for John Bratt's ranching firm, February 26, 1891. Notice the brand identifying information and the $100 reward posted at the bottom.

JOHN BRATT
Taken in the year 1892

Fig. 10. John Bratt in 1892. Bratt's experiences were interwoven with the history of horse stealing in western Nebraska in *Trails of Yesterday*. They include pursuing Big Turkey and other raiders in 1878, assisting in the capture of Doc Middleton, investigating rustlers in Grant County, and arguing for better working and living conditions for seasonal cowboys. Photographer unknown.

Fig. 11. This sketch, published in *Frank Leslie's Illustrated Newspaper* on
June 9, 1877, depicts Crazy Horse and his band on their way to surrender at
Fort Robinson. Upon their arrival they were forced to surrender all of their
ponies as well as their arms. Library of Congress, LC-USZC2–769.

Fig. 12. Wooden Leg holding a Custer rifle from the Battle of Little Bighorn, 1927. Wooden Leg fought in the battle and recounted the stories of many horse raiding expeditions to reservation physician Thomas Marquis. Photo by Thomas Bailey Marquis, Buffalo Bill Center of the West, Cody, Wyoming; Thomas Marquis Collection, PN.165.1.48.

Fig. 13. Grant County welcome sign. This part of the Sandhills was famous for its ranching and infamous for its rustlers. Photo by the author.

Fig. 14. Studio portrait of Doc Middleton, who was perhaps America's best-known—and most prolific—horse thief. It was taken after his release from prison. Photographer unknown, Denver Public Library, Western History Collection, x-31309.

Fig. 15. An actor playing a horse thief in Buffalo Bill's Wild West, ca. 1892. Photo by Nate Salsbury, Salsbury Collection, Buffalo Bill's Wild West Show, album 2 (A. R. Dresser photographs), Denver Public Library, Western History Collection, NS-531.

Fig. 16. Horse thieves were routinely hanged as part of the Wild West show,
ca. 1892. Cropped from original. Photo by Nate Salsbury, Salsbury Collection,
Buffalo Bill's Wild West Show, album 2 (A. R. Dresser photographs),
Denver Public Library, Western History Collection, NS-494.

Fig. 17. Horse thieves were often hanged in movies as well. In this early promotional poster for *The Arizona Raiders* (*Bad Men of Arizona* was an early working title), the "Horsethief" comes closer to the center of the noose than either the "Killer" or the "Murderer." *Bad Men of Arizona* promotional poster, 1936.

Fig. 18. Buffalo Bill Cody cutout at Fort Cody, North Platte, Nebraska, 2017. Before becoming a world-renowned showman, Cody led army scouts throughout the region and claimed to have stolen multiple Indian horses during his career. Photo by the author.

Fig. 19. Horse at a farm near Hickman, Nebraska, 2015. Although horses are less ubiquitous today, they are still an integral part of Nebraska's history and culture. Photo by Erik Johnson.

4

A Most Tempting Business

It is the fashion to laugh at the severity with which horse-stealing is
punished on the border, but the reasons are evident. Horses are the
most valuable property of the frontiersman, whether cowboy, hunter,
or settler, and are often absolutely essential to his well-being, and
even to his life. They are always marketable, and they are very easily
stolen, for they carry themselves off, instead of having to be carried.
Horse-stealing is thus a most tempting business, especially to the more
reckless ruffians, and it is always followed by armed men; and
they can only be kept in check by ruthless severity.

—THEODORE ROOSEVELT, *Ranch Life and the Hunting-Trail*

Intermittent, tit-for-tat horse raiding between American
Indians, military units, and even ranchers created a theft
culture in western Nebraska in which these various groups,
none of whom completely controlled the region, legitimized
the stealing of horses from the "other." This kind of mutual
horse stealing did not end until the late 1870s. But during that
decade the size of the local criminal class grew along with the
region's homesteading population. Many of these crooks were
out stealing reservation horses, thus fueling the massive stolen-
pony trade discussed in the previous chapter. These horses
helped sustain the growth of large horse-stealing gangs, such
as the one led by Doc Middleton, which stole animals on an
unprecedented scale while evading both state authorities and
vigilance mobs.

This new surge of theft created a parallel white horse-stealing gang crisis. As thieves struck growing numbers of people who had smaller herds, in addition to ranches or the military, concerns over the crime's severity on the frontier mounted among those settlers who were most vulnerable: families or businesses that relied on one or two horses to survive but who could not muster the manpower or create the safeguards necessary to protect those horses from theft. Media reports of horse-stealing gangs and American Indian breakouts exacerbated this crisis, introducing recently arrived migrants to both the fears and realities of just a few years earlier, when the legal system was less developed and a state of open warfare with the Lakotas existed. What settlers believed was a safe country for settlement was suddenly not safe anymore.

Yet when compared to the Plains Indian horse-stealing crisis of the late 1870s, the white horse-stealing gang crisis was different in one important respect: it never really went away. Long after the Lakotas and Cheyennes had been sent to their reservations, and even after whites had despoiled the defeated tribes of much of their horse wealth, gangs continued to rustle horses and cattle. By the 1880s, however, growing populations and law enforcement budgets forced them into hiding. Once gangs could no longer argue that they principally stole reservation horses, they lost their only claim to social and moral legitimacy and instantly forfeited their folk hero status. Gangs grew more mafia-like in their composition and operation, valuing secrecy and profit over adventure and survival.

Secrecy might have kept many of these bandits hidden from the law, but their discretion does no favors for the historian. Horse-stealing gangs did not leave constitutions, meeting minutes, or newspaper notices behind. As a result, gangs are difficult to track across time and space, and scholars must be inventive when researching them. Military correspondence, legal documents (including depositions), and detailed personal reminiscences can often be used to triangulate a gang's activities, members, and location, provided that they exist and are discoverable. Newspaper reports can also be helpful, though edi-

A MOST TEMPTING BUSINESS

tors often published rumors and hearsay when discussing gang activity. Nevertheless, more or less detailed descriptions of several different gangs appear in the pages that follow, including Doc Middleton and his infamous band of thieves out of Texas.

This horse-stealing crisis mirrored Nebraska's transition toward an agricultural economy. Since this shift was partial and, at a certain point west of the 100th meridian, impossible to complete, it ensured that the region straddled two incompatible cultural, economic, and political worlds: free-range ranching and independent yeoman farming. The tensions between these two visions of the future of the plains played out in corrals and canyons across western Nebraska as horse-thieving gangs made headlines stealing from ranchers and Plains Indians, to the approval of homesteaders throughout the region. They also shaped the nature and fortunes of rustling gangs themselves since stockmen possessed both the ability to marshal enough resources to pursue and destroy thieving gangs as well as the social hierarchy necessary to create their own gangs. Organizationally, ranches and gangs had more in common than most would have cared to admit. These little fiefdoms, both legitimate and invisible, were common throughout western Nebraska.

An Amoral Country

The crisis came like a bolt from the blue. The range was largely quiet during the early 1870s, prompting commentators to congratulate themselves on bringing American law to the region so quickly. Soon after the September 1874 term of the district court had adjourned without hearing a single criminal indictment, one newspaper editor in North Platte lauded his neighbors for creating "a moral county."[1] This period of relative calm was short-lived, however, and within two years an almost decade-long crime wave began to plague the Platte Valley. Between 1876 and 1884 the number of reported horse thefts in Lincoln County exploded, along with corresponding increases in personal and other forms of property crime. Thirteen men were convicted and three acquitted in district court of horse stealing during this period. Accusers swore out an additional dozen or so warrants, but for one reason or another the suspects were not caught or arraigned. These years corresponded with a population boom as North Platte organized itself as a city and as land in the eastern half of the county filled up with farmers. Ranchers such as John Bratt depended on a growing labor pool of ranch hands to increase their own stock herds, and the Union Pacific Railroad attracted workers, travelers, and tramps to the city. As settlers moved into or passed through the county, the wave of settlement brought growing pains in the form of increased crime.

The looming possibility of Lakota or Northern Cheyenne horse raids gave Lincoln County settlers an exogenous cause for anxiety, but the actual crisis of horse stealing in the region reflected a noticeable rise in the number of criminal indictments for horse theft. In 1872 recorded reports of personal and property crime reached a statistical high of 1,200 incidents per 100,000 people (fig. 20). The number of reports then dropped precipitously between 1873 and 1876, paralleling North Platte's incorporation as a second-class city in 1875 and the establishment of a municipal police force in 1876.[2] However, during the same period of time reports of horse stealing rose in relation to the overall population of Lincoln County.[3] In fact, five out of six property crimes reported in 1876 were horse thefts. The stealing of horses from ranches and farms outside of town placed those incidents outside of the immediate jurisdiction of the newly established police force in North Platte, so the rate of horse theft was likely immune from any downward pressure the police placed on crime rates. Later, personal and property crime incidents rose again, in 1878 and 1880, and horse theft reports spiked in 1878 and 1881, but after 1882 all three indicators fell gradually throughout the rest of the decade. While the overall trend line for horse-stealing reports closely mirrors that of other property crimes as well as personal crimes, the eight-year period between 1874 and 1881 represents the only time between 1872 and 1890 when Lincoln County's population was small enough, and the number of horse-stealing cases high enough, to make horse theft a statistically meaningful threat.

Horse thieves plagued Cheyenne County as well. Complain-

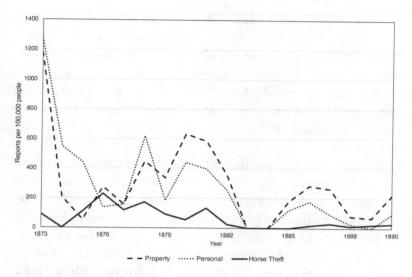

Fig. 20. Number of reported crimes in Lincoln County per 100,000 people, 1872–90; the years 1883 and 1884 are omitted due to absence of legal data. (See chap. 4, n. 3, for a complete rundown of my methodology for this figure.) Created by the author.

ants accused 18 defendants of stealing horses or mules between 1876 and the end of 1878, which was greater than the total number of grand larceny cases during that same time. Another 9 men stood accused of the crime in 1879, including Edgar D. King, who was charged with three separate counts. Considering that Cheyenne County's population was only 1,558 in 1880, 27 defendants is a staggering number even for a community whose Boot Hill cemetery contained over 200 bodies. While the court only referred 9 of the defendants to District Court for trial, the large number of individual accusers means that at least as many people reported that their horses were stolen.[4]

The widely publicized exploits of horse thief gangs compounded, and contributed to, worsening crime statistics in the region. Although these gangs committed the vast majority of their crimes elsewhere, newspapers filled their pages with reports of their misdeeds. Familiarity bred contempt as media reports attached names and reputations in people's minds to the otherwise shadowy ranks of horse thieves. At least one high-profile, comparatively well-documented gang of horse thieves operated in western Nebraska. Doc Middleton, one of the most famous horse thieves in the history of the West, and briefly a Lincoln County resident, was the leader. He and his gang allegedly stole over four thousand horses throughout Nebraska and across the Great Plains, enough animals to mount a Civil War cavalry brigade.

Though one might debate whether or not a famous criminal can be a representative one, in some ways Doc Middleton fit the generic profile of a typical horse thief: he came from humble origins, worked as a cowhand at one point, and enjoyed the thrill of stealing horses and not getting caught (fig. 21). Originally from Texas, Middleton's father was a Mexican War veteran. Middleton allegedly stole his first horse while in Texas and was rumored to have murdered three men there as well. In 1872 the prosecutor in Coryell County, Texas, indicted him for stealing a mare, and two years later he stole a gelding worth seventy-five dollars. These two crimes earned him a spot on the Texas Rangers' fugitive list in 1874. Middleton evaded the law by moving to North Platte, where the Powers Cattle Company hired him as a ranch hand in spite of his reputation as a lousy cowboy.[5] But Middleton was soon back to cutting herds, and in 1877 authorities arrested him near Julesburg, Colorado, for stealing thirty-four horses. Middleton escaped by digging out of his cell, which, like many prisons from that period, had a dirt floor.

After his escape Middleton's fame skyrocketed over the next two years. According to biographer Harold Hutton, Middleton's notoriety began in early 1877, when he and his gang fled Colorado for neighboring Nebraska, and soon thereafter the state seemed to be crawling with horse thieves, cattle rustlers, and other bandits. It did not take long for Middleton to get in trouble: a Cheyenne County grand jury indicted "Dock" Middleton on one count of second-degree murder for allegedly shooting and killing James Keefe on January 13, 1877. That spring Middleton's gang began focusing their efforts on the Niobrara River valley in northern Nebraska, but as their infamy spread,

146   A MOST TEMPTING BUSINESS

Fig. 21. Doc Middleton standing next to a horse, 1893. After his arrest and imprisonment, Middleton became a regional celebrity, but by that time most of his gang members were dead. David Cherry "Doc" Middleton, 1849–1913, collection (RG2248.AM), Nebraska State Historical Society, Lincoln, RG2248-5.

reports of gang activity surfaced farther west and south across the state. One Lincoln County local judge issued a warrant for the elusive Middleton in May 1879, just two months before the fugitive's capture in Columbus, Nebraska. Though the sheriff never served the warrant, it shows that people across the state were afraid of being struck by the gang. Some even believed that Middleton was the leader of a statewide criminal organization of robbers and highwaymen, though Hutton argued that the idea of "how such organization and discipline could be possible among as large a number of lawless and undisciplined men as were engaged in stock stealing baffle[s] the imagination."[6]

Unlike most horse thieves, Middleton was a widely recognizable character, and like Jesse James before him, Middleton deflected some of the outcry against him by skillfully manipulating his public image. He limited himself to stealing horses from the Lakotas and Cheyennes and left the rest of the thieving to his associates. Chief Little Wound complained in a letter to the Pine Ridge agent that Middleton had stolen 590 of the Lakotas' horses. Meanwhile, Bratt claimed that gang member Charles Fugit, not Middleton, had stolen 3 of his horses. People across the state also believed that Middleton contributed to charities in various communities and did other good deeds. By sticking to reservation horses, Nebraskans saw Middleton as an ally against Lakota horse raiding and a friend of the white man's civilization. After all, like Robin Hood, he was only stealing back that which had been stolen already, namely by the Lakotas, and then giving part of it back to the victimized community. Middleton beat the Plains Indians at their own game by raiding those bands that had earlier raided farms and ranches for horses.[7]

No one heaped any laurels upon Fugit, however, who was by all accounts an unrepentant, serial horse thief. Although he affiliated with the Middleton gang, Fugit was the only member to repeatedly appear in Lincoln County's legal record. On November 27, 1876, a Lincoln County resident accused Fugit of stealing horses and submitted a criminal complaint to the county court. The judge ordered Fugit to come to court, but he did not appear. The following year Fugit stole horses from several ranchers throughout the county. Once again, he escaped undetected, though in 1879 he was eventually convicted on these counts. In November 1878 Fugit stole three horses from John Bratt. The rancher suspected Fugit's involvement when he noted the loss of the horses in his records, but he did not file a legal complaint against the fugitive. Finally, authorities charged Fugit in 1879 for stealing horses from Charles Wood and Bernard Beer in 1877. When Sheriff Con Groner confronted Fugit in a bar and attempted to arrest him, the thief fired a shot at the officer's head. The bullet passed harmlessly through the sheriff's hat, but Fugit was soon convicted of attempted murder and horse stealing and sentenced to twenty years in jail. Fugit left prison a few years later on a pardon, but one year after being released from prison, he was killed in a gunfight.[8]

If Middleton's misdeeds sold newspapers, Fugit's crimes made the gang's actual work visible to and even dangerous for Nebraskans. Consequently, the Middleton gang's criminal activities across the state from 1877 to 1879, combined with a relative spike in horse theft and criminal reports overall during the same period, created another horse-stealing crisis. Not only did settlers fear losing their valuable animals to Fugit or other members of the gang, but the group's theft of reservation horses brought the region to the brink of open warfare between ranchers and reservation Lakotas. Fortunately, Bratt and other local ranchers who understood what was actually going on raised $1,300 in reward money to end Middleton's horse-stealing career, which in turn paid for the information that helped federal agents locate, surround, and apprehend the notorious villain.[9]

Doc Middleton's career sheds light on the motives and actions of a gang leader. Above all, Middleton wanted to be respected and admired by his gang, the public at large, and even his family. His letters to his father and sister reveal another side to the horse thief: a man desperate for his parents' love.[10] Middleton wrote several letters to his family while still in Texas in 1872 and 1873, in spite of his growing notoriety there as a horse thief. The letters indicate that the times were rough for Middleton and his wife, Lizzie, who had lost their baby boy in November 1871. In them he repeatedly complained about writing so many letters without getting a response from his family, even though he stated that he only began to write his family recently on account of his not being able to write very well. "I want you to right me as soon as you get this leter," he urged his father. "I hav rote severl leters havent got eny yet but one leter a bout 4 munts a go." He then asked his father to come and see him if he was not able to write back. His other letters made similar pleas, such as one written on April 21, 1871, in which he implored, "Well father I havent herd from you in a good while I wood like to her from you all I hav rote 5 leter and I havent got no one from you yet." By 1873, when Middleton's legal problems prevented him from ever returning home, he apologized profusely to his sister. "I am [sorry] to let you know that I will never come home againe," he wrote. "I cant help it now [and] I hope that you all wont take it hard." These letters display another side of the notorious horse thief, murder suspect, and supposed leader of over one hundred armed bandits: that of a family man, committed to his wife, grieving the loss of his son, and working to preserve his relationship with his parents and siblings.[11]

Middleton's first wife did not remain committed to him for long, but he soon found a partner who was more willing to give him—or less able to resist giving him—the adulation and unquestioned love he thought he deserved. In May 1879, two months before his capture, Middleton exchanged vows with Mary Richardson, who, in spite of her father's vocal opposition, decided to marry the outlaw celebrity. She continued Doc's corresponding with his family after he was arrested in 1879 and told his relatives in Texas that while her husband was in deep trouble, he would find a way to get through it. "He has got himself in a pretty bad shape up here [in Nebraska,]" Mary Middleton wrote in a letter to her mother-in-law, "but I guess he will get out all right." Mary then assured his mother that she would stand by her husband, possibly in reference to his first wife's decision to leave. "He has got a wife that will stick to him as long as he lives no matter what his fate is," she declared. "I will stay close to him in all trouble. [Everyone] has his trouble sooner or later." But like her predecessor, Mary Middleton also left her husband. Shortly after their divorce, Doc married Irene, Mary's sister.[12]

Fortunately for Doc Middleton, it all worked out in the end. Despite serving some jail time, his charisma, reputation, and fresh start after leaving prison gave Middleton the opportunity not only to begin a new life as a free man but also to repair his public image. Nebraskans learned that Middleton had been released early on good behavior and were surprised to discover that he had won a widely popularized horse race from Chadron, Nebraska, to Chicago. Doc Middleton eventually earned a place as an entertainer in Buffalo Bill's Wild West show, where he performed alongside war-whooping Plains Indians and target-shooting cowboys in a "realistic" depiction of what the western frontier was really like. As time passed, tales about the man

A MOST TEMPTING BUSINESS

who had allegedly stolen two thousand horses became legends, and the outlaw-turned-social-bandit acquired a mythic stature in Nebraska history. One chronicler wrote that while in prison, Middleton allegedly cut off the tip of his finger while working. He refused to take a sick leave, however, claiming that he owed it to the state to finish his task.[13]

John Bratt also revised his opinion of Middleton, and he reserved some space for the lately reformed outlaw in his autobiography. Bratt recalled one story of an old preacher in a frontier town where he happened to be during a roundup. After mingling with the town residents and resident cowboys for several days, the preacher urged them all to attend a church service the following evening. The service, held in the town dance hall, was lit by several gas lamps. When one cowboy tired of the sermon and shot out one of the lamps, however, Doc Middleton got up, stood next to the preacher, and threatened to kill the shooter if he tried to do that again. The guilty cowboy slunk out of the room, and Middleton emerged as a defender of frontier religion. Later Bratt issued a more direct compliment: "Some of the readers will agree with the writer in his estimate of 'Doc' Middleton, who may have committed some crimes, but nevertheless had a good heart in him and his later life seems to prove it."[14]

Middleton's fate, while remarkable, was uncommon. He craved fame and recognition more than he did horses; his criminal career after 1877, his activities upon being released from prison, and his family relationships suggest Middleton possessed a pathological need for approval. To that end he got what he wanted. Middleton found celebrity, respectability, and redemption in spite of being a convicted horse thief. However, his associates were not as lucky, and neither Charles Fugit nor the other members of the gang who had been responsible for doing the so-called dirty work found forgiveness or fortune. One of Middleton's biographers pointed out the difference in how the public perceived Middleton versus his associates while still sanctifying the gang's leader: "It's a fact that Doc did MOST of his stealing from the Indians and from the government, but he couldn't have been all bad . . . he had a pretty loyal band of cutthroats riding with him, most of whom came to a bad end. They were horse lovers and Indian haters every one."[15]

The difference between Middleton's and gang member Charlie Fugit's respective fates highlights the very unusual circumstances behind Middleton's redemption. Middleton enjoyed a strange combination of advantages: public notoriety, sympathetic neighbors, vocal advocates within both the community and his family, the fact that he was taken in alive (a fate that was not shared by Jesse James and other infamous outlaws), a keen sensitivity to his own public image, and a marketable personal history that landed him in Buffalo Bill's Wild West show as a performer. Meanwhile, Charles Fugit, who was shot and killed within a year after his release from jail, and most of western Nebraska's remaining convicted horse thieves faced a more ignominious, or at least anonymous, future: at least two members of Middleton's gang, Kid Wade and Jack Nolan, were later lynched, while Fugit faced a lengthy prison sentence. When Fugit was released, Buffalo Bill's touring company did not await him. Only the Wild West itself.

Profiles in Rustling

The disintegration of high-profile criminal gangs in the late 1870s and early 1880s, including those belonging to Doc Middleton and Jesse James, reflected more general declines in both actual and perceived violence. The 1880s witnessed fewer horse thefts throughout western Nebraska, at least with respect to the number of horse theft prosecutions relative to other forms of property crime during that period. However, the gangs themselves did not simply disappear from the landscape of western Nebraska. Instead, they evolved, keeping themselves hidden not just from the cavalry or federal marshals but also from their neighbors, friends, and associates. As the region's new residents continued to legitimize its economy, the days of settlers openly supporting and cheering on bandits like Middleton were over. Unfortunately, western Nebraska's economic, social, and legal bonds were not yet strong enough to impede the organization of rustling gangs.

A MOST TEMPTING BUSINESS

While regional crime statistics only partially capture the presence of baseline gang activity, the steady drumbeat of news reports suggest that rustling was a persistent and pervasive concern. During the early 1890s rumors and reports of rustling gangs swirled throughout western Nebraska. Within the span of just a few weeks in May 1891, two potential gangs emerged in different parts of the region. In Alliance, according to one newspaper correspondent, "the suspicion that there is a gang of horse and cattle thieves in this section of the country is pretty nearly a settled conviction with many." The writer blamed the belief on some "very curious" recent events: "There are a good many strangers in the country and cattle and horses have taken unaccountable notions to go where they were never known to go before, and entirely too far from their regular ranges to believe they have done so voluntarily." Meanwhile, down in Lincoln County, the sheriff arrested George Marcott on suspicion of running a gang near Brady Island for at least five years. His wife divulged the scheme to local authorities, adding that her husband had physically abused her and threatened to kill her if she ever exposed him. She arrived in North Platte on the 10:00 p.m. train and hurriedly sought out the police.[16]

The previous year a similar series of rumors and reports prompted John Bratt to investigate a potential cattle-rustling gang in Grant County, where his company had recently lost a number of stock. As Bratt's ranch interests reached deep into the Sandhills, business and criminal matters in faraway Grant County also began to interest the North Platte–based cattle baron. In 1890, as his losses mounted, he sent an agent to Hyannis to look into the matter. In addition to getting a detailed account of an alleged scheme to steal his company's cattle, Bratt received a pair of signed affidavits from two thieves whom his foremen had accused of stealing cattle in the area.[17] Although both depositions were given by suspected cattle thieves, their confessions contain a glimpse into the world of the horse thief as well, in which each perpetrator had to weigh both the risks and the rewards of his or her decision to carry away a horse they did not own. They reveal the hidden world of the rural rustling gang and its usually adversarial, though occasionally symbiotic, relationship with the region's ranchers.

Incorporated in 1887, Grant County has always been ranching country. Its demographic history reflects its distance from larger settlements: 458 people lived in the county in 1890, which reached its historical peak in 1920 with 1,486 persons. The population then began a gradual decline, and according to the 2010 census, it had decreased to 614. Even today, travelers heading north on Nebraska Highway 61 will quickly understand ranching's place in the local culture and economy when they see the large wooden welcome sign with a giant cow, which reads: "Grant County: This is no bull." But while motorists in the twenty-first century often nod while passing each other on the remote Sandhills highways, during the nineteenth century residents were less likely to give friendly acknowledgment to strangers. Grant County's low population density, its economic monoculture, a lopsided gender ratio (274 men in 1890 to 184 women), and the absence of authority figures beyond the ranches themselves created ripe conditions for rural gang activity throughout the region.[18] One local historian attributed the county's susceptibility to theft to its desolation: "Occasionally a small instance of cattle rustling comes to light yet, but its nothing like in the old days. It is a long ways across country between railroads . . . [which] provides plenty of isolation for rustlers and it was in these wide spaces that the cattle rustlers made their last strong stand against the law."[19]

Grant County was known both for its expansive prairie lands and its expensive rustling problem, which attracted respectable cattle barons, less respectable crooks, and perhaps a few people who stood somewhere in between. Bartlett Richards—a Chadron-based ranchman who was famously prosecuted in 1906 for fraud and conspiracy against the federal government after he and several employees fenced over 217,000 acres of public land—ranged many of his cattle around Hyannis and helped organize the Northwestern Nebraska Stock Growers Association. Like Bratt, his operation required vast amounts of pastureland that took his business interests well beyond his home

A MOST TEMPTING BUSINESS

range. However, high cattle populations and low human population densities in Grant and adjacent counties also made those herds an attractive target for theft. In 1886 the rustling problem was so severe that reports of gang rule in the region reached Governor John Milton Thayer's desk in Lincoln. In response Thayer appointed R. M. "Bud" Moran to serve as the new sheriff of Grant County. According to historian Nellie Snyder Yost, cattlemen throughout the state urged Thayer to "get Moran to clean it up."[20] It was almost as if everyone who had made their way to Grant County during the 1880s intended to either raise cows, steal cows, or chase cattle thieves.

Bud Moran served over two decades as sheriff of Grant County, and Bratt would find him to be a competent and honest collaborator. He was not risk-averse, however; Moran reportedly followed the trail of rustled cattle on several occasions toward the camps of those who had taken them. On one occasion he surprised three men butchering the cattle late in the evening. He then led them back to Hyannis, which required standing guard over the trio all night to make sure they would not get the jump on him. Moran also helped track a Cherokee bootlegger, a man who had allegedly killed nine U.S. marshals, all the way to Arkansas, where he and several officers cornered and killed the fugitive.[21] Clearly, Moran's recklessness bore some fruit, and when he received information that Thomas Campbell was burying Bratt-branded cattle hides, he would soon hit the trail again.

Thomas Campbell swore his deposition on February 8, 1890. Under oath he testified to having helped a rustling gang steal dozens of head of cattle from Thomas Lynch, John Bratt, and other ranchers in Grant County. Campbell claimed that he had taken several head of cattle from the Lynch farm, killed them at his own place sold the dressed meat to a butcher in Alliance, and buried the carcasses on his land. The butcher, Perry A. Yeast, promised Campbell a third of the profits from his scheme to purloin sirloin. But Yeast, a respected local stockman, also needed to exercise caution. He was then serving on the executive committee of the Northwest Nebraska Stock Growers Association and was therefore in charge of local efforts to protect ranches from thieves. By disposing of the branded parts of the cattle, Yeast hoped to safely profit from the now unidentifiable beef by butchering it in his shop and selling it for retail. However, the gang's activities were discovered when a neighbor witnessed Campbell burying his hides.[22]

On January 21, a few weeks before the arrests, Sheriff Moran wrote Bratt at the request of the rancher's foreman in the area, who had asked Bratt to "send a man up to him at once" since "there is a great amount of stealing going on in that country and [the authorities] will come down on the rustlers in a short time." The sheriff also indicated that he had found several of Bratt's cattle among the other head he had recently recovered from the gang. Bratt sent Hanson Grimes, an experienced North Platte attorney, to Grant County to collect information on the thefts and aid in the prosecution of the gang. Upon arriving, Grimes recorded Campbell's deposition, which implicated his fellow gang members, and subsequently gave a copy to Bratt. Meanwhile, the county prosecutor filed multiple charges against Yeast, as well as Campbell and several other associates, for stealing cattle on three separate occasions between April and December 1889. In total Yeast and his goons allegedly stole fifty head from Bratt, Lynch, and Daniel Egan.[23] But despite Campbell's sworn testimony, there is no evidence that Campbell, Yeast, or anyone else in the gang went to prison for their crimes.

Campbell shared several traits with the prototypical horse-stealing gang member: he worked with a group, had a willing and complicit fence waiting to buy and sell the stolen goods, mitigated personal risk by burying the carcasses on his claim, and wanted to turn a quick profit. He was also an unlikely culprit, at least in comparison to the evil, avaricious rustlers often encountered in Western literature. Campbell was a family man with a wife and three kids. Originally from Norton County, Kansas, the Campbells had staked a claim in Deuel County and moved there in 1888. Still three years away from filing eligibility, Campbell was probably stymied in his efforts to create a profitable farm by his poor choice of location within the Sandhills. Even in the twenty-first century, the region continues to defy cultivation and is still predominately a ranching district. By 1889 Campbell probably needed money for one reason or another, but regardless of his financial insecurity, a prison term was unlikely to improve his situation. Consequently, his deposition is ostensibly straightforward and sufficiently damning. He wasted no time in pointing out the involvement of others (he named his accomplices several times throughout) and did not hesitate to implicate others in giving him the idea to commit his misdeeds. His story is somewhat inconsistent, however, because at one point Campbell lied about the number of people responsible for burying the cowhides on his land. Perhaps in an effort to distribute even more blame among his accomplices, Campbell asserted that Yeast and two other suspects had helped him dispose of this evidence, while the neighbor who turned him in reported that Campbell had managed to finish the task with only one helper.[24]

After Yeast's arrest, the defense successfully delayed his trial for several months due to a series of courtroom motions to change the trial venue and summarily disqualify various jurors. In fairness to Yeast, though, it is not surprising that many of his neighbors would refuse to give him the benefit of the doubt, considering both his position within the regional stockman's association and his membership in the fraternity of Nebraska cattle barons. By the time the case went to trial, in December 1890, the prosecution alleged the group had stolen over one thousand cattle from at least ten different towns over five years. The thefts were timed to coincide with three different regional fairs, allowing the group to easily peddle their meat to large crowds without arousing too much suspicion. In spite of the state's deepening case, however, Yeast and his lawyers had used the intervening months to their advantage. In court Yeast's attorney produced a bill of sale from Bratt for many of the missing cattle. Bratt had signed the document and sold the cattle in Omaha at a time when it was well known that he had been in that city. Embarrassed, Bratt's firm withdrew its complaint, and the judge dismissed the case.[25]

Unfortunately for Yeast, his acquittal was not an exoneration. The cattleman's prestige and business took a big hit. His cattle sales declined after his trial, and when the Northwest Nebraska Stock Growers Association reincorporated in 1891, it did so without its most infamous member. But while it is plausible to argue that Bratt, his stock detective, the sheriff, and Campbell were all misinformed about Yeast's involvement, Bratt's habit of carefully tracking his herd counts suggests that the cattle that went missing were not the same as those he sold. Moreover, it is unlikely that so many of Bratt's sold cattle hides would have been secretly interred if not for some nefarious motive. After all, the hides would have been bought and paid for and would not have required a nocturnal burial. In any event Yeast did not escape his fate: he was convicted in 1908 on a conspiracy charge for fraudulently obtaining homestead land. Yeast served three months in jail, only to face more serious charges soon thereafter, when local settlers accused him, his son Frank, and nearly thirty others under Yeast's direction of intimidating several homesteaders and forcing them to vacate the region.

While Grant County already had a long-standing reputation as a ranching preserve, the 1904 Kinkaid Act quadrupled the amount of claimable land for public entry in Grant and other Sandhills counties in an attempt to encourage homesteading in the area. Now accustomed to having uninhibited access to these rangelands, Yeast led a small army against the settlers, some of whom were threatened at gunpoint. One victim even claimed that Yeast and his cowboys arrived uninvited at his home, threatened him and his family with death, and then "broke his machinery, cut his harness to pieces, and in other ways mistreated him. Later . . . Yeast [met] with members of the county's insanity board and secured [his] incarceration in the asylum." The settler was not released until the asylum superintendent, upon examining the incoming patient, concluded there was nothing wrong with him. Another local homesteader had so little faith in the sheriff's ability to end the persecution that he wrote to President William Howard Taft for help. This letter reportedly initiated the state's investigation, leading to Yeast's indictment.[26]

A MOST TEMPTING BUSINESS

Regardless of whether Yeast was guilty of stealing hides in 1890 or threatening Kinkaiders in 1910, both cases paint a portrait of a gang leader. Yeast used his employees, allies, and neighbors for stealing cattle, illegally fencing land, and intimidating innocent homesteaders. One person's name, Leslie Ballinger, shows up in both indictments, suggesting that several allies worked in his orbit. Meanwhile, his public persona exuded wealth, respect, and influence. The *Alliance Herald* noted Yeast's arrival when he visited the town on business in 1911, which was the newspaper's practice whenever an important businessman or other well-known individual passed through Alliance. Three months later the paper announced that Yeast and his son were passing through on their way to Omaha, where his wife, Nancy, was to "undergo a surgical operation" at the Presbyterian hospital. This reputation was durable enough to affect what historians wrote about him years, even decades, later. Grant Shumway, while writing his *History of Western Nebraska*, blandly remarked that "Yeast was adept at the work of discovering unbranded stock on the range." Shumway also mentioned Yeast's "palatial" home in Lincoln twice, in addition to his "magnificent" ranch in Alaska. Allegedly worth "a million," Yeast amassed a fortune through years of grifting and manipulation. Even Nellie Snyder Yost, who did not shy away from criticizing other cattlemen in her history of the Nebraska ranching industry, only quoted Shumway's "unbranded stock" comment and mentioned the location of Yeast's ranch. The stockman's many legal troubles did not appear in her otherwise exhaustively researched text, though in fairness she may not have believed the accusations herself.[27]

When Yeast's complicated legacy is compared to that of a more genuinely infamous cattle baron, the dynamics of the region's historical memory start to become clearer. Notorious rancher and "one-man-mafia" Isom Print "I.P." Olive had few friends. Chased out of Williamson County, Texas, and later convicted of murder in Nebraska, Olive offered "one-way tickets to hell" to anyone who threatened to steal his cattle or horses. He often levied these threats at neighbors whose ranges Olive's cattle happened to wander upon, and in both Texas and Nebraska he managed to alienate ranchers, homesteaders, and sheriffs alike. His notoriety peaked in 1878, when he and his associates killed Ami Ketchum and Luther Mitchell for fighting back against his efforts to muscle homesteaders out of his desired range in Custer County. Olive then burned the bodies and buried the charred remains under a thin layer of frozen prairie sod. Over the next several months Olive fought the state's prosecutors and judicial establishment with a veritable army of Texas cowboys and a mountain of cash, which ultimately helped him reverse his murder conviction. The following year, realizing he was running out of luck in Nebraska, Olive relocated to Kansas. However, his fortunes were even worse in the Sunflower State, where cowboy drifter Joe Sparrow fatally shot the scandalous rancher whom Nebraskans had started calling the "Man Burner."[28]

Olive could solve many of his problems with money and a fiercely loyal gang, but he would not have faced these situations at all if he had simply learned to charm, rather than char, his enemies. His brutal reputation suggests that in the social-political world of Great Plains ranching power—and name recognition—depended primarily on one's ability to get along with others, rather than on one's willingness to pistol-whip sodbusters. In the near term his heavy-handed tactics worked; Olive's personal shortcomings did not prevent the cattle baron from amassing a large herd, possibly at the expense of some of his neighbors in Texas. Like other unscrupulous ranchers, Olive hired unscrupulous cowboys to carry out his orders. They also helped him carve out large ranges for his cattle in already crowded districts. Yet his tactics quickly wore thin, requiring him to move every few years and frequently placing him at odds with the law. Even after his death, Olive's historical legacy has been nothing short of contentious—Mari Sandoz once referred to him as "a furious-eyed man whose name came to be associated with hideous forms of death for those who opposed him or simply got in his path." A rancher with as many enemies and with so few friends as Olive could not survive long in business or in life, as evidenced by his escape from one state, his conviction in another, and eventually, his murder in a third.[29]

Olive's poor reputation was easily surpassed by Perry Yeast's, who despite operating an informal gang for many years and running afoul of the law multiple times, was only infrequently mentioned as a possible bad guy himself. Amid ongoing legal troubles and rumors about his complicity in the Bratt cattle theft case, the *Grant County Tribune* refused to comment directly on the matter. "For the good of the town the *Tribune* has refrained from exposing some very spicy bits of news concerning the actions of several parties in this vicinity," it proclaimed at one point, presumably in reference to Yeast. This journalistic coyness continued long past the trial date. Years later one local historian referenced the Yeast case when discussing Sheriff Bud Moran's career but decided to keep the parties anonymous: "The first [district court] case was a cattle stealing case, but I would rather not mention the names of the parties most interested in the matter, as I believe some of them are still living and carry names pretty well and favorably known now over the state, and to retell the story might seem embarrassing to them." Yeast himself is mostly excised from the book of pioneer reminiscences and biographies, except for a short blurb about his marriage to Nancy Jane Markland, which suggests that in later years more than a few locals did not remember him too favorably.[30] Nonetheless, the sharp difference in how western Nebraskans remembered Olive and Yeast in later years underscores just how powerful a good name and a positive reputation were in the region, and it probably allowed strongmen like Yeast to operate in plain sight.

If Campbell was unapologetic and perhaps a bit cold in his deposition, G. A. Fane was anxious and contrite. Also accused of stealing cattle, Fane's deposition was dated on October 12, 1891, in an incident separate from Campbell's. Like Campbell, Fane portrayed himself as a less-than-eager participant in the crime. When Frank Smith approached Fane about stealing some cattle from a local rancher named "Merill," Fane hesitated. "I told him I did not want to steal cattle for we would get in trouble," he replied, but he relented when Smith told him that they could "steal them easy" and that a mortgage was going to be closed on the cattle soon. "If he was a single man," Smith reportedly told Fane, "he knowed what he would do," and "he would make a fortune" if he went through with it. Fane later claimed that he attempted to back out of the theft while it was in progress but was angrily rebuffed. "I said to Frank we was doing wrong," he said, but Frank angrily replied, "Who hell you are not going to back down now." Fane tried to limit the take to just two yearlings, but Frank insisted on taking more. Later Smith talked Fane into trading the stolen cattle in for a gold watch, fourteen dollars, and a horse since Fane was apparently under less suspicion than Smith. Fane refused to do any additional work after delivering the watch to Smith's accomplice John Foster. However, the pair warned Fane that he would be killed "or put away" if he "squealed." To Foster's credit, he allowed Fane the privilege of wearing the fancy gold watch "once or twice," provided that he answer any inquiries about how he acquired it by saying that he bought it off of someone for five dollars.[31]

Fane's deposition illustrates what the inside of a rustling gang might have looked like. This is important since most Americans' impressions of how gangs operated come from western cinema, novels, and pulp fiction. And to a degree these impressions are not far off the mark: Fane was young, single, and naive; his leaders, who had more to lose but also more to gain from their involvement, intimidated, manipulated, and browbeat Fane to get their way. However, movies also understate, if not ignore, the ties that connect gang members to their leaders and overlook any rituals or other group dynamics that held them together. Fane's connection to Smith and Foster was not merely casual or instrumental—even before he was threatened, Fane did not want to disappoint the pair.

Without knowing anything else about the internal dynamics of this gang, Fane's interactions with Smith and Foster resemble the characteristics that define what historian Eric Hobsbawm called "mafia" in his classic work *Primitive Rebels*. Setting aside the conventional American understanding of "the Mafia" as a family-based crime syndicate, Hobsbawm identified loosely structured, rural criminal networks that flourished in the absence of strong state authority in late-nineteenth-century Sicily as a possible prototype for similar networks elsewhere. In particular, these networks coalesced around local strongmen who, given the absence of centralized state power, employed local laborers, padded their profits by stealing, and used their labor power to subdue noncompliant criminals or others who resisted their authority.[32] Fane saw Foster as a kind of role model, and given the apparent lack of previous contact between Smith and Fane, it seems that Foster may have recommended Fane to Smith as someone who might undertake a rustling job. Later, when Fane had second thoughts, Smith and Foster told the young man that it was too late to back out and that they would kill him if he told the authorities.

Hobsbawm's model illuminates how other regional criminal rings operated, and Campbell's deposition suggests that his gang operated in a similar manner. Perry A. Yeast—stock owner, stock association executive committee member, and secret rustler—exemplified the role of "local strong-man" who commanded the respect of criminals and law-abiding colleagues alike and who compelled their accomplices to stay silent through a rough-hewn, rural honor code resembling the Sicilian tradition of omertà. In addition, if the stories about Jack Morrow are true, then his ranch closely resembled a Hobsbawmian mafia in the way Morrow used cowboys, soldiers, and even American Indians to steal livestock and control the surrounding area. Senator Thayer's plea that the secretary of interior furnish honest, "unapproachable" stock inspectors to monitor Morrow's contract work hints at Morrow's reputation for sucking newcomers into his criminal orbit. So does a photograph of Morrow, taken by Arundel C. Hall in 1868 or so, that shows the road rancher in the center of the frame, sitting on a barrel, elevated, and surrounded by thirteen men (fig. 22). It is labeled "Jack Morrow at Benton." In person as well as in photographs, Morrow was the center of attention.[33]

It is difficult to categorize these or any similar operations in the American West as mafia organizations when, as Hobsbawm himself points out, historians have little evidence tying local bosses to local crimes. These relationships were informal and are thus difficult to map with precision. Nonetheless, many con-

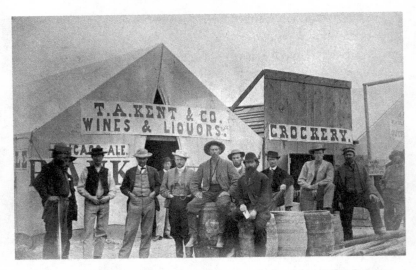

Fig. 22. Jack Morrow, sitting tall on a barrel in the middle of this 1868 photograph, always seemed to be the center of attention. C Photo Collection 155. Eugene Arundel Miller Collection, Denver Public Library, Western History Collection, z-5803.

temporaries suspected high-profile criminals, ranchers, agents, and even some sheriffs of operating similar networks throughout the West, so their existence would not have surprised anyone. Otto Uhlig, a grocer from Lincoln, described such a network to authorities at Fort McPherson in 1870, when he reported seeing four government mules being sold at an auction in Denver. Uhlig, who supplemented his income by tracking stolen property for the government, followed the animals to Colorado. He persuaded the authorities in Denver to arrest the man responsible for stealing the mules, but Uhlig believed that the suspect, named Clark, was "an accomplice" to a group of several other citizens spread out across Nebraska, Colorado, and Kansas who conspired to have their henchman steal the team while they reaped the profits. Since Clark was under bond and facing trial for a separate offense at the time of his second arrest, it is possible that the four mules stolen from Fort McPherson represented only a small percentage of the actual number of animals stolen by this cabal.[34]

A MOST TEMPTING BUSINESS

One should not discount the possibility that Fane was lying. Just as gang leaders were aware of how their reputations affected their luck, gang members were more than capable of playing on the public's sympathies as well, especially once they were caught. In 1893 six Nebraskans from Box Butte County faced trial in Wyoming for allegedly stealing and killing cattle. When one of the defendants testified, his story allegedly brought the courtroom to tears: he claimed that they were all family men who were hard up and unable to provide for their families. The prosecution asked that the minimum sentence of one-year imprisonment be imposed, and the court obliged. A Box Butte County–based correspondent, however, had a decidedly less charitable view of the affair. "The sympathy racket worked well on the court," noted the reporter, "but the fact is all those parties were doing a great deal better than many people in this county, and the story about starvation is absolutely without foundation. In fact, there is not a man in Box Butte County who is so hard up as to have to either steal or go to the poorhouse."[35]

Alternatively, if Fane was telling the truth, then many cattle and horse thieves appear to have been reluctant crooks. Peer pressure, false assurances of a lucrative profit, financial exigency, and the supposed ease of getting away with the crime all made cattle and horse theft a seductive trade. While it seems that Fane had second thoughts about his new vocation soon after stealing two heifers, it is an open question as to how many horse thieves started out this way. Perhaps the three rewards for Fane and Smith's crime represented the overall material gains horse and cattle thieves attempted to make through their crimes. His gold watch signified social and economic status, while the fourteen dollars in cash was worth about two weeks' wages for many ranch hands. The horse, however, represented both. Regardless of his integrity or incredibility, the material rewards he sought appear to align well with what he and most other local cowpokes and farmhands wanted: more money and more respect.

Between Campbell, Fane, Yeast, and others like them, Moran had his work cut out for him. In fact, his successor, Albert Metcalf, reportedly broke up the county's last major rustling outfit during the 1920s. The Hooky Wilson gang was named for its leader, W. A. Wilson, a one-eyed, one-armed man who wore a prosthetic limb with a hook attached. In his reward notice Metcalf also observed he was "a slouchy dresser . . . smokes a pipe and liable to frequent places where there is liquor." The gang stole ninety head of cattle from Joe Minor's sprawling ranch, and Metcalf was tipped off by one of the crooks who believed he was getting stiffed on the proceeds from the haul. After obtaining a confession from the accomplice, Metcalf rode down to find Hooky Wilson. However, the man apparently left his hovel in a hurry, and the sheriff could not find him after that.[36] Nonetheless, the rustling stopped, the accomplice went to jail, and for all intents and purposes, "the old days" of cattle thieving were officially over.

Horse and cattle rustling gangs were pervasive throughout the Sandhills and elsewhere on the Great Plains. Unfortunately, discovering and uncovering these groups long after their members and victims have passed away is like playing a solo game of Battleship. There is no easy way to tell where a gang begins or ends, when it starts or when it stops, or how successful it is in pilfering stock. In addition, there is a broad expanse of organizational and criminal diversity between high-profile and heavily investigated groups, like the Doc Middleton gang, and the machinations of men like Perry Yeast, who hid in plain sight. Court documents, newspaper reports, memoirs, and the occasional deposition give us some breadcrumbs to follow, but most gang secrets died along with their members.

Nevertheless, while rustling gang information may be difficult to obtain, their impact on western Nebraska is abundantly clear. During the 1870s they contributed to higher crime rates and made the range more dangerous for stockmen, reservation Indians, and the army. The theft of reservation ponies in particular brought western Nebraska to the brink of conflict between the Lakotas and its stockmen. Later, after the disintegration or apprehension of several major gangs, the region's white horse-stealing gang crisis slowly came to an end. But while gangs could no longer operate with some degree of impunity

A MOST TEMPTING BUSINESS

or at least insularity from the law, they continued to plague the region, albeit in secret. In time rustling gangs eroded public confidence in law enforcement while also sowing dissention and mistrust between farmers, ranchers, cowboys, and other persons throughout the plains. Although these thieves seemed to prefer stealing cows to horses, especially given the former's value upon being butchered for meat, the hidden world of the secret gang did not encourage would-be victims to believe that their horses were safer than their stock. If anything, it heightened suspicions by casting doubt on neighbors and strangers alike and by creating an underground economy that could carry off stolen horses and move them far beyond the protective veneer of the regional stockmen's associations and well past locally printed "missing" notices. Rustling gangs reoriented and upended rural economies and social networks by fostering and rewarding violent entrepreneurs who could manipulate and bully less-powerful local actors to their own selfish ends. With plenty of places to hide, lots of cash money to make from cattle and beef sales, and a number of ranchers and homesteaders who precariously teetered on the brink of bankruptcy, these criminal entrepreneurs in Grant County found no shortage of opportunities to carry the region's theft culture well into the twentieth century.

Horse stealing was by no means limited to gang activity. The majority of documented horse thieves appear to have been lone actors or members of small, unorganized groups. But studying rustling gangs can help historians bridge the transition from the raiding and theft culture that predominated until the 1870s to the more settled homesteading and small ranching economies that took root in the region during the early 1880s. Not only do they represent a continuation of the former, but they also illustrate the tenuousness of the latter. It took many years for the rustlers to disappear, and their persistence was due in large part to the vast swaths of unpatrolled, underpopulated, cash-poor, sandy-soiled, and sometimes bone-dry land that contained little of value except for the thousands of livestock feeding upon its bluestem grasses. Back during the "old days" and beyond, rustling was indeed a most tempting business.

5

From Thieves to Villains

It's awfully easy to rush into a profession you don't really like,
and awfully hard to get out of it.

—WILLA CATHER, *O Pioneers!*

The Wild West rolled into Omaha on May 15, 1883. Nine
railroad cars unloaded the cast, animals, and scenery for Buffalo Bill Cody's world debut of the "Wild
West, Rocky Mountain, and Prairie Exhibition." They depos-
ited eighty men (including sixty Lakotas, Pawnees, and Omahas); forty bronco ponies; and numerous elaborate set pieces
at the Union Pacific shop. Three days later the show's center-
piece—a coach from the Deadwood Stage line—arrived in town
for the next day's performance.[1] Cody's first major production
in Omaha sparked his rapid rise to national fame, and by that
summer Buffalo Bill and his company were touring the East.
For many Omahans, and most Americans east of the Missouri
River, the Wild West exhibition and show provided their first
"real" glimpse of the frontier. Plains Indian raiders, gunfighters, cowboys, and other legendary characters from the nation's
recent past came to life, and viewers left with what they thought
was a more experiential understanding of westward expansion.

Although Cody's soon-to-be famous Wild West set up in
Omaha in 1883, its namesake era had left southwestern Nebraska
long before. A period of relative calm followed the twin horse-
stealing crises that threatened, frightened, and mobilized hun-

dreds of ranchers, farmers, and other settlers across western Nebraska during the late 1870s. As the region's population grew, reports of horse theft steadily dropped. Partly, this was a result of a growing consensus among citizens of the region that the state should criminalize certain kinds of behavior. This emerging legal culture mirrored what had developed in the eastern and central parts of the state. Property crime declined as the state typologized and vilified a range of different kinds of offenses that all involved the taking or destruction of horses or horse equipment. In short the West was considerably less wild than it used to be.

Yet few people took notice. Just as the overall trend line of horse stealing started to fall in some places, the stakes only grew for many residents in the region. More families began buying land and filing for homesteads, which led to the proliferation of small herds on which the success of those new family-run enterprises depended. Horse stealing existentially threatened these businesses, which already suffered from non-anthropomorphic threats, including drought, grasshopper invasions, and severe winters. If the late 1870s witnessed the smashing of theft culture across the northern plains, the 1880s signified the building of something new: a yeoman farming culture, the financial, social, and moral tenets of which demanded the protection of valuable, indispensable private property. But this culture, and the small herds it employed across the plains, was not always easily protected, much to the herds' owners chagrin. Unfortunately for horse thieves, it was much easier for homesteaders to blame a human bogeyman for their problems than it was to condemn insects, the soil, the drought, the railroad companies, commodity prices, epizootics, inefficient and biased policing, ungovernably large jurisdictions, or even God. And unlike locusts or the weather, horse thieves were easier to hang.

Growing Cities, Wild Towns, and Magic Places

Western Nebraska, like Walt Whitman, is self-contradictory: it is large and contains multitudes. From the Platte River valley to Pine Ridge, the western half of the state contains a great deal of geographic, demographic, and historical diversity. But a close examination of three different jurisdictions—Lincoln, Cheyenne, and Dawes Counties—reveals not only how each of these places is different from the others but how together they tell a larger story about the history of horse theft on the Great Plains.

Lincoln County

Emigrants began passing through what is now Lincoln County in the 1830s, but permanent settlement in the region did not begin until the Civil War. The first settlers opened road ranches or other businesses that catered to passing migrants, and when Post Cottonwood opened in 1863, several locals secured supply contracts or work as freighters for the garrison. Ranchers John Burke and Jack Morrow, among others, made their fortunes finding, cutting, and hauling timber for the Union Pacific in the mid-1860s.[2] Once the railroad rolled its way west past the Platte forks in 1866, it rendered the Overland Trail obsolete almost overnight and connected the region to nearly fifty thousand miles of track east of the Missouri River. The Hell on Wheels railroad worker encampment at the forks soon grew into the permanent town of North Platte. With the Transcontinental Railroad's completion in 1869, North Platte became a major hub for the line, connecting the eastern and western halves of the continent.

The end of the Civil War and the arrival of the railroad facilitated new kinds of movement into the Platte Valley. Ranchers drove longhorn cattle from Texas—which had overpopulated on the range during the Civil War—to Abilene, Ogallala, and other points along the railroads to meet the growing postwar demand for beef. While the northern terminus of the nearest Texas cattle trail lay to the west, nutritious bluestem grasses blanketed the Sandhills. Lincoln County and other places along the rail lines became valuable ranching areas, where Texas longhorns could be purchased wholesale for a few dollars a head, fattened up, and resold to wholesalers in the East at a higher cost. Later, the end of the Plains Indian Wars coincided with the beginning of a major population boom in Lincoln County as streams of settlers moved into the region. Although some of these new arrivals tried their hand at livestock raising, most either moved to North Platte to take advantage of the opportunities carried to it by the Union Pacific or settled elsewhere in the county to become farmers. The number of 100- to 500-acre farms in Lincoln County, which stayed the same size from its founding in 1867 through 1890, jumped from 88 in 1880 to 1,142 in 1890—an increase of almost 1,300 percent. At the same time, the average farm's size decreased from 402 to 267 acres, meaning that more people were farming smaller plots of land. However, the number of farms over 1,000 acres in size tripled between 1880 and 1890, which suggests that in spite of the homesteading wave, some ranchers and farmers consolidated large landholdings during this decade.[3]

Several waves of destructive Indian raiding, significant horse and cattle rustling activity, and a few wild periods during the first few years of settlement inured Lincoln County residents to the dangers of horse theft. But in spite of Crazy Horse's murder and Doc Middleton's arrest, settlers across Lincoln County continued to believe that horse thieves were a pervasive threat to their lives and livelihoods after 1880, even though the rate of horse stealing and other horse-related crimes had fallen substantially by the mid-1880s. Demography was one of the main reasons for this dramatic decline. The rate of horse stealing in proportion to the total population dropped precipitously. Figure 23 illustrates this trend with a scatterplot of two different variables: reports of horse theft per 100,000 people and the population of Lincoln County. As this graph shows, years when rates of horse theft were high corresponded to years with lower county populations. Fewer residents meant less support for county law enforcement and greater opportunities for criminals to steal with relative impunity. Conversely, no more than 30.9 horse thefts per 100,000 people occurred during years when the county population surpassed 5,000. As more people moved into the region, the Sheriff's Department relied on a growing customer base of service fee–paying residents. In addition, farming grew at the expense of ranching, insofar as farms

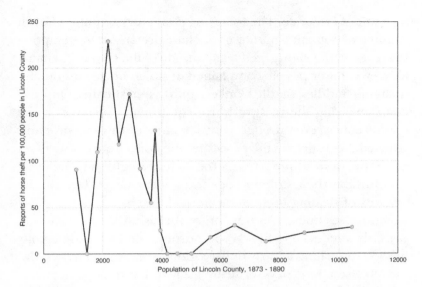

Fig. 23. Scatterplot of horse theft reports per 100,000 people and population of Lincoln County, 1873–90. This scatterplot combines the overall number of horse theft reports in criminal courts with the projected annual population. (See chap. 4, n. 3, for a complete rundown of my methodology for this figure.) Created by the author.

replaced big ranches and their large horse herds with smaller farming plots and much less livestock. With better law enforcement, more potential witnesses, and fewer large horse herds, horse stealing became much less attractive to would-be thieves. Although the courts processed more horse-stealing cases as the decade progressed, the actual rate of horse stealing relative to the total population stayed about the same.

Other horse-related property crime rates dropped as well. Lincoln County residents only accused a handful of men of obtaining money or goods under false pretenses. This crime charged suspects with misrepresenting facts to complete a transaction that likely would not have occurred had both parties known all of the facts before making the exchange. For instance, John Colfer accused George Dudley of acquiring a horse under false pretenses when Dudley allegedly traded Colfer a horse that he had previously stolen, but the district court judge dismissed the case for want of evidence. The following year a jury acquitted Calvin Bunnell of obtaining money under false pretenses by attempting to sell a recently mortgaged team outside of the county.[4] Remarkably, even fewer people complained of stolen horse equipment, including saddles, saddle blankets, quirts, and stirrups. Only five cases involving the theft of horse equipment appeared in the county courts, even though petty larcenies of this sort probably reached the justices of the peace and the police court more often or simply went unreported as the victims might have believed that finding their stolen goods was a lost cause. After all, the rewards of stealing these items were almost as high as those of stolen horses but with a fraction of the risk. Charles Robinson was only sentenced to five days in prison when he pleaded guilty in 1886 to stealing a thirty-dollar saddle, and in 1890 Jesse Grayble was given thirty days for stealing a forty-five-dollar buggy. The difference between stealing a forty-five-dollar buggy and a fifty-dollar horse in 1890, incidentally, was the difference between one and twelve months in jail, since the mandatory minimum sentence for horse stealing was a year in prison.[5]

Another reason for this paradox of growing fears of horse stealing in spite of declining horse-stealing crime rates was that the crime constituted a disproportionate percentage of property violations in the county. Relative to other offenses, horse theft was one of the most commonly filed charges in county court: of the 193 property crime charges filed between 1878 and 1890, 34 charged the defendants with horse stealing. When one includes other crimes that involved the loss, theft, or maiming of a horse (grand larceny, disposing of mortgaged property, killing horses, and obtaining horses under false pretenses), the number of horse-related crimes jumps to 47, or just over one-fifth of all property crimes. This percentage may be inflated by the severity of horse stealing as a crime relative to lesser property offenses (such as petty theft), but the number of horse-related crimes is high when we control for the value of the property stolen or destroyed. During this eighteen-year period, citizens filed more horse theft complaints than all of the charges of burglary, forgery, robbery, embezzlement, and arson combined.[6]

FROM THIEVES TO VILLAINS

Lincoln County residents not only suffered from horse stealing more often than other property crimes; they were also more likely to read about horse theft in the newspaper. Citizens and local newspapers sensationalized horse stealing, portraying it as an existential menace. They had plenty of material to work with: by the late 1880s reports of horse stealing had increased once again. Ten horse thefts or horse theft–related crimes appear in the Lincoln County District Court docket from 1885 to 1890, and several more cases are dismissed or unresolved on the county level. Some publicized reports never even made it to the sheriff's office, such as when an unidentified thief stole Lincoln County school superintendent R. H. Langford's horse and buggy team between eight and nine o'clock in the evening, right in front of the Methodist church, where Langford was attending an Oxford League meeting. Given the quality and speed of the horses stolen, the *Lincoln County Tribune* reckoned that the thief could have been "fifty miles away by daylight."[7] Even though horse owners had little to fear from thieves, at least from a statistical perspective, this high-profile crime grabbed readers' attention.

Horse owners also feared what they did not know, and as with any crime, most successful horse thieves stole their animals anonymously. Criminal warrants issued by the Lincoln County Criminal Court, for instance, list "John Doe" six times as a suspect, including once for a theft that occurred four days before Middleton allegedly purloined a local horse in 1879. In addition, many of those thieves who alerted victims and enforcers to their presence eluded capture. Con Groner unsuccessfully searched western Nebraska for several days in pursuit of three men accused of stealing two horses in May 1881 and brought home little more than a bill for mileage and expenses amounting to one hundred dollars.[8] Despite the growing ease with which authorities could track down suspects using the telegraph and the railroad, western Nebraska was a vast country where trails grew cold before even the most intrepid pursuers.

Horse stealing was underreported as well. Although indictments for horse stealing declined during the 1880s, reports of stray livestock skyrocketed. Upon discovering that a horse was missing, owners had to decide whether the animal had broken out of a stable or fenced-in pasture or if a thief had broken into it. During the 1870s citizens filed twenty-one stray horse reports in the Lincoln County estray catalog, in which those who found lost livestock posted a report. This meant that ranchers and farmers found, but were not able to locate the owner of, twenty-one different horses. Residents logged other stray animals as well, such as hogs and cattle. Between 1881 and 1885 the number of reported horse strays jumped over 500 percent, from about two to ten per year, while the number of reported stray cows and hogs remained about the same. Stray horse reports also increased during the second half of the decade, when county residents reported sixty-one horses as strays between 1886 and 1890.[9]

Stray reports confuse and complicate horse theft crime statistics for two reasons. First, as Lincoln County filled with settlers, residents often could not tell whether their horses had been stolen or if they had wandered off to a neighbor's farm. With less acreage to graze horses on and fewer sources of water on a homestead, unsecured horses were more likely to roam in search of food and fresh water. Residents also had more neighbors than ever before; rather than sharing a section of land with one or two other families, farmers and ranchers were gradually surrounded by crowded communities. Missing horses could easily migrate to areas that the owner did not know and had no right to access, making it far more difficult to locate a missing horse as a part of a growing community than when one knew many or most of one's neighbors in a sparsely settled area. In addition, citizens risked paying the costs of prosecution if a county judge decided to quash their criminal complaint. For this reason a combination of wishful thinking and pragmatism likely motivated some horse owners to report missing animals as strays, rather than assuming that they had been stolen.

The intersection of stray logs and stolen horses represents a broader point in how effective and successful the legal apparatus was for preventing, documenting, and adjudicating horse thefts. Overall, Lincoln County judges only sent fourteen men to prison for stealing horses. But those fourteen convicted thieves represented the apex of a much larger criminal pyramid. Each layer down—district court acquittals, county court case dismissals, corroborated reports, uncorroborated reports, and unreported thefts—included more incidents of theft than the last. North Platte's relatively urbanized community, compared to other western Nebraska towns in the late nineteenth century, only compounded the problems residents had keeping tabs on the crime. But North Platters were hardly alone in their struggle.

Cheyenne County

Cheyenne County witnessed a more dramatic shift in its crime statistics. Sidney's early history more closely corresponds to the "Wild West" stereotype than North Platte's, both in terms of reputation and documented fact. However, there is little evidence that North Platte's relatively more violent counterpart witnessed any comparable escalations in horse theft. Between 1872 and 1880 the Cheyenne County District Court adjudicated approximately seventy crimes. Half of these indictments were for violent crimes, and eleven defendants faced trial for murder. Two other suspected murderers never made it to trial: mobs lynched Charles H. Patterson and Charles Reed in 1875 and 1879, respectively. Several others escaped justice, extralegal or otherwise: of the 211 people buried at Sidney's Boot Hill cemetery between 1867 and the end of 1882, at least 30 died as a direct result of violence. The most common non-violent crime during this period was horse theft, with nine men standing trial for stealing geldings, mares, or mules. But since four of the men were tried in pairs, the grand jury only issued seven separate indictments. "Pedro," a local vaquero, would have also likely faced trial for stealing a horse, but the sheriff shot and killed him as he tried to escape. Four other cases involved cattle theft or horse stealing–related crimes, including two defendants who were accused of breaking horses with the intent to steal them. Notably, the court also arraigned three men for malfeasance in office and adjudicated several disputed elections.[10] This suggests that Sidney's early leaders, like those of many other frontier towns, had a fondness for graft and abuse of power.

After a tumultuous first decade as a "wild and wooly" rail-road town, by 1882 the community had settled down considerably. During the next eight years only 19 percent of the district court's cases concerned murder, felonious assault, or assault with an intent to kill. The number of defendants accused of murder dropped by half, even though the county's population had more than tripled between 1880 and 1890. The court only arraigned one man for assault with an intent to kill, as opposed to nine defendants facing similar charges before 1881, suggesting a dramatic reduction in the number of brawls and barroom fights. Meanwhile, non-horse-related property crimes skyrocketed: the court indicted nine men for grand larceny, five for burglary, and four on forgery charges. The number of horse-stealing indictments declined as well, from seven to five.

Between the lower number of horse theft arraignments and the county's fast-growing population, Cheyenne County's falling rate of horse stealing echoed similarly dramatic declines in Lincoln County. Not only did just five men face horse-stealing charges in district court, but the justice of the peace dockets suggest that few horse-stealing cases were dismissed prior to being referred over to the district court for trial. Robert Shuman served as a justice of the peace in Sidney from 1884 through 1887, and his court near Sidney heard over 170 cases during that time. Of those cases 126 were criminal complaints. The vast majority were misdemeanor charges: 24 cases of vagrancy, an equal number of assault and battery counts, and various other crimes, including one count of indecent exposure and 7 cases of prostitution (with several more defendants in each matter who were arraigned together). Of the 24 theft-related charges, only one directly involved stolen horses. Most thefts either targeted smaller, more easily fenced kinds of property (a fifteen-dollar watch, a saddle, three blankets, and an overcoat from the Metropolitan Hotel in Sidney) or less distinguishable items that could not be readily identified (barbed wire, fence posts, and bales of hay). Four other defendants allegedly stole or butchered cattle from area ranches, and three others burgled area homes. Shuman also referred two different murder charges to the district court. On a granular level Shuman's docket represents the criminal landscape of Cheyenne County during the mid-1880s: many people were arrested for vagrancy and prostitution, two dozen were tried for various types of larceny, and two men were accused of murder. Only one defendant allegedly stole horses.[11]

Dawes County

Dawes County, the youngest of the three jurisdictions, filled up quickly after its establishment in 1885 due to the rapid and simultaneous growth of two different towns. Like North Platte and Sidney, the county seat of Chadron owed its existence to the railroad. The Chicago and Northwestern tracks connected the Nebraska Panhandle with Chicago and Iowa to the east and with Casper, Wyoming Territory, to the west. In 1885 the tracks reached the present town site, located roughly thirteen miles west-southwest from the abandoned Camp Sheridan military reservation. Sitting on the north slope of the Pine Ridge, Chadron is flanked by vertical bluffs and ponderosa pines. On a clear day visitors can see the Black Hills from the top of the range. Along the same ridge, about twenty-five miles west-southwest, local boosters founded the town of Crawford the following year. Perched upon Fort Robinson's eastern border, the new village offered some long-desired services and entertainments to the adjacent military post, which had been isolated since its founding. Crawford also offered service to travelers on the Sidney–Black Hills trail, which connected Deadwood with Sidney. The Chicago, Burlington, and Quincy Railroad Company's arrival in 1889, however, rendered the trail obsolete while eventually connecting Dawes County to Wyoming's coal country and to the Black Hills.

Chadron, the "Magic City of the West," appeared almost overnight. Homesteaders and their families flocked to the new town. "It seemed beyond belief how rapidly the town was built, and [how quickly] comfortable homes and business houses were put up," recalled pioneer resident Lola Byington.[12] Some pioneers fondly remembered Chadron's early years. In many ways the opposite of rough-and-tumble Sidney, Chadron immediately became a decent place to live. Phyllis Holding recorded her grandfather L. H. Cartwright's stories about the town: "Thru all that time the price of gasoline did not trouble us. The horse was always on the picket rope, and a ten-cent box of axle grease would keep the old buggy hitting on all four cylinders for a year or more." Others had a less sanguine view. "This town is the greatest fraud that ever existed in the western county," wrote carpenter George Walter Scott. "Lots of men are actually starving to death . . . I tell you Cheyenne is a paradise to this place."[13]

As in many other railroad towns, a procession of villains and ne'er-do-wells kept its courts busy. The Dawes County District Court, plus the county, justice of the peace, and police courts, heard 909 criminal cases between 1885 and 1895. Of these, according to historian Benjamin Watson, 85 cases were "crimes against people," while 163 cases were "crimes against property." The vast majority of the remainder—nearly 700 cases—concerned public order, morality, and comparable crimes.[14] Residents did not have to wait long to watch the county's first horse-stealing trial either, which arrived before the district court, only two months after Chadron had officially organized as a community and a mere six months after the county had been established. George W. Smith complained to Justice of the Peace James A. Wilson in Chadron that on October 26, 1885, an unknown person had stolen two bay horses from him. Wally Church soon emerged as the primary suspect, and in November the justice of the peace heard Smith's case against the defendant. Despite Church pleading not guilty, Wilson bound the case over to the district court. Shortly thereafter, John Dykeman was named as an accomplice, when authorities discovered that Dykeman had planned the theft. In February the pair appeared before Judge Francis Hamer at the county's first district court session. The jury found both men guilty.[15]

These numbers should be kept in perspective. Compared to the sheer amount of violence that afflicted Sidney's early years, Chadron might as well have been Mayberry. Between 1885 and 1895 twelve men were arraigned for horse stealing, and another six were tried for murder. But as horse stealing became less

FROM THIEVES TO VILLAINS

fashionable as a crime, criminals in Dawes County continued to find ways to use horses for ill-gotten gain. At least six defendants tried before 1890 faced various charges related to horse-related fraud, either by illegally disposing of mortgaged property or obtaining money under false pretenses. Also, thieves in the region preferred to target smaller, more easily transportable or disposable property. Several succeeded in stealing far more money than they would have earned pilfering an animal team. For instance, John O'Brien allegedly stole a chest containing 2,750 cigars, while John W. Wood accused Lewis Dillon of having stolen over $500 worth of watches and other jewelry.[16]

As in Lincoln and Cheyenne Counties, the Dawes County District Court adjudicated few horse-stealing cases in Chadron during the 1880s. The county's relative youth compared to the former two jurisdictions make the absence of accused horse thieves even more significant, especially since Chadron in the late 1880s was still a "frontier" community. Unlike Cheyenne and Lincoln Counties, however, Dawes had been founded only a few months before the great open range ranching collapse began, during the winter of 1885–86, which weakened or destroyed many ranches across the plains. Homesteaders encountered little resistance from cattlemen as they claimed their land and quickly dominated the new county's politics. "The cattle barons who had been using all that vast territory for grazing their thousands of cattle of course were not too happy about the nesters," one pioneer later wrote. "[They] tried their best to discourage people [from coming and taking land] but there never was any violence in that neighborhood." Later "there was some controversy about herd law and range law, so it was put to a vote. The fence law won out."[17] Once the railroad construction crews moved on, hundreds of families moved in to begin filling the surrounding land. This ensured that the local sprinkling of drunks, rabble-rousers, and thieves that generally accompanied new towns along railroads was quickly diluted with a flood of families.

Horse stealing's infrequency in Chadron and Crawford also had much to do with the absence of horses to steal. Most of the county's farms were homesteads: in 1890 over 96 percent of the county's 1,581 farms claimed between one hundred and five hundred acres. Only five farms claimed to own more than a thousand acres. Moreover, at least 95 percent of the county's farms were operated by their owners, indicating a high incidence of homesteading and land mortgaging by farm operators and relatively few renters or sharecroppers. But while most farmers in Dawes County claimed, owned, or financed their own land, they had few horses between them: about 6,115 horses and mules for 9,722 residents, many of which were owned by a few ranching firms in the county. Technically, the average number of horses per farm was about 3.8, but in reality it was far less. "When my father's people came to Nebraska [in 1882], there were few good horses, though many had one good team and they had to sleep on a pile of hay behind their trusty team," recalled Lena Jones Anderson, whose family settled in neighboring Sheridan County. "No horse was safe in an unwatched pasture."[18] Horses, already a precious resource, were both hard for thieves to find and relatively difficult to carry off.

Overall, Chadron and Crawford residents had little to fear from horse thieves. Both towns had managed to escape much of the violence and unsettledness that characterized the early years of North Platte and Sidney. Yet even though few horses were stolen, horses were also valuable enough to be used for other kinds of theft and fraud. Because of this, residents did not lapse into complacency within their reasonably well-ordered neighborhoods. Seemingly omnipresent, horse thieves lurked throughout even the safest domains.

Thieves

Regardless of whether someone stole a horse in North Plate, Sidney, or Chadron, their motivations were often similar. Some of the most common reasons were primal: revenge, jealousy, desperation, or simple drunken foolishness. Whatever the motive, most people usually stole horses out of necessity or on the spur of the moment, which suggests that most incidents of theft were not premeditated. At the very least most thieves were not in the habit of thinking too carefully about their decisions. Historian Mark Ellis recounts two such instances in his book *Law and Order in Buffalo Bill's County*, noting that Charlie Short stole a horse in 1876 while attempting to break out of jail and that penniless German immigrant Peter Wesselgarter stole a horse after being stranded in North Platte. Alcohol was a factor in some of these cases. Frank Massey was drunk when he hopped on and rode away with James Johnson's gelding on September 17, 1878, and his attorney urged the court to take his client's intoxication into consideration when deciding Massey's fate.[19] But at other times accused thieves could not offer any kind of excuse for their crimes. In neighboring Keith County, Henry Johnson offered a mea culpa of sorts when the judge sentenced him in 1883 to three years in prison for stealing a horse worth forty-five dollars. "[I am] corralled," he reportedly exclaimed when asked if he had anything to say for himself, "and ready for sentence!"[20]

Some thieves wanted to make a quick profit. Stolen horses were valuable commodities and were sometimes worth up to three or four times what a laborer or ranch hand could earn in a month. Horses were also portable, and thieves could sell them at distant points of sale or via fences without locals being aware of who was missing animals and being able to identify different brands. Sometimes the search for money did not even require the physical abduction of a horse—a few men were accused of falsely claiming horses as collateral for bank loans or running off mortgaged property with the intent to defraud their lenders. For example, Jacob Shields was convicted of obtaining money under false pretenses in 1889. He was sentenced to a year in prison for the crime of claiming two horses and a wagon as collateral for a loan from the First National Bank of North Platte. The bank processed the loan and gave Shields over $57 in cash, but it soon learned that Shield's collateral actually belonged to someone else. A similar incident occurred in Dawes County, but in this case a man walked out of the Citizens State Bank with $225 for claiming that an entire team of horses belonged to him.[21]

One striking fact about the "typical" horse thief in western Nebraska is that he was male. While there is little evidence that women were responsible for stealing any horses in the region, women did steal horses elsewhere on the plains. The *Lincoln County Tribune* reported in 1888 that a schoolteacher in Columbus, Kansas, who was otherwise known for being a "pretty, smart bachelorette," led a gang in the area. "The organization embraced horse thieves, various styles of burglars, several murderers and other choice malefactors," it reported, "and their doings were all directed by Miss Blalock, the woman spoken of." The article went on to explain that local vigilantes initially targeted her for summary justice, but the author apparently thought the subject too rare to be spoiled by a hangman's noose: "Within a few months she will probably secure an engagement as the star attraction of a museum and live happily ever after."[22] In other words, male horse thieves had to be exterminated, while women horse thieves needed to be exhibited.

In less-sensationalized cases suspected women seemed to be given some benefit of the doubt. Investigators were reluctant to apply the horse thief label to women, perhaps because the label itself was masculinized and could not be easily reconciled with late-nineteenth-century gender norms. In one case near Grand Island, a woman hired out a pair of horses for a three-hour period, but she did not return that day or evening. The owner began searching for the woman and the hired team, believing it had been stolen. The next day, however, the suspect's male companion telegraphed the owner and called on him to reclaim his property from Hansen, about twenty miles south of Grand Island. Not wanting to get arrested for the woman's alleged theft, he called the owner and then fled the area. But while the horses made it back to their owner, local authorities promised to investigate the suspects. Meanwhile, the *Grant County Tribune* published the report under the headline "Was It a Theft," leaving the matter open to interpretation. Tellingly, the woman was not named in the article, which was a courtesy that newspapers almost never extended to male suspects.[23]

Nearly all non-native horse theft suspects were white as well.

FROM THIEVES TO VILLAINS

Although relatively few African Americans lived in western Nebraska during the late nineteenth century, the ones who did reside there were careful not to risk an almost certainly macabre response were they to steal a horse during the Jim Crow era. Beginning in 1885, buffalo soldiers from the Ninth and Tenth Cavalry regiments were stationed at Fort Robinson, where they served with distinction for nearly two decades. None of the cavalrymen apparently stole any local horses, but the potential for violence among the troops and between civilians and soldiers off the reservation was a real possibility, as when First Sergeant Emanuel Stance was reportedly shot and killed by his own men in response to his mistreatment of them. Incidentally, Stance earned a Congressional Medal of Honor for having seized several ponies and rescuing two white prisoners from a Kickapoo raiding party in Texas. For the most part, however, black soldiers stuck together and possessed both the wherewithal and in many cases the institutional support needed to defend themselves from white civilians. This mutuality also discouraged buffalo soldiers and cavalrymen from deserting, and across the frontier buffalo soldier desertion rates were only a fraction of those of their white counterparts. While fears of being caught with a stolen cavalry horse undoubtedly factored into a black soldier's decision to stay put, group identity and the difficulty of blending into local white populations were more important considerations.[24]

Black soldiers did not have to go so far as to steal a horse in order to get into trouble; they typically received harsher punishments than white enlisted men, and racially motivated animosity by white superiors often created a hostile environment for black troops. Henry V. Plummer, Fort Robinson's first black chaplain, was court-martialed in 1894 after he was caught sharing a drink with some off-duty enlisted men. Plummer was widely known and locally reviled both for his temperance preaching and his antiracist writing, and his commanders dismissed him from the army on a technicality. Elsewhere, white officers seized on racist explanations when rationalizing the loss of army horses by Indian raiders, as when Captain Ambrose Hooker blamed the

E Troop herders of the Ninth Cavalry for "losing" sixty-eight horses to the Apaches in 1867.[25]

Outside of the military few African Americans lived in western Nebraska during the late nineteenth century. According to the 1880 census, only six resided in Lincoln County, while fifty-three lived in Dawson County, and another forty-two lived in Cheyenne. Dawson County contained Overton, western Nebraska's first Exoduster community, while in Cheyenne many worked as cooks, cowhands, and laborers in the county's ranches.[26] In this labor environment, given the long hours, hot sun, back-breaking labor, and poor wages that ranch jobs often entailed, black men often earned the respect, if not the acceptance, of their employers and colleagues. In fact, at least one suspected black horse thief in Nebraska was so beyond reproach that his prosecution in a neighboring state angered his white neighbors and employers.

In 1890 Grant County sheriff Bud Moran arrested Ed Stringfellow, a black rancher living about twenty-five miles northwest of Hyannis, at the request of a Wyoming sheriff who wanted him on suspicion of horse stealing. Stringfellow allegedly stole a horse while driving cattle with the Dunn brothers in Wyoming. His neighbors vouched for him, however, and told the *Grant County Tribune* that the suspect legally owned the horse and had the paperwork to prove his claim. Stringfellow quietly submitted to the arrest and appeared "confident of an acquittal." Unfortunately, though, a Wyoming jury did not buy his story, and the judge sentenced Stringfellow to two years in jail. After his release the *Grant County Tribune* welcomed him back to Hyannis. "Ed was more sinned against than sinned in that deal," it declared, "and [he] says they will never catch him again in any such proceeding." In Cherry County the Twenty-Fifth Buffalo Soldier regiment stationed at Fort Niobrara may have enjoyed a similar presumption of innocence when several soldiers on leave allegedly "borrowed" civilian horses and used them to return to their barracks. Although they turned the horses loose upon reaching the fort, the regional predisposition to react viscerally and swiftly in response to horse thieves was likely muted by the comparatively good relationship the soldiers there enjoyed with the mostly white town of Valentine.[27]

No such allowances were made for "Pedro," a vaquero in Cheyenne County who allegedly stole two horses from the Loomis and Jorgan Ranch in September 1876. While vaqueros were common throughout much of the Great Plains, few seemed to make their way to Nebraska. According to the 1880 census, only fourteen residents throughout the state claimed to have been born in Mexico. In any case Pedro found work in Cheyenne County as a cowhand, but he was fired for allegedly getting drunk on the job. The horse-stealing complaint came only two weeks after his termination. Pedro took the stock to Ogallala—presumably in order to sell them for extra cash given his recent unemployment—with Deputy Sheriff John Zweifel hot on his trail. Upon entering Keith County, the Cheyenne County sheriff evidently deputized two citizens of the former jurisdiction, and they caught up with Pedro about nine miles west of Ogallala. The suspect reportedly fired two shots at the arresting party, wounding one, before being shot and killed by the deputies. Zweifel carried Pedro's body back to Sidney and displayed the corpse outside the county jail as a warning to other would-be criminals before burying it. If there were any other vaqueros in the vicinity, they undoubtedly received the message loud and clear.[28]

Gender and race notwithstanding, the most important thing that horse thieves had in common was what the public thought of them. *Horse thief* was an especially offensive name to call someone, and writers and editors sometimes used the term to condemn individuals not accused of any specific crimes. Hardware merchant James Belton berated an anonymous letter writer to the *Lincoln County Tribune* for signing his or her name "No One" and claimed that "every time I see a poor fellow rolling in the gutter, a fellow execution proof, a constitutional liar or a horse thief, it will come into my mind that he may be 'No One.'" On another occasion a clergyman compared saloon-keepers to criminals in his Sunday sermon, arguing that they were worse than horse thieves. Contemporaries assumed that horse thieves wanted easy profits; one newspaper sarcastically encouraged "young men out of employment to enter the business [of horse theft]" since "the profits were large, the work light, and the risk nothing—after the officials get after you."[29]

The degree to which both the public and the courts believed horse thieves were unambiguously bad and beyond redemption notwithstanding, thieves defied easy labeling. Most horse thieves did not identify themselves as such: they were principally cowboys, farmers, laborers, or soldiers. Furthermore, many people who joined horse-stealing gangs had only tenuous connections with the gangs' leaders and dubious affiliations with their organizations. Instead, local figureheads such as ranchers, farmers, or even sheriffs used informal, exploitative relationships with lower-status men to compel them to work or steal on the leaders' behalf. While cowboys, homesteaders, and rustlers did not self-identify as horse thieves, each group represented cultures of resistance whose roots lay within the marginal economies and ecological borderlands of Lincoln County. These cultures of resistance did not create horse thieves, but they did create new opportunities for marginalized workers to secure economic windfalls. They also reflected the conditions that made economic success so rare for so many of these workers.[30]

Many Americans are surprised that cowboys were not only working-class wage earners but that they were often beaten down by the Great Plains labor economy. While most fictional cowboys seemed to enjoy job security and fair wages, the cold economic realities of ranch work on the high plains turned some cowboys into horse thieves. According to John Bratt's 1885–86 time book, the average monthly wage for an employee who worked over twenty-five days during the month of January was $36.56. To put this into perspective, the average price that Bratt paid for his horses between 1875 and 1883 was $46.75 per head, and good saddle horses often cost as much as $60 or $70.[31] Thus, a cowboy who needed to buy a horse might have to save two months' worth of his earnings to afford one. Of course, this also meant that a stolen horse was worth about two months' pay.

Like many other ranchers, Bratt hired and later laid off most

FROM THIEVES TO VILLAINS

of his workers according to seasonal cycles and only paid a dollar a day to most of his temporary workers. These wages did not include sick days or other involuntary absences. Some employees missed weeks at a time for one reason or another and did not receive pay for those periods. Those employees who worked on a seasonal basis needed to find something else to do during the winter months, but their options were limited. Unemployed workers could either perform odd jobs around the county, stay at home with their family, or move to another town to find work. Those who had little luck finding extra employment faced other dangers besides not having enough money. Cheyenne County sheriffs and judges worked vigorously to rid their jurisdiction of tramps and loafers, and as a result, the county's court dockets were crowded with vagrancy cases. Justice of the Peace Robert Shuman sent dozens of men to hard labor at the county jail for terms ranging between five days and three months. Upon hearing the state's vagrancy case against Alexander Maine and Thomas Whitehead in October 1885, Shuman summarily found the pair guilty, declaring that the men were "entirely destitute of means for support and that they . . . [were] loafing about the town without employment." Shuman sentenced both to thirty days in jail.[32]

While some cowboys stole, most did not. Bratt had high praise for most of his workers: "We had during our twenty-five years' activity in the cattle and horse growing business, hundreds of good, faithful men, many whose names I cannot now recall." Bratt was nevertheless well aware of the temptation for a luckless cowboy to steal a cow or a horse, and he articulated his concerns in his autobiography. After discussing his experiences as a member of the Wyoming Stock Growers Association (WSGA) executive committee, he recalled expressing incredulity at his colleagues' labor practices. Bratt allowed his employees to stay on the ranch over the course of the winter, which reduced the financial pressures they faced during the slow work months between roundups. Other ranchers apparently left their cowboys to their own devices during the winter, and the lack of income during this season drove many of them to steal. "We paid our men good wages, gave them good food and cared the best we could for their moral and physical welfare," Bratt argued in defense of his own fairness. "We kept them winter and summer, unlike some of our Western stock growers, who discharged most of their men in the fall, thus doing more to make horse and cattle thieves out of them than anything they could do." Ultimately, the typical ranch hand's income was small enough to require careful management by the wage earner. According to Bratt: "The summer's wages of a cowboy would often be spent in a night. What was he to do through the winter? He had to live, and to live he was forced to steal."[33]

Bratt objected to what his colleagues were doing. "I frankly told the members of this committee that they did everything they could, indirectly, to make horse and cattle thieves out of their employees." His advice had some effect: "Some agreed with me, and later allowed many of these employees to remain at their ranches through the winter, boarding them without charge, while others paid their men half wages and boarded them for the little work they did around the ranches."[34] Bratt had identified a crucial labor problem within the cattle economy: ranchers paid laborers meager wages for seasonal work, turned them loose for the winter with few other job prospects awaiting them, and then expressed surprise when their employees stole their horses.

Bratt's neighbors in the cattle business knew this problem well. Although most cases were not legally adjudicated—either because the ranchers never learned that their employees had stolen horses from them (as Bratt suggested) or the ranchers somehow dealt with these cases internally—sometimes these incidents made it to court. In 1885 Antelopeville rancher E. Witcher accused Joe Crawford, one of his ranch hands, of stealing a team of mules. At justice court Witcher testified that he had sent Crawford with the mules to go "seven or eight miles" out and "gather bones from the prairie." Instead, Crawford took the mules to town, where he attempted to sell them. "[I] do not know what induced me to come to Sidney," Crawford told the judge. "[I] acknowledge that I offered the mules for sale, but [I] was under the influence of whiskey." The judge referred the matter to the Cheyenne County District Court. Fortunately for Crawford, who faced several years in jail for his crime, the prosecutors dropped the charges, and the case was dismissed.[35]

Another rancher near the then-abandoned Fort McPherson filed a complaint in 1890 against an employee, William M. Jaycox, for allegedly taking "a team of horses . . . and accompanied by a woman not his wife, departed for parts unknown." The sheriff set out to find Jaycox and apprehended the suspect several days later. However, the county judge accepted the defense's argument that the young laborer had been slandered and had some kind of claim on the horses in question and dismissed the case. In the Panhandle near Harrison, rancher James Cook lamented his thieving employees as well, though some of their indiscretions hit closer to home than others. When his family's housekeeper, Lalee, married their ranch hand, Pete, Cook approved of the union. "Pete was a surly sort," recalled Harold Cook, James's son, "but [he was] a good worker." Soon after they married, Pete grabbed one of James's "good horses" and fled for Montana. When the ranchman told Pete's estranged bride about the crime, Lalee immediately demanded an annulment.[36]

Other cowboys ran off ponies that they believed belonged to them for one reason or another. Asa T. Marcellus, a laborer who worked at two different Lincoln County ranches, took a horse that his most recent employer had sold as part of a herd to Wendel Waldo and his partner, Evans. At one point prior to the sale, Marcellus claimed the horse in question. Even though he was allegedly present when his employer sold the herd, he later objected to the transaction and decided to take the horse for himself. He attempted to ride to Kansas with his reclaimed property, but the authorities caught up to him before he left the state. Charged with horse stealing, the defendant pleaded not guilty in court two days later. Shortly thereafter, the judge decided to dismiss the case. Even though a newspaper story on the incident reported that the two parties continued to contest the ownership of the horse after the charges were dropped,

Marcellus's attempt to steal what he thought was his was successful, at least in the short term. Stealing one's own property, rather than seeking redress through the courts, was not theft in the eyes of cowboys and the law alike.[37]

Marcellus's actions, though juvenile, reflected how the ranching industry gendered young men working as cowboys. According to historian Jacqueline Moore, ranch owners, or "cattle men," acted as if they were the patriarchs of their ranches. Ranchers preached civility, hard work, forbearance, and other virtues, while their cowboys were like children: dependent, adolescent in their pursuit of hard living, and in need of guidance and control from both ranchers and townspeople. As a result, cowboys "saw their masculinity in terms of their skills on the job, their control over their working conditions, and their ability to make independent decisions." Acts such as defending against raiders and outlaws, performing acts of bravado, and doing their jobs with consummate skill and without complaint became means of assessing and asserting manliness. To that end, developmentally arrested cowboy horse thieves were also acting out their urges whenever they decided to take a horse from an employer. Reclaiming a horse was, in a sense, like reclaiming one's masculinity. Marcellus, who married a few years later and settled down to raise a family in Kansas, had a lot more to gain by repossessing his horse in 1888 than he had to lose at that time.[38]

Outside of western Nebraska's ranches, economic privation also drove homesteaders and farmworkers to steal. For instance, at least four of the men who were convicted of horse stealing in Lincoln County were farmers. But while cowboys could steal horses undetected and sell them to supplement their income, farmers had to keep their businesses afloat in spite of falling crop prices and scant rainfall. To make matters worse, a devastating grasshopper invasion in the mid-1870s wiped out entire fields of crops, sending already fledgling farms into a struggle for survival. A series of bad winters, including the one in 1885–86 that killed millions of livestock across the plains, also reduced herd sizes on homesteads as well as ranches. Conditions were so bad in October 1874 that thirty-five soldiers hunted bison near Red Willow Creek to distribute to starving settlers. After marching 334 miles over two weeks, however, they only killed twenty-seven head.[39]

Dire necessity did not always lead to horse stealing, at least in the conventional sense of the term. The cash-poor economy of high plains homesteading could not operate without horse power, but many of the homesteaders who relied on horses, like ranch hands and cowboys, could not afford them. When securing horses for their farms, some farmers took out horse chattel mortgages. Like home mortgages or car loans today, debtors borrowed money from a creditor for the purpose of buying a horse. In turn the lender collateralized the loan by placing a lien on the animal. Farmers made installment payments, including interest on the principal borrowed, toward their loans. This process worked for an unknown but presumably large number of borrowers who grew their herds, and their productivity, on credit. The McCoy family in Chadron decided to mortgage a horse team from the Upper 33 Ranch after their original animals wore themselves out breaking the tough prairie sod in the White River valley. "They brought back a well-matched team of buckskin horses, giving a mortgage on both teams as payment," recalled Arthur McCoy. "They were not broke to work, but Irve and I soon trained them." But if farmers could not pay off their mortgages, their loans were called due, and the lenders sent men to round up their collateralized horses. Farmers who lost mortgaged horses also lost their ability to plow fields, move goods to market, haul heavy equipment, and travel. Without horses or money, farmers often had no choice but to sell their land or abandon it altogether.[40]

It is difficult to know how most of the farmers who forfeited their horses coped with their losses, but some of the debtors took matters into their own hands and tried to sell, trade, or even escape with their animals before they were repossessed. Several cases involving the disposal of mortgaged property appear in the court records, two of which made it to the Lincoln County District Court. In 1890 rancher William Hubbart accused Aleck

McCann of attempting to sell both of his mortgaged mules in Omaha, and merchant Charles McDonald filed charges against Marion Stout for attempting to do the same. Neither defendant was convicted, however, although local lenders were obviously growing more aggressive in defense of their investments. Later someone discovered McCann in Iowa more than a year after allegedly taking the mules, and the state of Nebraska extradited the suspect. Similarly, in Dawes County, Oscar V. Harris mortgaged a cream-colored horse, a bay horse, and a saddle to William Comstock on June 18, 1887. Twelve days later Comstock illegally took the mortgaged team to Cherry County. Believing that Comstock intended to sell the team, Harris filed a complaint. However, a jury acquitted him of the charges on November 22, 1887.[41]

While lenders often defined the loss of mortgaged property as stealing, occasionally the borrowers themselves tried to keep their animals by accusing the foreclosing authorities of theft. When North Platte livery owner Daniel Besack was brought into court on charges of horse stealing in September 1889, few people—including the judge, who summarily dismissed the case—doubted his innocence. It probably surprised no one, however, that somebody had maliciously pressed charges against Besack for stealing a horse. The owner of the Brick Livery Stable was one of Lincoln County's most prominent repossession agents. Besack rounded up mortgaged horses from local farms, housed the animals in his stable, and either returned them to the original lenders or auctioned them off to the public to pay off the balance of the debt. He advertised at least three auctions in the *Lincoln County Tribune* between 1886 and 1889, at which he auctioned off six mortgaged horse teams.[42]

This indictment illustrates the extent of the public's contempt for the booming horse mortgage business. Since whoever charged Besack with horse stealing was aware that the defendant was collecting—not stealing—mortgaged property, considering Besack's well-publicized role in collecting and auctioning off foreclosed horses, the accuser wanted to get back at the livery owner for taking his horses by pressing charges. But while

FROM THIEVES TO VILLAINS

most people did not go so far as to falsely accuse a repossession agent of horse stealing, few settlers envied or admired his work. In January 1888 the *Lincoln County Tribune*'s correspondent in Wellfleet reported on Besack's visits to the community, which left "several parties in bad shape and one in a critical position with the law and the people." A week later the same writer predicted that if Besack visited the village "much oftener" to "round up horses," then local residents would soon "not have enough teams to put in our crops next spring."[43]

Partial ownership stakes in horses were even more problematic for smaller farmers. John Tilford, an Irish immigrant in his late fifties, ran a farm with his family in North Platte in 1880. The farm was so small—it probably brought in less than one hundred dollars a year—that Tilford did not actually own his own team. Instead, he owned a twenty-five-dollar special interest in two horses, which he used and cared for on his farm. Yet Tilford lost more than his ownership share when both horses were taken from his horse pen sometime during the spring of 1881. On March 29, 1881, Tilford swore out a warrant accusing Con Hill and Henry Miller of horse stealing. Although Hill and Miller had taken the horses, Hill apparently owned a share of these horses as well. Judge William Peniston quashed the complaint when he ruled that one cannot feloniously steal one's own property. A few days later Tilford filed a second complaint against Hill and Miller, accusing the pair of simple larceny. The second charge resulted in a jury trial, but by the time deliberations began, Tilford had dropped the charges for unknown reasons.[44] The case might have been resolved to Tilford's satisfaction, or perhaps it became clear to Tilford that if he were to lose, then he might be held liable for the costs of prosecution. Either way, Tilford could not afford the loss of even one horse, let alone both.

While Tilford's case is an unusual one, the devastating consequences—and fears—of horse stealing for settlers in western Nebraska were all too common. Ranchers often absorbed losses from horse and cattle theft and could afford to augment, subsidize, or otherwise influence state responses to livestock theft from their ranches. Other locals, however, had no such luck. Farmers, laborers, businesspeople, town dwellers, and railroad employees did not rely on vast herds of livestock and often could not purchase or mortgage more than a team of horses. Farmers and homesteaders in particular faced a perilous economic existence on the plains, and most of the dangers they endured could not be controlled. But since human beings can be arrested, imprisoned, and killed, unlike railroad corporations or the weather, farmers could potentially control horse thieves. In spite of falling rates of horse stealing in western Nebraska, other economic and environmental dangers to small-herd owners continued unabated. Settlers personified this spectrum of calamity into the form of a horse thief.

Victims

Many reports of depredations and horse-stealing gangs were overblown, but settlers had good reasons to be concerned. Few individuals could afford to lose their horses to thieves. This was especially true for farmers. Like most homesteaders west of the 100th meridian, farmers in Lincoln County had very little margin for error: low amounts of rainfall, sandy soil, and usurious freight rates conspired to keep crop yields low and profits lower. Consequently, farmers were especially vulnerable to horse theft, as they could ill afford to replace a part of their operation that was as vital and expensive as a horse. In 1882 Boyd Wilkinson stole two horses from Richard Dalton, a homesteader near Fort McPherson. The loss must have been severe to Dalton, who reported the incident and helped authorities capture and convict Wilkinson. Dalton's farm in 1885 was small by any measure: both the total value of his livestock and the total output of his farm production were priced at five hundred dollars, and only 20 of his 160 acres were tilled. Dalton reported owning only two horses, so in effect Wilkinson stole what would have been Dalton's entire stock of horses in 1885. It is impossible to know whether the two horses Dalton owned in 1885 were replacements for his 1882 losses or the remnants of his herd after the theft. In either case, though, the losses would be severe. Con-

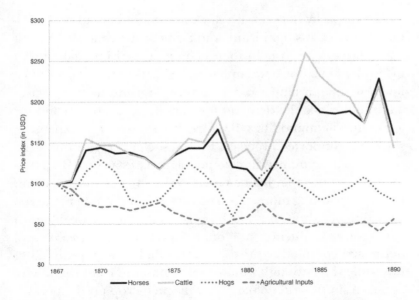

Fig. 24. Deflated price index for horses, cattle, and hogs relative to other agricultural inputs, 1867–90. Data was compiled from *Historical Statistics of the United States* and then indexed to the year 1867. Created by the author.

sidering that the average price of a horse was over fifty-eight dollars in 1882, these two stolen horses probably represented one-fifth of Dalton's total livestock investment.[45]

Dalton's loss of about one hundred dollars' worth of horses was devastating, but the actual economic, financial, and utility value of the stolen horses was likely much greater. A deflated price index demonstrates how the lost value of a horse can affect a farmer's ability to operate at a profit, pointing to even wilder changes in the real value of horses over time (fig. 24).[46] When the price of horses rose, as it did after the Civil War and during the mid-1880s, the price of other commodities (e.g., hay, oats, and corn) dropped. In 1883 the average price for a horse was about seventy-three dollars, which was six dollars less than the average price in 1867. However, since the prices of agricultural commodities had plummeted across the board, the deflated value of the horse more than doubled by this time. Horse prices rose dramatically as a result.

The disparity between livestock and other agricultural commodity prices was significant, and farmers' awareness of it must have played a key role in their economic decision-making. An investment in a horse was much more likely to turn a profit in a few years than a similar investment of time and money in crop cultivation since the demand for horses outpaced demand for agricultural commodities. Biology also limited herd expansion since even imported breeds of horses, such as Percherons, were bred from an extremely limited population of stallions. Crop production, on the other hand, was easily scaled up to meet demand by simply planting more of a crop on a greater number of acres. This practice, however, has long been a systemic problem in agricultural production, as it often leads to overproduction and depressed commodity prices. As a result, livestock production was somewhat (though not entirely) immune from the fluctuations in supply and demand that plagued crop production.[47]

These changes mirrored a larger trend in the American economy during the Gilded Age: deflation. A long period of deflation, stretching from the early 1870s until the turn of the century, resulted from a contraction of the money supply following the recall of greenbacks after the Civil War. As the economy grew, the money supply could not grow in response to the demand for money, so money itself became more valuable. This drove prices for most commodities down. As the index shows, however, horses were somewhat immune from the overall deflationary trend, at least until the early 1890s. Horses became an investment, as they often appreciated in value over the course of time. And while cattle prices fluctuated even more radically during this era, the lower unit cost of an individual steer and the nearly total lack of productive power for a cow made investing in cattle a speculative enterprise. Two head of cattle were worth one horse, which meant having to feed and care for two animals as opposed to one. Cattle thus required more input (especially food) than horses, which were hungry yet efficient animals. These inputs lowered profits, and although there was a greater demand (or perhaps appetite) for cattle, they had less profit potential per unit than horses.

In addition to the financial cost of horse theft, the productive cost of losing one or more horses was a danger to farms as well. After the Civil War horses and mules were essential machines for every farmer—they enabled their owners to plow, sow, and ultimately harvest more acres than they could with oxen or man-power. The most useful horses—four to eight years old, in good health, large enough to pull draft or quickly carry a human, and well trained—were also the most expensive horses and were thus the most likely animals to be stolen. An old, broken-down horse was easier to replace than a healthy, adult horse, but when given the choice between the two, a thief would obvi-ously choose the latter. So the combined financial cost and productive value of horses made stealing them an activity that could bankrupt an owner.[48]

Nebraskans reduced the risk of losing their investment by taking proactive steps to prevent and cure equine illness, being extra vigilant when guarding and protecting their livestock, and insuring their animals against theft, death, or injury. However, these measures were often difficult to implement. Overworked, underfed, or otherwise neglected horses were susceptible to a wide range of ailments. Even healthy animals contracted conta-gious diseases, as when the Great Horse Influenza Epizootic of 1872 killed thousands of horses across the country without warn-ing. Livestock insurance advertisements claimed that lightning killed scores of horses each year, while other potential killers included rattlesnakes, trains, and the heavy labor of their day-to-day duties. Horses and mules also suffered from exhaustion, as many owners relied exclusively on a single team. Finally, guard-ing one's horses was a labor-intensive activity, and few individ-uals or families could watch their livestock around the clock.[49]

Insurance was the best option for those owners who could afford it, but its availability was limited. The Western Horse and Cattle Insurance Company (WHCIC), based in Omaha, was the only licensed, specialized insurance company for livestock in Nebraska. Since the company effectively had the state's livestock insurance business to itself, it could name its price. The premi-ums would have been high anyway—cattle and horses are much more prone to the elements and to the vicissitudes of nature than humans and their dwellings, which meant that they died more frequently and unexpectedly. But in any case the premiums were likely cost-prohibitive for most farmers, families, and businesses. One man in Adams County, Claus Timm, insured a team of two mules with the WHCIC in 1884 for $21. The policy covered them up to $150 and was good for two years. At $5.05 a mule per year, his policy seemed like a bargain. However, the company demanded that the premiums be paid up front, requiring a $21 payment at the beginning of the policy. This was a month's salary for many workingmen and a hard amount to collect for nearly anyone in an economy as cash-poor as western Nebraska's was in the 1870s and 1880s. And while policyholders were able to pay for their policy with a promissory note, the company reserved the right to refuse payment of a claim to any customer who owed anything on their note. So in effect some of the company's customers were borrowing money to pay for a policy that was null and void so long as the premium balance was outstanding. Some may have even borrowed money to protect borrowed or mortgaged cows. These policies did not reassure small-herd owners who wanted insurance against horse stealing but who could not afford to keep their account current, let alone replace a missing horse.[50]

The WHCIC also reserved the right to refuse payment when, in its judgment, the policyholder had directly or indirectly caused the death of his or her stock. This gave the company the ability to deny claims based on the charge that its policyholder had overworked or neglected his or her stock, which it did when Timm issued a claim after his two mules died shortly after taking out the policy. Although Timm won a judgment in the Adams County District Court for $300 when he proved that he had finished paying off his promissory note before his mules died, the appeals court reversed the judgment when it determined that the company's charge that the mules had been killed from overwork warranted an investigation.[51]

With rumors of raids, the potential for fraudulent or unreported cases of theft, and the growing numbers of missing animals wandering around, it is difficult to pinpoint the number of Nebraskan settlers who lost horses to thieves. But in spite of all the confusion, the consequences were clear. A stolen horse represented the immediate and usually irrevocable loss of a large investment of time and money. Yet settlers could not effectively guard their herds. Unlike Lakota, Northern Cheyenne, United States Army, or ranch-based herd managers, farmers, families, and individuals did not command the labor necessary to protect horse herds around the clock. Less-successful farmers often mortgaged their teams, and even those homesteaders who bought horses could not afford expensive livestock insurance. While most settlers did not experience horse theft firsthand, those who did suffered considerable damage.

Horse stealing was a high-profile, sensational, and infrequent crime—it was more common than other forms of larceny, it involved the loss of a greater amount of money and labor than other personal possessions, and it was often associated with hostile Plains Indians or violent criminal gangs. In the fragile economic world of the late-nineteenth-century Great Plains, where high shipping costs, wild market fluctuations in distant cities, and the sheer force of nature could quickly destroy a farm or business, horse thieves were a tangible—and more easily punished—scapegoat for victims and non-victims alike. From the victim's perspective horse theft was an urgent problem that came at a terrible cost. Horses were an essential commodity whose economic, productive, and financial value could make or break a farm, ranch, or other business. Demand for horses was inelastic between the beginning of the Civil War and the Panic of 1893, meaning that demand stayed constant in spite of fluctuations in price or supply. But like with any other commodity, those who had a lot of it were in better shape to recover from the loss of that commodity than others who had less.

Horse thieves also took a heavy toll on western Nebraska's ranches. When one considers the likely high number of unreported thefts on ranches by unscrupulous or disgruntled employees, thieves would have stolen more horses from ranches than from any other type of business or farm. Yet these numbers do not tell the whole story since these victims also had far more horses on the whole than their non-ranching neighbors. A stockman with a hundred horses was much better equipped to recover from the loss of a horse than a farmer who only owned two or three. Also, reports of theft on ranches gradually declined, at least relative to the overall number of horses and cattle grazing in the region. From a loss prevention standpoint, theft was a moderate threat to ranchers' herds, somewhat more damaging than disease but not nearly as deadly as drought and cold. However, unlike drought and cold, horse thieves were a problem that ranchers had at least some hope of controlling.

In Lincoln County the large number of horses on ranches was proportional to a much larger number of cattle. According to the 1880 agricultural census, over 52,000 head of cattle grazed in the county, excluding milch cows, and 1,750 horses were on hand to herd them. With a population of 3,632 people, Lincoln County had a two-to-one ratio of people to horses. Since there were over 14 head of cattle to every person in the county, many of the available horses were used almost exclusively for ranging and herding cattle. Consequently, there was a lower ratio of horses to people in Lincoln County than the records seem to indicate since all of the extra cattle would mean that a substantial percentage of the county's available horse power was necessary to round up the cattle. Bratt's records demonstrate this fact—at any given time between 1875 and 1883, Bratt had about one horse on hand for roughly every one hundred head of cattle.[52] If that ratio applies throughout the county, then cattlemen used nearly one-third of the available horse supply for ranching purposes. Thus, a handful of people in the county owned a sizable percentage of the county's horse population, meaning that the herds at their ranches were large and, comparatively speaking, easier to steal.

Bratt's livestock records illustrate how the economics of ranching required large horse populations. In 1875 Bratt ranged 4,500 cattle near Fort McPherson, which included his thoroughbred and native herds. Over the next eight years he tripled his livestock holdings—in 1883 he had over 14,000 "thoroughbreds," and his "native" and "common" herds included thousands more. A large percentage of this growth came from natural increase: as early as 1876, Bratt estimated that his thoroughbred cows had given birth to 1,395 calves, and this number increased to 2,895 in 1883. These births alone outpaced his estimated winter losses, which could be as high as 750 head. Bratt also bought cattle from other ranchers; between two different transactions in July 1882, he bought nearly 3,000 head. For all of this trouble Bratt relied on monthly cattle sales to the fort, where he held a contract as the post's beef supplier, and regular sales to other locals via his meat market in North Platte. On several occasions he unloaded hundreds of cattle at a time, usually three- or four-year-old steers and cows that had been sufficiently fattened. When prices were high, these large transactions raised enormous amounts of cash, especially by late-nineteenth-century rural America standards—on September 9, 1880, Bratt sold 500 cattle to the McKee Brothers for $15,729.45. A month later he unloaded another 280 head for $9,798.30.[53]

Bratt's horse population grew along with his cattle population. In August 1875 Bratt kept 33 horses near Fort McPherson. This number had doubled by May 1877, and the herd doubled again by August 1879. His horse population reached 202 in June 1882, after which the population leveled off in 1883 to around 185, where it stayed until the end of the extant record. But unlike his self-sustaining cattle population, Bratt had to continually refresh his horse stock with trades and purchases. In August 1879 Bratt bought 49 horses from J. Coe, and in September 1880 he bought 10 horses and one mule from Jon P. Hale for $412.50. Although Bratt's colt population continued to grow with his mare stock during this period, natural increase could not keep up with the demand for horses on the ranch.[54] Bratt needed to keep his horse herds large enough to accommodate and manage his much larger cattle population. As Bratt raised more cattle for sale, he needed horses to round up and track down his cattle when necessary. A population of cows and steers as large as Bratt's needed nearly constant human intervention and maintenance, and on the open range this was best done on horseback. Yet while cows stood around all day and leisurely chewed the prairie grasses, horses worked long hours under harsh conditions, and for these reasons many were needed. In a letter to his son, rancher Raymond Gentry outlined the equine requirements for a "well equipped [sic] trail outfit": a remuda that included about ten horses per rider, extra mounts for the foreman, and four head of horses or mules to pull the chuck wagon. Cowboys frequently swapped horses along the way in order to keep the animals well rested and fresh.[55] Since Bratt likely conformed to similar guidelines for his remudas, it is no wonder that his horse population was slow to reach self-sustainability.

As the years passed, Bratt's ability to breed, purchase, and barter for more horses outpaced his losses. This was fortunate since Bratt's horses often died. Of the 104 horses Bratt lost between 1875 and 1883, according to his records, 79 perished. He carefully noted the cause of death for each horse whenever possible, and the list of various causes was long: starvation, fever, exposure, snakebite, and getting caught in barbed wire were some of the more common causes. At least 2 horses were hit by trains while wandering along the Union Pacific railroad tracks. Many horses also died of old age, though Bratt also tended to trade some of his older horses for younger ones that could handle the workload. Harsh Nebraska winters claimed a few horses as well.[56]

Most of the remaining lost horses simply disappeared. In his records Bratt recorded seventeen horses as being "missing." This was not synonymous with "stolen." A careful accountant, Bratt did not let such an important detail slip by without careful consideration—if he believed that a horse was missing, he did not assume (though he might have suspected) foul play. The majority of these horses went missing on or before May 25, 1880, when Bratt discovered that twelve mares and several colts were absent. Bratt did not know what happened to them, and he provided no clues in his records.[57] They most likely wandered off since it seems unlikely that thieves would have easily absconded with so many mares and colts unnoticed or that they would have elected to steal colts over adult horses in the first place. Much like missing cattle, missing horses were an occupational hazard for Bratt, who noted losing more on three other occasions. But like dead horses, the missing ones were replaced.

The economies of scale that dictated herd size on Nebraska ranches did not preclude the kind of human-to-animal relationships that compassionate horse owners and riders tend to have with their own ponies today. "Our horses always were given names," quipped Raymond Gentry, "[though] sometimes they might not be very complimentary." Bratt recorded names for most of his horses, which were noted along with their color and brand in his inventory book. Some of the names—like Prince, Beauty, and Butter—hinted at the kinds of relationships the horses had with the men who rode or cared for them most often.[58] Bratt probably did not name all of these horses himself but, rather, recorded the nicknames given to the horses by those who used them most frequently. Yet even in this environment, in which dozens of ranch hands used, groomed, fed, and grew attached to the hundreds of animals Bratt had on hand, over one hundred horses and mares had no names. Some horses were given names eventually, such as Pin and Johnny, but the majority of them were bought, used, and later sold, traded, or found dead without a nickname.[59] Although the long lives led by Bratt's animals and the high resale value they commanded suggest that the animals were well cared for by the ranch hands, Bratt owned so many horses that the regular cowboys could not give names to them all. Had it not been for Bratt's meticulous record keeping, it is possible that many of these horses would have been stolen and he would have never known. And on ranches without such record keeping, which were the vast majority, this is probably what happened.

Over the course of one particular year, between the fall of 1877 and the following autumn, thieves stole eight horses from John Bratt's ranch near North Platte. Bratt believed that three different culprits were responsible: Big Turkey's Brulé band, which struck during one of the last raids to occur in western Nebraska; Charlie Fugit, a member of the Doc Middleton gang;

and an unknown person who snuck off undetected with two horses. According to Bratt, no additional thefts occurred on his ranch between 1875 and 1883, the years for which his horse inventory records are available. However, Bratt's careful accounting was not the norm, and less meticulous ranchers may have suffered greater losses. But even those ranchers who left no lasting record of their inventory, and likely took none to begin with, retained a major asset: a large population of horses and a much larger population of beef cattle.

Ranches were larger economic units (in terms of horse ownership) than most farms and other businesses. Ranchers owned dozens or even hundreds of horses, whereas individuals seldom owned more than a few. Compared to other businesses, only the Union Pacific Railroad and freighting firms such as Russell, Majors and Waddell owned similar numbers of livestock. Therefore, horse herd management on ranches had much in common with Lakota, Northern Cheyenne, and United States military management practices. All four groups maintained enough resources to sustain large horse herds, allocated labor for guarding horses, and rallied enforcers to their cause whenever someone raided their herds.

Horse thieves preyed upon ranches more than any other business. Of the fifty people in Lincoln County who filed complaints for horse theft between 1878 and 1890, at least fifteen were ranchers.[60] In Cheyenne County at least two of the ten complainant parties owned or represented ranches. There were several reasons for this. For instance, unlike other businesses, ranching was a capital-intensive enterprise. Large numbers of horses on ranches made them appealing targets. Guy C. Barton, who was robbed twice in 1877 and 1879, was one of the region's most prominent ranchmen. He claimed 156 horses and over $361,000 in livestock during the 1880 census.[61] John Bratt owned about 150 horses during this period as well. Ranching was land intensive, which made horses more difficult to track than they would be on smaller farms or stables. A handful of stockmen controlled much of the land in western Nebraska, including Bratt, who grazed his cattle over 200,000 acres in several differ-

FROM THIEVES TO VILLAINS

ent counties. The combination of large horse populations and an indefensible perimeter resulting from the vast amount of land needed for horses and cattle to graze upon was too inviting for thieves to ignore.

Ranchers in the 1880s did not despise horse thieves because they threatened their bottom line but because the thieves themselves reminded them of, and gave them an opportunity to reverse, their loss of local economic and political power. In spite of the confidence that many government officials, writers, and migrants placed in homesteading as the transformative institution capable of "civilizing" the West, ranchers believed—and not without cause—that homesteading would never take root in the high plains. Homestead grants, which gave 160 acres to settlers who were able to improve the land they claimed, were not large enough to sustain free-range ranches, nor were they sufficient for agriculture. Later pieces of legislation directed toward making the high plains region more amenable to homesteading—such as the 1904 Kinkade Act, which granted 640 acres to interested settlers in the Sandhills—failed to turn western Nebraska into a facsimile of Iowa, Illinois, or even the eastern half of the state.

Legislators, government officials, and settlers pressured ranchers to forfeit their use of public land on the high plains to would-be homesteaders, but the cattlemen saw their role in a different light. They believed that they were the true "civilizers" of the region. Ranchers brought commerce, community, and law to their domains, and they endeavored to lead their communities. Bratt, for instance, served as mayor of North Platte as well as on the local school board. Nebraska's ranches were patriarchal organizations: the ranchers saw themselves as the "men" of their estates, treated their hired hands as if they were their "boys," and believed that they had at least some responsibility for law and order on their range. Horse and cattle rustling posed a direct challenge to this hierarchical system of ranch management, especially if the ranchers were worried that some of their workers may have been encouraged to try their hand at stealing their livestock.[62]

Rustling did not seriously threaten the ranchers' businesses, at least with respect to their horse populations. Large herds were both subject to and insulated from theft—it was as easy for a cowhand to steal a horse from his employer as it was for that employer to then purchase or trade for a new one. Economies of scale also worked to the advantage of ranchers, who could call upon the same workers used to herd cattle with their horses to protect their mounts as well. But horse thieves presented a moral threat to ranches that other sources of herd attrition did not. Thus, when western Nebraska's theft culture disintegrated in the face of homesteading and American Indian land dispossession, ranchers were among those leaders who clamored the loudest for the state to assume a powerful new role in apprehending horse thieves.

Herd size determined how horse stealing affected its victims. Ranchers in the Platte Valley who had survived the early chaos of the Plains Indians Wars found themselves in a much more congenial climate for business: horse raids had declined, national demand for beef had risen, and new railroad lines in Nebraska and Kansas connected the Great Plains to eastern markets. As a result, ranchers grew their horse herds, which were necessary for rounding up cattle on the open range. By virtue of their investment in cattle, ranchers also had greater access to capital. This made it easier for ranchers such as Bratt to replace herd loss from theft, while some ranchers were so oblivious to horse herd skimming by their employees that they simply added their "missing" horses to their balance sheet and obtained replacements. Similarly, a much larger institutional and economic unit, the army, also had to cope with the risk of losing its already limited access to equine wealth, but in time even Uncle Sam's cash-strapped and largely unsupported frontier forces discovered new means of augmenting their horse wealth. Farmers and small businessmen had fewer options open to them, and the loss of a horse for any reason could result in decreased productivity, the unexpected costs of having to buy new horses, the loss of borrowing collateral, and financial meltdown.

Although herd size made a difference in how the consequences of horse theft were felt, virtually all horse owners shared a deep and intense hatred of horse thieves. Small-herd owners lamented the loss of any horses, but horse stealing evoked an even more powerful reaction. Owners felt empathy for their horses, and whenever one was stolen, the owner must have also believed the horse was victimized as well. These feelings were more common between small-herd owners and their stolen horses since large-herd owners had less emotional attachment to some or most of their horses. As a result, small-herd owners had a visceral dislike of horse thieves. This hatred was codified into the law, as horse theft was a Class II felony with a minimum sentence of several years in prison, a punishment comparable only to lesser categories of homicide, rape, and violent crime.

Ranchers had reason to hate horse thieves as well. On the surface they were a significant threat to profits, and their stealing imperiled smaller ranchers as they did farmers and other micro-herd owners. Some larger ranch owners such as Bratt began to view their seasonal, underpaid labor force as a potential incubator for horse thieves. This affected how they treated their ranch hands. While much of this treatment worked to the laborers' advantage (e.g., they were provided with cheap winter housing, free meals, and odd jobs during the off-season), it also cast each employee as a potential horse thief. A mere suspicion of horse theft by a cowboy could lead to his dismissal and possible blacklisting among other ranchers. But there was a moral reason for ranchers to combat horse thieves as well. As the civilizers of the range, ranchers had to prove to their communities, their crews, and their compatriots that they were just as capable of and successful in turning the plains into civilized districts as homesteaders. This in turn protected the ranchers' hold on their land from the incursions of land-hungry homesteaders while also validating their exploitative and ruthless appropriation of the plains. Horse thieves were anathema to this vision of the region, as they were a menace to the good, honest workers of the land and a danger to the region's prospects for becoming fully incorporated into the American nation.

Enforcers

Fortunately for both farmers and ranchers, horse stealing had long been against the law in Nebraska and in the United States, thus making the question of its enforcement somewhat moot following statehood in 1867. These laws were a relic from a long-standing Euro-American legal tradition that penalized the theft of horses more than the stealing of other forms of property, including cattle and other livestock. In ancient Rome statutes against theft only specified two kinds of property crime that could lead to a more severe penalty: rustling livestock and stealing a bather's clothes. Cattle and horse thieves, known as "abigei," and their fences faced death or banishment when caught transferring stolen livestock. Centuries later, in 1760s England, William Blackstone noted in his *Commentaries* that horse stealing was not only a felony, but it was also the only larceny offense not subject to the benefit of clergy. It was punishable by death. In the English colonies, meanwhile, a softer approach was taken to the crime. Horse thieves in early-nineteenth-century Virginia risked several years of hard labor, for example, in addition to paying for the value of the horse.[63]

Nebraska's law against horse theft did not originate in the state assembly. When legislators rewrote the state constitution in 1875, like other western states, Nebraska adopted another state's criminal code. Nebraska borrowed Ohio's, which passed most of its criminal law statutes in 1835. The original code included a statute identifying horse stealing as a felony offense regardless of the value of the animals stolen.[64] This fact is not surprising when one compares the historical background of Ohio's criminal code with Nebraska's own unique historical context, considering that the laws adopted by the representatives of Nebraskan homesteaders, ranchers, and railroad interests mirrored those written nearly four decades earlier by officials who represented midwestern farmers. It also explains why horse theft was enshrined in Nebraska's criminal law. Few Ohioans operated ranches or farms on the scale of those in Nebraska and other Great Plains states, and therefore, like the homesteaders who flocked to Nebraska, they were severely affected by horse stealing.

Nebraskans did not write the original law, nor did they move to change it. Horses remained the only livestock exempt from value-based larceny classifications until 1899, when the state legislature explicitly prohibited cattle theft. The only modification to the law against horse stealing was made in 1883, when the maximum sentence for horse theft was lowered from fifteen to ten years and the minimum sentence was reduced from three years to one. Although the law was changed with little fanfare or public discussion, judges who had sought to reduce the sentences of convicted horse thieves for one reason or another welcomed the news. A Nebraska state supreme court decision in 1881 prohibited district court judges from prosecuting suspected horse thieves with a lesser crime, thus forcing reluctant judges to adhere to the mandatory sentencing law. In spite of this adjustment, the legislature did not eliminate the minimum sentence altogether or otherwise subject horse theft to the same kind of value-based assessments that dictated the charges levied against cattle rustlers and other livestock thieves.[65] Within Nebraska criminal law, as well as that of Ohio, horses were a special kind of property.

The various county sheriffs' departments were principally responsible for enforcing the felony law against horse stealing. County law enforcement was effective and efficient, in spite of the government's early age and its status as a "frontier" outpost.[66] From 1868 onward Lincoln County had a functioning and accessible district court, a full-time sheriff, and a population that was usually willing to utilize both when settling disputes or reporting crimes. As time passed and the country grew, the criminal justice system in the county became more elaborate and professionalized. When North Platte became a city in 1875, it established a police court for misdemeanor crime and founded a municipal police force. By 1880 it had a dedicated county criminal court that served as an appellate court for police court convictions and an examining court for felony cases. Although occasional vigilante activity occurred within the county, most citizens supported and worked with the county's criminal justice apparatus.[67]

The sheriff was not usually a professional policeman. Most sheriffs only served for one term, and few had any experience in law enforcement. The majority of a sheriff's day-to-day work was administrative, which consisted of serving papers for civil and legal cases, posting election notices, and conducting other necessary county business. Rather than rewarding on-the-job experience, Lincoln County voters elected sheriffs on the basis of their trustworthiness and reputation. In addition, the position paid very little since it was completely reliant on the collection of fees, so there was very little room for professional development or patrolling in the sheriff's schedule. The office would not become salaried until 1907.[68]

Beginning in 1876, when North Platte became a second-class city, residents could elect a city marshal to help combat crime within the city limits. To that end city marshals were also responsible for pursuing thieves.[69] On a Sunday evening in 1876, Marshal A. L. Walker caught Charlie Short, a young bronco trainer who had recently breezed into town, with a stolen horse belonging to William Dickenson. Short had arranged to rendezvous with two friends under a bridge that night, each of whom was to steal a horse as well, and the three had planned on riding south to Kansas. Walker caught wind of the plot, however, and arrested Short. His companions, meanwhile, allegedly heard about Short's arrest. Neither of them appeared at the designated time and place. Walker waited all night at the meeting place but with no luck. Unlike the sheriff, however, the marshal was the highest-paid official in the city. He made $784 a year in the late 1890s, which was more than what rancher John Bratt's highest-paid foremen earned.[70] Walker could afford to wait for Short.

Other law enforcement organizations and officials played a role in the policing of Lincoln County as well. By the late 1870s the city of North Platte had a night watchman as well as a city marshal. It also established a police force, which served to patrol the city and enforce misdemeanor offenses, and a police court to adjudicate misdemeanor cases. Through the 1880s federal marshals operated in the region. Their principal goals were to prevent the sale of liquor to American Indians and enforce other federal laws. By the late 1880s railroad detectives established a presence in North Platte, where they worked with local authorities to police the area and secure company property against theft. Their strength grew over time, and by 1891 they had a centralized police department that was headquartered in Omaha.[71] On occasion these law enforcement organizations were called upon to solve a horse theft or apprehend a suspect, such as during the effort to capture Doc Middleton. Mostly, though, these enforcers were busy with their own work.

The Sheriff's Department was responsible for carrying out a variety of functions that competed and conflicted with its law enforcement duties. Many of these functions provided the department with a substantial share of its annual revenue, which came primarily from user fees. Whenever a litigant needed to send a summons, deliver a subpoena, garnish wages, foreclose on property, or claim property through a replevin action, the sheriff would carry out the order. The successful completion of that order would result in a fee, for which the requester would be initially responsible. Since the sheriff did not draw a stipend or budget allocation from the cash-strapped county government, his department depended on the revenue collected from these fees.

Of course, the Sheriff's Department did not function as a business. Law enforcement trumped its civil duties, and the department charged the county for mileage accrued during manhunts and when carrying out warrants. It also received revenue for housing prisoners and providing security. However, an analysis of the department's fee-based revenue during the mid-1880s shows that there was a noticeable imbalance between civil and criminal fee collection.[72] Between 1884 and 1885 at least one-quarter of the department's fee-based revenue came from issuing and delivering summons. Although some of these went to defendants in criminal cases, the vast majority were issued for civil cases. Even those summonses that were used in criminal cases were seldom issued by the state but, rather, by the accuser's attorney, who initiated the action. The accuser was thus potentially liable for paying those costs in the event that a judge quashed the complaint before it reached the grand jury.

In addition, while 11 percent of the fees came from subpoenas delivered to witnesses, almost twice as much money came from garnishments and writs of replevin, in which cases the sheriff collected money or other property from negligent debtors. Foreclosures and attachments netted over 4 and 11 percent, respectively. Foreclosures were also the most profitable actions since the sheriff's office received a portion of the proceeds from the sale of foreclosed-upon property. The average foreclosure yielded about fourteen dollars for the department, which dwarfed the next-highest average yield for a specific fee-based action, and subpoenas generated an average of six dollars per case. In sum, creditor-initiated actions constituted over a third of the collected fee-based revenue for the department, while warrants only made up about 13.5 percent of the total amount.

The potential for civil case fee collection often surpassed the potential for criminal fee-based revenue (fig. 25). This was because the various services available to civil litigants by the Sheriff's Department, such as foreclosures and writs of replevin, were less likely to result in a flat fee. Logistics conspired to make criminal apprehension a less financially expedient activity. After all, suspected horse thieves and murderers were more likely to cut and run from the law in anticipation of being arrested than a defendant in a civil case, who was more likely to be surprised by the arrival of a sheriff's deputy on official business. While the sheriff could charge mileage whenever he had to leave North Platte, which sometimes resulted in some large fee payouts, whenever the sheriff embarked on a manhunt, travel was never free; it cost money to outfit a party and purchase provisions. The fee-based revenue stream for the Sheriff's Department did not necessarily mean that the sheriff took his law enforcement duties lightly, but this imbalance likely influenced his efforts to police the county.[73]

It is important to note that the Lincoln County Sheriff's

FROM THIEVES TO VILLAINS

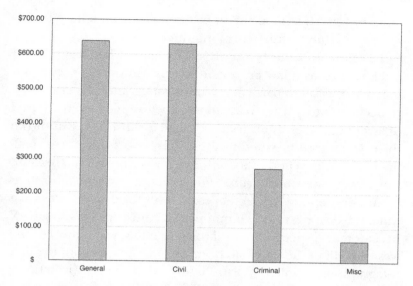

Fig. 25. Fees collected by the Lincoln County Sheriff's Department by category, 1882–86. Note that "general" fees include subpoenas and summonses and can be either criminal or civil, depending on the case. Sheriff Day Book, Lincoln County Records, NSHS. Created by the author.

Department, and to some degree the North Platte police, operated to respond to crime rather than to prevent it. Crime prevention is a relatively recent phenomenon in both police science and in law enforcement policy.[74] During the late nineteenth century the nation's unparalleled economic and demographic expansion, its rapidly growing cities, and a rise in urban crime led to new concerns over the frequency, impetus, and effects of crime. These concerns led in part to a new focus on criminal activity as not simply the result of bad or evil decision-making but as a manifestation of socioeconomic ills. Crimes such as vagrancy and public drunkenness were prosecuted relentlessly, and policy makers explored new options for ridding their communities of tramps, hobos, and vagrants. Up until that time potential threats among the citizenry were not criminalized and branded as future troublemakers nearly as often as they would be during the twentieth century.[75] This reduced the amount of time the Sheriff's Department or the police would have had to spend "on duty" while patrolling the region.

The Lincoln County Sheriff's Department had a successful track record as a law enforcement institution. Its record on horse theft cases in particular is impressive. Since the crime carried a mandatory three-year jail term before 1883, men accused of stealing horses often tried to make a run for it. But of the thirty-five warrants issued by the county courts for horse stealing between 1873 and 1890, only seven were not served because the suspect was on the run.[76] On multiple occasions the sheriff and his deputies tracked horse thieves for days or weeks at a time, traversing a mostly unpopulated landscape on horseback in search of suspects. Up until the late 1880s, when most of the western half of the state had been carved into new counties and telegraph lines linked North Platte to these new jurisdictions, the sheriff was primarily responsible for tracking down thieves, regardless of where they went. These manhunts, while long and difficult, also generated revenue since the sheriff could assess fees based on mileage. These exploits gave several sheriffs some well-deserved acclaim. Con Groner, who had nearly been shot while trying to apprehend notorious horse thief Charles Fugit, developed enough of a reputation as a crime-fighting lawman that he later toured with Buffalo Bill's Wild West show as the "frontier sheriff of the Plains."[77]

Like any elected office, the sheriff's office was not immune to political intrigue and charges of fiscal or fiduciary incompetence. The *North Platte Republican* accused Sheriff Bradley of costing the taxpayers more money during his tenure than the previous two sheriffs combined and alleged that Bradley had refused to investigate complaints made against the Union Pacific Railroad. The editors also argued that Bradley won the office of sheriff by a twenty-vote majority, barely beating an opponent who, in their words, "was a most disreputable man, a drunken bully and a ne'er-do-well." That he won the office at all was due only to his loyalty to Union Pacific and to Barton, Keith, and the other cattle "bosses." These charges, which came while Bradley was running for Congress, show how arbi-

trary the discretion of the sheriff's office could be when deciding how and where to allocate its resources.[78] They also reveal
the depth of feeling against the cattle barons in Lincoln County.

Perhaps the most cumbersome impediment to the Sheriff
Department's ability to enforce the law was that the fee-based
system of carrying out criminal and civil actions alike occasionally held the victims of crimes responsible for the costs of prosecution. Before a criminal action entered the district court,
whereupon the county assumed the costs of prosecution, actions
brought at the county court level or below were subject to the
same kind of discretionary penalties that plaintiffs in civil cases
faced if their causes were dismissed. As a result, the victim of a
crime was sometimes held liable for the costs of prosecution.[79]
This rarely happened. Of the approximately 450 criminal cases
to be heard before a Lincoln County court between 1873 and
1890, fewer than 15 were ruled against the plaintiff. Yet whenever the plaintiff was held liable, the costs to the accuser were
substantial. An unnamed plaintiff was charged over twenty-four
dollars in fees when his case against Jake Durr was dropped.
Durr had allegedly stolen a span of horses from the plaintiff.
Years later, in a similar case, O. D. Lyle was charged court costs
after accusing former employee H. M. Jaycox of stealing two
horses worth seventy-five dollars. Jaycox made a run for it, but
when he was caught and returned to North Platte for a criminal examination, he claimed that Lyle was slandering him. Evidently, the judge agreed.[80]

While these cases were unusual, they happened often enough
that the lessons hit home for many settlers in the county. If someone who was suspected of a property crime secured the services
of an adept defense attorney, as most of the court-appointed
defense attorneys were, the victims knew that there was a reasonable chance that their case might be thrown out, in which
case they would be liable.[81] Sometimes the fees for such cases
ran upward of forty or fifty dollars. When facing such a potential loss, one may wonder how many horse thieves escaped for
want of prosecution. This could explain why so many of the
horse thief victims who appear in the records are ranchers or

successful businessmen. Small farmers or homesteaders could not afford to face the consequences of a failed suit, particularly if they were smarting from the loss of a valuable horse. Many thefts were never reported, or victims responded in other ways. In either case this circumstance limited the public's access to its own law enforcement institutions, which, in spite of the best efforts of their lawmen, created substantial structural inequalities within the state and county criminal justice system.[82]

Some of these barriers included procedural issues that arose when the courts' efforts to ensure due process clashed with limited available judicial resources to quickly adjudicate crimes. The district courts in western Nebraska rotated from county to county like a traveling circus, holding sessions in each courthouse between two and four times a year. On occasion enough legal business piled up to justify calling a special session of the district court. One such session was convened in December 1885 in Cheyenne County, owing to the court's inability to seat a petit jury in the previous session and to the "accumulation" of "important criminal business" in that county. But usually the judge and county clerk labored to cram as many cases and hearings into those limited time schedules as possible. Once court was in session, the judge would then convene a grand jury for indictments, adjudicate civil cases, give citizenship to qualified immigrants, and grant divorce decrees to self-disqualified couples. On top of all this, the court had to hear criminal felony cases as well. Since cases sometimes spanned several months or even years, the district court relied on the recognizance of both defendants and prosecution witnesses. As a result, the nonappearance of critical parties to either case sometimes delayed cases indefinitely and even forced the dismissal of charges.

One horse-stealing case in Cheyenne County typified this not-uncommon process: on October 1, 1878, Edgar King allegedly stole three horses from Thomas Lawrence and George Bosley. With over one thousand sections of land and as many as fifty thousand cattle, the Boslers operated one of the largest and most prominent ranches in the Panhandle. Nevertheless, they still had to wait a year for the culprit to be caught and for the case to be heard in district court. When the grand jury indicted King for horse theft, the court issued a recognizance to Lawrence and Bosley, as well as two additional witnesses, for $500. When the district court reconvened in April 1880, one of the plaintiff's witnesses did not appear, and the case could not move forward. Later, during the October 1880 session, Edgar King did not show up for his third date in court. His surety, A. M. Bruce, forfeited his $800 bond to guarantee King's appearance in court. But Bruce was also missing. Two years had passed since the crime, and now, much like Lawrence and Bosley's horses, neither party could be found.[83]

The legal system's inadequacies annoyed but did not hinder ranchers and corporations. Large-herd owners used their capital to hire guards to protect their property and detectives to find anything that was stolen. The railroads employed this kind of power directly by operating their own police forces, and the Union Pacific police successfully augmented civilian law enforcement while safeguarding private property. Unlike corporations, ranchers could not field their own professional police agencies, but they could work together to organize a strong response to those they deemed a threat to their property and their business. Ranchers established the Western Nebraska Stock Growers Association (WNSGA) to meet this need for mutual protection, and while it could not be called a "vigilante organization," its vigilance against crime profoundly influenced county governance and law enforcement in Lincoln County and beyond.

Stock associations were the primary organizations responsible for promoting and protecting the interests of the cattle industry, and like the cattle industry itself, they were imported from elsewhere. In colonial Mexico organizations called "mestas" controlled brands, managed roundups and estrays, regulated ranchlands, and pursued rustlers. These organizations also carried the rule of law. *Mestas* remained in use by ranchers throughout the Southwest through the Mexican-American War. Later, when Texas attracted American ranchers in the early nineteenth century, they faced similar problems. Comanche raids, cattle rustlers, growing numbers of stockmen, and an open range created a wide range of issues and conflicts that prompted ranchers to form and join cattlemen associations. Unlike the *mestas*, however, these organizations did not supplement or replace existing law enforcement. Rather, they became vehicles for promoting stock growers' interests.

After the Civil War cattle associations not only assumed an important role in regulating, protecting, and promoting the stock business; they also became pivotal players in the development of western communities and states. Perhaps the most important institution on the scene during the 1870s and 1880s was the Wyoming Stock Growers Association. Founded in 1873 as the Laramie County Stock Association, it soon changed its name to reflect its growing influence. For the next twelve years the WSGA became a political powerhouse in the Wyoming Territory, where it controlled the legislature for several years. The WSGA pursued rustlers, but it also lobbied for several important agricultural reforms. It established protocols for quarantining diseased cattle from entering the territory and strictly regulated the use of brands.[84]

However, the WGSA is perhaps best known for orchestrating one of the strangest and most brazen acts of corporate violence in American history: the Johnson County War. The trouble began in Johnson County, Wyoming, which was among the least violent and criminally active jurisdictions in the state, if not the entire Great Plains. This quietude was due in large part to the growing number of homesteaders and sheepherders moving into the area. As these newcomers squeezed established cattlemen off of the public range, however, the WGSA began a campaign of violence to reclaim their grazing land. The cattlemen turned to Frank Canton, Johnson County's new sheriff and an ex-convict who had previously moved to the plains under an assumed name, for protection. Canton had earned a reputation as an enforcer for the WGSA before being elected sheriff in 1885. As a lawman, Canton filled local newspapers with reports about horse and cattle rustling in the area, which he used as a pretext to kill at least three people who had run afoul of the region's powerful cattle barons. He worked with four other men, all of whom had connections with the WGSA. One of their victims, a successful horse dealer named Tom Wagoner, was hanged for allegedly stealing his animals from local ranches. But according to historian Christopher Knowlton, "a posthumous investigation into Wagoner's operation revealed that not one of his eleven hundred horses was stolen." Over the next few years the murders continued, and by 1892 the residents of Buffalo, Wyoming, began to suspect that the killing had been orchestrated by Canton and other cattle barons. And something even more sinister was afoot: on April 5 twenty-five gunmen out of Texas, most of whom were recruited by WGSA range detective Tom Smith, traveled north by train to Buffalo to kill several local citizens and opponents of the cattlemen, including Canton's successor as Johnson County sheriff, Red Angus. Eleven men on the WGSA Executive Committee joined them on their killing expedition.[85]

What happened next is the stuff of legend. The invaders first lay siege to Nate Champion and three companions at the KC Ranch. All four were captured or killed but not before Champion fought off the four dozen attackers for most of the day, wounding and killing several. The expedition continued to suffer one setback after another, and soon word got out that cattlemen from Cheyenne had invaded the Johnson County range. The expedition ended with over four hundred local cowboys, settlers, and residents besieging the invaders at the TA Ranch. They were saved when a company of troops from the Sixth Cavalry arrived just in time to stop the surrounding army from using the cattlemen's own dynamite (seized earlier from a teamster who had orders to deliver it and thousands of rounds of ammunition to the attackers) to blow up the ranch. But despite being arrested, the cattlemen escaped justice. As their lawyers launched one delaying tactic after another, Johnson County's legal bills exploded as it paid to house and feed forty-five prisoners. Later none of the Texans would return to the state to face trial after leaving Wyoming.[86]

Contrary to its mission to protect honest businesspeople from theft and grift, the WGSA in 1892 bore all the signs of a rustling cabal, its leaders composed generally of avaricious, entitled, and morally unscrupulous men. The story of the Johnson County War, now mostly demythologized and laid bare, is both a shocking tale of violent economic conquest during the late Gilded Age (followed two months later by the fateful July 6 battle in Homestead, Pennsylvania, between strikers and Pinkerton agents) and a peerless example of a rural gang syndicate whose leaders successfully managed the law, media, and local economy to maintain their power. The WGSA cattlemen's claims of vigilantism were dog whistle appeals for justice, but regardless of the pretext, their crimes were no less premeditated and heavy-handed than Perry Yeast threatening to send a sodbuster to an insane asylum. The only real differences lie in the scale of the two enterprises and with the fact that only the WGSA had the veneer and the benefit of operating on the right side of the law.

The WGSA claimed hundreds of members across several states, expanding its influence across the region. Bratt was a member as well as several other Nebraskan stockmen.[87] But by the mid-1870s the Platte Valley had its own organization. The Western Nebraska Stock Growers' Association attempted to consolidate countywide societies across the western half of the state, though during the 1870s at least, it was mostly based in North Platte. The WNSGA organized local cattle ranchers, kept track of each ranch's cattle shipments and brands, hired detectives to locate missing stock, and lobbied on behalf of the ranchers in state and local politics.

The WNSGA and allied associations magnified and focused the efforts already being made by ranchers attempting to recover stolen stock. Unlike homesteaders, laborers, and businesspeople, ranchers could call on their workers to chase, track down, and sometimes even apprehend suspected horse thieves. In the larger outfits a veritable cowboy army could be raised to deal with the scourge of theft or safeguard the property of a single individual or company. Bratt employed his men to protect his herds from raids in the early 1870s, ordering them to sleep in stables and keep night watches for thieves. At one point he even told his men to sleep with their horses tied to them.[88] However, stock growers' associations made it possible for ranchers to

FROM THIEVES TO VILLAINS

trust one another enough to collaborate against thieves, thus reducing individual ranchers' needs to hire their own people. By selling unclaimed mavericks, the WNSGA could afford to hire detectives and offer rewards for the capture of suspected thieves. The organization sponsored its own policing.

Stock associations made roundups easier to carry out and less likely to result in lost or stolen livestock. If uncoordinated and conducted independently of one's neighbors, the roundup of free-range cattle to send to market became a chaotic, labor-intensive mess. Multiple parties of men might canvass the same land, take up cattle belonging to their employers, and inevitably claim some that did not belong to them. Horses were especially subject to being mistaken for one's own property since they were less likely to display an unmistakable brand belonging to a single ranch. Owners traded horses often, so many animals had multiple brands. Ranchers spilled a considerable amount of ink in the county court over disputes arising from falsely claimed cattle and horses.

The stock growers' association solved many of these problems by centralizing the process of rounding up cattle. Depending on the size of their herd, ranchers sent a predetermined number of men to assist with the roundup, and together they fanned out and collected all of the livestock they came across. Once the stock was brought in, the ranchers met and divvied up the steers and horses based on their brands and settled any issues arising from disputed ownership right away. Mavericks were then sold to the public, the proceeds of which were to fund the organization. Coordinated roundups reduced the number of horses and cattle stolen from the participating ranches while also saving them court and labor costs.[89]

Stock associations also registered the brands belonging to their members, which allowed members to work together to recover and redistribute stolen animals once they were found. When 250 head of stolen cattle were discovered in Dawson County, Bratt and several other Lincoln County ranchers rushed over to present a list of local brands to the sheriff. Bratt then telegraphed those ranchers whose brands were found among the herd.[90] Brand inspectors ensured that all livestock transactions were legal and proper and used brand registries to investigate reports of stolen cattle or horses.

The benefits of joining a stock association were not always apparent to ranchers, but their interest in organizing eventually coalesced around a common issue: the prevention of theft. In his annual address as president of the Lincoln County Stock Growers Association in 1877, Bratt recalled that "the time was not far back" when ranchers refused to organize, primarily because "each thought the other a thief (perhaps not without cause.)" In time, however, it became clear that their individual interests demanded collective organization. "There are thieving bands whose business is to run off cattle and horses," Bratt warned. "[They are] operating today under your very nose." The threat of stealing threatened their industry as a whole and demanded a unified, organized response. Bratt's point resonated with members of the dozens of livestock associations that appeared throughout the Great Plains during this era.[91] The best thing that ranchers could do to prevent livestock theft, it turns out, was to start trusting other ranchers.

Collective action against horse and cattle thieves provided only one reason for cattlemen to band together, but for many stock growers it seems to have been the original impetus. Stock grower organizations brought self-imposed regulation to the once wild and woolly range, where ranchers could steal from one another but could not chase rustlers far beyond their own territory. The WNSGA gave Nebraska ranchers power in numbers, and aside from the kind of cynical decision-making that doomed other organizations such as the WSGA to failure in 1892, the western Nebraska association and its successors on the federal level brought stability and order to the ranching industry. Unlike the homesteaders and settlers who employed vigilante rhetoric to make up for the perceived inadequacies of law enforcement, ranchers relied on an individualistic, libertarian ethos and rhetoric that fought federal range regulation, on the one hand, while promoting advances in veterinary science, on the other. Much of this cooperation stemmed from

FROM THIEVES TO VILLAINS

the ranchers' original goal of banding together and busting up the gangs of horse thieves and cattle rustlers that once preyed on their ranches.

While the inspiration for stock grower associations came from Texas and Mexico, farmers' organized responses to horse stealing could be found farther east. After the Civil War hundreds of thousands of farmers across the Midwest joined local, state, and even national anti–horse thief societies.[92] Similar in organization to stock grower associations, these groups usually collected dues for income, relied on an executive committee to disseminate stolen horse information and pursue thieves, and often filed articles of incorporation and formally adopted constitutions with county and state authorities. Unlike their western counterparts, however, anti–horse thief associations borrowed heavily from the Freemasons. Members frequently gathered in secret and often incorporated rituals into their meetings.

Organized extralegal responses to horse stealing are older than the United States itself, dating back to at least 1769, when the South Carolina Regulators began whipping and branding suspected thieves in the backcountry. But the national anti–horse thief association movement began during the Civil War, when few law enforcement authorities were around to prevent thieves from stealing horses in several midwestern states. Many former and would-be sheriffs, police officers, and constables were serving in the Union and Confederate armies, leaving open large swaths of unpatrolled rural areas throughout the Mississippi Valley. According to one member of the Kirksville, Missouri, Anti–Horse Thief Association, horse thieves operated freely during the Civil War, unleashing a massive crime wave upon the civilians who were not off fighting in the war. "The horse thieves taking advantage of the situation," he noted, "grew to a magnificent cluster of thorns and it seemed that everything they came in contact with stuck to them." Unfortunately, locking the thieves up was futile: "The civil war had so completely destroyed the courts that to prosecute criminals was out of the question."[93]

In spite of this law enforcement vacuum, locals were not quite willing to back down and submit to the spike in crime. The Anti–

Horse Thief Association (AHTA) was founded by David McKee in 1854 as a local protective society in Clark County, Missouri. It was a small, local organization for the first decade of its existence, and in fact its membership declined during the first few years of the Civil War, as many of its members enlisted. Beginning in 1863, however, the society began to grow again with the help of discharged soldiers and other noncombatants. Elsewhere in the state, which was plagued by the Quantrill gang and other disaffected Confederate bandits, Clay County farmers founded the Central Protective Association. After the war thousands of midwestern men who arrived back home after their service ended noticed the emergence of these societies, which began to assume responsibility for the welfare of those on the home front. The tight organization of these groups must have also appealed to the veterans. During the next forty years many began to establish their own local societies and national chapters across the country. The AHTA expanded into several neighboring states within the next few decades, and by 1900 it had over fifty thousand members.[94]

Anti–horse thief societies usually declared themselves to be nonviolent and publicly announced their intention to work with local authorities. However, some of these societies used their organizational clout on a local level to legitimize racially motivated lynchings and other sporadic violence. For instance, several members of the Waseca County Horse Thief Society in Minnesota participated in an attempted lynching. Although the society itself took no official action, most members of the Waseca County society were open to violence, and those who participated used the nonviolent cloak of the anti–horse thief society to defend themselves afterward. Farther south, in Iowa, local anti–horse thief societies allegedly plotted and carried out Charles Howard's lynching in Des Moines on December 15, 1874. The vigilante mob's actions, which included busting Howard out of his cell in the middle of the night, created considerable controversy in the region. "The whole proceeding is most bitterly felt by the citizens here," reported one correspondent, "and the perpetrators are denounced in most unmeasured

FROM THIEVES TO VILLAINS

terms." Nonetheless, the anti–horse thief society movement continued to grow there too. At the annual AHTA meeting in 1886, held in Des Moines that year, the national organization claimed to represent eighty local chapters and over two thousand members in Iowa.[95]

Localized violent aberrations aside, these societies grew quickly and over a wide area because anti–horse thief societies were a tailor-made response to horse stealing. They channeled the concerns of worried farmers across the Midwest, alleviated anxieties over inefficacious law enforcement, and in general expressed the precariousness of the postbellum agricultural economy. In one sense they can be viewed alongside the Grange and Populist movements as an organized response to the many pressures facing farmers during the Gilded Age—both as an organizational framework for responding to horse stealing as one of these particular problems and as an outgrowth of Populist political culture that emphasized peaceful movement building. Moreover, these societies' relative harmlessness when compared to the premeditated violence of the WGSA, the San Francisco Vigilance Committees of 1851 and 1856, and the 1863 Montana vigilante movement helps illustrate why many of them lasted well into the twentieth century. Many chapters found a second life as rural community social clubs and in some cases even gained members who drove their cars to meetings. Because of these factors, it is possible that anti–horse thief societies, while occasionally serving as vehicles for extralegal or lynching violence, may have actually prevented such acts against horse thieves by giving rural farmers a means to organize and a place to vent. It was a reasonably cheap, proactive, and socially satisfying way to cope with an often terrifying problem.

Despite the popularity of anti–horse thief societies across the Midwest, western Nebraskans expressed little enthusiasm for the concept. This was likely because the conditions that made homesteading in western Nebraska so difficult overall—poor rainfall, sandy soil, high freight rates, and dwindling returns on commodity production—prompted many sodbusters to leave the state before they had firmed up their land patents. Farmers often moved into and out of townships, creating demographic and population turnover and resulting in the more economically successful and socially connected people in most communities throughout the region being ranchers, not farmers. Homesteaders in Nebraska had common cause with one another, but because too few people stayed on their claims long enough to build stable communities, they could not effectively direct their anxieties into productive group building. This explains why stock growers' associations were the primary organizational tool in the region for combating rustlers as well as why homesteaders and other farmers in western Nebraska often embraced violent solutions and rhetoric when dealing with horse thieves.

Overall, in western Nebraska, the wealthier that a rancher was, the more protection he or she enjoyed. Large-herd managers called on the military and county police for assistance, whereas small-herd owners were not deemed worthy of special military protection. Crime prevention was not a zero-sum game. Success in enforcing and upholding the law was not merely a matter of low crime rates and an absence of vigilantism. It required fairness, equity, and equal access by all to the scales of justice. The problem in western Nebraska and in other western jurisdictions was not that the law specifically benefited one group of people over another but that it was structurally incapable of treating everyone the same way. Low budgets, technological limitations, a huge amount of territory, and a lack of training ensured that the sheriff and municipal police departments were not a ubiquitous presence in the region. For those who could afford it, detective agencies and other private parties filled in the gap by providing security and supplemental law enforcement. For those who could not, in spite of the massive influx of cash, wealth, and property that flowed into and out of the plains, all that they had was each other.

Horse stealing grew less common even as it became more immediate in the minds of potential victims. North Platte and Sidney both witnessed declines in horse theft during the 1880s, and even during Chadron's rough-and-tumble early years, few horses were stolen. At the same time, horse thieves themselves increasingly represented and reflected the winners and losers of the western Nebraska economy, which granted few favors to its beleaguered ranchers and luckless homesteaders. Neither declines in horse theft nor the de-professionalization of horse stealing seemed to matter to small-herd owners and managers, however, as they rightfully dreaded the consequences of losing their animals. Furthermore, the growing presence of professional law enforcement did little to allay their fears. In other words, falling crime rates could not mitigate horse theft's outsized influence on plains culture and society, nor could they prevent the thieves themselves from earning evil reputations.

Horse thieves were not always villains or bogeymen. Back during Buffalo Bill's heyday as a scout, horse stealing was a cyclical phenomenon. Cody allegedly stole a horse from Tall Bull, whose band stole horses from Nebraska ranchers, who themselves might have stolen horses from passing migrants who happened to be grazing their horses on Lakota and Northern Cheyenne land. Even as the horse-raiding and trading economy proved to be unstable and asymmetrical in its outcomes, it at least contained its own logical consistency. But the growing homesteader class and the erasure of horse appropriation as a form of warfare created a new legal and moral landscape in which only evil people stole horses—except, of course, for the members of Buffalo Bill's touring company, who continued to act out the battles of westward expansion over and over in front of audiences across the world. One way or the other, in real life or in fantasy, horse thieves were primed to become villains in the post-frontier West.

6

When Horse Thieves Were Hanged

Men are not hang'd for stealing horses,
but that horses may not be stolen.

—GEORGE SAVILE, *Political, Moral, and Miscellaneous Reflections*

In 1966, when historian and Lincoln County native Nellie Snyder Yost wrote the definitive book on stock associations in Nebraska, she tackled the subject of vigilantism among ranchers and farmers in a chapter entitled "A Rustler Was Never Caught Twice." She argued that rustlers and horse thieves who managed to escape the authorities or repeat their crimes usually met their untimely end at the hands of a vigilante killer. Yost relates a series of lynchings in the state, ranging from the famous killing of the notorious horse thief Kid Wade to the slightly more mundane murders attributed to the Niobrara vigilance committee.[1] The book, written for the members of the Nebraska Stock Growers Association who commissioned it, entertained readers with violent stories about the state's past.

It is true in a broader sense that most horse thieves were never caught twice. In fact, as previous chapters have shown, many were never caught at all. But even among those thieves who were, most escaped conviction or justice for various reasons. Among those who were convicted, most received substantial jail sentences or, in some cases, the mercy of the court. Recidivism was low: no one convicted of horse stealing in Cheyenne, Dawes, Grant, or Lincoln County before 1890 was ever caught in those jurisdictions doing it again, with the singular exception of Doc Middleton and other members of his gang. And as for those suspects who were known by the community to be thieves but for one reason or another were not apprehended, tried, and sent to prison by the law, the public responded with rage, scorn, and even threats but not lethal violence. Overall, the vast majority of horse thieves were never hanged for their crimes. Out of the seven people known to have been lynched in western Nebraska, not a single one was killed for stealing horses.[2]

One reason why horse thieves are so often believed to have been hanged is because the crime is more or less extinct. One of the least-appreciated elements of horse stealing's criminological history is that it, unlike most personal or property crimes, is both uniquely severe in its consequences and technologically irrelevant today. While humans have been murdering, assaulting, scamming, raping, and stealing from one another for thousands of years, horse stealing is not nearly as socially and economically impactful in the twenty-first century as it was during the nineteenth. This gradual obsolescence has had a curious effect on the historical memory of horse stealing. While contemporary Americans inevitably and understandably filter modern crime through their own lived experience and through friends, family, or media consumption, horse stealing is usually experienced as a historical subject first. Consequently, Americans who do not own, manage, or ride horses (which are, of course, stolen even today) generally only visualize horse thieves through the lens of the Western films that they have seen or from stories they heard from their pioneer grandparents or great-grandparents. And this image of horse stealing is, one might imagine, incredibly distorted.

If even diligent and historically self-aware authors such as Nellie Snyder Yost can fail to see the honor in some (though certainly not all) horse thieves or contend with the kaleidoscope of outcomes for theft that ranged from lynching to prison to power to legitimate social and economic rewards, then it is worth thinking about why that is indeed the case today. Why are horse thieves almost universally reviled in America's historical memory

WHEN HORSE THIEVES WERE HANGED

and generally consigned to the end of a rope? The answer lies in the daily experience of those men and women who suffered from the crime itself or who feared that their horses would be stolen. Horse stealing posed a grave risk for small-herd managers, farms, and businesses. And while late-nineteenth-century Americans generally had faith in their military defenders and law enforcement institutions, they probably did not have as much faith in them as people do today. After all, a farmer in 1880 could not dial 911 on his cellular phone after witnessing a break-in, and the sheriff could not be expected to show up in a Ford Police Interceptor suv. Western Nebraska's law enforcement institutions, while well-organized, competent, and semi-professional, were hardly omnipresent.

Ironically, the story of horse stealing's demonization and the radicalization of its victims does not end with the organization of frontier law enforcement. Rather, vigilante rhetoric and legal professionalization are concurrent. Even today, most Americans seem to believe that the "Wild West" ended when sheriffs, marshals, and police emerged in bloody, dusty frontier backwaters to bring justice to an unsettled world. Movies like *High Noon, The Man Who Shot Liberty Valance,* and *Tombstone* reinforce this collective mythology, suggesting that justice workers were the people who ultimately established order amid chaos. Even revisionist Westerns such as *The Unforgiven* fail to question this central assumption, going only so far as to say that order can be corruptible and that criminals can be reformed. However, once late-nineteenth-century ambivalence over the efficacy (though not the necessity) of law enforcement is squared with contemporary American justifications for armed self-defense as an indispensable auxiliary to police protection, it quickly becomes clear that twenty-first-century Nebraskans have many beliefs in common with their 1885 counterparts. Consequently, the Old West should not be defined as a society with an absence of law enforcement; rather, it was a culture that legitimized and endorsed vigilante violence. Much like the theft culture that abetted horse stealing until the late 1870s, vigilante culture aids and abets the deployment of extralegal violence as a means of guaranteeing justice or promoting order. But unlike theft culture, which few people in Nebraska seemed to miss after 1880, many Americans throughout the plains continued to pine for a return to vigilante culture long after vigilantism itself became culturally undesirable and legally impermissible. Horse thieves, who could not defend their motives or recast themselves as sympathetic characters as a result of their own historical obsolescence, were an ideal bogeyman for imagined acts of vigilante justice.[3]

Regulators and Militias

In the early days of settlement, vigilantism and self-protection were not mutually exclusive goals. Road ranchers, for instance, depended on their cowboys to lend a hand when trouble struck. When a raiding party hit Morrow's ranch in 1868, his men "interrupted" the raid in time to prevent the theft of all but three mules.[4] However, during the Plains Indian Wars, the army protected North Platte, Sutherland (near O'Fallon's Bluff), and the Morrow Ranch with small detachments. But other communities spread throughout the region had much less strategic value, and thus their residents were more exposed to danger. Some of these citizens attempted to procure arms for their own local militias. Captain Dudley politely refused a request from a civilian on Brady Island, which is located only a few miles from Fort McPherson, to supply him and his neighbors with arms in case of an attack. The civilian claimed to see Plains Indians in the area, but when forwarding the citizen's letter to the department headquarters in Omaha, Dudley denied that there had been any raids in that section "for many months." Nevertheless, anxiety over additional attacks persisted long after the war against the Lakotas had moved to Wyoming and Montana.[5]

Nebraska's vigilante tradition is firmly rooted in its settlers' encounters with Plains Indian raiding parties. As residents, ranchers, and investment capital continued to flood into the region, citizens demanded increased protection from raids. While the overall threat decreased rapidly with the removal of the remaining non-agency Plains Indians to reservations in

Dakota and Indian Territories, civilians were hyperaware of Plains Indian raids both in their own backyard and elsewhere in Nebraska and Kansas. Each raid put additional pressure on the army and its resources as civilians clamored for total security. In 1874, after a small band of Lakotas killed a settler on Brady Island, ran off several horses, and nearly caught Sheriff Alex Struthers and several deputies off guard and mostly unarmed, Fort McPherson sent a small squad in pursuit of the party. This response did not satisfy the people of North Platte, and the sheriff rounded up a posse of civilians to conduct an expedition of their own. But when Struthers petitioned the post commander to furnish the group with guns, General Dudley rejected the request, insisting that it would require formal permission from the Department of the Platte in Omaha. The sheriff and other civilians objected to the commander's refusal, and the *North Platte Enterprise* penned an editorial the following week calling on the military to assist civilian efforts to combat native horse thieves whenever the need arose. There were "plenty of muskets" at the fort, the editorial insisted, and so long as the majority of its forces were engaged in fighting a war "hundreds of miles away," to not volunteer the use of army arms for the purpose of protecting the town was to create "a great injustice" against the civilian population.[6]

Both military and civil authorities were reluctant to empower local, ad hoc citizen militias, but sometimes even soldiers flirted with vigilante justice. Corporal Lauren Aldrich recalled one instance when he and a small detachment of troops attempted to apprehend a group of five rustlers operating in Wyoming. After discovering, surrounding, and disarming the party, they told the prisoners that they should say their prayers. "The penalty for rustling in accordance with Western code was hanging," Aldrich recalled, "and [Poole] was ordered to assume the role as hangman." Poole approached the rustlers with a lariat in his hands, proclaiming, "'As there seems to be no trees near by sufficiently large with which to decorate your ornery carcasses, I shall proceed to sever your domes with this lariate [*sic*] and a lively running horse.'" According to Aldrich, "The pleadings by the rustlers were pathetic to the extreme." But it was all an act, and "for the time being the farce continued" as the soldiers promised to stay the rustlers' execution in exchange for them revealing the names of everyone they worked with. "Within a short time the entire gang were captured," Aldrich recalled, "and thus ended this gang of horse thieves without bloodshed."[7]

Over time settlers doubtlessly noticed that the army's protective services favored ranchers over farmers. Good relationships with officers helped ensure that ranchers' claims of depredations and stolen property would get a favorable hearing. When J. B. Mackle claimed that nine of his horses had been stolen, a detachment set out for his ranch, camped there, and set out in pursuit. They were able to find and return the horses. The officer reported that Mackle was "a reliable citizen." Ranchers with especially good reputations and enough money could commission their own scouting parties. A more suspect intervention occurred when Keith and Barton requested that a detachment of troops be sent by "special agreement" to investigate a horse-stealing raid on their ranch. In the official report the commander noted that the mission was "free of expense to the government." On the other hand, when commanders refused to help ranchers, they often referenced the civilians' reputed dishonesty as opposed to the impropriety of protecting privately owned enterprises. When Jack Morrow asked for help after a raiding party stole several horses from his ranch, the fort did not send it. The commander made this decision two days after he had written a letter to Morrow explaining that as long as the rancher refused to "make any promises for future correct behavior," he would not be allowed on the military reservation.[8]

On occasion the army worked in concert with armed cowboy detachments when attempting to apprehend horse raiders. In the early morning hours of June 6, 1870, forty Lakotas stole seventy-five horses from Bratt's herd, more than half of the mounts the rancher owned at the time. Fearing depredations the night before the attack, Bratt had ordered twelve herders to tie themselves to the horses in the stable while they slept. When the raiding party cut away Bratt's horses, one of the cowboys did not loosen himself in time and was almost dragged to death by the stampeding animal. Bratt immediately responded to the raid by sending most of his remaining men after the party, while he personally petitioned the army for assistance. The post adjutant general furnished a company from the Fifth Cavalry, commanded by First Lieutenant Earl Thomas, who led the detachment to where the raiders were camping. William Cody, who still worked at McPherson as a scout, picked up the trail.[9] The cavalry detachment joined up with Bratt's men before dawn, and the group encircled the Lakota camp, located near Red Willow Creek in southeastern Lincoln County. At daybreak they attacked the sleeping party. The combined force of cavalry and cowboys killed three raiders in the ensuing battle and wounded several others. The whites seized most of Bratt's stolen horses, and Buffalo Bill won some new fans when he wrote a letter of his exploits to the *New York Daily Standard*. "I came nearer losing my hair there than I have for a time!" Cody exclaimed to its readers. "It was one of the liveliest little fight[s] I ever was in. I wish you all could have been there!" Lieutenant Thomas, however, probably wished that he had been someplace else. His commanders understood that Thomas had violated the terms of engagement by firing on the sleeping party and relieved him of his command a week later.[10]

Ranchers benefited more from the army's presence than the homesteaders, but they, too, were seldom satisfied with the protection they received. Sometimes the troops were overbearing or too demanding, such as during the Platte Valley War in 1865, when road ranch owner Dan Smith complained that the garrison protecting his outpost took up more than half of his stabling, calling it an "outrage." At other times the military was too distant. General Philip Sheridan noted in a letter to Governor Albinus Nance that "the cattle interests of Northern Nebraska" demanded a new military post at the mouth of the Snake River, which is located directly north of Lincoln County. The post was to provide a buffer between the cattle ranches in Nebraska and the Rosebud Agency, where Spotted Tail's Brulé Lakotas had recently been moved and who in the eyes of the cattlemen were still committed to stealing horses. Department of the Platte commander William T. Sherman, however, rejected the request, stating that such a post would require special permission from Congress. The *Western Nebraskian*, which represented the region's cattle interests, frequently penned scathing editorials against the military's policies and its inability to protect cattlemen against depredations.[11]

Lincoln County's "official" militia company, which organized itself as a military unit and sought official approval by the state, did not form until after the Plains Indian Wars were almost over. Its leaders established the group in time, however, for it to see some action in the field. In 1878 the North Platte Guards organized what was intended to become a formal state militia. Frank North, recently retired from service as the captain in charge of the Pawnee Scouts, was elected captain of the Guards. The members elected Bratt second-in-command, which made him a first lieutenant. They organized just in time for Dull Knife's exodus from Oklahoma. As reports of the Cheyenne Breakout reached Nebraska, Lincoln County residents panicked, but the North Platte Guards did not yet have an armament. Mayor James Belton wrote Governor Silas Garber on their behalf and asked him to furnish the company with two hundred rifles and twenty thousand cartridges. The request was forwarded to the adjutant general of the Nebraska State Militia, Bruno Tochuck, who denied it. In writing about his decision to deny sending arms to the militia, Tochuck told the governor that the reports of imminent depredations were exaggerated, remarking that not "one hostile Indian" was "within one hundred and fifty miles" of the state.[12]

At any other time Tochuck would have been correct. But only a few weeks after this request was made, the Guards gathered their own weapons and mustered in response to reports that Brulé raiders were bearing down on western Nebraska. On December 20 news of a horse raid raced across the county as several ranchers reported having lost horses to a raiding party. The Guards gathered several dozen of their members and deployed that evening. Two days later they caught up with the thieves and engaged them in a firefight, killing one suspect and wounding another. The Guards got their horses back, however, as well as a few that did not originally belong to them. They took the spoils back to North Platte.[13]

Ranchers who could not join Bratt's militia or who were otherwise unable to call up an army of ranch hands also had access to these institutions. Helen Randall, a woman who owned a large ranch and employed a handful of men, could do neither as one of the victims of the raid. An important rancher in her own right, Helen Randall had moved west in 1872, after her husband, former Wisconsin governor Alexander Randall, died. Upon arriving in Nebraska she purchased a cattle ranch near North Platte. According to the 1880 agricultural census, her business was successful—she owned over 800 head of cattle and 45 horses on nine hundred acres of land and sold 184 head to livestock buyers. The estimated value of her farm was over $45,000, making it one of the most valuable ranches in the region. By comparison, noted rancher Morrell C. Keith's ranch was worth about $65,000, and Buffalo Bill Cody's ranch was valued at just over $11,000.[14] In addition to raising cattle, Randall was also responsible for bringing up several orphan girls whom she fostered. She continued to run the ranch by herself until at least 1885, when she remarried and moved into a house in North Platte. At the time of the raid Randall owned more than four times as many horses as the leader of the expedition, Major Leicester Walker. When the North Platte Guards set out to recover her horses, Randall did not accompany them. Her employees apparently stayed behind as well, as Bratt makes no mention of her herders until the end of his narrative, when upon returning Randall's stolen horses, "her man at the ranch" complained that the halters were missing. It is unclear why none of her workers joined the expedition, though one possible reason was so that they could stay behind to protect her and her property in case of another attack. Bratt and other local ranchers respected Randall and her operation enough to go after her horses and return them upon recovery. And at least one member of the party would in time become very close to Randall: William C. Ritner, a marble worker, who would eventually become her husband.[15]

The Guards' fateful encounter seems unlikely in retrospect. Their formation was ill-timed with respect to the historical trajectory of the Plains Indian Wars and their impact on Lincoln County. Yet their creation was also a sign of the region's population growth and the treasure trove of wealth created in and from area ranches, railroads, and homesteads. Before 1875, when the threat of raiding was substantially higher, locals benefited from the army's peacekeeping enforcement policies, which greatly reduced the number of raids in the region by turning allied Plains Indian bands into informers and by systematically patrolling the region. There were also fewer people in the area, which justified the army's presence in the region. With the arrival of homesteaders and the urbanization of North Platte, however, the perceived need to keep peace in the region subsided as policy makers and army officers decided that settlement was thick enough in the area that a well-armed, semi-disciplined, and vigilant citizenry could prevent raids.

When reports of Brulé raiders entering northern Nebraska and Dull Knife's bloody march through northwestern Kansas reached the Platte, a perfect storm threatened to inundate the Platte Valley. With so much property and so many lives at stake, and with the military unable to lend aid to such a well-settled area, the members of the North Platte Guards mimicked the kind of protection they would have gladly accepted from a now mostly powerless Fort McPherson just four years earlier. Unfortunately, the militia also lacked the broader vision of events held by many of the officers on the ground at the fort. The army could choose who to attack and when to do it since for most of the period after 1865 the garrison owed its earthly existence to the overwhelming resources, logistics, and manpower of the Union army, rather than to the whims of its enemies. The North Platte Guards, caught between a war and a wilderness, had no such assurances for their long-term safety, and they responded as if backed into a corner. Help did not come in time to save those thirty settlers killed in Kansas, and

WHEN HORSE THIEVES WERE HANGED

from the militia members' perspective, there was no guarantee that it would come for them either.

Even as locals hesitated to organize a militia against American Indian horse raiders, their fears of criminal activity had motivated North Platters to organize a vigilance committee much earlier. In 1870 North Platte was still a very young settlement. Lincoln County had only been established three years earlier, and the railroad had barely started to facilitate the town's growth. By that time the town was protected by a county sheriff and a small army garrison but not by much else. In spite of the settlement's diminutive size, it seemed to attract a disproportionate share of the criminal element that came through on the railroad as well as thieves who were after livestock.[16] As a result, like many other "frontier" towns, North Platte was briefly the scene of a small vigilante movement. Toward the end of 1869, according to Adamson, North Platte's "leading citizens" formed a vigilance committee. At first the committee resorted to threats in an attempt to get tramps and suspected thieves to leave town. "Undesirables . . . were notified by a letter containing a skull and cross bones," wrote Adamson, "and a piece of rope with a noose." The postmaster, who reportedly delivered several such letters, recalled that the recipients usually left town in a hurry.[17]

Unfortunately, the committee's actions did not stop there. In February 1870 North Platters lynched two suspected thieves. The incident occurred after two burglaries took place on the same day: two men robbed a section foreman at gunpoint, and later someone robbed the McLucas jewelry store. Soon two suspects were arrested near the railroad bridge. When their home was searched, authorities found the loot under the house, and evidence of the two men's involvement in a gang of thieves implicated them even further. Before deciding to lynch the men, a crowd gathered and hunted for a possible accomplice. They found one, interrogated him, exacted a confession, and hanged him by the railroad bridge. Then they grabbed the two prisoners. One escaped, but the other one was not so lucky. Adamson claimed that the man "who placed the rope round the neck of one of the victims, [still] lives, and [he] bitterly regrets that he got mixed up in this disgraceful affair." But the damage had been done. Lynching is a one-way ticket.[18]

The vigilante impulse in Lincoln County was not confined solely to property crime. On April 9, 1871, Kate Manning was murdered. Her brother, Peter Manning, became the prime suspect. He reportedly wanted his sister's land claim and murdered her to acquire it. The sheriff arrested him and temporarily put Manning up in his home. Meanwhile, in North Platte an angry crowd assembled, demanding the suspect's immediate release. They then marched to the jail to claim the prisoner. Once they arrived, however, the sheriff was away on business. Instead, his wife appeared. In spite of the crowd's protestations, she stood her ground, refused to let the crowd enter, and told the leader of the mob that she did not approve of a lynching. Once the sheriff returned home, he hired a guard to protect the prisoner, and the group continued to harass the sheriff outside his home for protecting a murderer. They besieged the jail for several days. However, the sheriff outsmarted the mob by dressing Manning in a soldier's outfit and then marching him out with the other guards when they were relieved. The ruse worked, and the sheriff moved Manning to Fort McPherson to be guarded there. Later, when the mob sent a committee to the fort to demand the prisoner's release, the commander gave them ten minutes to leave the reservation. Once the excitement died down, the sheriff sent Manning to the prison in Hall County.[19]

Sidney, located about 123 miles west of North Platte on the Union Pacific, is perhaps better known for its rough-and-tumble history. By 1880 the town had earned a reputation as one of the most dangerous stops along the railroad, owing in large part to local thieves and robbers who held up passengers as they tried to exit the train for a meal and a drink. By early 1881 passenger trains began flying through the town without stopping and with locked doors. During the town's early years the city's original "Boot Hill" cemetery collected over 211 bodies, which a government contractor later discovered while attempting to excavate the remains of 21 soldiers buried there in 1922. Although most of the residents had died of natural causes—

typhoid, pneumonia, and consumption were some of the most common culprits—a handful of men were either murdered, lynched, or killed by police. For example, in response to the town's growing criminal dangers, approximately 200 residents, calling themselves "Regulators," began posting notices across town warning "ALL MURDERERS, THIEVES, PIMPS AND SLEEK FINGERED 'GENTLEMEN'" to leave town at once. With the help of a phalanx of Union Pacific detectives, Sidneyites began cleaning the town of its criminal element. One of the most notorious lawbreakers , gambler and suspected gang leader Jack McDonald, disregarded the notices and threatened to destroy the city. The Regulators responded by hanging him from a telegraph pole on April 3, 1881. Before that, Sidneyites lynched two other men, both of whom were suspected of murder—one in 1875 and another in 1879.[20]

Perhaps the largest outbreak of vigilante activity in the state occurred in the Niobrara River region east of Cherry County. Despite the region's duly constituted law enforcement and judicial institutions, three different vigilante organizations—the Niobrara Mutual Protective Association, the Farmers' Protective Association, and the Holt County Regulators—killed at least seven men in response to various crimes. All were suspected of stealing horses, cattle, or in the case of Holt County treasurer Barrett Scott, public funds. Kid Wade is undoubtedly the most famous victim of the Niobrara vigilantes, having once ridden with Doc Middleton's gang in the late 1870s. After leaving the gang and serving a brief prison sentence in Iowa, Wade returned to the Niobrara region to live with his father, John Wade, on his homestead claim. Before long, however, Wade returned to the horse-stealing business and stole several animals in the area. Believing the father and son to be in cahoots, local vigilantes shot John Wade on November 10, 1883, after kidnapping him during his arraignment on charges of aiding horse thieves. John's disappearance forced Kid Wade into hiding, but by January the vigilantes had tracked him down. After the vigilantes paraded the horse thief around the region like a trophy bass before hundreds of gawking settlers, the Holt County sheriff forced the group to turn the prisoner over for legal due process. On February 6, 1884, however, the vigilantes returned and forced the sheriff to release Wade from his custody at gunpoint. They hanged him that night. One other suspected horse thief, Kit Murphy, was hanged in nearby Keya Paha County in November 1883, the same month when John Wade was shot.[21]

The Niobrara Valley vigilance committees' killings represented about 12 percent of Nebraska's fifty-eight documented lynchings between 1859 and 1919. More significantly, Niobrara Valley residents killed three of the nine men lynched across Nebraska for allegedly stealing horses. Of the remaining six, three were killed in the late 1850s, before Nebraska became a state. In 1858 one man was hanged in Richardson County, near the Kansas border, while in January the following year two others met their end near Omaha. The other three men were hanged during the dual horse-stealing crises of the mid- to late 1870s: in 1874 Richardson County residents killed their second accused horse thief, and in May 1879 two more were hanged in Furnas County. Although the latter jurisdiction is only about seventy-five miles south-southeast of Lincoln County in the Republican River valley, the crowd there also charged the pair with assault and breaking out of jail.[22]

The common assumption that horse thieves were hanged contains a deadly kernel of truth, as evidenced by the nine people who died for allegedly committing that crime. However, the death toll needs to be contextualized. For one, the number of suspected horse thieves who were lynched across the state is dwarfed by the number who were legally charged, indicted, tried, convicted, and sentenced for their crimes. Between 1867 and 1890 thirty-four suspects received criminal warrants for horse stealing in Lincoln County alone, while Dawes County charged sixteen more. None of these suspects were killed before, during, or after their cases were heard in court. During the same period twenty-four inmates convicted of horse theft in western Nebraska—nearly three times the number who were lynched for that crime statewide—submitted applications to the parole board for early release in hopes of restarting their lives.[23]

WHEN HORSE THIEVES WERE HANGED

The historical preoccupation with hanged horse thieves across the state also obscures a more devastating legacy in Nebraska's vigilante story: between 1878 and 1919 Nebraskans lynched five African Americans and two Mexicans. Even though blacks made up less than a percent of Nebraska's population, they comprised nearly a tenth of its lynchings. Nebraska's newspapers often echoed those of the Jim Crow South in portraying black men as brutes and rapists. Not surprisingly, two of the victims—George Smith and Will Brown—were accused of rape in Omaha and killed nearly twenty-eight years apart, in 1891 and 1919, respectively. Another man, Jerry White, was hanged in Valentine for allegedly assaulting a woman in 1887. In addition, mobs savagely beat Smith and Brown before hanging them, whereas none of the alleged horse thieves—all of whom were white—faced similar assaults. Comparative murder conviction rates in Douglas County (where Omaha is located) tell a similar story: 85 percent of black defendants were convicted of murder in that jurisdiction, versus 34 percent of whites, which suggests that racial bias was just as present in the courtroom as it was outside. Of the two Mexicans who were lynched, Luciano Padillo was accused of rape and hanged by a mob in 1884, while in 1915 vigilantes shot Juan Gonzalez near Scribner for allegedly killing a policeman. And while it was not a lynching, Doc Middleton gang member Jack Nolan murdered José Valdez in 1879 for being "a s—n of a b— of a Mexican." Although both men were in a Sidney brothel, Nolan took offense at Valdez occupying the same room as a white prostitute.[24] Because of these racially motivated killings, it was far more dangerous to be a person of color in Nebraska than it was to be a horse thief.

Nebraska's bloody vigilante past does not compete with some of the more sensational examples of extralegal violence elsewhere, many of which have done more to fuel the narrative that horse thieves were routinely hanged. One of these examples can be found in Montana, where Stuart Granville's Stranglers, acting on behalf of the recently constituted Montana Stock Growers' Association, hanged dozens of men according to one historian. "After each execution," notes Christopher Knowlton, "they pinned a card to the dead man's chest that read HORSE THIEF or CATTLE THIEF." Even though the men acted in secret, the corpses and the pinned notes had a habit of being discovered. Word soon spread of the fates of these men and of the violence exhibited by their pursuers.[25] The signature chest cards used by Stuart's Stranglers and others would soon assume a bizarre memetic importance during both the height of the Jim Crow era and the heyday of the TV and movie Western, with similar cards appearing on the chests of lynched African American men and fictional Western villains. While these flashes of memory and call signs to mortality did not appear as frequently in Nebraska, they certainly resonated far beyond Montana.

While historians continue the necessary if macabre labor of counting those killed by vigilante activities, it is impossible to enumerate the number of lynchings that were prevented at the last moment, either by persuasion or by violent threats in kind. According to Harold Cook, a deserter from Fort Meade was almost hanged after he stole a mare from his Uncle Jack, who lived in a shack on the Niobrara River. After escaping the post, the authorities caught the deserter and jailed him, whereupon the soldier fled once again. After traveling to Harrison by foot and coming upon Uncle Jack's shack, the surprised host invited the deserter inside for dinner. As they ate supper together, during which time Jack noticed that "the man's pants were covered with horse hair" and having already learned of his escape from jail, "[he] put two and two together." In addition, Jack "also knew—as everyone else did in those days—that a man never walked unless there was some unusual reason for it." Jack invited his guest to stay the night, and after breakfast the following morning, he produced a gun and ordered the thief to accompany him to the 04 Ranch, where the sheriff would collect the prisoner. As they waited for the law to arrive, a group of men arrived at the jail and demanded the prisoner's release. The posse, "looking for excitement . . . Announced they were going to hang the horse thief." James Cook stood his ground, however, and his son Harold recalled him shouting:

"You won't hang any man here. This is my home." The rancher threatened to shoot the first vigilante to enter his home, and the posse soon retreated. Cook then offered the deserter a horse to ride so that he could go and collect his stolen mare, which he had abandoned on the river nearby. Accompanied by Patricio, a vaquero in Cook's employ, the prisoner collected the mare and returned to Harrison with the stolen horse.[26]

"Vigilance" did not always entail "vigilantism," and a watchful eye on one's property did not necessarily lead to extralegal justice. But civilians did assist law enforcement from time to time. On occasion a victim caught a horse thief in the act, sometimes chasing and apprehending the thief him- or herself. Since law enforcement and even neighbors were too far away to get word of and respond quickly to an emergency, when horse owners caught thieves in the act, they usually had no choice but to take care of the situation themselves. When Peter Wesselgarter attempted to steal several mules from Cain Brunt near North Platte in 1878, Brunt and his brother hopped on their horses and chased the thief down. They caught up with him near Fox Creek and brought him to town. The Brunts turned him over to the authorities, and a jury later convicted Wesselgarter of horse stealing.[27] Citizens who could not make the chase found other ways to contribute to the apprehension of horse thieves, such as advertising rewards for stolen cattle and horses in local newspapers. B. A. Sheidley and Brothers published an announcement in the *Western Nebraskian*, offering fifty dollars for any information about stolen horses or cattle that displayed any of their brands. In addition, stockmen associations and other groups of cattlemen frequently published illustrated "brands and awards" columns in local newspapers. They featured pictures of cows branded with each outfit's symbol, along with the ranch's name, thus allowing anyone who encountered a stolen cow with the legal owner's brand to turn the animal's thief in for a reward.[28]

Settlers' threats of extralegal justice for less severe infractions amplified horse stealing's comparative severity. One of the worst non-larceny offenses was fence cutting, which occurred whenever cowboys decided to ignore a homesteader's property claim by cutting a fence and moving his or her cattle across the homestead without the claimant's permission. After catching a group of cowboys cutting their way across his property, James Cook issued a stern warning: "You were lucky to run into a group of peaceful citizens up here. Some of the settlers east of here are rough . . . For your own good, I would advise you not to cut fences down the river, or you might run into somebody that's quick tempered, and you just might get hurt." Vigilante rhetoric targeted white-collar wrongdoers as well, especially those who had breached the public's trust. In 1895 a correspondent to the *Omaha Bee* lamented the latest scandal raging in Illinois, arguing that "sooner or later the people will have to settle with recreant representatives as they used to do with horse thieves and highwaymen." Only "when legislative bribery is made high treason and punishable as a capital crime we may possibly be able to eradicate the cancer that is eating out the vitals of the republic." But perhaps the most famous (and cutting) political comparison belonged to Horace Greeley, who once quipped that "all Democrats are not horse thieves, but all horse thieves are Democrats."[29]

The mere possibility of vigilantism loomed large as part of the public discourse against horse stealing and other forms of property crime. Calls for the use of violent retribution against horse thieves recalled what had already become a mythologized past of righteous violence in the region. As late as 1890, the *Lincoln County Tribune* took note of the apparent rise in horse stealing over the previous several months and suggested that an "old" course of action be taken in dealing with the crime wave. The fact that this call was made at all shows that the prospect was not far from people's minds. Some people even acted on this suggestion, as when H. M. Slack "sent several load of shot" at a thief he caught stealing a horse from his stable.[30] No vigilance movement appeared after this announcement, but vigilante reports from elsewhere were treated with editorial approval, as when a group of ranchers in Red Willow County dispensed "the old system of giving horse thieves justice" to three suspects. Another article reported on the fate of two horse thieves who "were well known" to Lincoln County: James Smith and Fred Ferguson. Both "paid the penalty of their crimes" when they were caught and murdered in Furnas County after allegedly killing a local farmer, "thus visiting quick and summary vengeance upon the notorious horse thieves and desperados." While there is evidence to suggest that both Smith and Ferguson were hanged for some combination of assault, murder, jailbreaking, and horse stealing, no such record exists of anyone being hanged in Red Willow County. Sometimes newspapers threatened even petty thieves with vigilante action. One article claimed that if a local coal thief were to "wake up some morning and find half a pound of bird shot around under his infernal hole, he will have no one to blame but himself." And the *Tribune* warned that "if this horse stealing business continues it would be well for the citizens to organize a society known as vigilantes." The sheriff amplified the sense of urgency by posting reward notices in the county papers during the late 1880s, offering fifty-dollar rewards to anyone offering any information in a case involving horse theft.[31]

By 1890 homesteaders played a major role in local governance. Even when a rancher such as John Bratt was elected mayor of North Platte in the late 1890s, he could only attain that office by appealing to the vast majority of the county's voters: railroad workers, ranch hands, businesspeople, and homesteaders. The cattle barony ceased to exist outside of places like Wyoming, and even there settlers decisively challenged the ranchers' authority during the Johnson County War. The police and the sheriff in the county were thus better suited to defend everyone and all property in the county, rather than the people with the most property. Also, policing in general was more efficient, thanks to the proliferation of counties that now surrounded Lincoln and to which the sheriff could telegraph descriptions of horse thieves before they could even manage to leave the county.

Despite law enforcement's growing powers, the perceived inefficiencies in county policing and the public's concern that there was little they could proactively do to prevent horse theft in a now-crowded county contributed to the continued rhetorical importance of vigilantism. Residents anxious about the possibility of their horses being stolen by thieves who could quickly fence their property and be on a train out of state communicated these fears by alluding to vigilantism. There was no social safety net to catch the victimized homesteader, and so the law— and violence outside of the law—became the only means of protecting oneself against economic disaster at the hands of a thief. That these threats were not actualized in the West against thieves as frequently as they were against African Americans in the southern states does not mean that the threat of violence itself did not hang ominously over the region like a bank of thunderclouds over a darkening horizon. Vigilantism's real power, like the power that whites wielded like a cudgel in the South (or in Omaha, for that matter), lay in how it influenced and affected those people who were not immediately destroyed by it.[32] In towns throughout Nebraska, especially those in the Niobrara Valley, vigilantism was a stark reality for many property criminals, including horse thieves.[33] But even in places like western Nebraska, where no one was hanged for horse stealing, the thought of doing so often entered people's minds.

The Horse Thief's Last Ride

The impulse to hang horse thieves has long outlived the crime itself. Horse stealing declined dramatically during the 1890s, and within twenty years the practice had begun to fade from public view as more Nebraskans bought gas-powered vehicles and tractors. While official statewide statistics do not exist, the state of Nebraska's register of prisoners from western Nebraska who applied for parole board between 1870 and 1990 provides the baseline data necessary to track the crime's statistical decline (fig. 26). For instance, about 5.2 percent of parole applicants between 1870 and 1891 served time for stealing horses. By comparison, from 1870 through 1891 a nearly equal number of western Nebraskan applicants (23) sought parole for burglary convictions. Assuming that prisoners convicted of various prop-

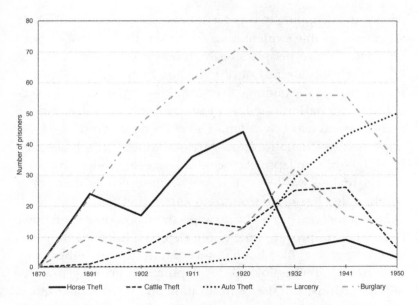

Fig. 26. Number of convicted horse thieves versus other property criminals applying for parole in western Nebraska, 1870–1950. Nebraska Prisoner Records Database, NSHS. Created by the author.

erty crimes sought parole at roughly the same rate, the number of burglars versus horse thieves began to change after 1890, when 47 burglars, representing about 16 percent of the prison population, applied for parole between 1891 and 1902. During that period the proportion of horse thieves increased only slightly, to 5.8 percent, with 17 prisoners seeking early release out of 292 total applicants.[34] In other words, burglaries rose dramatically, while horse thefts decreased slightly in terms of absolute numbers. People were still robbing and stealing, but their targets changed from horses to smaller, more portable, and easily concealable pieces of property.

Although the most dangerous period of horse stealing peaked during the late 1870s, over half of western Nebraska's parole-seeking horse thieves were arrested later, during the first two decades of the twentieth century. More than 13 percent of parole applicants between 1902 and 1911 were horse thieves, with the proportion dropping to 11 percent between 1911 and 1920. There are a few possible explanations for this, with the most obvious being that more people simply stole more horses. However, horse theft was already on the decline by 1900. The Panic of 1893 realigned the national livestock economy, severely depressing demand nationwide for horses and further restricting the cash necessary to buy them. The collapse of credit and the implosion of the nation's overstressed money supply resulted in a large-scale collapse of prices for horses and other livestock. Horse stealing was less profitable because horses themselves commanded less money on the open market.[35]

Law enforcement's ability to apprehend and prosecute horse thieves also improved, which both deterred horse stealing and ensured a greater likelihood of successfully capturing those who stole horses. Technological development, a growing number of jurisdictions, and the centralization and professionalization of law enforcement reshaped sheriffs' departments throughout the region. By 1900 sheriffs had new tools at their disposal, including telephones and better means of identifying suspects. Older, larger counties split into smaller, more manageable ones; these new jurisdictions established more sheriffs' departments to patrol them. Growing populations also meant larger tax bases. Most important, sheriffs and their deputies professionalized and modernized their departments. After 1900 voters expected new sheriffs to have law enforcement experience, and as the technology available to law enforcement agencies evolved, so, too, did the amount of training necessary to effectively use it.[36]

Meanwhile, other civic improvements, including the installation of streetlamps and the proliferation of telephones, further complicated efforts to steal horses in the dead of night and without anyone discovering the crime for several hours afterward. For instance, North Platters had telephone service by 1896, and the municipal government ordered the first electric streetlamps in 1899. While linking growing horse thief prison populations to better law enforcement can be problematic, these decades coincide with a similar explosion in prisoners convicted of burglary. Between 1902 and 1911 nearly 25 percent of parole appli-

WHEN HORSE THIEVES WERE HANGED

cants were sent to prison on burglary charges, suggesting that either improved lighting, telephones, or professional police services led to more burglar apprehensions or that houses were unusually attractive targets for theft during this period.[37]

Shifting commodity landscapes and improved law enforcement both had a pronounced effect on overall rates of horse stealing, but these paled in comparison to the impact of horse replacement technology. The internal combustion engine provided more than just the final nail in the equine economy's coffin—it supplied the hammers, most of the pine, and a host of willing pallbearers. The public's fascination with motor vehicles increased during the mid-1890s with newspaper and magazine reports of car races in Europe. On May 26, 1896, the *Valentine Democrat* notified Nebraskans that they would be able to view a horseless carriage in person at the upcoming Sioux City Fair, and the Nebraska State Fair in Omaha the following year featured a daily race between a motor vehicle and "the fastest horse on the grounds." Within a few years automobiles were common enough that residents in many towns had gotten a closer look at them, whether they wanted to or not. "Captain Corbin recreates now-a-days in his horseless carriage," the *Alliance Herald* announced in 1902. "And when he whirls through the streets at the rate of ninety miles per hour—more or less—pedestrians hug the fronts of the buildings, with eyes peeled for an open door." Within a decade the town of Alliance had its own car dealer, Lowry & Henry, which sold Fords and Studebakers in addition to servicing motor vehicles in its garage. Rather than urging its readers to dive for cover, the *Herald* instead suggested they move fast to take advantage of the firm's new shipment of 1913 Ford touring cars, which were "selling like hot cakes."[38]

By the 1920s, as farmers purchased cars of their own and their children moved to cities to find work, the legal, military, and cultural significance of horse stealing almost disappeared. The overall number of horse-stealing convictions in western Nebraska reflected this shift: between 1920 and 1926 only 3 out of 288 parole applicants appealed for early release for prior horse-stealing convictions, and only 15 out of 1,873 early-release candidates between 1926 and 1950 had stolen horses, compared to 109 burglars. While horses have been and continue to be stolen from ranches, farms, breeders, and others through the present day, these concerns rarely echo outside of those communities of horse owners and riders who continue to purchase, care for, depend on, and love their equine friends. In its place the more urban and modern specter of car theft has captured the fear and imagination of most Americans. Between 1926 and 1950, 103 parole applicants from western Nebraska were in prison for auto theft, and over 400 more convicted car thieves applied between 1950 and 1990. To date, the crime has inspired count-less movies, an entire industry of car alarms and other anti-theft gadgetry, and even a popular video game franchise, *Grand Theft Auto.* Much of the latter's gameplay revolves around carjacking unsuspecting drivers, taking their vehicles to body shops, and either customizing them or using them to commit additional crimes. Meanwhile, terms such as *drive-by shooting* and *carjacking* have entered America's real-life vernacular, becoming terrify-ing crimes in their own right, with far more dangerous conse-quences for the personal safety of their victims.

Vox Populi

In spite of horse theft's declining phenomenological influence, the severity of the crime looms large in historical memory. In fact, for what little historians know about horse stealing as a cross-cultural, transnational, and economically deterministic phenomenon, most people seem to have an opinion on the sub-ject. Pronouncements on the frequency of horse stealing (it hap-pened all the time) and the fate of those convicted of it (they were hanged) are common in historical texts, popular culture, and the collective historical imagination. Most Americans prob-ably would have agreed with one editor's assessment in 1908: "When [horse thieves were] caught the rope cure was admin-istered and a second treatment was never found necessary."[39]

Newspaper mentions of the crime help trace the historical shouts and sounds of horse theft as they echo through an increas-ingly motor vehicle–dominated landscape. In the early 1890s

Nebraska papers breathlessly reported on horse thief hangings in Oklahoma, Tennessee, and elsewhere with dire headlines, including "To Lynch Murderous Horse Thieves" and "HORSE THIEVES HANGED" printed in extra-large letters. By the turn of the century, however, horse stealing had lost some of its editorial urgency. In 1907 the *Omaha Daily Bee* was ready to write the crime's epitaph. "Out in this country the horse thief is about as extinct as the dodo and the great awk," claimed one editorial. "The horse thief saw his finish and left the West for the more attractive field in New York," which had reportedly become a hotbed for horse stealing in part due to the absence of vigilante activity there. The following year the same newspaper published an article entitled "Silence Followed Duty" in its women's section. The story describes how a Mount Pleasant, Kansas, "committee" pursued and "disposed" of a band of horse thieves. Without explicitly mentioning their fate, the paper instead noted that "all questions as to what [the committee] did with the thieves were met with silence." Meanwhile, columnist Allan D. May nostalgically recalled the days when cattlemen murdered horse thieves; he described a gun shop whose owner fixed old firearms and a man who brought in a broken shotgun that must have been old enough to "shoot geese in Canada, alligators in Florida, Indians in Nebraska, and horse thieves in Wyoming."[40]

By 1917, as the United States mobilized to enter a Great War being fought with tanks and airplanes in Europe, Americans back home increasingly complained about car thieves. The *Alliance Herald* argued that "stealing automobiles seems to be a much more profitable risk than stealing horses." One reason was that horse thieves, unlike their modern counterparts, were "promptly suspended from the nearest tree." Technology, however, remained the biggest factor. "The great difficulty in detecting this form of crime is that the machines can be taken to distant states, where they are sold to dealers without difficulty." Later, in 1921, horse stealing was a light enough subject that the Box Butte county commissioners joked to a *Herald* reporter that since there was so little to report on for that day's meeting, he should go ahead and write that the commissioners were all horse thieves: "No, don't say that—it isn't exactly true. Say that we have been stealing horses all winter, but since the bottom dropped out of the horse market, we've quit. There isn't any profit in stealing horses any more. In fact, the price of hay is so high that as soon as the grazing season is over we may have to take some of 'em back because we can't feed them."[41]

As the 1920s roared with the growl of gasoline engines, horse stealing became the punch line to a joke. But in the years following Black Tuesday and the 1929 Wall Street crash, pioneer reminiscences reinforced both the apologetics behind and the supposed ubiquity of horse thief hangings. For commentators living in an age of scarcity, horse stealing was no laughing matter. "In the early history of Lexington, Nebraska, as in all western states," according to Benjamin Krier, a newspaper editor in Dawson County, "there was no crime committed more reprehensible than that of stealing a horse. One might kill a man and it would be overlooked or excused, but the offense of stealing a horse was a crime that nothing could atone for but the 'wiping out' of the thief." In fact, the crime was so severe that "it mattered but little to whom the horse belonged or whether the owner was present to take a hand in the execution. The culprit was dealt with in such manner that he never stole another animal." Krier later recalled how two Pawnees accused a lone "half-breed Sioux," who had stopped in town for a meal, of stealing their horse, causing the traveler to be brought before the local justice of the peace. After a brief, informal trial, the justice summarily sentenced the alleged thief to hang, prompting one of the observers to point out that "as we are now organized into a county and have to go by law, you can't sentence a man to hang fer stealin' a hoss." After a moment's reflection, the judge rescinded the original sentence and ordered the suspect to leave the state "within fifteen minutes."[42]

Historians of the Wild West continued to assert horse theft's lethality in their works. In a 1933 issue of *Nebraska History Magazine*, Olive Gass discussed "the Vigilantes" of Cass County, located along the Missouri River in the eastern part of the state.

WHEN HORSE THIEVES WERE HANGED

The organization, composed of approximately three hundred justice-seeking men, attacked claim jumpers and other criminals. However, they apparently saved most of their energy for horse thieves. When Sheriff Perry Gass, the father of the article's author, arrested blacksmith Jim Tibbits and a lawyer named "Hunt" near Plattsmouth, he and Judge Jim Doom determined to prosecute the pair legally, despite the Vigilantes' calls for a hanging. Doom eloquently defended the legal process, and the Vigilantes relented, while the accused were convicted and subsequently sent to jail. Soon after their arrival, however, they escaped and began stealing horses again. This time the Vigilantes and other roused civilians cornered the pair of thieves and lynched them. "A horse thief in those days, you know, was despised as much or even more than a murderer," recalled Gass. She defended her father's membership in the Vigilantes organization, despite his reluctance to hang Tibbits and Hunt. "We see the founding of these . . . [vigilance] Committees as self-defense," she argued. "Unless the settlers used drastic measures in dealing with claim jumpers and horse thieves, they might as well give up their claims and their visions of independent, happy homes in the west and return to the east from whence they came."[43]

Not all chroniclers of Nebraska history believe that vigilantes had the public's best interests at heart, however. In *Old Jules*— Mari Sandoz's 1935 classic and widely beloved biography of her father, Jules Sandoz, a settler on the Sandhills in Sheridan County—the author minces no words about the Niobrara vigilantes. "They took Kid Wade from the sheriff at Bassett only a month ago," Sandoz wrote. "Hung him to a telegraph pole and sold the rope at fifty cents an inch. They said he was a horse thief. That dodge always worked." Later many of the vigilantes themselves ended up in jail, having been "charged with doing considerable horse stealing on the side."[44]

Surprisingly, Hollywood filmmakers were less likely to sensationalize horse thieves than local and regional historians were. In general, the Western genre immortalized relatively few individuals known primarily for stealing horses. Horse thieves wore many hats, and some murdered as well as stole. But people feared horse thieves who did not murder less than murderers who did not steal, and confrontations with horse thieves who could not defend themselves with lethal violence did not inspire the same kind of climactic, narrative tension as a murderer facing off against the hero. Thus, the smug, exciting gunfighter, rather than the sly and clever bandit, morphed into the archetype of western criminality.[45] However, there were some exceptions, including Laramie Nelson (played by Buster Crabbe), who transforms from a falsely accused horse thief who is nearly hanged to a ranch hand who discovers and tracks down a gang of actual horse thieves in *The Arizona Raiders* (1936). One of the film's promotional posters prominently shows a noose, with images of three characters—labeled "Killer," "Horsethief," and "Murderer," respectively—pasted over it. The horse thief's head comes closest to the center of the noose. After the war "King of the Cowboys" Roy Rogers chased a gang of horse thieves who had horse-napped his famous equestrian pal and costar, Trigger, in the 1948 classic film *Under California Stars*.

In some ways horse thieves were better suited as heroes than as villains, especially when they were depicted as antihero characters facing off against vigilante strongmen antagonists. In the 1940s film *The Westerner*, Cole Harden (played by Gary Cooper) is caught stealing a horse belonging to one of "Judge" Roy Bean's associates. Harden is able to escape the hangman's noose by leveraging the judge's infatuation with an English actress. He later becomes a sheriff, uses the actress to lure the judge into a theater, and then kills him in a shootout. Decades later *The Missouri Breaks* followed a gang of horse thieves whose efforts to establish a relay ranch for disposing of rustled animals are harried by Robert E. Lee Clayton, a flamboyant regulator played by Marlon Brando. The film begins with David Braxton, a local cattle baron, and his chief enforcer leading a member of the horse-stealing gang to a festive party in a grassy meadow, where a rope slung over a cottonwood tree awaits him. Later, after Braxton finds his chief lieutenant hanged from the same tree as the rustler, he hires Lee to finish the job and kill the remaining horse thieves. Apart from a brief encounter with some Canadian Mounties, little mention is made of duly constituted law enforcement. Although Braxton had the time, money, and wherewithal to haul thirty-five hundred books up the Missouri and across the prairie to his ranch library, he and his community peers never bothered to appoint an effective sheriff.

Filmmakers preferred to present gunfighters, gangs, cattle barons, and renegade sheriffs as primary characters over horse thieves, but serialized television writers could afford to play with different kinds of career criminals. *Gunsmoke,* one of the most successful and influential American television dramas ever produced, featured at least a dozen episodes dealing with horse thieves. Throughout the series many of the characters imply that horse stealing is a capital crime in Kansas, even though Marshal Matt Dillon clearly believes that thieves will go to jail for their crime, not to their deaths. Nonetheless, while the viewer is led to believe that Dillon does not enjoy hangings and certainly would never condone extralegal justice, vigilante violence frequently stalks those accused of horse stealing in the series. When a pair of thieves frames half-Comanche blacksmith Quint Asper (played by Burt Reynolds) for stealing a settler's horse, the town turns on him. One night a gang of eight men breaks into his shop and beats him unconscious. Although Dillon blames the attack on drifters and is careful not to implicate anyone living in Dodge City, at several points during the episode, the townspeople suggest that they kill the "half-breed horse thief."

One *Gunsmoke* episode in particular, "Lynching Man," serves as a manifesto on the moral superiority of law and order when faced with popular vigilante impulses as well as a historiographical document arguing for the widespread acceptance of vigilantism. The episode begins when two cowboys come across Hank Blemis, a "green" would-be homesteader from Ohio, and they hang him above his campsite and steal his horse. When Dillon discovers the body, he assumes that Blemis was a horse thief who had been lynched for his crime. Later Charlie Gray, a stockman, approaches Dillon in Miss Kitty's bar and gives the marshal information on a man named Hank Mather, whose horses were recently stolen. Gray, motivated by his own father's lynching when he was a child, demands that Dillon bring the murderer to justice, or else (remarkably and without any irony) he will bring the man to justice himself. In the next scene Dillon rides out to the suspect's ranch to confront him. When Dillon asks Mather if he knows who stole his horses, Mather replies, "If I knew, there'd be a man hanging from a limb somewhere." Dillon then explains that a suspected horse thief had been lynched nearby, and Mather declares his innocence while adding parenthetically, "Well, horse thieves have got to be hung, though."

The marshal returns to town without Mather, and the stockman returns to the bar, once again demanding action. He tries to rile up the patrons to "do something" about "the lynchers." Later that evening the two cowboys who murdered Blemis approach Gray and claim that they know who committed the crime. They offer to provide the information for one hundred dollars apiece, and then they leave with Gray, supposedly to confront the accused vigilante. Dillon soon realizes that Blemis was a farmer rather than a horse thief, and after receiving a report about suspicious activity at Mather's place, he and his partner, Curtis, ride over to check it out. There he and Curtis discover Gray, the two cowboys, Mather's body, and Blemis's stolen bay. Gray, realizing he was deceived, pulls his gun on the cowboys, who then shoot him down. When Gray exclaims with his dying breath that the cowboys were "dirty lynchers," Dillon replies, "What do you think you are?" Dillon later philosophizes with Curtis, telling him that sometimes "hate can twist [a man] until he doesn't know the truth anymore."

"Lynching Man" is more than a mere morality play about a rancher whose hatred turns him into the very same kind of monster he despises. It is an extended discourse between Dillon, Curtis, and Doc Adams, who all revile lynchings and extralegal hangings, and Gray and Mather, who both support vigilantism as a means of bringing justice when the law ostensibly does not move fast enough. Although law and order wins in the end, it does so in spite of the almost universal and matter-of-fact understanding among many horse owners that horse thieves "have got to be hung, though." Much like the series as a whole, this episode of *Gunsmoke* lionizes Dillon's efforts to monopolize violence in the name of the law, both by reserving for the courts (and, on an emergency basis, for himself) the right to mete out punishment to wrongdoers and, in the case of Gray's angry tirade about Dillon not moving fast enough, by accepting responsibility when the wheels of justice grind along at a snail's pace. Despite the show's proclivity to depict the plains surrounding Dodge City by filming its scenes in the mountains surrounding Los Angeles, *Gunsmoke* is right about one thing: legal and extralegal law enforcement often coexisted in the West, with the inadequacies of one serving as a sop for the other. Although horse thieves were certainly not lynched nearly as often as the show implies, *Gunsmoke* reflects the historical memory of horse stealing as an existentially destructive crime warranting extralegal punishment while also, in all likelihood, helping produce generations of fans who would make similar assumptions about horse theft and hangings in the old West.

While *Gunsmoke* frequently dealt with complex issues, the wildly popular 1989 miniseries *Lonesome Dove* explored horse stealing within an array of less-nuanced scenarios. It also frequently echoed the myth that horse thieves were usually hanged. The protagonists, retired Texas Rangers captain Gus McCrae and captain Woodrow F. Call (played by Robert Duvall and Tommy Lee Jones, respectively), rustle over twenty-five hundred horses and cattle from a ranch in Mexico and set out for Montana in hopes of finding some adventure and making a new start. As they begin heading north, Arkansas sheriff July Johnson pursues Jake Spoon, who is heading north separately with prostitute Lorie Wood. Shortly after July's departure, however, his deputy, Roscoe Brown, tries to track him down in order to tell him that his wife, Elmyra, has left him for her supposedly dead ex-lover, Dee Boot, in Ogallala. Brown is soon joined by Janey, a runaway girl, before being attacked by a pair of horse thieves, who bizarrely order him to strip off his clothes in addition to forfeiting his horse. Janey then throws rocks at the thieves, who try to shoot her. Fortunately, Sheriff Johnson is within earshot of the gunfire, and he rides up and rescues the pair.

Lonesome Dove also tells the story of how four horse thieves were hanged. Jake Spoon falls in with a new gang in Fort Worth, who invite him along to help them rob banks in Kansas. Spoon quickly realizes that his new gang is more interested in stealing horses. When Spoon tells the leader of the gang, Dan, that he does not recall them agreeing to take a pair of horses from a small group of men on the road, Dan replies, "What have you got against stealing horses?" "It don't happen to be my line of work, that's all," Spoon answered. The leader threatens to kill Spoon if he refuses to help and then forces Spoon to fire on the wranglers. The gang ambushes the men, killing all but one, who gets away in time to warn Captains McCrae and Call, who are with their herd nearby. Call and McCrae and two men set out to find the horse thieves. When Lorie protests, not wanting them to leave her by herself on the prairie, Call explains that "he can't let a horse thief off, particularly one that's killed a boy." The captains soon pick up the trail and discover the murdered wranglers. Not long after that they realize that Spoon was a member of the gang.

Meanwhile, Dan kills a couple of sodbusters, steals a watch, and—in a dramatic flourish perhaps inspired by Print Olive himself—forces his men to hang and burn the bodies. "Pretty sight, ain't it?" asks an exultant Dan. "Damn sodbusters!" When the outfit discovers the corpses, Call sighs: "That's a bad bunch we're after. Bad as I ever seen." Soon Captains McRae and Call, Deets, Pea, and Newt catch up with and surround the thieves by the side of the creek. Call orders Newt and Pea to bring their ropes over. Although Spoon protests, he and the others are tied up, and McCrae tells Jake he is going to hang with the others. After the other three are dispatched, McCrae tells Spoon he has found Lorie and that he is sorry "it's us that's got to do this, Jake." "Well, hell, boys," Spoon replied, "I'd rather be hung by my friends than a bunch of damn strangers." He apologized to his friends and then spurred his own horse out from under him. When they leave the four bodies hanging from the tree, they pinned a note on Dan's chest: "MAN BURNER AND HORSE THEEF."

Horse stealing drives much of the narrative action in *Lonesome Dove*. It constantly serves as a means to move its protagonists from one place to another as well as a rationale for its antagonists to behave badly. Moreover, the almost-always-lethal response to the crime throughout the series reinforces the idea that horse thieves were hanged. Even Jake Spoon, who obviously did not participate in the killing of five settlers and horse wranglers, does not escape his noose in the end. Horse stealing also motivates Blue Duck's plot to abduct Lorie, which consumes the second episode. He promises his gang an ownership interest in his captive in exchange for their horses and then tells them they can keep both the girl and the horses if they stay and kill Gus, who is in pursuit. Although Gus ends up killing the entire gang and rescuing Lorie, it comes at a price: Blue Duck murders Roscoe, Janey, and July's stepson, Joe (who was traveling along with the group), when the sheriff links up with Gus to take down the gang. Soon the whole setup is revealed to be a gambit for Blue Duck, who uses the opportunity to steal nearly everyone's horses. By the end of the series, hundreds of horses have been stolen and several people have been killed as a result. While hardly delicate in its discourse, *Lonesome Dove* at least conveys the idea that horse stealing was a pervasive, multifaceted problem, which it was.

American Indian raiding complicates horse stealing's historical memory even further since it often serves to help whites characterize indigenous culture as inherently brutish or, paradoxically, as pure and noble. In this way horse raiding is a sort of Rorschach test for modern Americans who can fit the practice into whatever biases or ideas they may already hold about Indians. In the 1990 Academy Award–winning film *Dances with Wolves*, for instance, horse raiding is probably the most controversial thing the Lakotas do, and even then it is such an innocent activity that three children attempt to take a cavalry horse while Lieutenant John J. Dunbar (played by Kevin Costner) is sleeping nearby. Although the raid goes south when Dunbar catches them in the act, causing one of the boys to fall off his pony, the escapade starts off as good, harmless fun. Not long after that a single adult Lakota, Kicking Bird (played by Graham Greene), casually walks up to and tries to steal the same horse while Dunbar is bathing. By contrast, when an unfriendly Pawnee war party finds Timmons, the freighter who delivered Dunbar to a mysteriously abandoned Fort Sedgwick, they murder and scalp him before stealing his wagon and mule team. Setting aside the movie's numerous historical inaccuracies (some of which are contradicted by portions of this book), the film uses horse stealing as a device to introduce Dunbar to the Lakota while simultaneously humanizing them, whereas the Pawnee raiders more appropriately fit Timmons's earlier characterization of Indians being "nothing but thieves and beggars."

Not surprisingly, literary and historical depictions of horse raids by native authors reveal a more complex interpretation of horse raiding. James Welch's 1986 novel *Fools Crow* begins with eighteen-year-old White Man's Dog joining Yellow Kidney's planned horse raid against the Crows, whose camp is located about a two-week walk away from their own band, the Lone Eaters of the Blackfeet. White Man's Dog laments not having already captured any horses of his own (his younger brother, at sixteen, had already captured two), and he hopes that his luck will change this time. Welch fully develops many of the characters out on the raid—the quiet and calm White Man's Dog, the headstrong and overconfident Fast Horse, and the aging Yellow Kidney, who struggles to manage the youthful zeal surrounding him. Once the party reaches the Crow herd, the raid has mixed success: White Man's Dog and the other adolescent warriors successfully steal 150 Crow ponies and lead them back to camp, while Yellow Kidney is captured trying to seize one of the prized buffalo-running horses kept apart from the main herd. Although Yellow Kidney is later discovered to have survived his capture (but not without being mutilated first by the Crows), after the rest of the party arrives at camp with the Crow pony herd, the people initially believe he has been killed. As Yellow Kidney's family mourns, White Man's Dog's parents are upset by the unsanctioned raid's mixed success but are visibly relieved by their eldest son's safe return.

Movies like *The Westerner* and *The Missouri Breaks* as well as television programs like *Gunsmoke* and novels like *Fool's Crow* confer a degree of moral ambiguity onto horse thieves. Contemporary Westerns, and pop culture in general, make it possible for a horse thief to be a sympathetic character. But once horse thieves were deprived of their unique status as bogeymen, they also ceased to be integral to modern understandings of the West. Outlaws in general, especially of the Clint Eastwood / Will Munny variety, can change, chameleonlike, in accordance with whatever circumstances the narrative sets forth. It does not matter if they are horse thieves, murderers, drunks, or inveterate gamblers like Doc Holliday in *Tombstone*.

Moreover, as Western films and television shows continued to evolve in parallel to decisive, generation-altering events like the Vietnam War, Watergate, and September 11, other character types—lawless sheriffs, evil land barons, and even unscrupulous district attorneys, such as Hedley Lamarr in *Blazing Saddles*—offered more flexibility and liminal ambivalence than the predictably bad horse thieves. And throughout, as the genre itself exploded into a globalized phenomenon—with Japanese anime Westerns like *Outlaw Star* and *Cowboy Bebop* emerging as cultural icons in their own right and South Korean filmmaker Kim Jee-woon remaking Italian director Sergio Leone's famous 1966 spaghetti Western *The Good, the Bad and the Ugly* and setting it in 1930s Manchuria (*The Good, the Bad, the Weird* of 2008)—horse thieves disappeared from relevance. After all, when producer and director Vince Gilligan paid homage to the Western genre in *Breaking Bad*'s final season, he dispatched iconic TV villain Walter White to rob a train as opposed to a stable. But one constant historical element about horse thieves has remained unchanged since the late nineteenth century. Like a faint echo, or the last ripple of a thrown stone after it hits a still pond, the belief that horse thieves were usually, summarily, and justifiably hanged continues to persist in the popular historical imagination.

References to horse thieves continue to appear in Western as well as non-Western movie, music, and literary genres. In Bone Thugs-n-Harmony's 1998 song "Ghetto Cowboy," for instance, the rapper Krayzie Bone narrates a tale of traveling west in search of a couple of banks to rob, when he is interrupted by a noise from a nearby bush. After threatening to let his shotgun "sing" into the shrubs, a woman reveals herself. When Krayzie Bone asks her who she is and why she is hiding, she responds that she is the Thug Queen Horse Stealer. "I'm wanted in four coun-teez, for armed robbery, killed two sheriffs, six of his best men wit' my hands," she claims. "Stole two horses, thought you was the law." Perhaps the horse theft metaphor rings even more truthfully for hip-hop artists, who often respond to twenty-first-century racial imbalances in police protection and criminal apprehension, as well as the overwhelming influence of white privilege on all levels of state power, in their music. From dime novels to hip-hop, most horse thieves personify irredeemable criminality. However, the kinds of people who steal horses vary and defy easy categorization. Ranchers and cowboys, American Indians and the U.S. Army, desperadoes and the desperate alike, all stole horses. Only some of those groups were prosecuted—or persecuted—for appropriating horses, and as legal responses to horse theft evolved in western Nebraska, it soon became apparent that even in the pursuit of justice, there would be winners and losers.

If one thing is clear, though, it is that hip-hop is not only embracing the horse and the Western genre; it is now perhaps the key to ensuring the Western's continued relevance in a changing world. In December 2018 rapper Lil Nas X released his hit single "Old Town Road," and over the next several months it became a viral sensation. In April 2019 he released a remix of the song featuring country music icon Billy Ray Cyrus, and during the next two months over two hundred million viewers watched the music video on YouTube. The lyrics describe how a rider finds peace and freedom when he takes his horse on an old country road into town. While the song does not explicitly mention horse stealing, its massive popularity may lead to some new interpretations on the subject. It also helps restore black cowboys and pioneers to their rightful place in the history and mythos of the American West, which has long whitewashed its settlers while turning American Indians into set pieces. If Westerns are going to survive in an increasingly multicultural America, they are going to have to shed the conventions and biases of the past while finding new audiences and reasons to be relevant. It will be interesting to see how interpretations of horse thieves evolve over time as the old myths of white western moral austerity unspool and give way to more inclusive understandings of a shared frontier past.

In dime novels and Westerns, horse thieves have no shortage of enemies. Mounted cavalrymen chase them up and down the plains, running them down with military efficiency. Sheriffs and marshals march confidently down the dusty main streets of their towns, coolly walking into violent bars and shadowy brothels in search of information and calmly announcing to trigger-happy suspects that they are under arrest, like John Wayne in *Rio Bravo*. And the lynch mob, as fast as it is furious, catches the thief in the middle of the night and brings him to a necktie party before melting back into civil society. Almost everyone in the Wild West who is *not* a horse thief seems to want to capture or kill one.

Among certain groups, that may have been true. After all, when one follows the short-yet-striking historical trajectory from horse raiding along the Platte to vigilante violence in towns across Nebraska, two important variables stand out: the exponential growth of private property in the region and the corresponding increase in the per capita percentage of horse wealth to total household and business wealth. During the 1860s theft was common among both the American Indians and the whites in the region. There was no real monopoly on law enforcement, and the most dominant institution in the region capable of policing against theft—the military—was more interested in keeping the region's inhabitants from killing one another than they were in ensuring the sanctity of private property. But enforcement against horse raiding constituted an essential part of the military's mission, as the signs, tactics, and objectives of a horse-stealing raid closely resembled those of a more overtly aggressive raid against a settlement, military force, or enemy tribe. The protection and recovery of horses against raiding attained both military and diplomatic significance as the threat of constant tit-for-tat raiding against American Indians and whites alike threatened the region's stability. Some leaders, including Spotted Tail, decided to aid the military in its efforts to curb horse theft by other tribes in order to curry favor with the government and undermine enemy bands while also partaking in their own raiding expeditions. In short, the army conducted its mission in spite of the wide acceptance of raiding and stealing as legitimate means of livestock accumulation among both some whites and some American Indians.

These circumstances changed in the 1870s, however, as homesteaders, farmers, and small businesspeople began to outnumber the ranchers and ranch hands in the region. These smaller-scale economic actors wrung as much as they could from both the land and the commerce that passed through it on the railroad, but in a deflationary economy, profits were hard-earned. With a diminished threshold for failure in mind and memories of well-established property law and policing back east, western Nebraska's newer residents brought with them a near-consensus about the sanctity of private property. As a result, both the military and the county's new law enforcement organs were called forth to police against property crime and bring thieves to justice. While mostly successful, both institutions were visibly and publicly inefficient in several respects. Citizens quickly lost faith in the state's ability to fight property crime, so they took extra-legal measures to extend the reach of policing power in the county while simultaneously trying to alleviate their anxiety over the possibility that some random crook was about to steal away their life's work.

These efforts manifested themselves in different ways. Citizens formed militias out of fear that American Indians would raid their settlements with impunity and without the threat of military reprisal. Ranchers relied on their aggregate pool of capital, influence, and managerial ability to create stock associations, which took upon themselves the imperative of guaranteeing personal property. They also gave ranchers an opportunity to move beyond the free-range, free-for-all culture that reigned during the early days of the cattle kingdom and forfeit a measure of autonomy in exchange for the assurance that their neighbors would not only refrain from stealing from them but would also be on the lookout for their mutual enemies: the cattle rustler and the horse thief. Eventually, these organizations advocated for a series of government regulations, reforms, and programs, ranging from the Taylor Grazing Act in 1934 to the Beef Promotion and Research Act in 1985. The cattle industry, rather than acting on the philosophy of self-reliance, instead chose to enshrine cultural and economic libertarianism, on the one hand, while constructing an interventionist, proactive state apparatus, on the other.

Conversely, most residents did not have the ability to create elaborate organizational mechanisms that acted on their behalf to curb property crime. Instead, they turned to fear and intimidation as their greatest weapons in crime fighting. Rather than replacing the policing power of the state with vigilantism, these citizens used vigilance as a corollary of the public police. Private property, particularly horses and other livestock, were so valuable to these residents that terrorism became a legitimate tool for protecting them. Whether they joined local ad hoc militias in response to potential horse raids or gathered late at night to march a suspected thief off to a stout tree someplace, the effect was the same: citizens consciously and deliberately bypassed due process and state monopolies on force in order to exact their own justice. What began as a theft culture turned into something far more insidious: a culture of violence.

It is no wonder why so many Americans continue to associate hangings with the fate of horse thieves. Local historians, screenwriters, novelists, and other purveyors of western Americana throughout the past century have largely agreed with Nellie Snyder Yost's contention that a horse thief was "never caught twice." The essential villainy of the rustler has become so hard-wired into our historical memory that the argument hardly seems controversial. Nevertheless, the time has come to challenge that narrative. Today, from "stand your ground" laws to superhero movies, Americans remain fascinated by vigilantism. And while every person inherently possesses the right to protect themselves when attacked, vigilante culture often encompasses and imagines solutions to less existentially threatening transgressions, including property crime.

In light of westward expansion's central place in the American mythos of self-determination and its ostensible legacy of establishing civilization in frontier spaces, it is critical that horse stealing be understood and remembered for what it really was: a severe problem with unusually far-reaching and sometimes terrible consequences. And the horse thieves themselves, although hanged on occasion, were much more likely to either go to prison or escape punishment entirely. By addressing the problem itself, as opposed to its mythological solution, historians can begin the work of decoupling horse stealing and other frontier crimes from more modern—and for our purposes vastly more consequential—vigilante apologetics.

Epilogue

The Old West in Miniature

I felt only as a man can feel who is roaming over the prairies of the far
West, well-armed, and mounted on a fleet and gallant steed.

—BUFFALO BILL CODY

This is really not much of a fort.

—DONNA Q. on Fort Cody TripAdvisor.com

Fort Cody, a sprawling tourist fortress in North Platte
for travelers passing through Nebraska on Interstate
80, offers visitors a familiar and digestible glimpse into
life on the frontier. It features multiple exhibits and shows, a
variety of artifacts both inside and outside of the building, and
of course a large store where visitors can buy anything from
T-shirts and bumper stickers to jars of chokecherry jam and
John Wayne novelty toilet paper and hot chocolate mix ("A real
man's drink!" according to the label). The featured attractions
include a miniature Buffalo Bill Wild West show, complete with
parading Indians and a cowboy riding a bucking bull. An enormous metal cutout of Buffalo Bill looms watchfully over the
parking lot, greeting visitors and celebrating the memory of the
business's larger-than-life namesake. Fort Cody celebrates and
perpetuates the same narrative that movies, television, literature, song, Broadway musicals, and tourist traps throughout the
West promote—that chaos, lawlessness, and uncertainty on the
western frontier gave way to order, regulation, and optimism.

271

Horse stealing complicates this story. American Indian horse raiding heaped opportunities for glory, coup counting, wealth acquisition, and revenge among and within tribes, but the practice also helped destabilize internal and external relationships while ensuring that herd health would become a critical and exploitable Achilles' heel for their enemies. Furthermore, hanged horse thieves do not represent the absence of law enforcement so much as its forfeiture; the thieves themselves were more likely to be underemployed cowboys, struggling homesteaders, staggering drunks, frustrated soldiers, or otherwise foolish young men than career criminals and gang leaders. For victims of horse stealing there was little comfort in America's impending and perhaps inevitable conquest of the Great Plains. Instead, stolen horses stoked settlers' worst fears of failure and privation, which in turn encouraged some of their worse impulses.

Historical research can shed light on the true transactional costs of horse stealing and raiding across the plains, but the collective historical memory of horse theft recalls a crime with readily identifiable winners, losers, and villains. Perhaps that is how those who became, chased, or were the victims of horse thieves remembered their own participation in the great equine property struggles of the late nineteenth century. In some ways we all create our own personal Fort Codys—manicured stockades and storefronts containing curated exhibits and dioramas of past accomplishments and formative memories populate Facebook posts and YouTube videos. We are lucky to have a few surviving memoirs, interviews, and autobiographies from participants in Nebraska's nineteenth-century theft culture. Their stories were not always nuanced, nor were they always easy to tell, but their perspectives are invaluable.

John Bratt, whose ranch was located just a short distance from Fort Cody's current location, was one of many former cowboys and ranchers who wrote books about their experiences in the early twentieth century. As the remaining members of Nebraska's first generation of ranchers, cowboys, and farmers began to retire their saddles, many of these men also felt as though they had lost something. The world was changing around them—sometimes through their own efforts, sometimes in spite of them. The collapse of the free-range ranching industry and the subsequent depression of land values hit western Nebraska hard, though the Sandhills ranches escaped the worst. Ranchers such as Bratt, who had managed to accumulate thousands of acres of land from the railroad companies and other holders, had difficulty downsizing their operations and liquidating their holdings. The Homestead and Kinkaid Acts opened up land to anyone who wanted it, and in the absence of irrigation canals, the land was of little use to anyone besides ranchers. Meanwhile, fewer cowboys worked in the region by the end of the 1890s, partly because the ranchers themselves made their businesses more efficient and less prone to fluctuations in beef prices and transportation costs. As a result, the 1890s brought a spurt of irrigation canal building in the county and elsewhere in western Nebraska.[1]

Bratt's herds shrunk in size as the rancher himself advanced in years. During this decade he slowly retired from ranching to focus on his other businesses, which included real estate. Bratt also lobbied the state to build an experimental dry farming research station in the area and tried to convince prospective buyers of the benefits of growing alfalfa. But while Bratt encouraged and even helped subsidize agricultural innovation and economic diversification, he never forgot his days in the saddle, and he turned to writing in an effort to preserve their memory. In 1917 he wrote and published an essay, "Pioneer Freighting Days with Ox Teams in 1866," chronicling his adventures as a government contractor after the Civil War. He focused most of his labors on his autobiography, however, which he never had the opportunity to publish while he was alive. When he died, in 1918, Bratt had only four horses to his name, a far cry from the hundreds he had owned and used during the heyday of his ranching business. Three years later, however, Bratt's daughter Elizabeth published her father's work, *Trails of Yesterday*, which ensured that the late rancher's once large remudas would not be soon forgotten.[2]

Bratt concluded *Trails of Yesterday* with a few words about the new world developing around him. He was proud of the results. "Law and order have taken the place of the vigilance committee," he remarked. "The desperado has either met his fate or become good. The church and Sunday school have driven out the frontier gambling halls and lewd dance houses, and while we have some bad people with us yet, I believe the world is growing better." Bratt also believed that efforts to encourage farming among American Indians and to educate their children were successful, though notably he expresses no regret for the cultural genocide that continued to erode tribal traditions and beliefs. "With a little more civilization and education," wrote Bratt, "the Indian will take his place among our best type of citizens and even to-day they are preferable to many illiterate, criminal foreigners who are coming to our shores."[3] Bratt does not mention horse thieves specifically in his conclusion, but it is clear that he does not miss their presence. Ultimately, the disappearance of "desperadoes" and raiders represented the West's moral and religious redemption.

Though pleased with the region's progress, Bratt had mixed feelings about the fate of those friends and employees who worked and traveled with him on the ranch. Attributing his own moral purity to a "Guardian Angel . . . [that] filled me with courage and confidence," he lamented how the vices he scrupulously avoided on the trail seemed to bedevil his friends later in life. "I have met and talked with many of our old employees who have made good [but] I sometimes meet some less fortunate. Drink, cards, and other weaknesses have been their curses." Meetings with old associates inevitably led to requests for charity. "They often ask me for aid, sometimes a meal, a night's lodging or railroad fare. I usually give these, which they promise to return, but they forget, poor fellows! They are to be pitied. I listen to their stories, give them the benefit of the doubt, and if I cannot find them work, help them to their destination." Bratt seemed to believe that his autobiography would be instructive to these men. Perhaps by better understanding his own moral credo, the old cowboys would find their own courage and confidence to reform. "If I knew the addresses of these old associates, who have shared these hardships with me, I would gladly mail them a copy of this book before I pass 'under the wire.' It would remind them of many familiar scenes."[4]

Soldiers and officers also waxed nostalgic about the old days during the Plains Indian Wars but often without the camaraderie and social organization enjoyed by veterans of other wars. Associated with America's barbarous legacy of indigenous conquest and genocide and punctuated by a series of massacres and one-sided battles on both sides, the Plains Indian Wars lacked the narrative coherence and moral gravitas of the Civil War, the giddy triumphalism of the Spanish-American War, the colossal horrors of the Great War, and the immediacy of America's disastrous occupation of the Philippines. War veteran Lauren Aldrich bemoaned the lack of recognition and community among other veterans as he aged: "Sixty years have passed since [my service on the plains] and the writer has not had the good pleasure of meeting a single [veteran] during that time. At this late date in life, we can only hope to meet them where the flowers bloom."[5]

By the 1920s Aldrich was working to help build this veterans' community, which now competed for space in America's historical memory with over four million recently minted veterans of World War I. In 1925 the National Indian War Veterans organization named Aldrich state commander of the Iowa chapter, but even this distinction did not help him reconnect with any of his old comrades. Ten years later he wrote to the *Winners of the West* newspaper, proposing a shooting match among the aging veterans of the Indian Wars in hopes of getting them together. The editors demurred, citing the "lack of a 'Get Up and Go' spirit" among his fellow veterans, but promised to announce the possibility in the next issue. Apparently, many former officers and soldiers read *Winners of the West*, but few were willing to write in and seek or volunteer information that might lead to reunions. Thus, many "winners of the West," who often relied on their independent spirit to survive their pioneering days, surrendered to isolation in their later years. Perhaps more than a few, like Aldrich, wrote their stories down because they knew no one who would understand their experiences.[6]

Plains Indian horse raiders, unlike the cavalry troops that pursued them, were more likely to maintain close connections with former friends and allies whenever possible. Aging horse raiders told tales of their exploits and those of the larger community during wartime to their children and grandchildren, and these stories continue to circulate today within each Plains tribe's oral history. But for many American Indians who had stories to share, fears of white reprisal and legal repercussions years after the fact dissuaded survivors from telling their stories to outsiders. Disregarding concerns among his friends about revealing his actions during the Battle of Little Bighorn, Wooden Leg told his story to reservation physician and historian Thomas Marquis, who then published it as a dictated autobiography. Wooden Leg served for many years as a reservation policeman and judge, traveled to Washington DC and New York to give talks about Cheyenne culture, and courageously spoke about his experiences to a gathering of whites and Indians at a 1906 event commemorating the forty-year anniversary of Little Bighorn. He passed away in 1940.

While Wooden Leg's white audiences wanted to hear his tale, whites who were themselves targeted by horse raids or otherwise caught in the crossfire were less forgiving. For instance, although Bratt forgave Middleton in his autobiography, he did not extend that courtesy to Big Turkey, even though the chief had converted to Christianity and lived a quiet life at the St. Francis Mission at Rosebud until he died in 1920. Big Turkey opened up to the Jesuit missionaries, producing a brief autobiography that cataloged some of his raiding exploits. However, he is best remembered today for his cartographic, as opposed to his literary, contributions to the historical record. During his later years Big Turkey used his photographic memory to create an accurate, detailed map of the Lakota nation for the resident Jesuits, who often had difficulty navigating a country with relatively few roads and signs (fig. 27). The map included

Fig. 27. Big Turkey hand-drawing a map for the missionaries at the St. Francis Mission. Courtesy St. Francis Mission and Marquette University, St. Francis Mission Records, ID 06-6.

everything from the Yellowstone to the Missouri River, including the Black Hills and the Bighorn mountains.[7]

John Bratt, Lauren Aldrich, Wooden Leg, and Big Turkey all addressed and understood horse stealing within the context of their roles within Nebraska's theft culture. When taken together, these stories reveal a larger truth about horse stealing: that whites and natives alike own and share its legacy in ways that are scarcely conceivable when thieves and raiders are discussed separately. Lakota and Cheyenne owners mourned, raged, and suffered whenever their horses were stolen and often sought violent retribution. Similarly, whites stole horses with relative impunity at certain points, and white managers of large herds viewed both loss and acquisition via horse theft in a comparable manner to the Lakotas and Cheyennes. Both whites and Plains Indians believed that horses were private property, and few people on the plains possessed anything of remotely comparable worth. Consequently, horse raiding and horse stealing should not only be understood in connection with one another, but the two seemingly separate historical subjects should never have been split off in the first place.

It may be sufficient to come away from a deep-dive study of horse stealing with a better understanding of and appreciation for its corrosive impact on Great Plains culture, law, and society. After all, the phenomenon frequently spurred historical action, reaction, and change, ranging from massacres and murders to subtler shifts in the evolving relationship between civilians and the state. For these reasons scholars need to take horse stealing more seriously and on its own terms when discussing western history. But it may be more satisfying to consider the history of horse theft and raiding together as something akin to the Old West in miniature. Rather than representing a mysterious and impenetrable history of ghosts, shadows, and rumors, horses and horse theft bind the many disparate human dramas of the Great Plains together. One can set aside the extreme dissonance and divergence of the white and native worldviews for a moment and contemplate the one factor that inextricably drew them together into the same frame of reference. The horse's universal and astonishing importance, its intimate relationship to humanity, and its essential utility on the plains never dimmed, as it was equally indispensable across ethnic and agrarian cultures. Like the "Buffalo Bill's Wild West in Miniature" show at Fort Cody, which depicts western expansion on a grand scale using over twenty thousand hand-painted carvings, models, and animatronics, horse theft similarly functions as a narrative device that glues together many unlike parts. When viewed as a parade, the procession of stolen horses across the plains and across time follows a route that touches nearly every corner of the history of the West.

Yet horse stealing says as much about who Americans are today as it does about their shared western history. Old tropes about horse thieves always being hanged, as well as family stories about Great-Great-Uncle So-and-So meeting an untimely end at the hands of a lynch mob in Montana, reveal much about how many modern Americans view property ownership and personal protection through the prism of a nineteenth-century crime. For instance, horses represent how sacrosanct private property has become, and the dread surrounding their loss helps legitimize the use of violence to protect them. This in turn highlights a central paradox in modern American political discourse: the notion that while police are almost always blameless agents when imposing violence (usually in the context of assaulting and killing people of color, especially men), the police themselves cannot be counted on to arrive at a crime in time to stop it. Perhaps the history of horse stealing will help Americans develop a more holistic, empathetic, and pragmatic understanding of criminal justice and guns rights issues that reconciles both urban and rural perspectives with respect to the limitations of institutional policing. Late-nineteenth-century Americans dealt with comparable problems when investing new law enforcement institutions with the resources and public trust necessary for them to expediently and safely carry out their duties while also bemoaning, and in many cases trying to compensate for, their perceived lack of protection. Structural inequalities and institutional inefficiencies alike contributed to their mistrust. An understanding of these historical issues might help break the logjam of partisan bickering and lead to the kind of fresh, collaborative thinking that enabled Congress to pass the bipartisan First Step Act in 2018.

Horse thieves will likely remain in the shadows of western history for now, even as Buffalo Bill casts both a literal and figurative shadow over Fort Cody and other tourist monuments throughout the Great Plains. In the meantime visitors to Fort Cody will receive a vivid, entertaining lesson in the exaggerated-yet-riveting drama of American expansion across the West. The exhibits, the building's aesthetics, and even the merchandise all celebrate the inexorable wave of progress in the form of law and order as it crashed ashore upon Nebraska's sandy plains after the Civil War. And Buffalo Bill's Wild West in Miniature will continue to run every thirty minutes, like clockwork, its hand-carved Indians, cowboys, and horses moving around their displays in a perpetual animatronic procession.

The exhibit is worth visiting, even though it does not reference another story that unfolded across the plains and sandhills surrounding the fictionalized outpost. It is a story of how horses transformed and transcended cultures, improved living standards, and offered protection and transportation while simultaneously becoming indispensable to their owners. It is an allegory for how the theft or appropriation of a kind of property so essential, so valuable, to all of the different groups in an area can lead to jealousy, betrayal, murder, war, vengeance, and distorted views of right and wrong. And it is a reminder that no revolutions come cheap, not even equestrian ones. But in any event these lessons may be lost on tired, road-hypnotized visitors as they shop for souvenirs, dine in one of the chain restaurants lining Jeffers Street, and then ride off in their gasoline-powered cars and trucks toward the hazy blue-gray horizon.

NOTES

Preface

1. See Griffith, *Outlaw Tales of Nebraska*; Avery, *Lynchings, Legends, and Law-lessness*; Burchill, *Bullets, Badges, and Bridles*. Incidentally, Burchill's book came out the same year I filed my dissertation, and since it is not bound by any regional or temporal limitations, he is able to profile several horse thieves and discuss several other fascinating actors in the world of horse stealing.

2. Blackhawk, *Violence over the Land*, 265.

3. The term *emigrant* was frequently used by migrants along the Overland Trail and has since been adopted by historians as well. See Bagley, *Across the Plains, Mountains, and Deserts*.

Introduction

1. Western Nebraska Tourism Coalition, "Journey to Western Nebraska," *Nebraska Life* (2018).

2. The Western Nebraska Travel Coalition's map excludes those counties within the Republican River valley, specifically Chase, Dundy, Frontier, Hays, Hitchcock, and Red Willow. I called the Coalition's office and asked why it had left them out. The person I spoke to responded, "We had to stop some-where . . . we already had twenty counties, and that's about a third of the state." This struck me as a perfectly reasonable explanation.

3. Bratt, *Trails of Yesterday*, 8–9.

4. For more information on Lakota hunting, camping, and migration patterns in western Nebraska, see Hedren, *After Custer*, 8. Note that *Oglala* is spelled differently than the town of Ogallala, which, like Scottsbluff and Kear-ney, suggests that Nebraska town founders had the strange and etymologi-cally confusing habit of misspelling the names of the very people for which they named their towns in the first place.

5. Sandoz, *Old Jules*, 6; Hewitt, "Fatal Fall of Barrett Scott," 107–20.

6. For the classic work, see Geographical and Geological Survey of the Rocky Mountain Region (U.S.), *Report on the Lands of the Arid Region of the United States: With a More Detailed Account of the Lands of Utah, with Maps*, 2nd ed. (Washington DC: GPO 1879). The most influential work on how the geography of the Great Plains environment has impacted its history is Webb, *Great Plains*. The line also resonates in popular culture, such as in the Tragically Hip's 1992 single "At the Hundredth Meridian."

7. Hämäläinen, "Rise and Fall of Plains Horse Cultures," 833–62.

8. West, *Contested Plains*, 52; White, "Winning of the West," 319–43.

9. This model was popularized in large part by William Cronon in his magnificent economic and financial history of the city of Chicago during the late nineteenth century. See Cronon, *Nature's Metropolis*, 49. For more information, see Johann Heinrich Von Thünen, *Von Thünen's Isolated State: An English Edition of Der Isolierte Staat*, ed. Peter Hall, trans. Carla M. Wartenberg (New York: Pergamon Press, 1966); and Blaug and Lloyd, *Famous Figures and Diagrams in Economics*, 170–72.

10. Bay State Livestock Co., *Description of the Bay State Livestock Co.'s Lands*; see also Wishart, *Last Days of the Rainbelt*, xiii–xviii.

11. This is not a new idea. See Webb, *Great Plains*, 8–9.

12. Moore, *Cow Boys and Cattle Men*, 38–39, 100–101.

13. Reid, *Law for the Elephant*, 332–33.

14. This is similar to Stephen Aron's argument that although hunters made Kentucky safe from American Indians, soon the settlers who followed made Kentucky unsafe for hunting. See Aron, *How the West Was Lost*, 56–57. For a discussion of how moral ecology and lawbreaking are related relative to the conservation movement, see Jacoby, *Crimes against Nature*, 1–10.

15. For some notable examples, check out Ewers, "Were the Blackfoot Rich in Horses," 602–10; Roe, *Indian and the Horse*; and Hämäläinen, *Comanche Empire*, 66–67, 85.

16. Ewers, "Were the Blackfoot Rich in Horses," 602–10.

17. Roe, *Indian and the Horse*, 223; McGinnis, *Counting Coup and Cutting Horses*, 16, 181.

18. White, "Winning of the West," 201; DeLay, *War of a Thousand Deserts*, 138.

19. Hämäläinen, *Comanche Empire*, 66–67, 85. A similar process occurred in the northern plains, where the Lakota and Cheyenne successfully transitioned to a nomadic, equestrian culture. See West, *Contested Plains*, 33–62.

20. Hanson, "Adjustment and Adaptation on the Northern Plains," 93–107. See also Brooks, *Captives and Cousins*, 179; Red Shirt, *Turtle Lung Woman's Granddaughter*, 55.

21. Hämäläinen, "Rise and Fall of Plains Horse Cultures," 833–62.

22. Many historians have explored the impact of the horse on American Indian society. Authoritative works on the subject include Hämäläinen, *Comanche Empire*; and West, *Contested Plains*.

23. Stands in Timber and Liberty, *Cheyenne Memories*, 102–3.

24. Red Shirt, *Turtle Lung Woman's Granddaughter*, 44; Standing Bear, *Stories of the Sioux*, 61–64. There are several stories in this book that tell other tales of friendship between man and horse. Chaps. 7 and 12 also contain good examples.

25. Red Shirt, *Turtle Lung Woman's Granddaughter*, 130.

26. Pearce, *Women and Ledger Art*, 29–52.

27. Brooks, *Captives and Cousins*, 174–80.

28. Hämäläinen, "Rise and Fall of Plains Horse Cultures," 833–62.

29. Several scholars have recently explored the importance of horses in nineteenth-century America, and they have provided a great deal of insight into how horse power and transport was applied throughout the Gilded Age. Historians Clay McShane and Joel Tarr argue that city residents, merchants, and manufacturers relied on horses as much if not more than they did on rail transport after the Civil War. They also maintain that the horse and horse travel helped shape the urban landscape in significant ways, such as the role horses played in nineteenth-century mass transit and in opening up the areas outside of cities to suburban settlement. Ann Norton Greene took a slightly different approach in her 2008 book, *Horses at Work*, which describes the mechanics of horse power and the history of its application in the Northeast and Midwest. See McShane and Tarr, *Horse in the City*, 10; Greene, *Horses at Work*, 1–9. In addition to this pair of books, a recent graduate of the UCLA Urban Planning graduate program, Eric Andrew Morris, wrote an exemplary master's thesis on how horse manure created an urban pollution problem of immense proportions. Much like the concerns Americans have today about the impact of automobile emissions on greenhouse gases, city dwellers during the 1890s fretted about the possible consequences of maintaining a horse economy in an increasingly dense urban environment. As millions of people moved into cities across America and Europe, the horse population ballooned as well. According to an article published in the *Times of London* in 1894, one writer predicted that if London's growth rate remained fixed, then by 1950 the streets of that city would be layered with nine feet of manure. Morris, "Horse Power to Horsepower," 2.

30. Flint, *American Farmer*, 548.

31. Goodwyn, *Democratic Promise*, xix, 32, 58, 65, 86.

32. Cronon, *Nature's Metropolis*, 90.

33. Knowlton, *Cattle Kingdom*, xiii–xxii.

34. According to Terry Jordan-Bychkov, multiple ranching cultures predominated in North America, only some of which relied primarily on horse power. California and Florida ranchers, for example, did not use horses nearly as often as those from Texas and, earlier, Mexico. The use of horses in ranching is a prime characteristic of the Spanish Andalusian ranching culture, which was transferred to New Spain with colonization and then rooted

in the southern Great Plains haciendas and their workers, the vaqueros. See Jordan-Bychkov, *North American Cattle-Ranching Frontiers*. See also de Steiguer, *Wild Horses of the West*, 132.

35. Savage, *Cowboy Hero*, 40.

36. Siringo, *Texas Cowboy*, 119.

37. I created a database of these horses, which contains information on when each horse was acquired as well as its departure (when it was sold, killed, or stolen). The horses were inventoried each month. Account of Horses, Mules-McPherson Herd, 1875–83, Bratt Collection, JBP.

38. "Local News," *North Platte (NE) Republican*, November 9, 1878.

39. "Local News," *Western Nebraskian* (North Platte), June 14, 1879; Local News, *Grant County Tribune*, February 12, 1891.

40. Kennon and Adams, *From the Pecos to the Powder*, 41.

41. To underscore this point, when I was giving a talk based on this part of the chapter at the Western History Association annual conference in 2012, a professor in the audience approached me afterward and informed me that on her family's farm growing up, they had, indeed, named their milk cow.

1. You Must Watch Your Horses

1. Hoig, *White Man's Paper Trail*, 90.

2. Hoig, *White Man's Paper Trail*, 85–96.

3. "Big Turkey," in Stars, Iron Shell, Buechel, and Manhart, *Lakota Tales and Texts*, 690–91.

4. Marquis, *Wooden Leg*, 58–59.

5. See White, "Winning of the West," 319–43. For a fantastic (and more recent) narrative survey of Lakota history, see Hämäläinen, *Lakota America*.

6. Greene and Thornton, *Year the Stars Fell*, 74–84.

7. Lewis, *Robidoux Chronicles*, 157; George Ledbetter, "Historian Recounts the Many Crow Butte Naming Stories," *Rapid City Journal*, November 3, 2009, https://rapidcityjournal.com/thechadronnews/news/historian-recounts -the-many-crow-butte-naming-stories/article_082f7663-fa22–53a3–890e -186902332de7.html.

8. Wishart, *Last Days of the Rainbelt*, 31; Flores, "Bringing Home All the Pretty Horses," 5.

9. Hämäläinen, "Rise and Fall of Plains Horse Cultures," 845–54.

10. McGinnis, *Counting Coup and Cutting Horses*, 16; Green and Thornton, *Year the Stars Fell*, 109.

11. Paul, *Autobiography of Red Cloud*, 39; Marquis, *Wooden Leg*, 91–92.

12. McGinnis, *Counting Coup and Cutting Horses*, 16; Green and Thornton, *Year the Stars Fell*, 175–76, 224–25, 248, 250–55.

13. Marquis, *Wooden Leg*, 107–9.

14. Llewellyn and Hoebel, *Cheyenne Way*, 127–28, 223–28.

15. Green and Thornton, *Year the Stars Fell,* 224–25, 248, 250–55; Red Shirt, *Turtle Lung Woman's Granddaughter,* 5; Maj. John DuBois, Fort McPherson, to Assistant Adjutant General, Department of the Platte, May 8, 1873, Letters Sent, vol. 4, NARA. For more information on how western tribes covered the dead, see Reid, "Principles of Vengeance," 21–43; and White, *Middle Ground,* 40, 77, 142, 404, and 423.

16. Marquis, *Wooden Leg,* 21–22.

17. Marquis, *Wooden Leg,* 23–25.

18. Marquis, *Wooden Leg,* 29–30.

19. Grinnell, *Fighting Cheyennes,* 63–69.

20. Red Shirt, *Turtle Lung Woman's Granddaughter,* 9–10.

21. Paul, *Autobiography of Red Cloud,* 34–37.

22. Paul, *Autobiography of Red Cloud,* 48–54.

23. Marquis, *Wooden Leg,* 116–18, 140.

24. For my Overland Trail analysis and discussion, I assembled over fifty different travel diaries, memoirs, and autobiographies. In light of my already expansive and far-flung source base, I focused on using material that was readily available online, preferably at Archive.org. I omitted the ones I did not directly cite from my bibliography. Will Bagley's exhaustive bibliography of Oregon and California Trail primary sources was invaluable in this effort. See Bagley, *Across the Plains, Mountains, and Deserts.*

25. Wyeth, *Correspondence and Journals of Captain Nathaniel J. Wyeth;* Young, "Diary of Rev. Jason Lee [1834]," 122.

26. First Lt. Henry Heth, Post Commander, Fort Kearny, to Maj. Francis Page, Adjutant General, Jefferson Barracks, September 24, 1854; Capt. Robert H. Chilton, Post Commander, Fort Kearny, to Maj. Gen. Roger Jones, Adjutant General U.S. Army, November 2, 1849; Capt. Robert H. Chilton, Post Commander, Fort Kearny, to Maj. Don Carlos Buell, Adjutant General, Jefferson Barracks, January 14, 1850, Letters Sent, vol. 1, Fort Kearny, NARA. See also Unruh, *Plains Across,* 210, for another description of the Ogle affair.

27. Maj. Benjamin Bonneville, Post Commander, Fort Kearny, to Maj. Gen. Roger Jones, Adjutant General's Office, Washington DC, July 2, 1849; Capt. Robert H. Chilton, Post Commander, Fort Kearny, to Maj. Gen. Roger Jones, Adjutant General of the U.S. Army, Washington DC, June 7, 1850, Letters Sent, vol. 1, Fort Kearny, NARA.

28. Capt. Henry W. Wharton, Post Commander, Fort Kearny, to Capt. Irvin McDowell, Jefferson Barracks, June 1852; Capt. Henry W. Wharton, Post Commander, Fort Kearny, to Maj. Francis Page, Adjutant General, Jefferson Barracks, May 20, 1854, Letters Sent, vol. 1, Fort Kearny, NARA.

29. Capt. Henry W. Wharton, Post Commander, Fort Kearny, to Maj. Gen. Roger Jones, Adjutant General of the United States, December 1851; 1st Lt. Henry Heth, Post Commander, Fort Kearny, to Maj. Oscar F. Winship, Adjutant General, Jefferson Barracks, March 19, 1855, Letters Sent, vol. 1; Maj.

Charles A. May, Post Commander, Fort Kearny, to Adjutant General, Department of the West, June 7, 1860, Letters Sent, vol. 2, Fort Kearny, NARA.

30. Capt. Robert H. Chilton, Post Commander, Fort Kearny, to John E. Barron, Indian Agent, Council Bluffs Agency, March 1850, Letters Sent, vol. 1, Fort Kearny, NARA.

31. Wyllis Alden, "Overland Journey to Oregon" (1851), 45; Williams, *Narrative of a Tour from the State of Indiana to the Oregon Territory*.

32. 1st Lt. Henry Heth, Post Commander, Fort Kearny, to Maj. Oscar F. Winship, Adjutant General, Jefferson Barracks, February 6, 1855, Letters Sent, vol. 1, Capt. Alfred Sully, Post Commander, Fort Kearny, to Adjutant General, Department of the West, August 17, 1860, Letters Sent, vol. 2, Fort Kearny, NARA.

33. Capt. Robert H. Chilton, Post Commander, Fort Kearny, to Maj. Don Carlos Buell, Adjutant General, Jefferson Barracks, June 27, 1850, Letters Sent, vol. 1, Fort Kearny, NARA.

34. William G. Johnston, *Experiences of a Forty-Niner by William G. Johnston, a Member of the First Wagon Train to Enter California in the Memorable Year 1849*; and Charles D. Ferguson, *The Experiences of a Forty-Niner during a Third of a Century in the Gold Fields*, both quoted in Munkres, "Plains Indian Threat on the Oregon Trail," 207–8.

35. Manly, *Death Valley in '49*, 66.

36. William Kirby, "Crossing the Plains from Kansas City to Salt Lake" (1854); "Leaving Salt Lake City for Green River" and "From Green River to St. Joseph: Incidents by the Way" (1856), *Mormonism Exposed and Refuted*, 100–108. For another example of the Latter-day Saint magistrate anecdote, see Langworthy, *Scenery of the Plains, Mountains and Mines*, 108–9.

37. Sarah Sutton, Diary 1854 (Oregon Historical Society, MSS 2280), quoted in Munkres, "Independence Rock and Devil's Gate," 38; Delano, *Life on the Plains and among the Diggings*, 323–24.

38. Ingalls, *Journal of a Trip to California*; Leonard, *Narrative of the Adventures of Zenas Leonard*, 7–8; Capt. Robert H. Chilton, Post Commander, Fort Kearny, to Maj. Don Carlos Buell, Adjutant General, Jefferson Barracks, June 3, 1850, Letters Sent, vol. 1, Fort Kearny, NARA.

39. Burnap, *What Happened during One Man's Lifetime*; Stewart, "Overland Trip to California" (1850), 184–85.

40. Capt. Robert H. Chilton, Post Commander, Fort Kearny, to Maj. Don Carlos Buell, Adjutant General, Jefferson Barracks, June 27, 1850; Capt. Henry W. Wharton, Post Commander, Fort Kearny, to Capt. Irvin McDowell, Jefferson Barracks, June 1852, Letters Sent, vol. 1, Fort Kearny, NARA.

41. Cummins, *Autobiography and Reminiscences of Sarah J. Cummins*, 27–28.

42. Leonard, *Narrative of the Adventures of Zenas Leonard*, 7; Bassett, *Buffalo County, Nebraska, and Its People*, 68.

43. Gibson, *Recollections of a Pioneer*, 25.

44. Thissell, *Crossing the Plains in '49*; Delano, *Life on the Plains and among the Diggings*, 208–9; Potter, intro., *Trail to California*, 45.

45. Mattes, *Great Platte River Road*, 37–38.

46. For example (and for additional information on the event), see Utley and Washburn, *Indian Wars*, 185–86; and Bray, *Crazy Horse*, 31–32.

47. Paul, *Blue Water Creek and the First Sioux War*, 20–21.

48. Paul, *Blue Water Creek and the First Sioux War*, 18–24, 107.

49. First Lt. Henry Heth, Post Commander, Fort Kearny, to Indian Agent of the Sioux, September 22, 1854; 1st Lt. Henry Heth, Post Commander, Fort Kearny, to Maj. Francis Page, Adjutant General, Jefferson Barracks, November 15, 1854; 1st Lt. Henry Heth, Post Commander, Fort Kearny, to Maj. Oscar F. Winship, Adjutant General, Jefferson Barracks, January 24, 1855; February 6, 1855; and March 19, 1855, Letters Sent, vol. 1, Fort Kearny, NARA; Paul, *Blue Water Creek and the First Sioux War*, 81.

50. Chalfant, *Cheyennes and Horse Soldiers*, 25–33.

51. Chalfant, *Cheyennes and Horse Soldiers*, 34–36.

52. Chalfant, *Cheyennes and Horse Soldiers*, 38–41.

53. Capt. Henry W. Wharton, Post Commander, Fort Kearny, to Assistant Adjutant General, Fort Pierre, June 7, 1856; Capt. Henry W. Wharton, Post Commander, Fort Kearny, to Lt. Thomas Twiss, Indian Agent, Fort Laramie, September 9, 1856, Letters Sent, vol. 2, Fort Kearny, NARA; Chalfant, *Cheyennes and Horse Soldiers*, 41–44.

54. First Lt. Elisha G. Marshall, Post Commander, Fort Kearny, to Col. Samuel Cooper, Adjutant General, Washington DC, August 2, 1857; Notice to Persons on the Road (August 4, 1857); 1st Lt. Elisha G. Marshall, Post Commander, Fort Kearny, to Col. Samuel Cooper, Adjutant General, Washington DC, August 4, 1857, Letters Sent, vol. 2, Fort Kearny, NARA.

55. Chalfant, *Cheyennes and Horse Soldiers*, 201.

56. West, *Contested Plains*, xxiii.

2. Theft Cultures

1. Coleman, *Pre-Statehood History of Lincoln County, Nebraska*, 23–24.

2. Clark, *Trip to Pike's Peak*, 47. See also Gilman, *Pump on the Prairie*, 123.

3. In 1864 and 1865 Fort McPherson was known as Cottonwood Post. See Holmes, *Fort McPherson, Nebraska*, 2–4. For a detailed history of the fort using Post Returns, see Wrehe, "'Thus Glory Does Fade,'" 53–105.

4. Holmes, *Fort McPherson, Nebraska*, 5–11; McChristian, *Fort Laramie*, 158–60.

5. McChristian, *Fort Laramie*, 174–75.

6. Utley, *Frontiersmen in Blue*, 285–87.

7. Hutton, "Early History of North Platte," 28. See also Holmes, *Fort McPherson*, 13; and Johnson, *Johnson's History of Nebraska*, 159–61. Historians who have written in detail about these raids include Hagerty, "Indian Raids along the

Platte and Little Blue Rivers," 176–86, 239–60; and Becher, *Massacre along the Medicine Road.*

8. R. R. Livingston, in the field near Fort Rankin, to Commanding Officer (CO), Cottonwood Post, February 6, 1865, Letters Received, box 1, Fort McPherson, NARA; Brig. Gen. Robert B. Mitchell, Fort Kearny, to Maj. George M. O'Brien, Cottonwood Post, May 23, 1864, Telegrams Sent, vol. 1, Fort McPherson, NARA; Maj. George M. O'Brien, Post Commander, Cottonwood Post, to Brig. Gen. Robert B. Mitchell, Fort Kearny, May 25, 1864, Telegrams Sent, vol. 1, Fort McPherson, NARA.

9. Cottonwood Post Post Returns (1863–65), December 31, 1864, jpeg image (digital scan of original records in the National Archives, Washington DC), subscription database, http://www.ancestry.com/. See also Holmes, *Fort McPherson,* 8–13.

10. Grinnell, *Fighting Cheyennes,* 174.

11. Utley, *Frontiersmen in Blue,* 302–3. There is a rich literature on the Indian War of 1865, which is also known as the "Colorado War." It is also sometimes lumped together with the Powder River Expedition. A recent and reliable narrative of the war can be found in McDermott, *Circle of Fire.* Elliot West also gives a brief but excellent discussion of the conflict in West, *Contested Plains,* 271–316.

12. Maj. George M. O'Brien, Cottonwood Post, to Col. R. R. Livingston, May 12, 1865, Maj. George M. O'Brien, Cottonwood Post, to Col. R. R. Livingston, May 13, 1865, Post Commander, Fort McPherson, to Capt. George Price, July 14, 1865, Capt. John Wilcox, Seventh Iowa Cavalry, to Lt. William Bowen, September 25, 1865, Telegraphs Sent, vol. 2, Fort McPherson, NARA.

13. Thomas O'Donnell, "Experiences of Thomas O'Donnell while a Workman in Building the Union Pacific Railroad," Thomas O'Donnell Collection, MS 1284, NSHS; Adamson, *North Platte and Its Associations,* 15–19; Lauren Aldrich, "Brief Reminiscences of the Soldiers Life on the Plains and in the Mountains during the Early Days of 1867-8-9 to 70," Lauren Winfield Aldrich Papers, Huntington Library (HL), 3; Hutton, "Early History of North Platte," 41–44.

14. Greene, *Horses at Work,* 166.

15. Marquis, *Wooden Leg,* 14.

16. Olson and Naugle, *History of Nebraska,* 129.

17. Bratt, *Trails of Yesterday,* 181–83; Yost, *Call of the Range,* 39, 117.

18. Becher, *Massacre along the Medicine Road,* 264–67, 420–21.

19. Fort McPherson Post Returns, April 1872 and April 1873; Holmes, *Fort McPherson, Nebraska,* 51.

20. Lauren Aldrich, "Brief Reminiscences of the Soldiers Life," HL, 16.

21. Buecker, *Fort Robinson and the American West,* 48.

22. Endorsement on report of C. V. Petteys, A.A. Surgeon, March 30, 1875, Endorsements Sent, vol. 1, Camp Sheridan, NARA.

23. Maj. Nathaniel Dudley, Endorsement on communication from Amos Mills, Julesburg, to 2nd Lt. H. R. Lemley, Third Cavalry, November 6, 1874; Capt. Deane Monahan, Endorsement on letter from Thomas Grady to Gen. George Crook, June 3, 1875, Endorsements Sent, vol. 1 Sidney Barracks, NARA.

24. Capt. Gilbert S. Carpenter, Sidney Barracks, to A.A.G., Department of the Platte, January 25, 1872; Capt. Gilbert S. Carpenter, Sidney Barracks, to Col. John E. Smith, Fort Laramie, February 5, 1872, Letters Sent, vol. 1, Sidney Barracks, NARA; Yost, *Call of the Range*, 69.

25. 1st Lt. James R. Hardenbergh, Sidney Barracks, to Lt. William Miller, Fort Sedgwick, May 3, 1870, Letters Sent, vol. 1, Sidney Barracks, NARA.

26. James R. Hardenbergh, Sidney Barracks, to Lt. William Miller, Ninth Infantry, May 17, 1870, Letters Sent, vol. 1, Sidney Barracks, NARA.

27. Col. Henry B. Carrington, Fort McPherson, to Maj. Henry G. Litchfield, Department of the Platte, May 6, 1867, and Carrington to Litchfield, May 8, 1867, Telegrams Sent, vol. 2, McPherson, NARA; Col. Henry B. Carrington, Fort McPherson, to Gen. Christopher Augur, Department of the Platte, May 29, 1867, and Lt. Henry Wessels, Fort McPherson, to Col. Patrick, U.S. Indian Agent, July 30, 1867, Letters Received, box 1, Fort McPherson, NARA; Hutton, "Early History of North Platte," 29, 60; Fort McPherson Post Returns, April 1868, May 31, 1868; Bratt, *Trails of Yesterday*, 177.

28. The Battle of Summit Springs succeeded in pushing the Lakota and Cheyenne out of the Republican River valley. Although raids would continue for another decade, one author claimed that as a result of the battle, the Republican River valley was made "safe for settlement." See James T. King, "Republican River Expedition, June–July, 1869," in Paul, *Nebraska Indian War Reader*, 31–70; and and Proceedings of a Board of Inquiry, July 11, 1869, box 2, Letters Received, Fort McPherson, NARA.

29. Cody, *Autobiography of Buffalo Bill*, 117–20. See also Spring, *Buffalo Bill and His Horses*.

30. Proceedings of a Board of Inquiry, July 11, 1869, box 2, Letters Received, Fort McPherson, NARA; Proceedings of a Board of Inquiry for J. A. Moore, July 23, 1869, box 2, Letters Received, Fort McPherson, NARA; Proceedings of a Board of Inquiry, July 31, 1869, box 2, Letters Received, Fort McPherson, NARA; John Burke, Lincoln County, to Col. William Emory, Fort McPherson, September 28, 1869, box 2, Letters Received, Fort McPherson, NARA; Proceedings of a Board of Inquiry for John Burke, October 1, 1869, box 2, Letters Received, Fort McPherson, NARA; Jacob Schnell, Lincoln County, to Post Commander, Fort McPherson, July 18, 1870, Letters Received, box 2, Fort McPherson, NARA. There is no evidence of a board of survey in the general orders or in the letters received. However, there is a two-year gap in the Fort McPherson collection of letters sent, so there is no evidence of the sort of reply, if any, given to Schnell.

31. Hutton, "Early History of North Platte," 50–51; Fort McPherson Post Returns (1865–72), March 31, 1871; Local News, *Western Nebraskian*, October

21, 1876; E. B. Fowler to Mrs. Barnes, Fowler Collection, Nebraska State Historical Society, Lincoln.

32. Dudley to Ruggles, November 24, 1874, Fort McPherson, Letters Sent, vol. 5, NARA; Leiker and Powers, *Northern Cheyenne Exodus in History and Memory*, 51; Local News, *Western Nebraskian*, December 4, 1874; Greene and Thornton, *Year the Stars Fell*, 374–76.

33. Fort McPherson Post Returns, April 1871, May 1871, June 1871. See Maj. George Ruggles, Department of the Platte, to Lt. J. B. Babcock, North Platte Post, July 6, 1871, Letters Received, Fort McPherson, NARA; General Orders No. 26, August 24, 1871, General Orders, Fort McPherson, NARA.

34. Capt. James Curtis, Fort McPherson, to Maj. George Ruggles, Department of the Platte, February 1, 1872, Letters Sent, Fort McPherson, NARA; Lt. Col. James B. Fry, Department of the Platte, to Brig. Gen. Edward Ord, Division of the Missouri, February 13, 1872, Letters Received, box 3, Fort McPherson, NARA.

35. Lt. Col. William Banner, Fort McPherson, to Lt. William Bowen, September 4, 1865, Telegrams Sent, vol. 2, Fort McPherson, NARA; R. E. Fleming, Post Adjutant, Fort McPherson, to Officer of the Day, Cottonwood Post, February 19, 1866, Lt. Col. R. E. Fleming, Fort McPherson, to Lt. William B. Raper, February 23, 1866, R. E. Fleming, Post Adjutant, Fort McPherson, to Officer of the Day, Cottonwood Post, February 28, 1866, Letters Sent, vol. 1, Fort McPherson, NARA; Lt. Col. R. E. Fleming, Fort McPherson, to Lt. William Bowen, February 10, 1866, Telegrams Sent, vol. 2, Fort McPherson, NARA.

36. Yost, *Call of the Range*, 113.

37. John Milton Thayer, "Letter [MS]: Omaha, Neb., to J. D. Cox, 1870 Oct. 17" (1870), VAULT box, Ayer MS 882, Edward E. Ayer Collection, Newberry Library, Chicago, http://www.aihc.amdigital.co.uk/Documents/Details /Ayer_ms_882#.

38. Bratt, *Trails of Yesterday*, 61–62, 169; Ware, *Indian War of 1864*, 70–72. See also Coleman, *Pre-Statehood History of Lincoln County*, 43–44; and Miller, *Shutters West*, 104–16.

39. Maj. John O'Brien, Cottonwood Post, to Maj. Loree, Fort Laramie, July 4, 1864, Telegrams Sent, Fort McPherson, NARA; Bratt, *Trails of Yesterday*, 169; Ware, *Indian War of 1864*, 70–72; Coleman, *Pre-Statehood History of Lincoln County*, 43–44; and Miller, *Shutters West*, 104–16; Carrington, *Absaraka*, 57.

40. Brig. Gen. J. N. Palmer to Maj. Henry G. Litchfield, Department of the Platte, December 18, 1864, James A. Ekin, Quartermaster General's Office, to Maj. Gen. Philip St. George Cooke, Department of the Platte, November 6, 1866, James Geary Affadavit, January 6, 1867, Letters Received, box 1, Fort McPherson, NARA; Affadavit of John Saylor, July 13, 1870, Letters Received, box 2, Fort McPherson, NARA.

41. Eugene Sheffield, Post Adjutant, Fort McPherson, to Lt. Samuel A. Lux, June 12, 1865, Letters Sent, vol. 1, Fort McPherson, NARA; Gen. Chris-

topher Augur, Department of the Platte, to Col. Henry Carrington, Cottonwood Post, May 8, 1867; Col. Henry B. Carrington, Fort McPherson, to CO, Fort Sedgwick, April 13, 1867, Telegraphs Sent, vol. 2, Fort McPherson, NARA.

42. Albert Bruman, Post Adjutant, Fort McPherson CO, Plum Creek Station, January 3, 1866, Telegraphs Sent, vol. 2, Fort McPherson, NARA; John Mizner, Fort McPherson, to Maj. Henry G. Litchfield, Department of the Platte, August 27, 1866, Letters Sent, vol. 2, Fort McPherson, NARA.

43. Ware, *Indian War of 1864*, 141. I added up this total using two letterbooks in the McPherson records: Telegrams Sent, vol. 2, and Letters Sent, vol. 2, Fort McPherson, NARA.

44. Albert Bruman, Post Adjutant, Fort McPherson, to Telegraph Operator, Box Elder, July 26, 1866, Albert Bruman, Post Adjutant, Fort McPherson, to CO, Company B, U.S. Cavalry, August 25, 1866, Letters Sent, vol. 1, Fort McPherson, NARA; Albert Bruman, Post Adjutant, Fort McPherson, to Lt. Robinson, CO, Company A, Second Cavalry, July 26, 1866, Albert Bruman, Post Adjutant, Fort McPherson, to Lt. Col. Mizner, CO, Company B, Second Cavalry, July 26, 1866, and Lt. Col. John Mizner, Fort McPherson, to Edward D. Townsend, Adjutant General, U.S. Army, Washington DC, January 20, 1867, Letters Sent, vol. 2, Fort McPherson, NARA; Deposition of George N. Woodard, September 1, 1866, Letters Received, box 1, Fort McPherson, NARA.

45. Utley, *Frontiersmen in Blue*, 38–39.

46. I tallied the number of desertions using the Cottonwood Post Post Returns (1863–65) and Fort McPherson Post Returns (1866–80), jpeg images (digital scan of original records in the National Archives, Washington DC), subscription database, http://www.ancestry.com/.

47. Charles E. Lathorpe's letter likely kept the private, who only enlisted a few months prior to his arrest, from being booted out of the Army. But Lathorpe deserted again four months later, and he was promptly discharged soon thereafter. See Charles E. Lathorpe, Ninth Infantry to Post Adjutant, Camp Sheridan, June 14, 1876, Letters Received, box 1, Camp Sheridan, NARA; Ninth Cavalry Regimental Return, Jan. 1870–Dec. 1879, M665, Roll 104 (jpeg images [digital scan of original records in the National Archives, Washington DC], subscription database, http:// www.ancestry.com/.)

48. Gretchen Cassel Eick, "U.S. Indian Policy, 1865–90, as Illuminated through the Lives of Charles A. Eastman and Elaine Goodale Eastman," *Great Plains Quarterly* 28 (2008): 27–47.

49. Col. Henry B. Carrington, Fort McPherson, to Maj. Henry G. Litchfield, Department of the Platte, May 19, 1867, Telegrams Sent, McPherson, NARA.

50. Col. Henry B. Carrington, Fort McPherson, to Gen. George Custer, Seventh Cavalry, April 12, 1867, and Lt. Henry Wessels, McPherson, to Col. Patrick, U.S. Indian Agent, July 30, 1867, Letters Received, box 1, Fort McPherson, NARA.

51. Col. Joseph J. Reynolds, McPherson, to Assistant Adjutant General, Department of the Platte, March 9, 1872, and 1st Lt. Joseph Lawson to Capt. Charles Meinhold, January 4, 1873, Letters Sent, vol. 4, Fort McPherson, NARA; Gen. Philip Sheridan, District of the Missouri, to Gen. Edward Ord, Department of the Platte, March 21, 1872, copy, Letters Received, box 3, Fort McPherson, NARA.

52. Petition of the Citizens of North Platte, May 15, 1871, Letters Received, box 3, Fort McPherson, NARA; William A. Reed, deputy sheriff of Lincoln County, to Post Commander at Fort McPherson, August 15, 1873, Letters Received, Fort McPherson, NARA; General Order No. 37, September 15, 1873, General Orders, vol. 4, Fort McPherson, NARA.

53. First Lt. John B. Johnson, McPherson, to Daniel Freeman, Plum Creek, March 26, 1872, Letters Sent, vol. 4, Fort McPherson, NARA; Daniel Freeman, Plum Creek, to Gen. Edward Ord, Omaha, March 30, 1872, Letters Received, box 3, Fort McPherson, NARA; George Roberts, Hitchcock County, to Governor Robert W. Furnas, Lincoln, October 26, 1873 (copy).

54. Maj. Nathan A. Dudley, Endorsement on papers connected with the buying of the mule from an Indian by Mr. J. A. Moore of Sidney Nebraska, April 7, 1873, Endorsements Sent, vol. 1, Sidney Barracks, NARA.

55. Maj. Nathan A. Dudley, Endorsement on papers connected with the buying of the mule from an Indian by Mr. J. A. Moore of Sidney Nebraska, April 7, 1873; Maj. Nathan A. Dudley, Endorsement on communication to the Sub-Department of the Platte, enclosing the bid of Mr. Carrigan of Sidney, Nebraska, April 18, 1873, Endorsements Sent, vol. 1, Sidney Barracks, NARA.

56. George H. Plummer, McPherson Station, to Gen. Nathan Dudley, McPherson, September 21, 1874 (two letters), Maj. Nathan Dudley, Fort McPherson, to George H. Plummer, McPherson Station, September 21, 1874, Letters Received, box 4, Reuben Wood, to Post Commander, Fort McPherson, January 21, 1871, Letters Received, box 3, Fort McPherson, NARA.

57. Maj. Nathan Dudley, McPherson, to Lt. A. C. Paul, Third Cavalry, September 16, 1874, Letters Sent, McPherson, NARA.

58. Col. George Woodward, McPherson, to Assistant Adjutant General, Department of the Platte, May 6, 1874, Letters Sent, vol. 5, Fort McPherson, NARA.

59. General Order No. 29, September 28, 1869, General Order No. 10, September 15, 1869, General Orders, vol. 2, Fort McPherson, NARA.

60. Stars, Iron Shell, Buechel, and Manhart, *Lakota Tales and Texts*, 691; Ware, *Indian War of 1864*, 273.

61. Linda Darus Clark, "Sioux Treaty of 1868," National Archives, https://www.archives.gov/education/lessons/sioux-treaty.

3. The Horse Wars

1. U.S. War Department, *Annual Report of the Secretary of War, 1872*, 52.

2. "The Grand Duke—He Is Going on a Buffalo Hunt, and Will Visit Leavenworth," *Leavenworth (KS) Weekly Times,* January 4, 1872.

3. Col. Henry B. Carrington, Fort McPherson, to Gen. George Custer, Seventh Cavalry, April 12, 1867, Letters Received, box 1, Fort McPherson, Records of U.S. Army Continental Commands, 1817–1947, Record Group 393, National Archives, Washington DC. Letters and telegrams from the Fort McPherson records at the National Archives will hereafter be cited in this format: series, volume or box (when applicable), Fort McPherson, NARA. This is the same expedition that resulted in the Kidder Massacre.

4. Hyde, *Spotted Tail's Folk,* 150–52; Col. Joseph J. Reynolds, McPherson, to Assistant Adjutant General, Department of the Platte, March 5, 1873, Letters Sent, vol. 4, Fort McPherson, NARA; Maj. John DuBois, Fort McPherson, to Assistant Adjutant General, Department of the Platte, May 8, 1873, Letters Sent, vol. 4, NARA.

5. McGinnis, *Counting Coup and Cutting Horses,* 48; Wishart, *Unspeakable Sadness,* 124.

6. Col. Joseph J. Reynolds, McPherson, Third Cavalry, to Post Adjutant, Fort McPherson, April 10, 1873, Letters Sent, vol. 4, Fort McPherson, NARA. See also J. Randall, North Platte, to Lt. Col. James A. Palmer, McPherson, April 26, 1868, Letters Received, box 1, Fort McPherson, NARA.

7. "Sioux Treaty of 1868," Teaching with Documents: Sioux Treaty of 1868, Archives.gov, http://www.archives.gov/education/lessons/sioux-treaty/.

8. Lt. Col. Henry Wessels, Fort McPherson, to Assistant Adjutant General, Department of the Platte, October 6, 1867, Letters Sent, vol. 2, Fort McPherson, NARA.

9. Lt. Col. John K. Mizner, McPherson, to Maj. Henry G. Litchfield, Department of the Platte, February 28, 1866, Letters Received, box 1, Fort McPherson, NARA.

10. Wrehe, "'Thus Glory Does Fade,'" 65, 70; Maj. Nathan Dudley, McPherson, to Gen. George D. Ruggles, Omaha, September 10, 1874, Maj. Dudley, McPherson, to Ruggles, Omaha, September 12, 1874, Dudley to Acting Assistant Adjutant General, Department of the Republican, Sidney Barracks, September 13, 1874, Dudley to Acting Assistant Adjutant General, Department of the Republican, Sidney Barracks, September 14, 1874, Letters Sent, vol. 5, NARA.

11. Fort McPherson Post Returns, April 1873.

12. Holmes, *Fort McPherson, Nebraska,* 51; and Fort McPherson Post Returns (1872–80), April 1873, jpeg image (digital scan of original records in the National Archives, Washington DC), subscription database, http://www.ancestry.com/.

13. First Lt. Joseph Lawson to Capt. Anson Mills, April 21, 1873, Letters Sent, vol. 4, Fort McPherson, NARA. A sequential reading of these reports provides a striking narrative of the fort, the Plains Indian Wars, and the wave of homesteaders flooding the region. See Scouting Reports, Fort McPherson, NARA.

14. Van de Logt, *War Party in Blue*, 4, 36, 99.

15. Thomas O'Donnell, "Reminiscences: 1867–1868," Thomas O'Donnell Collection (1844–1935), Record Group 1284, AM, Nebraska State Historical Society, Lincoln, 8. See also Van de Logt, *War Party in Blue*, 90.

16. Capt. Henry E. Noyes, Second Cavalry, to 1st Lt. A. E. Bates, McPherson, Letters Received, box 2, McPherson, NARA.

17. Unknown correspondent on Swift Bear to Post Commander at McPherson, n.d., Letters Received, box 2, McPherson, NARA. This letter was likely written by Spotted Tail, on both his and Swift Bear's behalf, or by an agent or translator who was capable of writing. Spotted Tail learned English while at Fort Leavenworth, but there is no evidence that he wrote this letter. It is written in the first person, however, and at the very least it was dictated by a duly appointed representative of his people, which would have probably been Spotted Tail.

18. Hyde, *Spotted Tail's Folk*, 162–65.

19. McGinnis, *Counting Coup and Cutting Horses*, 70.

20. Williamson, "Last Buffalo Hunt of the Pawnees." Richard White argues that the Lakota were primarily responsible for the decline of the Pawnees and that horse theft was one of several contributing factors. I agree with this assessment, but I would stress that horses were necessary in order for the Pawnees to reach the hunting grounds that lay far from their reservation and that hunting was a key source of protein for the Pawnees. Thus, horses were necessary for the Pawnees in order to maintain their food supply, though this was only the case during the late 1860s and 1870s, when bison herds retreated westward. See White, *Roots of Dependency*, 201, 211.

21. Fire Lightning, Big Springs, Nebraska, to Post Commander, Fort McPherson, February 25, 1867, Letters Received, box 4, Fort McPherson, NARA.

22. Cozzens, *Earth Is Weeping*, 208–12.

23. First Lt. William Rogers, Ninth Infantry, to 2nd Lt. William Abbot, Camp Sheridan Post Adjutant, May 3, 1875, Letters Received, box 1, Camp Sheridan, NARA; Camp Sheridan Post Returns, May 1875 and June 1875.

24. Second Lt. Frederick Schwarka, Third Cavalry to William Abbot, Camp Sheridan Post Adjutant, July 1, 1875; E. A. Howard, Spotted Tail Agency, to Capt. Anson Mills, Camp Sheridan Post Commander, August 23, 1875, Letters Received, box 1, Camp Sheridan, NARA.

25. Brig. Gen. Edward Ord, Department of the Platte, to HQ, District of the Black Hills, October 8, 1874, Letters Received, box 1, Camp Sheridan, NARA.

26. Gen. Sherman, St. Louis, to CO, Camp Sheridan, March 17, 1875, Letters Received, box 1, Camp Sheridan, NARA.

27. Moulton, *Valentine T. Mcgillycuddy*, 61–62.

28. Marquis, *Wooden Leg*, 169.

29. Waggoner, *Witness*, 130.

30. Hedren, *Great Sioux War Orders of Battle*, 63, 112.

31. Marquis, *Wooden Leg*, 161–62.

32. Hedren, *Great Sioux War Orders of Battle*, 132–33; Moulton, *Valentine T. Mcgillycuddy*, 91. For more information on the pony seizures at the agencies, see Clow, "General Philip Sheridan's Legacy," 460–77.

33. Bray, *Crazy Horse*, 97, 100.

34. QM Letters Received 1876, no. 5366, November 27, 1876.

35. U.S. War Department, *Annual Report of the Secretary of War, 1878*, 534.

36. See Military Service Institution, "Fifth Regiment of Infantry," 477; de Stiguer, *Wild Horses of the West*, 120–21.

37. U.S. War Department, *Annual Report of the Secretary of War, 1878*, 534, 536–37; Waggoner, *Witness*, 615N10.

38. U.S. War Department, *Annual Report of the Secretary of War, 1878*, 534, 536–37.

39. Contracts for Property Received from U.S. Army to Indian Scouts, Cheyenne Agency, D.T., folder 1, box 74, Enlistment Papers of Indian Scouts, 1866–1914, Records of the Adjutant General's Office, Record Group 94, NARA; Fort Bennett, Post Return, June 1877.

40. The most accurate summary of this information can be found in Waggoner, *Witness*, 615N10. See also Donald F. Danker, "The North Brothers and the Pawnee Scouts," in Paul, *Nebraska Indian Wars Reader*, 82–83; "Act to Divide a Portion of the Reservation of the Sioux Nation;" Clow, "General Philip Sheridan's Legacy," 466.

41. De Stiguer, *Wild Horses of the West*, 120.

42. Visit of Sioux Delegation to Washington, tablet 37, Ricker Collection, MS008, 28; Bratt, *Trails of Yesterday*, 261; Sorenson, "Quarter Century on the Plains," 204–5.

43. Lt. Col. L. H. Bradley, District of the Black Hills, to Capt. D. Monahan, June 20, 1877, Letters Received, box 2, Camp Sheridan, NARA; Bratt, *Trails of Yesterday*, 216; Letter from Citizens of Indianola, Red Willow County NE, to Post Commander, March 1875, box 4, Letters Received, Fort McPherson, NARA.

44. Endorsement on letter, D. B. Ball, U.S. Marshal, to Chief QM, Department of the Platte, November 6, 1879, Endorsements Sent, vol. 3, Camp Sheridan, NARA.

45. Capt. Deane Monahan, Third Cavalry, to R. Williams, Department of the Platte, October 23, 1878, Endorsements Sent, vol. 3, Camp Sheridan, NARA.

46. J. H. Hammond, Ogalalla Agency, to Capt. Deane Monahan, Camp Sheridan, December 1, 1878, Letters Received, box 2, Camp Sheridan, NARA.

47. Moulton, *Valentine T. Mcgillycuddy*, 166. I planned to retrieve this document and other agency records during a planned trip to Missouri in late 2018, but due to the government shutdown, the National Archives at Kansas City, facility was closed.

48. Second Lt. Frederick Schwartka, Third Cavalry, to Capt. Daniel W. Burke, CO, Camp Sheridan, July 9, 1877; Endorsements Sent, vol. 3, Camp

Sheridan, NARA; Mardi Anderson, "Gilbert C. Fosdick II, Stagecoach Driver," *Grand Island Independent,* February 20, 2003.

49. Capt. Deane Monahan, Third Cavalry, to R. Williams, Department of the Platte, October 23, 1878, Endorsements Sent, vol. 3, Camp Sheridan, NARA; Camp Sheridan General Orders & Special Orders, 1:78.

50. 2nd Lt. Joseph Dorst, Fourth Cavalry, to CO Camp Sheridan, May 7, 1877, Letters Received, box 2, Camp Sheridan, NARA.

51. R. Williams, Department of the Platte, to CO, Camp Sheridan, September 19, 1877, Letters Received, box 2, Camp Sheridan, NARA; 1st Lt. W. P. Clark, Second Cavalry, to CO, Camp Sheridan, May 20, 1877, Letters Received, box 2, Camp Sheridan, NARA.

52. Endorsement on letter from Lt. J. M. Lee, September 25, 1877; Endorsement on additional report of Lt. J. M. Lee, September 25, 1877; Endorsements Sent, vol. 3, Camp Sheridan, NARA (63).

53. Leiker and Powers, *Northern Cheyenne Exodus in History and Memory,* 34, 49–50, 59.

54. Endorsement on Maj. Caleb H. Carlton, Third Cavalry, to Camp Sheridan, October 13, 1878, Endorsement on Maj. Caleb H. Carlton, Third Cavalry to Camp Sheridan, October 31, 1878, Endorsements Sent, vol. 3, Camp Sheridan, NARA (107).

55. Monnett, *Tell Them We Are Going Home,* 97–99; Endorsement on letter of J. H. Hammond, Indian Inspector, December 5, 1878, Endorsements Sent, Camp Sheridan, NARA.

56. Alfred Sorenson, "A Quarter of a Century on the Frontier, or the Adventures of Major Frank North, 'The White Chief of the Pawnees,'" Frank North Collection, MS448, Nebraska State Historical Society, Lincoln, 203–6; Bratt, *Trails of Yesterday,* 262; "Murder and Robbery by Indians," *Daily Los Angeles Herald,* November 23, 1878; Account of Horses, Mules-McPherson Herd, 1875–83, Bratt Collection; John Bratt, North Platte, to Maj. Eugene Carr, Fort McPherson, December 23, 1878, Letters Sent, Fort McPherson, NARA.

57. Account of Horses, Mules-McPherson Herd, 1875–83, Bratt Collection; Bratt, *Trails of Yesterday,* 262–67; Sorenson, "Quarter of a Century on the Frontier," 207. The North Platte Guards were a large citizen militia group formed the previous month in response to the threat of Indian raids on Lincoln County. They will be discussed in much further detail in chap. 4.

58. Sorenson, "Quarter of a Century on the Frontier," 203–5.

59. Bratt, *Trails of Yesterday,* 261, 270–73.

60. Endorsement on letter from "Woman's Dress," Indian Soldier, at Pine Ridge Agency, May 15, 1879, Endorsements Sent, vol. 3, Camp Sheridan, NARA; see also McGinnis, *Counting Coup and Cutting Horses,* 173–94.

61. Maj. Eugene Carr, Fort McPherson, to Adjutant General, Department of the Platte, August 21, 1877, Telegrams Sent, Fort McPherson, NARA; Fort McPherson Post Returns, September 1878 and March 1880.

62. Maj. John DuBois, Fort McPherson, to Assistant Adjutant General, Department of the Platte, May 8, 1873, Letters Sent, vol. 4, NARA.

63. Copy of endorsement sent from Gen. Philip Sheridan, Military District of the Missouri, to the commander of the Department of the Platte, May 20, 1873, forwarded from James W. Forsyth to the post commander at Fort McPherson, May 22, 1873, Letters Received, box 4, Col. Joseph J. Reynolds to Assistant Adjutant General of the Military District of the Missouri, October 31, 1873, Letters Sent, Fort McPherson, NARA.

64. Paine, *Pioneers, Indians, and Buffalos*, 65–72.

65. For more information on the dispossession of American Indians in Nebraska, see Wishart, *Unspeakable Sadness*, 187–238; and Hyde, *Spotted Tail's Folk*, 219–46.

66. Capt. Henry Wessels, Third Cavalry, to Post Adjutant, Fort McPherson, June 19, 1876, Scouting Reports, Fort McPherson, NARA.

4. A Most Tempting Business

1. "A Moral County," *Western Nebraskian*, October 2, 1874.

2. Ellis, *Law and Order in Buffalo Bill's Country*, 112, 116.

3. Reports of personal and property crime are compiled from the following sources: Lincoln County Criminal Court (Docket A), Lincoln County Court (Docket A), and Lincoln County Probate Court (Dockets A–B). Illegible entries and "victimless crimes" (e.g., drunkenness) are omitted. The years 1883 and 1884 are excluded since the county criminal court journals did not record any court hearings for much of that time. The number of horse thief incidents are annualized from the data in fig. 1. Population is calculated using the following formula: using data points from the 1870, 1880, 1885, and 1890 census population tables (Nebraska held a state census in 1885), I computed population growth from 1870 to 1880 using the following linear equation: $361.5x + 17$. I used a cubic equation for the period between 1880 and 1890 in order to express the accelerating growth pattern indicated by the 1885 census estimate. The equation is: $y = 5.27203x^3 + -155.981x^2 + 1669.92x + -2741.09$. To request a copy of this data, please email the author at luckethistory@gmail.com. The census data can be accessed at U.S. Bureau of the Census, *Statistics of the Population of the United States*, 1870: Population, vol. 1, pt. 1, 46; U.S. Bureau of the Census, *Statistics of Population of the United States at the Tenth Census*, 1880: Population, vol. 1, pt. 1, 70; U.S. Bureau of the Census, *Report on Population of the United States at the Eleventh Census*, 1890: Population, vol. 1, pt. 1, 243. For a county-by-county breakdown of the 1885 Nebraska State Census, see "Marvellous Increase of People," *McCook Tribune*, August 27, 1885.

4. Cheyenne County Court Docket, vols. 2–5; Cheyenne County District Court, vols. A–B, CCC. According to the Cheyenne County clerk, vol. 1 of the County Court Docket is missing.

5. Best, *Doc Middleton*, 5.

6. Hutton, *Doc Middleton*, 35; Cheyenne County Case Files, CCC; Lincoln County Criminal Court Dockets, A-106, NSHS. Much of the hyperbole that emerged about Middleton came from the pens of newspaper writers, correspondents, and editors. The editor of the *Red Cloud Chief*, in describing Middleton to his readers, expressed a fairly typical assessment of the horse thief at that time: "For the benefit of those who may not know the character of 'Doc' Middleton, we will say that he is the leader of a gang of a hundred or more desperados who, by their lawless acts have terrorized the whole Niobrara country in the northern part of this state." See *Red Cloud Chief* (Red Cloud NE), July 31, 1879.

7. Hutton, *Doc Middleton*, 33, 35, 37–44; Account of Horses, Mules-McPherson Herd, 1875–83, Bratt Collection. For more information on the "Robin Hood" archetype as applied to other bandits in history, see Hobsbawm, *Bandits*, 41–56. Richard White uses a similar approach in White, "Outlaws of the Middle Border: American Social Bandits," *Western Historical Quarterly* 12 (1981): 391–93.

8. Ellis, *Law and Order in Buffalo Bill's Country*, 46, 178; Lincoln County Court Dockets, A93–A95, NSHS; Lincoln County Probate Court, B151, NSHS; Account of Horses, Mules-McPherson Herd, 1875–83, Bratt Collection.

9. Bratt, *Trails of Yesterday*, 261.

10. See the Doc Middleton Correspondence, 1867–79, MS120, NSHS. The originals are not available for public use, but reproductions are. They were transcribed, typed, and microfilmed by Harold Hutton.

11. J. M. Reilly to J. B. Reilly, February 12, 1872, April 2, 1872, April 121, 872, J. M. Reilly to M. A. Reilly, June 7, 1873, Middleton Correspondence, NSHS. See also Hutton, *Doc Middleton*, 25. Based on these letters, Hutton argues that Middleton missed his home back in Texas and did not like being separated from his wife and child during cattle drives.

12. Hutton, *Doc Middleton*, 14, 96–98; J. M. Reilly to M. A. Reilly, June 7, 1873, Mary Middleton to Mrs. Reilly, July 29, 1879, Middleton Collection, NSHS; Best, *Doc Middleton*, 24–25.

13. Best, *Doc Middleton*, 25; Hutton, *Doc Middleton*, 48.

14. Bratt, *Trails of Yesterday*, 274–76.

15. Best, *Doc Middleton*, 15.

16. Local News, *Grant County Tribune*, May 21, 1891; "A Wife Charges Her Husband with Being an Outlaw," *Grant County Tribune*, May 14, 1891.

17. Unfortunately, these are the only two written depositions that the author could find. Lincoln County case files did not include written depositions from defendants. These two depositions were found in Bratt's private correspondence, suggesting that at some point he or his lawyer requested these depositions for some undetermined reason. See "Statement of Thomas Campbell" and "Deposition of G. A. Fane," Bratt, John, 1842–1918, Nebraska State Historical Society, Lincoln, box 3, folder 6, RG4157.AM (hereafter referred to as Bratt MSS).

18. Census Bulletin (no. 208), 1890 Census, 12.

19. Grant County Historical Society, *Grant County Neighbors and Friends*, 395.

20. Yost, *Call of the Range*, 214, 226–30, 272–73.

21. Grant County Historical Society, *Grant County Neighbors and Friends*, 312–13.

22. "Statement of Thomas Campbell," Bratt MSS; and "Cattle Thieves Bound Over," *Omaha Daily Bee*, February 16, 1890. The *Daily Bee* article claims that Yeast was on the executive committee of the cattle association responsible for bringing the action against him. Yeast also appears on the stationery letterhead of the Northwestern Nebraska Stock Growers Association, which was used for a letter Bratt received warning him about recent cattle thefts in Grant County. See M. B. Ocumpaugh to Bratt, January 21, 1890, Bratt MSS, box 2, folder 1.

23. R. M. Moran to Bratt, January 21, 1890, Bratt MSS, box 2, folder 1; "Cattle Thieves Bound Over," *Omaha Daily Bee*, February 16, 1890; State of Nebraska v. Perry Yeast et al., Grant County.

24. "Statement of Thomas Campbell," Bratt MSS; State of Nebraska v. Perry Yeast et al., Grant County.

25. State of Nebraska v. Perry Yeast et al., Grant County; "Cattle Thieves Bound Over," *Omaha Daily Bee*, February 16, 1890; "Cattle Thieves," *Omaha Daily Bee*, December 18, 1890; Shumway, *History of Western Nebraska*, 121.

26. Northwest Nebraska Stock Growers Association, Articles of Incorporation, Miscellaneous County Records, Vol. 1, GCC; "Sutton Ordered Acquitted," *Omaha Daily Bee*, January 9, 1908; "Perry A. Yeast Pays Fine," *Omaha Daily Bee*, September 15, 1908; "CONSPIRACY OF FARMERS," *Herald Democrat* (Leadville CO), November 4, 1910.

27. "Local Paragraphs," *Alliance Herald*, January 26, 1911; "Local Paragraphs," *Alliance Herald*, April 20, 1911; Shumway, *History of Western Nebraska*, 121; Yost, *Call of the Range*, 172.

28. John Feack, "One-Man Mafia of the Prairies," *True* 41 (1960): 24, 25, 90–97; Mari Sandoz, "Tyrant of the Plains," *Saturday Evening Post*, June 7, 1958.

29. Sandoz, "Tyrant of the Plains."

30. Local News, *Grant County Tribune*, October 15, 1891; *Grant County Neighbors and Friends*, 370, 391.

31. "Deposition of G. A. Fane," Bratt MSS.

32. Hobsbawm, *Primitive Rebels*, 30–56.

33. John Milton Thayer, "Letter [MS]: Omaha, Neb., to J. D. Cox, 1870 Oct. 17" (1870), Edward E. Ayer Collection, Newberry Library, Chicago, http://www.aihc.amdigital.co.uk/Documents/Details/Ayer_ms_882#; Miller, *Shutters West*, 102.

34. Hobsbawm, *Primitive Rebels*, 30–31; Capt. Campbell D. Emory, North Platte, to Maj. Eugene Carr, Fort McPherson, May 16, 1870, Register of Letters Received, Fort McPherson, NARA.

35. "Cattle Rustling," *Pioneer Grip* (Alliance NE), December 8, 1893.

36. Grant County Historical Society, *Grant County Neighbors and Friends*, 395–96.

5. From Thieves to Villains

1. "'The Wild West,'" *Omaha Daily Bee*, May 16, 1883; "The Lincoln Mannerchor Coming To-Morrow," *Omaha Daily Bee*, May 19, 1883.

2. Hutton, *Early History of North Platte*, 22–25; Coleman, *Pre-Statehood History of Lincoln County*, 82.

3. U.S. Department of the Interior, *Tenth Census: Statistics of Agriculture*, http://www.agcensus.usda.gov/Publications/Historical_Publications/1880 /1880a_v3–02.pdf, 72; U.S. Department of the Interior, *Eleventh Census: Statistics of Agriculture*, http://www.agcensus.usda.gov/Publications/Historical _Publications/1890/1890a_v5–08.pdf, 162.

4. Lincoln County Criminal Court Dockets, B-230, B-324, NSHS; Lincoln District Court Case Files, LCC C-30, C-32, C-67, C-284, C-463, C-464, LCC.

5. Lincoln County Court Dockets, C-233, B-511, C-363, NSHS; Ellis, *Law and Order in Buffalo Bill's Country*, 46; Lincoln County Criminal Court Dockets, C-231, C-232, C-233, NSHS.

6. Data compiled from the following legal sources: Nebraska, Lincoln County, County Court Docket A, Nebraska State Historical Society (NSHS), Lincoln; Criminal Court Docket A, NSHS; and Probate Court Dockets A and B, NSHS.

7. "A Team Stolen," *Lincoln County Tribune*, August 28, 1889; Ellis, *Law and Order in Buffalo Bill's Country*, 65.

8. Lincoln County Court Dockets, A-113, NSHS; Nebraska, Lincoln County, County Court Criminal Dockets, A-88, Nebraska State Historical Society, Lincoln (hereafter cited as "Lincoln County Criminal Court Dockets, volume-page, NSHS").

9. Lincoln County Estray Catalogue, 1870–90, RG218, NSHS. Note that some of these animals were lame, blind, or old and thus may have been "put out to pasture," or retired from service. However, it seems that no more than ten of the horses described fit that criteria, although some descriptions are not detailed enough to indicate the condition of the stray horse. A few were also found with saddles and saddle marks, indicating that they were in active use. Unfortunately, there is no reliable record of the number of horses reported missing during this period of time, but it can be assumed that the majority of people who lost horses consulted the estray catalog and called upon their neighbors to see whether their horses had ended up in someone else's herd.

10. Nebraska, Cheyenne County, District Court Journal, vols. A–C (hereafter cited as "Cheyenne County District Court Journal, volume-page, CCC").

11. Justice of the Peace Docket, Journal A, CCC.

12. Lola Byington, "Old Chadron Days," NSHS.

13. Phyllis Holding, "The Founding of Dawes County, 1884–1885," NSHS; George Walter Scott, *Chadron Democrat*, September 17, 1885, cited in Watson, *Prairie Justice*, 4.

14. Watson, *Prairie Justice*, 4.

15. Nebraska, Dawes County, District Court Case Files, Wally Church, Dawes County Courthouse, Chadron. Hereafter referred to as "Dawes District Court Case Files, DCC."

16. Lewis Dillon, John O'Brien, Dawes County Case Files, DCC.

17. Webster, *Memories of a Pioneer*, 3.

18. 1890 Agricultural Census, 162, 338; Lena Jones Anderson, "Pioneers," in *Dusting Off the Saddles*, 45–46.

19. Ellis, *Law and Order in Buffalo Bill's Country*, 46; Nebraska, Lincoln County, District Court Case Files, Frank Massey, Lincoln County Courthouse, North Platte, box 2. Hereafter referred to as "Lincoln District Court Case Files, LCC."

20. Keith County District Court Records, Journal A, NSHS.

21. Nebraska, Lincoln County, District Court Journal, c-284–85, c-290, Lincoln County Courthouse, North Platte (hereafter cited as "Lincoln County District Court Journal, volume-page, LCC"); George James, Case Files, DCC.

22. Lincoln County *Tribune*, March 31, 1888.

23. "Was It a Theft," *Grant County Tribune*, September 18, 1890.

24. Schubert, "Violent World of Emanuel Stance," 203–20; Leiker, "Black Soldiers at Fort Hays," 30–31.

25. Lamm, "Buffalo Soldier Chaplains of the Old West," 70–72; Kenner, *Buffalo Soldiers and Officers of the Ninth Cavalry*, 108–9.

26. Department of the Interior, Census Office, *Statistics of the Population of the United States at the Tenth Census*, 400.

27. "Arrested for Horse Stealing," *Grant County Tribune*, June 26, 1890; Local News, *Grant County Tribune*, September 1, 1892; *Sundance (WY) Gazette*, November 3, 1890; Buecker, "Prelude to Brownsville," 105–8, 111.

28. Yost, *Call of the Range*, 65–66; Potter, "'Wearing the Hempen Neck-Tie,'" 141.

29. 1880 U.S. Federal Census (Population Schedule), North Platte, 174, Lincoln, Nebraska, p. 437, line 493, James Belton, jpeg image, available online at Generations Network, 2009 (digital scan of original records in the National Archives, Washington DC), subscription database, http://www.ancestry.com/; James Belton, Letter to the Editor, *Lincoln County Tribune*, September 4, 1886; Middleton, Letter to the Editor, *Western Nebraskian*, May 10, 1879; *Omaha Daily Bee*, August 23, 1887.

30. See Hobsbawm, *Primitive Rebels*, 30–56.

31. Time Book, November 1885 to April 1886, and Account of Horses, Mules-McPherson Herd, 1875–83, Bratt Collection.

32. Justice of the Peace Docket, Case 69, vol. A, Cheyenne County Court, CCC.

33. Bratt, *Trails of Yesterday*, 221, 205–6.

34. Bratt, *Trails of Yesterday*, 206.

35. *Lincoln County Tribune*, October 31, 1885; Cheyenne County Justice Court Docket, Case 74, vol. A, css; Cheyenne County District Court Journals, A-205, ccc.

36. *Lincoln County Tribune*, July 16, 1890; Lincoln County Criminal Court Records, B-318, nshs; Cook, *Fifty Years on the Old Frontier*, 54.

37. Local News, *Lincoln County Tribune*, February 11, 1888; Lincoln County Court Dockets, A-255, nshs.

38. Moore, *Cow Boys and Cattle Men*, 21, 69, 83; 1900 U.S. Federal Census (Population Schedule), Highland, 96, Norton, Kansas, p. 89, line 15, Asa Marcellus, jpeg image, available online at Generations Network, 2009 (digital scan of original records in the National Archives, Washington dc), subscription database, http://www.ancestry.com/.

39. Fort McPherson Post Returns, October 1874.

40. McCoy, "Reminiscences," 21, nshs. For more information on how animal and other chattel mortgages worked in the late-nineteenth-century West and Midwest, see Bogue, Cannon, and Winkle, "Oxen to Organs," 420–52.

41. Lincoln County District Court Journal, c-401, c-4012, c-444, c-511, c-512, lcc; *Lincoln County Tribune*, July 16, 1890; William Comstock, Dawes County Case Files, dcc.

42. "Chattel Mortgage Sale," *Lincoln County Tribune*, September 4, 1886; "Notice of Chattel Mortgage Sale," *Lincoln County Tribune*, January 28, 1888; "Notice," *Lincoln County Tribune*, November 13, 1889.

43. "Wellfleet," *Lincoln County Tribune*, January 7, 1888; "Wellfleet," *Lincoln County Tribune*, January 14, 1888.

44. Case no. 62 and Case no. 63, Lincoln County Criminal Case Files, Nebraska State Historical Society, Lincoln; 1880 U.S. Federal Census (Population Schedule), North Platte, 174, Lincoln, Nebraska, p. 38, l. 625, John Tilford, jpeg image, available online at Generations Network, 2009 (digital scan of original records in the National Archives, Washington dc), subscription database, http://www.ancestry.com/. This charge was based on a statute passed by the Nebraska legislature in 1875 that extended the definition of *larceny* to include embezzlement of property by one co-owner against another. See State of Nebraska, "Laws Passed by the Legislature," 8–9.

45. See Lincoln County District Docket, B-322, B-366; Lincoln Count Criminal Docket, A-138; Lincoln County Census, 1880.

46. Data for figure 24 was compiled from Alan L. Olmstead and Paul W. Rhode, "Rice, Oats, Sorghum, and Soybeans—Acreage, Production, and Price: 1866–1998 [Annual]," table Da667–78; "Corn, Barley, and Flaxseed—Acreage, Production, Price, and Corn Stocks: 1866–1999 [Annual]," table Da693–706; "Wheat, Spring Wheat, and Winter Wheat—Acreage, Production, Price, and Stocks: 1866–1999 [Annual]," table Da717–29; "Hay, Rye, and

Buckwheat—Acreage, Production, and Price: 1866–1999 [Annual]," table Da733–45; "Cattle, Hogs, Sheep, Horses, and Mules—Number on Farms: 1868–2000 [Annual]," table Da968–82; "Horses and Mules—Number on Farms and Value per Head: 1867–1960 [Annual]," table Da983–87, in *Historical Statistics of the United States*, hsus.cambridge.org/ (by subscription).

47. This benefit of livestock production ceased to be a truism by the 1890s for horses. A leveling off of demand for horse power during the Panic of 1893 led to a large supply of horses, and in a very short time the horse market was a very competitive one. By the time the Model T was introduced, demand for horses began a steady and irreversible decline. Beef producers would face similar problems after World War I, when wartime demand for beef collapsed and the oversupply of meat depressed livestock production for decades. See Greene, *Horses at Work*, 202, 224.

48. Greene, *Horses at Work*, 191, 199.

49. Red Cloud *Chief*, April 2, 1886.

50. *Western Horse and Cattle Insurance Company v. Timm*, 23 Neb. 526 (1888); see also Kopf, "Origin, Development and Practices of Livestock Insurance."

51. *Western Horse and Cattle Insurance Company v. Timm*, 23 Neb. 526 (1888).

52. U.S. Department of the Interior, *Tenth Census: Statistics of Agriculture* and *Statistics of Population of the United States at the Tenth Census*, http://www2 .census.gov/prod2/decennial/documents/1880a_v1–01.pdf; Account of Horses, Mules-McPherson Herd, 1875–83, Bratt Collection.

53. Account of Cattle, McPherson Herd, August 1875 to December 31, 1883, Bratt Collection; Bratt, *Trails of Yesterday*, 192.

54. Account of Horses, Mules-McPherson Herd, 1875–83; Memo Book, November 30, 1877 to April 17, 1878; Memo Book, April 17 to August 19, 1878; and Memo Book, June 24 to October 16, 1880, Bratt Collection.

55. Gentry, *Letters to Bob*, 23.

56. Bratt, *Trails of Yesterday*.

57. Bratt, *Trails of Yesterday*.

58. Bratt, *Trails of Yesterday*.

59. Gentry, *Letters to Bob*, 42; Bratt, *Trails of Yesterday*.

60. I cross-referenced victims' names against the 1880 Federal Agricultural Census schedules for Lincoln County. Fifteen plaintiffs or complainants appear on these schedules as ranchers. I did not include self-identified ranchers from the Population schedules because I wanted to limit my results to ranchers with operations large enough to report on the agricultural census schedules. See 1880 U.S. Federal Census (Agriculture Schedules), Districts 72, 172–76, Lincoln, Nebraska, jpeg images, available online at Generations Network, 2009 (digital scan of original records in the National Archives, Washington DC), subscription database, http://www.ancestry.com/.

61. Other victimized ranchers claimed to have much smaller operations—A. M. Stoddard only claimed 4 horses in 1880, while August Johnson claimed

to have none—but it is possible that these owners simply did not want to disclose the true number of horses in their possession. For instance, John Bratt, who claimed to only have 30 horses when completing the 1885 Nebraska State Census, indicated in his personal records that he owned at least 440, which were divided between three different locations on his various tracts of land. See Account of Horses, Mules-McPherson Herd, 1875–83, Bratt Collection.

62. Moore, *Cow Boys and Cattle Men*, 21, 97. See Atherton, *Cattle Kings*, 45, for a more sympathetic view of the ranchers' quest to maintain morality on the plains.

63. Blackstone, Tucker, and Christian, *Blackstone's Commentaries*, 4:238–39.

64. Alan G. Gless, "Criminal Statutes," *History of Nebraska Law*, 30, 32.

65. Gless, "Criminal Statutes," 34; and 1881 Laws of Nebraska, 1394.

66. I will not give a detailed history of the Lincoln County Sheriff's Department in this chapter. Mark Ellis has already done that. Rather, I will limit my discussion to an analysis of how the various layers of law enforcement in Lincoln County enforced against horse theft. This is due in part to the rigor and completeness of Ellis's work and because the resources needed for a more substantive narrative lie mostly outside of my primary source base, with the exception of the Sheriff Day Book, which I will discuss later in this chapter. Readers who wish to read beyond that are highly encouraged to consult Mark Ellis's fantastic work on the subject. See Ellis, *Law and Order in Buffalo Bill's Country*. See also Eric Monkkonen, "History of Urban Police," *Crime and Justice* 15 (1992): 547–80; and Uchida, "Development of the American Police," 17–36.

67. Ellis, *Law and Order in Buffalo Bill's Country*, 17.

68. Ellis, *Law and Order in Buffalo Bill's Country*, 56–61.

69. Ellis, *Law and Order in Buffalo Bill's Country*, 116.

70. "Thief Caught," *North Platte Republican*, August 19, 1876; Salaries of City Officials, John Bratt Collection, box 3, folder 1, RG 4157.AM, NSHS; Time Books, box 2, Bratt Collection, NSHS.

71. Ellis, *Law and Order in Buffalo Bill's Country*, 55, 61–62, 74–78, 120.

72. The data for the foregoing analysis comes from the Sheriff Day Book at the North Platte courthouse. Although some of the data predates 1884, the record seems spotty during that time. See Nebraska, Lincoln County, Sheriff Day Book, Lincoln County Courthouse, North Platte.

73. Although I do not have the data to corroborate this assertion, the connection between departmental income sources and the distribution of public services has been observed and explored elsewhere. For instance, in 2013, an audit of the Los Angeles County Sheriff's Department found that the department's response time in unincorporated areas is higher than its response time in municipalities that subcontract their policing services to the Sheriff's Department. See Robert Faturechi, "Sheriff's Response Time Is Longer in Unincorporated Areas, Audit Finds," *Los Angeles Times*, January 29, 2013, http://articles.latimes.com/2013/jan/29/local/la-me-sheriff-audit-20130129.

Distributed politics literature also addresses this discussion by exploring how the public sector transfers rents to voters, contributors, and others in democracies. See Cox and McCubbins, "Electoral Politics as a Redistributive Game," 370–89. For information on the swing voter side of the debate, refer to Lindbeck and Weibull, "Balanced Budget Redistribution and the Outcome of Political Competition," 273–97; and Dixit and Londregan, "Determinants of Success of Special Interests in Redistributive Politics," 1132–55. For a historical discussion of these concepts in American history, one standout work is Edward L. Glaeser and Claudia Goldin, "Corruption and Reform: Introduction," *Corruption and Reform.*

74. Walker, "'Broken Windows' and Fractured History," 58.

75. Ellis, *Law and Order in Buffalo Bill's Country*, 110–40. Legal historian Jonathan Simon argues that the ubiquity of the police in the twenty-first century is the result of the use of crime since the 1960s as a political "wedge" by which both liberals and conservatives can justify government action. As a result, policing has gone from being a last-resort kind of state intervention to being something that is proactive in enforcing a much more sweeping criminal code. See Simon, *Governing through Crime*, 13–29. For other excellent works that are critical of the growth of the twentieth-century policing state, see Dubber, *Police Power;* and Foucault, *Discipline and Punish.*

76. Nebraska, Lincoln County, County Court Docket A, Nebraska State Historical Society, Lincoln; Nebraska, Lincoln County, Criminal Court Docket A, Nebraska State Historical Society, Lincoln; Nebraska, Lincoln County, Probate Court Dockets A and B, Nebraska State Historical Society, Lincoln.

77. Ellis, *Law and Order in Buffalo Bill's Country*, 56–61, 72.

78. Local News, *North Platte Republican*, November 2, 1878. Ellis makes a similar point. See Ellis, *Law and Order in Buffalo Bill's Country*, 63–64.

79. There is no singular law that forces plaintiffs to pay court costs for a dismissed claim. Rather, judges are given the option in some cases of charging costs to the plaintiff. This right is explicitly stated in several sections of the Nebraska State Statutes (1873, rev. 1881). See Neb. Gen. Stat., chap. 18, art. 2, sec. 8; chap. 26, sec. 270, 278.

80. Lincoln County Probate Court Dockets, A-51, NSHS; Lincoln County Criminal Court Dockets, A-318, NSHS; and Local News, *Lincoln County Tribune,* July 16, 1890,

81. Ellis, *Law and Order in Buffalo Bill's Country*, 208–9.

82. For more background on this phenomenon, see Williams and Murphy, "Evolving Strategy of Police," 27–50.

83. Cheyenne County District Court Journal, B-187, A-317, A-353, A-372, CCC; Yost, *Call of the Range*, 78–79.

84. For more information on the Wyoming Stock Growers Association and stock associations in general, see Burmeister, "Six Decades of Rugged Indi-

vidualism," 143–50; Jackson, "Wyoming Stock Growers' Association Political Power," 571–94; and Merrill, *Public Lands and Political Meaning.*

85. Knowlton, *Cattle Kingdom*, 257–71.

86. Knowlton, *Cattle Kingdom*, 272–99.

87. Bratt, *Trails of Yesterday*, 225.

88. Bratt, *Trails of Yesterday*, 183.

89. Local newspapers, especially the *Western Nebraskian*, often contained stories about local roundups. For one especially interesting narrative of a local roundup, see "The Round Up," *Western Nebraskian*, June 17, 1876.

90. Bratt, *Trails of Yesterday*, 121.

91. "Address of John Bratt," *Western Nebraskian*, March 30, 1878, 138.

92. Brown, *Strain of Violence*, 23.

93. E. Hitt Stewart, "Origin of the Anti–Horse Thief Association," in Gresham, *Story of Major David McKee*, 24; Burchill, *Bullets, Badges, and Bridles*, 53–56.

94. Gresham, *Story of Major David McKee*; Stanberry, *Protect the Innocent*; Burchill, *Bullets, Badges, and Bridles*, 56–58. For some examples of how and where these societies developed, see Luckett, "Wide-Awake Citizens," 16–27.

95. Nolan, *Vigilantes on the Middle Border*, 91–93, 171, and 234–35; "Lynch-Law at Des Moines," *Nebraska Herald* (Plattsmouth), December 24, 1874; and "Meeting of the Anti–Horse Thief Society," *Omaha Daily Bee*, October 25, 1886.

6. When Horse Thieves Were Hanged

1. Yost, *Call of the Range*, 266–74. A better work on the subject of Nebraska vigilantism is Hewitt, "Fatal Fall of Barrett Scott," 107–20.

2. James E. Potter has tallied up all the known cases of lynching in Nebraska, along with the names of the victims, their alleged crimes, and their locations. See Potter, "'Wearing the Hempen Neck-Tie,'" 149.

3. One recent study indicates that western Nebraska was a violent place in general, with homicide rates that compare to Dodge City and other enclaves of western violence. Of the eighty-eight homicides reportedly committed in the Panhandle, five were the result of vigilantism, while another nine were attributable to theft or robbery. See Reed, "Homicide on the Nebraska Panhandle Frontier," 137–60.

4. Jack Morrow to Post Commander, Fort McPherson, April 19, 1868, Letters Received, box 1, Fort McPherson, NARA.

5. Maj. Nathan Dudley, McPherson, to W. W. Newton, Brady Island, May 8, 1876; and Maj. Nathan Dudley, McPherson, to Lt. Col. R. Williams, Omaha, May 8, 1876, Letters Sent, vol. 6, Fort McPherson, NARA.

6. "Red Devils Abound," *North Platte Enterprise*, September 19, 1874; Maj. Nathan Dudley, Fort McPherson, to Maj. George Ruggles, Department of the

Platte, September 13, 1874, and Dudley to Ruggles, September 15, 1874, Letters Sent, McPherson, NARA.

7. Aldrich, "Brief Reminiscences of the Soldiers Life," 23–24.

8. First Lt. John B. Walker, Third Cavalry, to 2nd Lt. James Simpson, McPherson, June 25, 1875, Lt. Col. Innis N. Palmer, McPherson, to J. A. Morrow, Morrow Ranch, April 17, 1867, Letters Sent, J. A. Morrow, Morrow Ranch, to Lt. Col. Innis N. Palmer, April 19, 1868, Letters Received, box 1, Col. William Emory, Fifth Cavalry, to Commander, Department of the Platte, June 1, 1871, Scouting Reports, Fort McPherson, NARA.

9. Fort McPherson Post Returns, June 1870; Bratt, *Trails of Yesterday*, 183–84.

10. William F. Cody, "Letter from the Great Hunter—He Has a Lively Little Fight in Which He Succeeds in Killing Two Indians," *New York Daily Standard*, June 9, 1870, reprinted in the *Tiffin (OH) Tribune*, June 30, 1870; Bratt, *Trails of Yesterday*, 183–84.

11. Lt. Albert Brumer, McPherson, to Lt. Cutter et al., September 18, 1865, Letters Sent, vol. 1, McPherson, NARA; Philip H. Sherman to Army Headquarters, copy, Governor Albinus Nance Collection, Letters Received, folder 1, Record Group 1, NSHS. For just one example of such a report after the Battle of Little Bighorn, see "The Indian Situation," *Western Nebraskian*, July 15, 1876.

12. Capt.-Elect Frank North, North Platte Guards, to Asst. Adj. Gen. Bruno Tochuck, State of Nebraska, December 6, 1878, Mayor James Belton, North Platte, to Governor Silas Garber, State of Nebraska, December 2, 1878, and Tochuck to Garber, November 17, 1878, Governor Silas Garber Collection, Letters Received, folder 15, Record Group 1, NSHS.

13. This incident is discussed in much further detail in chap. 2. For more information on the event itself, see Bratt, *Trails of Yesterday*, 262–67; and Alfred Sorenson, "A Quarter of a Century on the Frontier, or the Adventures of Major Frank North, 'The White Chief of the Pawnees,'" Frank North Collection, MS448, Nebraska State Historical Society, Lincoln, 207.

14. 1880 U.S. Federal Census (Agriculture Schedules), District 174, Lincoln, Nebraska.

15. Bratt, *Trails of Yesterday*, 268; 1880 U.S. Federal Census (Agriculture Schedules), District 174, Lincoln, Nebraska; List of Names for Indian Fight on East Birdwood, folder 16, Bratt Collection.

16. This is not to say that there was absolutely no criminal justice apparatus in Lincoln County. Ellis points out that a major murder trial had already occurred in the county, in 1868, during which the suspect was investigated, arrested, tried, released on a technicality, retried on a different charge, and convicted according to law. Ellis sees this as evidence of a professional, fully functioning judiciary. See Ellis, *Law and Order in Buffalo Bill's Country*, 1–17.

17. Adamson, *North Plate and Its Associations*, 55.

18. Adamson, *North Plate and Its Associations*, 62–67.

19. Adamson, *North Platte and Its Associations*, 71–75; and Ellis, *Law and Order in Buffalo Bill's Country*, 85–86. Ellis cites Adamson, who presents no other evidence to corroborate this account. However, the petition filed by the vigilance committee to the commander at Fort McPherson is on file at the National Archives. Although it is unknown whether the commander actually gave the committee a ten-minute ultimatum, his reaction must have been swift and decisive, as no other comment on the incident appears in the post return or in the rest of the fort's correspondence. See Petition of the Citizens of North Platte, May 15, 1871, Letters Received, box 3, Fort McPherson, NARA.

20. Avery, *Lynchings, Legends, and Lawlessness*, 172–73; Department of the Interior, Census Office, *Statistics of the Population of the United States at the Tenth Census*, 495.

21. Hewitt, "Fatal Fall of Barrett Scott," 107–20. According to Potter, a total of nine people are known to have been lynched in the Niobrara Valley (specifically Boyd, Brown, Holt, Keya Paha, and Rock Counties), which is more than the seven people believed to have been lynched in western Nebraska. See Potter, "'Wearing the Hempen Neck-Tie,'" 141.

22. Nebraska Prisoner Records Database, NSHS.

23. Potter, "'Wearing the Hempen Neck-Tie,'" 144–45, 149; McGrath, *Homicide, Race, and Justice in the American West*, 61; Reed, "Homicide on the Nebraska Panhandle Frontier," 147–48.

24. Potter, "'Wearing the Hempen Neck-Tie,'" 149; Reed, "Homicide on the Nebraska Panhandle Frontier," 137–60.

25. Knowlton, *Cattle Kingdom*, 189–91.

26. Cook, *Fifty Years on the Old Frontier*, 19–20.

27. Local News, *North Platte Republican*, June 24, 1876.

28. Gentry, *Letters to Bob*, 187; "$50 Reward," *Western Nebraskian*, October 16, 1875.

29. Cook, *Fifty Years on the Old Frontier*, 53; *Omaha Daily Bee*, July 11, 1895.

30. Both the editorial and the news report of H. M. Stack shooting at a horse thief can be found in Local News, *Lincoln County Tribune*, August 28, 1889.

31. "Letter from Red Willow County," *Western Nebraskian*, June 10, 1876; Local News, *Western Nebraskian*, May 10, 1879; Potter, "'Wearing the Hempen Neck-Tie,'" 141, 149; "A Team Stolen," *Lincoln County Tribune*, August 28, 1889; Ellis, *Law and Order in Buffalo Bill's Country*, 65.

32. There is a vast literature on the subject of lynching. Some of the standout works include Tolnay and Beck, *Festival of Violence*, ix, 239–45; Pfeifer, *Rough Justice*; and Carrigan, *Making of a Lynching Culture*, 12–13.

33. See Hewitt, "Fatal Fall of Barrett Scott," 107–20. A lot more work can and should be done on this subject. Nebraska is currently lacking a book-length study of vigilantism within the state's borders, which is unfortunate because there are multiple countywide studies of crime in Nebraska—Ellis's

study of Lincoln County and Clare V. McKanna Jr.'s study of Douglas County, which is where Omaha is located. See McKanna, *Homicide, Race, and Justice in the American West*. A statewide survey of vigilante violence in Nebraska, when combined with a sampling of county-level crime data sets, could really shed a lot of light on the subject of late-nineteenth-century violence. For some good examples of statewide studies of vigilantism, see Leonard, *Lynching in Colorado*; Gonzalez-Day, *Lynching in the West*, which surveys lynching in California; Davis, *Goodbye, Judge Lynch*; and Bessler, *Legacy of Violence*.

34. Nebraska Prisoner Records Database, NSHS. I mined all of the prisoner data from twenty-seven western Nebraskan counties and then assigned each record (they are all undated) to a year range using the prisoner numbers. See *Nebraska Prison Records, 1870–1990*, by Gerald E. Sherard (2001).

35. Greene, *Horses at Work*, 224; McShane and Tarr, *Horse in the City*, 22–24. My own data corroborates this, as I have compiled CPI data for horse and other livestock prices during the late nineteenth century. This data is explained more fully in chap. 5.

36. See Ellis, *Law and Order in Buffalo Bill's County*, 78–79.

37. Bratt MSS, ser. 6, folder 2; also http://govdocs.nebraska.gov/epubs /h6000/b009.5215–2009.pdf.

38. "The Horseless Carriage," *Valentine Democrat*, May 28, 1896; "One Fare for Round Trip to the Omaha Races," *Nebraska Advertiser* (Nemaha City), May 28, 1897; front page, *Alliance Herald*, August 22, 1902; "Fine Weather for Cars," *Alliance Herald*, November 21, 1912.

39. "Horse Thieves in New York," *Omaha Daily Bee*, September 20, 1908.

40. "To Lynch Murderous Horse Thieves," *Omaha Daily Bee*, January 27, 1892; "Horse Thieves Hanged," *Red Cloud Chief*, July 5, 1895; "Horse Thieves in New York," *Omaha Daily Bee*, September 20, 1908; "Silence Followed Duty," *Omaha Daily Bee*, December 12, 1909; Allan D. May, "Facts and Fancies," *Falls City Tribune*, March 25, 1904.

41. "Stealing Automobiles," *Alliance Herald*, March 1, 1917; "Last Few Days Uneventful for Commissioners," *Alliance Herald*, August 23, 1921.

42. Krier, "Pioneer Justice," 72–73.

43. Gass, "Vigilantes of Eastern Nebraska," 3–18.

44. Sandoz, *Old Jules*, 6, 33.

45. For more information on the evolution of the archetypical gunfighter, see Slotkin, *Gunfighter Nation*, 3–28.

Epilogue

1. Olson and Nagle, *History of Nebraska*, 193–97; "Irrigation Canal and Lincoln County Nebraska, September, 1902," Bratt MSS, box 3, folder 3. See also Luckett, "'Nebraska Is, at Least, Not a Desert,'" 76–90.

2. See Nebraska, Lincoln County, Probate Dockets (1868–1972), vol. 11, Nebraska State Historical Society, Lincoln.

3. Bratt, *Trails of Yesterday*, 301–2.

4. Bratt, *Trails of Yesterday*, 299–300.

5. Aldrich, "Brief Reminiscences of the Soldiers Life on the Plains and in the Mountains," 47.

6. Aldrich, "Brief Reminiscences," 47; and C. E. Christiansen to Lauren Winfield Aldrich, August 21, 1935, HM 65819, Lauren Winfield Aldrich Collection.

7. "Big Turkey," in Stars, Iron Shell, Buechel, and Manhart, *Lakota Tales and Texts*, 690–91.

BIBLIOGRAPHY

Archives and Manuscript Materials

Autry Library, Autry National Institute, Los Angeles
    John Bratt Collection, 1869–1941
Cheyenne County Courthouse, Sidney, Nebraska (CCC)
    District Court Case Files
    County Court Dockets
    District Court Journals
Dawes County Courthouse, Chadron, Nebraska (DCC)
    District Court Case Files
Grant County Courthouse, Hyannis, Nebraska (GCC)
    District Court Case Files
    District Court Journals
    Northwestern Nebraska Stock Grower's Association Articles of
        Incorporation
Huntington Library, San Marino, California
    Lauren Winfield Aldrich Collection, 1848–1938
    Pierson Family Correspondence, 1850–99
    Russell, Majors and Waddell Records, 1838–1903
Lincoln County Courthouse, North Platte, Nebraska (LCC)
    District Court Case Files
    District Court Journals
    Sheriff Day Book
National Archives Building, Washington DC (NARA)
    Records of the Adjutant General's Office
    Records of the Office of the Quartermaster General
    Records of United States Army Continental Commands, 1821–1920
        (Camp Sheridan, Fort Kearny, Fort McPherson, Fort Niobrara,
        Sidney Barracks)

Nebraska State Historical Society, Lincoln, Nebraska (NSHS)
    Albinus Nance Papers, 1848–1911
    Bartlett Richards, 1862–1911
    David Cherry "Doc" Middleton Correspondence, 1849–1913
    Doc Middleton Vertical File
    E. B. Fowler Letter, 1873
    Fort McPherson, Nebraska Collection, 1854–1983
    Frank Joshua North Papers, 1840–85
    John Bratt Papers, 1842–1918
    Lincoln County, Nebraska Records, 1866–1981
    Nebraska Prisoner Records Database
    Paul Davis Riley Papers, 1936–81
    Silas Garber Papers, 1833–1905
    Thomas O'Donnell Collection, 1844–1935
Newberry Library, Chicago
    Christopher C. Augur Papers, 1780–1912
    Edward E. Ayer Collection

Published Works

"An Act to Divide a Portion of the Reservation of the Sioux Nation of Indians in Dakota into Separate Reservations and to Secure the Relinquishment of the Indian Title to the Remainder, and for Other Purposes." In *Indian Affairs: Laws and Treaties*, vol. 1: *Laws*, edited by Charles J. Kappler. Washington DC: GPO, 1904.

Adamson, Archibald R. *North Platte and Its Associations*. North Platte NE: Evening Telegraph, 1910.

Adelman, Jeremy, and Stephen Aron. "From Borderlands to Borders: Empires, Nation-States, and the Peoples in between in North American History." *American Historical Review* 104 (1999): 814–41.

Agonito, Joseph. *Lakota Portraits: Lives of the Legendary Plains People*. 1st ed. Guilford CT: TwoDot, 2011.

Alden, Wyllis. "Overland Journey to Oregon [1851]." In *The Ancestors and Descendents of Isaac Alden and Irene Smith, His Wife, 1590–1903*, edited by Harriett Chapman Fielding. Orange NJ: printed by the author, 1903. http://archive .org/stream/ancestorsdescend00fiel/ancestorsdescend00fiel_djvu.txt.

Alexander, Michelle. *The New Jim Crow: Mass Incarceration in the Age of Colorblindness*. New York: New Press, 2010.

Allen, Charles Wesley, Cloud Red, Sam Deon, and R. Eli Paul. *Autobiography of Red Cloud: War Leader of the Oglalas*. Helena: Montana Historical Society Press, 1997.

Allen, Frederick. *A Decent, Orderly Lynching: The Montana Vigilantes*. Norman: University of Oklahoma Press, 2004.

Alston, Felix, and Scott Alston. "Bronco Nell, a Woman Horse Thief." *Annals of Wyoming: The Wyoming History Journal* 76 (2004): 13–17.

Anderson, Lena Jones. "Pioneers." In *Dusting Off the Saddles, by Members of the Tri-State Old-Time Cowboys*, edited by Tri-State Old-Time Cowboys Memorial Museum. Chadron NE: B&B Printing, 1993.

Anderson, Terry Lee, and Peter Jensen Hill. *The Not So Wild, Wild West: Property Rights on the Frontier*. Stanford CA: Stanford Economics and Finance, 2004.

Aron, Stephen. *American Confluence: The Missouri Frontier from Borderland to Border State*. A History of the Trans-Appalachian Frontier. Bloomington: Indiana University Press, 2006.

———. "Frontiers, Borderlands, Wests." In *American History Now*, edited by Eric Foner and Lisa McGurr. Philadelphia: Temple University Press, 2011.

———. *How the West Was Lost: The Transformation of Kentucky from Daniel Boone to Henry Clay*. Baltimore: Johns Hopkins University Press, 1996.

Atherton, Lewis Eldon. *The Cattle Kings*. Bloomington: Indiana University Press, 1961.

Avery, Loren. *Lynchings, Legends, and Lawlessness: The Story of Historical Sidney, Nebraska*. Sidney NE: Hughes Design LLC, 2006.

Bagley, Will. *Across the Plains, Mountains, and Deserts: A Bibliography of the Oregon-California Trail, 1812–1912*. Prepared for the National Park Service. Salt Lake City: Prairie Dog Press, 2014. https://www.nps.gov/oreg/learn/historyculture/upload/nps-hrs-Biblio-Master-February2014_WillBagley.pdf.

———. *Overland West: The Story of the Oregon and California Trails*. Norman: University of Oklahoma Press, 2010.

Bancroft, Hubert Howe. *Popular Tribunals*. 2 vols. San Francisco: History Co., 1887.

———. *The Works of Hubert Howe Bancroft*. 39 vols. New York: Arno Press.

Banner, Stuart. *The Death Penalty: An American History*. Cambridge: Harvard University Press, 2002.

Bay State Livestock Co. *Description of the Bay State Livestock Co.'s Lands in Cheyenne County, Nebraska*. Omaha NE: Rees Printing, 1887.

Beal, M. D. "Rustlers and Robbers: Idaho Cattle Thieves in Frontier Days." *Idaho Yesterdays* 7 (1963): 24–28.

Becher, Ronald. *Massacre along the Medicine Road: A Social History of the Indian War of 1864 in Nebraska Territory*. Caldwell ID: Caxton Press, 1999.

Bessler, John D. *Legacy of Violence: Lynch Mobs and Executions in Minnesota*. Minneapolis: University of Minnesota Press, 2003.

Best, Jack Carson. *Doc Middleton*. Santa Fe NM: Press of the Territorian, 1966.

Bettelyoun, Susan Bordeaux, Josephine Waggoner, and Emily Levine. *With My Own Eyes: A Lakota Woman Tells Her People's History*. Lincoln: University of Nebraska Press, 1998.

Blackhawk, Ned. *Violence over the Land: Indians and Empires in the Early American West.* Cambridge: Harvard University Press, 2006.

Blackstone, William, St. George Tucker, Edward Christian, William C. Rives, Thomas Jefferson, Thomas Jefferson Library Collection (Library of Congress), and William Blackstone Collection (Library of Congress). *Blackstone's Commentaries: With Notes of Reference, to the Constitution and Laws, of the Federal Government of the United States, and of the Commonwealth of Virginia: In Five Volumes, with an Appendix to Each Volume, Containing Short Tracts upon Such Subjects as Appeared Necessary to Form a Connected View of the Laws of Virginia, as a Member of the Federal Union.* 5 vols. Philadelphia: Published by William Young Birch, and Abraham Small . . . Robert Carr, Printer, 1803. https://books.google.com/books?id=ntq0aqaamaaj&pg=pp7#v=onepage&q&f=false.

Blaug, Mark, and P. J. Lloyd. *Famous Figures and Diagrams in Economics.* Cheltenham: Edward Elgar, 2010.

Blok, Anton. *The Mafia of a Sicilian Village, 1860–1960: A Study of Violent Peasant Entrepreneurs.* Pavilion Series. Oxford: Blackwell, 1974.

Bogue, Allen G., Brian Q. Cannon, and Kenneth J. Winkle. "Oxen to Organs: Chattel Credit in Springdale Town, 1849–1900." *Agricultural History* 77 (2003): 420–52.

Bratt, John. *Trails of Yesterday.* Lincoln: University of Nebraska Press, 1980.

Bray, Kingsley M. *Crazy Horse: A Lakota Life.* Civilization of the American Indian Series. Norman: University of Oklahoma Press, 2006.

Brooks, James, and Omohundro Institute of Early American History and Culture. *Captives and Cousins: Slavery, Kinship, and Community in the Southwest Borderlands.* Chapel Hill NC: Published for the Omohundro Institute of Early American History and Culture, Williamsburg VA, by University of North Carolina Press, 2002.

Brown, Dee. *Bury My Heart at Wounded Knee: An Indian History of the American West.* 1st ed. New York: Holt, 1971.

Brown, Richard Maxwell. *No Duty to Retreat: Violence and Values in American History and Society.* New York: Oxford University Press, 1991.

———. *Strain of Violence: Historical Studies of American Violence and Vigilantism.* New York: Oxford University Press, 1975.

———. "Western Violence: Structure, Values, Myth." *Western Historical Quarterly* 24 (1993): 5–20.

Buecker, Thomas R. *Fort Robinson and the American West, 1874–1899.* Lincoln: Nebraska State Historical Society, 1999.

———. "Prelude to Brownsville: The Twenty-Fifth Infantry at Fort Niobrara, Nebraska, 1902–1906." In *African Americans on the Great Plains: An Anthology,* edited by Bruce A. Glasrud and Charles A. Braithwaite. Lincoln: University of Nebraska Press, 2009.

Burchill, John K. *Bullets, Badges, and Bridles: Horse Thieves and the Societies That Pursued Them.* Gretna LA: Pelican Publishing Co., 2014.

Burmeister, Charles A. "Six Decades of Rugged Individualism: The American National Cattlemen's Association, 1898–1955." *Agricultural History* 30 (1956): 143–50.

Burnap, William A. *What Happened during One Man's Lifetime, 1840–1920: A Review of Some Great, Near Great and Little Events [1859].* Fergus Falls MN: Burnap Estate, 1923. http://archive.org/details/whathappendduri00burn.

Calloway, Colin G. *One Vast Winter Count: The Native American West before Lewis and Clark.* History of the American West. Lincoln: University of Nebraska Press, 2003.

Carlson, Paul Howard. *The Plains Indians.* Elma Dill Russell Spencer Series in the West and Southwest. 1st ed. College Station: Texas A&M University Press, 1998.

Carrigan, William D. *The Making of a Lynching Culture: Violence and Vigilantism in Central Texas, 1836–1916.* Urbana: University of Illinois Press, 2004.

Carrington, Margaret Irvin. *Absaraka, Home of the Crows: Being the Experience of an Officer's Wife on the Plains.* 1st Bison Books ed. Lincoln: University of Nebraska Press, 1983.

Chalfant, William Y. *Cheyennes and Horse Soldiers: The 1857 Expedition and the Battle of Solomon's Fork.* 1st ed. Norman: University of Oklahoma Press, 1989.

Clark, Charles M. *A Trip to Pike's Peak and Notes by the Way [1861].* San Jose CA: Talisman Press, 1958. https://archive.org/stream/triptopikespeakn00clar/triptopikespeakn00clar_djvu.txt.

Clay, T. A. "A Call to Order: Law, Violence, and the Development of Montana's Early Stockmen's Associations." *Montana: Magazine of Western History* 58 (2008): 49–63.

Clow, Richmond L. "General Philip Sheridan's Legacy: The Sioux Pony Campaign of 1876." *Nebraska History* 57 (1976): 460–77.

Cody, William F. *An Autobiography of Buffalo Bill (Colonel W. F. Cody).* New York: Cosmopolitan Book Corp., 1920. https://archive.org/details/autobiographyofb00buff/page/n5.

Coleman, Ruby Roberts. *Pre-Statehood History of Lincoln County, Nebraska.* Bowie MD: Heritage Books, 1992.

Cook, James H. *Fifty Years on the Old Frontier as Cowboy, Hunter, Guide, Scout, and Ranchman.* New ed. Norman: University of Oklahoma Press, 1957.

Cox, Gary, and Mathew D. McCubbins. "Electoral Politics as a Redistributive Game." *Journal of Politics* 48 (1986): 370–89.

Cozzens, Peter. *The Earth Is Weeping: The Epic Story of the Indian Wars for the American West.* 1st ed. New York: Knopf, 2016.

Cronon, William. *Nature's Metropolis: Chicago and the Great West.* 1st ed. New York: Norton, 1991.

Crow Dog, Leonard, and Richard Erdoes. *Crow Dog: Four Generations of Sioux Medicine Men.* 1st ed. New York: HarperCollins, 1995.

Cummins, Sarah J. *Autobiography and Reminiscences of Sarah J. Cummins [1845].* La Grande OR: La Grande Printing Co., 1914. http://archive.org/details /autobiographyrem00cumm.

Davis, John W. *Goodbye, Judge Lynch: The End of a Lawless Era in Wyoming's Big Horn Basin.* Norman: University of Oklahoma Press, 2005.

Davis, Theodore. "A Summer on the Plains." *Harper's Monthly,* February 1868, 292–98.

Delano, Alonzo. *Life on the Plains and among the Diggings; Being Scenes and Adventures of an Overland Journey to California: With Particular Incidents of the Route, Mistakes and Sufferings of the Emigrants, the Indian Tribes, the Present and Future of the Great West.* Auburn NY: Miller, Orton & Mulligan, 1854. http://archive.org/details/lifeonplainsamon01dela.

DeLay, Brian. *War of a Thousand Deserts: Indian Raids and the U.S.-Mexican War.* Lamar Series in Western History. New Haven CT: Yale University Press, 2008.

De Steiguer, Joseph Edward. *Wild Horses of the West: History and Politics of America's Mustangs.* Tucson: University of Arizona Press, 2011.

Deverell, William Francis. *A Companion to the American West.* Blackwell Companions to American History. Malden MA: Blackwell, 2004.

DiMarco, Louis A. *War Horse: A History of the Military Horse and Rider.* 1st Westholme paperback ed. Yardley PA: Westholme, 2012.

Dixit, Avinash, and John Longregan. "The Determinants of Success of Special Interests in Redistributive Politics." *Journal of Politics* 58 (1996): 1132–55.

Drees, David James. "The Army and Horse Thieves." *Kansas History* 11 (1988): 35–53.

Dubber, Markus Dirk. *The Police Power: Patriarchy and the Foundations of American Government.* New York: Columbia University Press, 2005.

Dunham, Roger G., and Geoffrey P. Alpert. *Critical Issues in Policing: Contemporary Readings.* 6th ed. Long Grove IL: Waveland Press, 2010.

Dykestra, Robert R. "Body Counts and Murder Rates: The Contested Statistics of Western Violence." *Reviews in American History* 31 (2003): 554–63.

——. "Quantifying the West: The Problematic Statistics of Frontier Violence." *Western Historical Quarterly* 40 (2009): 321–47.

Edwards, Richard, Jacob K. Friefeld, and Rebecca S. Wingo. *Homesteading the Plains: Toward a New History.* Lincoln: University of Nebraska Press, 2017.

Ehrlich, Amy, and Dee Brown. *Wounded Knee; An Indian History of the American West.* 1st ed. New York: Holt, 1974.

Eick, Gretchen Cassel. "U.S. Indian Policy, 1865–1890, as Illuminated through the Lives of Charles A. Eastman and Elaine Goodale Eastman." *Great Plains Quarterly* 28 (2008): 27–47.

Ellis, Mark R. *Law and Order in Buffalo Bill's Country: Legal Culture and Community on the Great Plains, 1867–1910.* Law in the American West. Lincoln: University of Nebraska Press, 2007.

Elofson, Warren. "An Exceedingly Dicey Business: Frontier Horse Ranching on the Northern Great Plains." *Agricultural History* 79 (2005): 462–77.

Ewers, John Canfield. *The Horse in Blackfoot Indian Culture, with Comparative Material from Other Western Tribes.* Washington DC: GPO, 1955.

———. "Were the Blackfoot Rich in Horses?" *American Anthropologist* 45 (1943): 602–10.

Faragher, John Mack. *Eternity Street: Violence and Justice in Frontier Los Angeles.* 1st ed. New York: Norton, 2016.

Feack, John. "One-Man Mafia of the Prairies." *True* 41 (1960): 24, 25, 90–97.

Flint, Charles L. *The American Farmer: A Complete Agricultural Library, with Useful Facts for the Household, Devoted to Farming in All Its Departments and Details.* Hartford CT: R. H. Park, 1882.

Flores, Dan. "Bringing Home All the Pretty Horses: The Horse Trade and the Early American West, 1775–1825." *Montana: The Magazine of Western History* 58 (2008): 3–21.

Foucault, Michel. *Discipline and Punish: The Birth of the Prison.* 2nd Vintage Books ed. New York: Vintage Books, 1995.

Gass, Olivia. "Vigilantes of Eastern Nebraska." *Nebraska History Magazine* 14 (1933): 3–18.

Gentry, Raymond R. *Letters to Bob.* N.p.: printed by the author, 1973.

Gibson, J. Watt. *Recollections of a Pioneer [1849, 1852, 1854, 1865].* St. Joseph MO: Press of Nelson-Hanne Printing Co., 1912. http://archive.org/details /recollectionsofp00gibsrich.

Gilman, Musetta. *Pump on the Prairie: A Chronicle of a Road Ranch, 1859–1868.* Detroit: Harlo, 1975.

Glaeser, Edward L., and Claudia Dale Goldin. *Corruption and Reform: Lessons from America's Economic History.* National Bureau of Economic Research Conference Report. Chicago: University of Chicago Press, 2006.

Glasrud, Bruce A., and Charles A. Braithwaite. *African Americans on the Great Plains: An Anthology.* Lincoln: University of Nebraska Press, 2009.

Glasrud, Bruce A., and Michael N. Searles. *Buffalo Soldiers in the West: A Black Soldiers Anthology.* 1st ed. College Station: Texas A&M University Press, 2007.

Gless, Alan G. *The History of Nebraska Law.* Ohio University Press Series on Law, Society, and Politics in the Midwest. 1st ed. Athens: Ohio University Press, 2008.

Goldsby, Jacqueline Denise. *A Spectacular Secret: Lynching in American Life and Literature.* Chicago: University of Chicago Press, 2006.

Gonzales-Day, Ken. *Lynching in the West, 1850–1935.* Durham NC: Duke University Press, 2006.

Goodwyn, Lawrence. *Democratic Promise: The Populist Moment in America.* New York: Oxford University Press, 1976.

Graff, Jane. *Nebraska: Our Towns.* Seward NE: Second Century Publications, 1988.

Grant County (NE) Historical Society. *Grant County Neighbors and Friends.* N.p.: Society, 1980.

Graybill, Andrew R. *Policing the Great Plains: Rangers, Mounties, and the North American Frontier, 1875–1910.* Lincoln: University of Nebraska Press, 2007.

Greene, Ann Norton. *Horses at Work: Harnessing Power in Industrial America.* Cambridge: Harvard University Press, 2008.

Greene, Candace S., Russell Thornton, National Museum of Natural History (U.S.), and National Museum of the American Indian (U.S.). *The Year the Stars Fell: Lakota Winter Counts at the Smithsonian.* Washington DC: Smithsonian National Museum of Natural History, Smithsonian National Museum of the American Indian, and University of Nebraska Press, 2007.

Gresham, Hugh Cleveland. *The Story of Major David McKee, Founder of the Anti-Horse Thief Association.* Cheney KS: printed by the author, 1937.

Griffith, T. D. *Outlaw Tales of Nebraska: True Stories of the Cornhusker State's Most Infamous Crooks, Culprits, and Cutthroats.* Guilford CT: TwoDot, 2010.

Grinnell, George Bird. *The Fighting Cheyennes.* Civilization of the American Indian Series. Norman: University of Oklahoma Press, 1956.

Hagerty, Leroy W. "Indian Raids along the Platte and Little Blue Rivers." *Nebraska History* 28 (1947): 176–86, 239–60.

Hallwas, John E. *Dime Novel Desperadoes: The Notorious Maxwell Brothers.* Urbana: University of Illinois Press, 2008.

Hämäläinen, Pekka. *Lakota America: A New History of Indigenous Power.* Lamar Series in Western History. New Haven: Yale University Press, 2019.

———. "The Rise and Fall of Plains Horse Cultures." *Journal of American History* (2003): 833–62.

Hämäläinen, Pekka, and William P. Clements Center for Southwest Studies. *The Comanche Empire.* Lamar Series in Western History. New Haven: Yale University Press, 2008.

Hanson, Jeffrey R. "Adjustment and Adaptation on the Northern Plains: The Case of Equestrianism among the Hidatsa." *Plains Anthropologist* 31 (1986): 93–107.

Haugen, T. Josephine. "The Lynching of Kid Wade." *Nebraska History Magazine* 14 (1933): 18–34.

Hedren, Paul L. *After Custer: Loss and Transformation in Sioux Country.* Norman: University of Oklahoma Press, 2011.

———. *Great Sioux War Orders of Battle: How the United States Army Waged War on the Northern Plains, 1876–1877.* Frontier Military Series. Norman OK: Arthur H. Clark Co., 2011.

Hewitt, James W. "The Fatal Fall of Barrett Scott: Vigilantes on the Niobrara." *Great Plains Quarterly* 12 (1992): 107–20.

Historical Statistics of the United States, Earliest Times to the Present: Millennial Edition. Edited by Susan B. Carter, Scott Sigmund Gartner, Michael R. Haines, Alan L. Olmstead, Richard Sutch, and Gavin Wright. New York: Cambridge University Press, 2006.

Hobsbawm, E. J. *Bandits*. Rev. ed. New York: Pantheon Books, 1981.

———. *Primitive Rebels: Studies in Archaic Forms of Social Movements in the 19th and 20th Centuries*. Manchester: Manchester University Press, 1959.

Hoig, Stan. *White Man's Paper Trail: Grand Councils and Treaty-Making on the Central Plains*. Boulder: University Press of Colorado, 2006.

Holmes, Louis A. *Fort Mcpherson, Nebraska, Fort Cottonwood, N.T., Guardian of the Tracks and Trails*. Nebraska Heritage Series. Centennial ed. Lincoln: Johnsen Publishing Co., 1963.

Horses, Emil Her Many, George P. Horse Capture, and National Museum of the American Indian (U.S.). *A Song for the Horse Nation: Horses in Native American Cultures*. Golden CO: Fulcrum, 2006.

Hoy, Jim. "Chasing Cattle Thieves in the Flint Hills in 1899." *Kansas History* 28 (2005): 16–29.

Hudson, John C. *Making the Corn Belt: A Geographical History of Middle-Western Agriculture*. Midwestern History and Culture. Bloomington: Indiana University Press, 1994.

Hutton, Harold. *Doc Middleton: Life and Legends of the Notorious Plains Outlaw*. 1st ed. Chicago: Swallow Press, 1974.

Hutton, Mary. "An Early History of North Platte, Nebraska." Master's thesis, University of Nebraska–Lincoln, 1944.

Hyde, George E. *Spotted Tail's Folk: A History of the Brulé Sioux*. Civilization of the American Indian Series. 1st ed. Norman: University of Oklahoma Press, 1961.

Ingalls, Judge Eleazer Stillman. *Journal of a Trip to California by the Overland Route across the Plains in 1850–51*. Waukegan IL: Tobey & Co., Printers, 1852. http://archive.org/details/journalofatripto31780gut.

Isenberg, Andrew C. *Wyatt Earp: A Vigilante Life*. 1st ed. New York: Hill & Wang, 2013.

Jackson, W. Turrentine. "The Wyoming Stock Growers' Association Political Power in Wyoming Territory, 1873–1890." *Mississippi Valley Historical Review* 33 (1947): 571–94.

Jacoby, Karl. *Crimes against Nature: Squatters, Poachers, Thieves, and the Hidden History of American Conservation*. Berkeley: University of California Press, 2001.

———. *Shadows at Dawn: A Borderlands Massacre and the Violence of History*. Penguin History of American Life. New York: Penguin Press, 2008.

Johnson, Harrison. *Johnson's History of Nebraska*. Omaha: H. Gibson, 1880.

Jones, Spencer. "The Influence of Horse Supply upon Field Artillery in the American Civil War." *Journal of Military History* 74 (2010): 357–77.

Jordan-Bychkov, Terry G. *North American Cattle-Ranching Frontiers: Origins, Diffusion, and Differentiation.* Histories of the American Frontier. 1st ed. Albuquerque: University of New Mexico Press, 1993.

Kenner, Charles L. *Buffalo Soldiers and Officers of the Ninth Cavalry, 1867–1898: Black and White Together.* Norman: University of Oklahoma Press, 1999.

Kennon, Bob, and Ramon F. Adams. *From the Pecos to the Powder: A Cowboy's Autobiography, as Told to Ramon F. Adams by Bob Kennon.* 1st ed. Norman: University of Oklahoma Press, 1965.

Kirby, William. *Mormonism Exposed and Refuted; or, True and False Religion Contrasted: Forty Years' Experience and Observation among the Mormons.* Nashville: Gospel Advocate Publishing Co., 1893. http://archive.org/details /mormonismexposed00kirbrich.

Klein, Maury. *Union Pacific.* 1st ed. 2 vols. Garden City NY: Doubleday, 1987.

Knowlton, Christopher. *Cattle Kingdom: The Hidden History of the Cowboy West.* Boston: Houghton Mifflin Harcourt, 2017.

Kopf, Edwin W. "Origin, Development, and Practices of Livestock Insurance." *Proceedings of the Casualty Actuarial Society* 14, no. 3 (1928).

Krier, B. F. "Pioneer Justice." In *Collection of Nebraska Pioneer Reminiscences,* edited by Daughters of the American Revolution, Nebraska. Cedar Rapids IA: Torch Press, 1916. https://archive.org/details/collectionofnebr01daug /page/n8.

Lamm, Alan K. "Buffalo Soldier Chaplains of the Old West." In *Buffalo Soldiers in the West: A Black Soldiers Anthology,* edited by Bruce A. Glasrud and Michael N. Searles. College Station: Texas A&M University Press, 2007.

Langworthy, Franklin. *Scenery of the Plains, Mountains, and Mines: A Diary Kept upon the Overland Route to California, by Way of the Great Salt Lake. Travels in the Cities, Mines, and Agricultural District—Embracing the Return by the Pacific Ocean and Central America, in the Years 1850, '51, '52 and '53.* Ogdensburg NY: J. C. Sprague Bookseller, 1855. http://archive.org/details /sceneryofplainsm00languoft.

Lears, T. J. Jackson. *Rebirth of a Nation: The Making of Modern America, 1877–1920.* 1st ed. New York: HarperCollins, 2009.

Lee, Wayne C. *Wild Towns of Nebraska.* Caldwell ID: Caxton Printers, 1988.

Leiker, James N. "Black Soldiers at Fort Hayes, Kansas, 1867–1869: A Study in Civilian and Military Violence." In *African Americans on the Great Plains: An Anthology,* edited by Bruce A. Glasrud and Charles A. Braithwaite. Lincoln: University of Nebraska Press, 2009.

Leiker, James N., and Ramon Powers. *The Northern Cheyenne Exodus in History and Memory.* Norman: University of Oklahoma Press, 2011.

Leonard, Stephen J. *Lynching in Colorado, 1859–1919.* Boulder: University Press of Colorado, 2002.

Leonard, Zenas. *Narrative of the Adventures of Zenas Leonard, a Native of Clearfield County, Pa., Who Spent Five Years in Trapping for Furs, Trading with the*

Indians, &C., &C., of the Rocky Mountains; Written by Himself. Clearfield PA: D. W. Moore, 1839. http://archive.org/details/narrativeofadven00leon.

Lewis, Hugh M. *Robidoux Chronicles: French-Indian Ethnoculture of the Trans-Mississippi West.* Victoria BC: Trafford, 2004.

Limerick, Patricia Nelson. *The Legacy of Conquest: The Unbroken Past of the American West.* 1st ed. New York: Norton, 1987.

Lindbeck, Assar, and Jörgen W. Weibull. "Balanced Budget Redistribution and the Outcome of Political Competition." *Public Choice* 52 (1987): 273–97.

Linebaugh, Peter. *Stop, Thief! The Commons, Enclosures, and Resistance.* Oakland CA: PM Press, 2014.

Llewellyn, Karl N., and E. Adamson Hoebel. *The Cheyenne Way: Conflict and Case Law in Primitive Jurisprudence.* Buffalo NY: W. S. Hein & Co., 2002.

Luckett, Matthew S. "Cattle Associations." In *Encyclopedia of Politics in the American West,* edited by Steven L. Danver. Washington DC: CQ Press, 2013.

———. "Honor among Thieves: Horse Stealing, State Building, and Culture in Lincoln County, Nebraska, 1860–1890." Ph.D. diss., University of California–Los Angeles, 2014.

———. "'Nebraska Is, at Least, Not a Desert': Land Sales, False Promises, and Real Estate Borderlands on the Great Plains." In *The Interior Borderlands: Regional Identity in the Midwest and Great Plains,* edited by Jon Lauck, 76–90. Sioux Falls SD: Augustana Press, 2019.

———. "The Wide-Awake Citizens: Anti–Horse Thief Associations in South Central Wisconsin, 1865–1890." *Wisconsin Magazine of History* 91 (2007): 16–27.

Maher, Susan Naramore. *Deep Map Country: Literary Cartography of the Great Plains.* Lincoln: University of Nebraska Press, 2014.

Manly, William Lewis. *Death Valley in '49. Important Chapter of California Pioneer History. The Autobiography of a Pioneer, Detailing His Life from a Humble Home in the Green Mountains to the Gold Mines of California; and Particularly Reciting the Sufferings of the Band of Men, Women and Children Who Gave "Death Valley" Its Name.* San Jose CA: Pacific Tree & Vine Co., 1894. https://archive.org/details/deathvalleyinim00manlgoog.

Mattes, Merrill J. *The Great Platte River Road: The Covered Wagon Mainline via Fort Kearny to Fort Laramie.* Nebraska State Historical Society Publications. Lincoln: Nebraska State Historical Society, 1969.

McChristian, Douglas C. *Fort Laramie: Military Bastion of the High Plains.* Frontier Military Series. Norman OK: Arthur H. Clark Co., 2008.

McDermott, John D. *Circle of Fire: The Indian War of 1865.* 1st ed. Mechanicsburg PA: Stackpole Books, 2003.

McGinnis, Anthony. *Counting Coup and Cutting Horses: Intertribal Warfare on the Northern Plains, 1738–1889.* Lincoln: University of Nebraska Press, 2010.

McGrath, Roger D. *Gunfighters, Highwaymen and Vigilantes: Violence on the Frontier.* Berkeley: University of California Press, 1984.

McKanna, Clare V. *Homicide, Race, and Justice in the American West, 1880–1920.* Tucson: University of Arizona Press, 1997.

McLennan, Rebecca M. *The Crisis of Imprisonment: Protest, Politics, and the Making of the American Penal State, 1776–1941.* Cambridge Historical Studies in American Law and Society. Cambridge: Cambridge University Press, 2008.

McPherson, James M. *Battle Cry of Freedom: The Civil War Era.* Oxford History of the United States. New York: Oxford University Press, 1988.

McShane, Clay, and Joel A. Tarr. *The Horse in the City: Living Machines in the Nineteenth Century.* Animals, History, Culture. Baltimore: Johns Hopkins University Press, 2007.

Merrill, Karen R. *Public Lands and Political Meaning: Ranchers, the Government, and the Property between Them.* Berkeley: University of California Press, 2002.

Military Service Institution. "Fifth Regiment of Infantry." In *The Military of the United States: Historical Sketches of Staff and Line with Portraits of Generals in Chief,* edited by Theophilus Francis Rodenbough and William L. Haskin. New York: Maynard, Merrill & Co., 1896.

Miller, Nina Hull. *Shutters West.* Denver: Sage Books, 1962.

Monkkonon, Eric H. "Homicide in Los Angeles, 1827–2002." *Journal of Interdisciplinary History* 36 (2005): 167–83.

Monnett, John H. *Tell Them We Are Going Home: The Odyssey of the Northern Cheyennes.* Norman: University of Oklahoma Press, 2001.

Moore, Jacqueline M., and William P. Clements Center for Southwest Studies. *Cow Boys and Cattle Men: Class and Masculinities on the Texas Frontier, 1865–1900.* New York: New York University Press, 2010.

Morris, Eric Andrew. "Horse Power to Horsepower: The External Costs of Transportation in the 19th Century City." Master's thesis, University of California–Los Angeles, 2007.

Moulton, Candy. *Valentine T. Mcgillycuddy: Army Surgeon, Agent to the Sioux.* Western Frontiersmen Series. Norman OK: Arthur H. Clark, 2011.

Munkres, Robert L. "Independence Rock and Devil's Gate." *Annals of Wyoming* 40 (1968): 23–40.

———. "The Plains Indian Threat on the Oregon Trail before 1860." *Annals of Wyoming: The Wyoming History Journal* 40 (1968): 193–221.

Nebraska, State of. "Laws Passed by the Legislature of the State of Nebraska." Omaha: Omaha Daily Republican, State Printers, 1875.

Nimmo, Joseph, Jr. *Treasury Department Report on the Interior Commerce of the United States.* Washington DC: GPO, 1885.

Nobles, Gregory H. *American Frontiers: Cultural Encounters and Continental Conquest.* 1st ed. New York: Hill & Wang, 1997.

Olson, James C., and Ronald C. Naugle. *History of Nebraska.* 3rd ed. Lincoln: University of Nebraska Press, 1997.

Ostler, Jeffrey. *The Plains Sioux and U.S. Colonialism from Lewis and Clark to Wounded Knee*. Studies in North American Indian History. Cambridge: Cambridge University Press, 2004.

Paine, Bayard H. *Pioneers, Indians and Buffaloes*. Curtis NE: Curtis Enterprise, 1935.

Paul, R. Eli. *Blue Water Creek and the First Sioux War, 1854–1856*. Campaigns and Commanders. Norman: University of Oklahoma Press, 2004.

——. *The Nebraska Indian Wars Reader, 1865–1877*. Lincoln: University of Nebraska Press, 1998.

Pearce, Richard. *Women and Ledger Art: Four Contemporary Native American Artists*. Tucson: University of Arizona Press, 2013.

Pfeifer, Michael J. *Rough Justice: Lynching and American Society, 1874–1947*. Urbana: University of Illinois Press, 2004.

Postel, Charles. *The Populist Vision*. Oxford: Oxford University Press, 2007.

Potter, David M., ed. *Trail to California: The Overland Journal of Vincent Geiger and Wakeman Bryarly [1859]*. New Haven CT: Yale University Press, 1945.

Potter, James E. "'Wearing the Hempen Neck-Tie': Lynching in Nebraska, 1858–1919." *Nebraska History* 93 (2012): 138–53.

Ramsdell, Charles W. "General Robert E. Lee's Horse Supply, 1862–1865." *American Historical Review* 35 (1930): 758–77.

Red Shirt, Delphine. *Turtle Lung Woman's Granddaughter*. American Indian Lives. Lincoln: University of Nebraska Press, 2002.

Reed, Eric Melvin. "Homicide on the Nebraska Panhandle Frontier, 1867–1901." *Western Historical Quarterly* 50 (2019): 137–60.

Reid, John Phillip. *Law for the Elephant: Property and Social Behavior on the Overland Trail*. San Marino CA: Huntington Library, 1980.

——. "Principles of Vengeance: Fur Trappers, Indians, and Retaliation for Homicide in the Transboundary North American West." *Western Historical Quarterly* 24 (1993): 21–43.

Robbins, William G., and James C. Foster. *Land in the American West: Private Claims and the Common Good*. Seattle: University of Washington Press, 2000.

Roe, Frank Gilbert. *The Indian and the Horse*. Civilization of the American Indian 41. 1st ed. Norman: University of Oklahoma Press, 1955.

Roosevelt, Theodore. *Ranch Life and the Hunting-Trail*. Illustrated by Frederic Remington. New York: Century Co., 1888.

Sandoz, Mari. *Old Jules*. Bison Books ed. Lincoln: University of Nebraska Press, 2005.

——. "Tyrant of the Plains." *Saturday Evening Post*, June 7, 1958.

Savage, William W. *The Cowboy Hero: His Image in American History and Culture*. 1st ed. Norman: University of Oklahoma Press, 1979.

Schubert, Frank N. "The Violent World of Emanuel Stance, Fort Robinson, 1887." *Nebraska History* 55 (1974): 203–20.

Schusky, Ernest Lester. *The Forgotten Sioux: An Ethnohistory of the Lower Brule Reservation.* Chicago: Nelson-Hall, 1975.

Scott, James C. *Weapons of the Weak: Everyday Forms of Peasant Resistance.* New Haven CT: Yale University Press, 1985.

Shumway, Grant Lee. *History of Western Nebraska and Its People.* 2 vols. Lincoln NE: Western Publishing & Engraving Co., 1921.

Simon, Jonathan. *Governing through Crime: How the War on Crime Transformed American Democracy and Created a Culture of Fear.* Studies in Crime and Public Policy. Oxford: Oxford University Press, 2007.

Siringo, Charles A. *A Texas Cowboy; or, Fifteen Years on the Hurricane Deck of a Spanish Pony, Taken from Real Life.* New York: Sloane, 1950.

Slotkin, Richard. *Gunfighter Nation: The Myth of the Frontier in Twentieth-Century America.* New York: Maxwell Macmillan International, 1992.

Smith, Sherry L. *The View from Officers' Row: Army Perceptions of Western Indians.* Tucson: University of Arizona Press, 1990.

Spring, Agnes Wright. *Buffalo Bill and His Horses.* N.p.: Spring, 1953.

Stanberry, Lynn. "'Protect the Innocent and Bring the Guilty to Justice': The Anti–Horse Thief Association in Western Arkansas." Master's thesis, University of Arkansas, Fayetteville, 1995.

Standing Bear, Luther. *Stories of the Sioux.* New ed. Lincoln: University of Nebraska Press, 2006.

Stands in Timber, John, and Margot Liberty. *Cheyenne Memories.* Yale Western Americana Series. New Haven CT: Yale University Press, 1967.

Starita, Joe. *The Dull Knifes of Pine Ridge: A Lakota Odyssey.* New York: Putnam, 1995.

Starrs, Paul F. *Let the Cowboy Ride: Cattle Ranching in the American West.* Creating the North American Landscape. 1st ed. Baltimore: Johns Hopkins University Press, 1998.

Stars, Ivan, Peter Iron Shell, Eugene Buechel, and Paul Manhart. *Lakota Tales and Texts: Wisdom Stories, Customs, Lives, and Instruction of the Dakota Peoples.* Pine Ridge SD: Red Cloud Lakota Language and Cultural Center, 1978.

Sterns, Peter N. "Horse Thieves and Peasant Justice in Post-Emancipation Russia." *Journal of Social History* 21 (1987): 281–93.

Stewart, J. M. "Overland Trip to California [1850]." *Publications of the Historical Society of Southern California* 5 (1901): 176–85.

Stiles, T. J. *Jesse James: Last Rebel of the Civil War.* New York: Knopf, 2002.

Thissell, G. W. *Crossing the Plains in '49 [1850].* Oakland CA: printed by the author, 1901. http://archive.org/details/crossingplainsin00this.

Thompson, E. P. "The Moral Economy of the English Crowd in the Eighteenth Century." *Past & Present* 50 (1971): 76–136.

Thünen, Johann Heinrich von, and Peter Hall. *Isolated State: An English Edition of Der Isolierte Staat.* 1st ed. Oxford: Pergamon Press, 1966.

Tolnay, Stewart Emory, and E. M. Beck. *A Festival of Violence: An Analysis of Southern Lynchings, 1882–1930*. Urbana: University of Illinois Press, 1995.

Tompkins, Jane P. *West of Everything: The Inner Life of Westerns*. New York: Oxford University Press, 1992.

Trachtenberg, Alan, and Eric Foner. *The Incorporation of America: Culture and Society in the Gilded Age*. American Century Series. 1st ed. New York: Hill & Wang, 1982.

Truett, Samuel, and William P. Clements Center for Southwest Studies. *Fugitive Landscapes: The Forgotten History of the U.S.-Mexico Borderlands*. New Haven CT: Yale University Press, 2006.

Uchida, Craig D. "The Development of American Police: An Historical Overview." In *Critical Issues in Policing*, edited by Roger D. Dunham and Geoffrey P. Alpert, 17–36. Long Grove IL: Waveland Press, 2010.

Unruh, John David. *The Plains Across: The Overland Emigrants and the Trans-Mississippi West, 1840–60*. Urbana: University of Illinois Press, 1979.

U.S. Bureau of the Census. *Compendium of the Eleventh Census, 1890*. Pt. 1. Washington DC: GPO, 1892.

———. *Report on the Population of the United States at the Eleventh Census, 1890*. Washington DC: GPO, 1895.

———. *Report on the Productions of Agriculture as Recorded at the Tenth Census, 1880*. Washington DC: GPO, 1882.

———. *Report on the Statistics of Agriculture in the United States at the Eleventh Census, 1890*. Washington DC: GPO, 1892.

———. *Statistics of the Population of the United States, 1870*. Washington DC: GPO, 1872.

———. *Statistics of the Population of the United States at the Tenth Census, 1880*. Washington DC: GPO, 1882.

U.S. Geographical and Geological Survey of the Rocky Mountain Region. *Report on the Lands of the Arid Region of the United States: With a More Detailed Account of the Lands of Utah, with Maps*. 2nd ed. Washington DC: GPO, 1879.

U.S. War Department. *Annual Report of the Secretary of War, 1870*. Washington DC: GPO, 1870.

———. *Annual Report of the Secretary of War, 1872*. Washington DC: GPO, 1872.

———. *Annual Report of the Secretary of War, 1878*. Washington DC: GPO, 1878.

Utley, Robert Marshall. *Frontier Regulars: The United States Army and the Indian, 1866–1891*. The Wars of the United States. New York: Macmillan, 1973.

———. *Frontiersmen in Blue: The United States Army and the Indian, 1848–1865*. Lincoln: University of Nebraska Press, 1981.

Utley, Robert Marshall, and Wilcomb E. Washburn. *Indian Wars*. 1st Mariner Books ed. Boston: Houghton Mifflin, 2002.

Van de Logt, Mark. *War Party in Blue: Pawnee Scouts in the U.S. Army*. Norman: University of Oklahoma Press, 2010.

Waggoner, Josephine, and Emily Levine. *Witness: A Húŋkpapȟa Historian's Strong-Heart Song of the Lakotas*. Lincoln: University of Nebraska Press, 2013.

Waldrep, Christopher. *The Many Faces of Judge Lynch: Extralegal Violence and Punishment in America*. 1st ed. New York: Palgrave Macmillan, 2002.

Walker, Samuel. "'Broken Windows' and Fractured History: The Use and Misuse of History in Recent Police Patrol Analysis." In *The Police and Society*, edited by Victor E. Kappeler, 51–65. Long Grove IL: Waveland Press, 2006.

Ware, Eugene F. *The Indian War of 1864*. New York: St. Martin's Press, 1960.

Watson, George D., Jr. *Prairie Justice, 1885–1985: A One Hundred Year Legal Study of Chadron and Dawes County*. Chadron NE: B&B Printing, n.d.

Webb, Walter Prescott. *The Great Plains*. Boston: Ginn and Co., 1931.

Webster, Catherine Christensen Newman. *Memories of a Pioneer*. Crawford NE: Webster, 1957.

Welch, James. *Fools Crow*. New York: Penguin Books, 2011.

West, Elliott. *The Contested Plains: Indians, Goldseekers, and the Rush to Colorado*. Lawrence: University Press of Kansas, 1998.

Western Nebraska Tourism Coalition. "Journey to Western Nebraska." *Nebraska Life* (2018).

White, Richard. *The Middle Ground: Indians, Empires, and Republics in the Great Lakes Region, 1650–1815*. Cambridge Studies in North American Indian History. Cambridge: New York: Cambridge University Press, 1991.

———. *Railroaded: The Transcontinentals and the Making of Modern America*. 1st ed. New York: Norton, 2011.

———. *The Roots of Dependency: Subsistence, Environment, and Social Change among the Choctaws, Pawnees, and Navajos*. Lincoln: University of Nebraska Press, 1983.

———. "The Winning of the West: The Expansion of the Western Sioux in the Eighteenth and Nineteenth Centuries." *Journal of American History* 65 (1978): 319–43.

White, Richard, Patricia Nelson Limerick, James R. Grossman, and Newberry Library. *The Frontier in American Culture: An Exhibition at the Newberry Library, August 26, 1994–January 7, 1995*. Berkeley: University of California Press, 1994.

Williams, Hubert, and Patrick V. Murphy. "The Evolving Strategy of Police: A Minority View." In *The Police and Society*, edited by Victor E. Kappeler, 27–50. Long Grove IL: Waveland Press, 2006.

Williams, Joseph. *Narrative of a Tour from the State of Indiana to the Oregon Territory in the Years 1841–2*. Cincinnati: J. B. Wilson, for the author, 1843. Republished as "The Joseph Williams Tour." In *To the Rockies and Oregon, 1839–1842*, edited by LeRoy R. and Ann W. Hafen. 1955. Reprint, Fairfield WA: Ye Galleon Press, 1977. http://archive.org/stream/narrativeoftourf00willrich/narrativeoftourf00willrich_djvu.txt.

Williamson, John W. "Last Buffalo Hunt of the Pawnees." In *History of Buffalo County and Its People: A Record of Settlement, Organization, Progress and Achievement*, edited by Samuel Clay Bassett. Chicago: C. S. Clarke Publishing Co., 1916. https://archive.org/details/buffalocountyneb01bass /page/n1.

Wishart, David J. *The Last Days of the Rainbelt*. Lincoln: University of Nebraska Press, 2013.

———. *An Unspeakable Sadness: The Dispossession of the Nebraska Indians*. Lincoln: University of Nebraska Press, 1994.

Wooden, Leg, and Thomas Bailey Marquis. *Wooden Leg: A Warrior Who Fought Custer*. Lincoln: University of Nebraska Press, 1962.

Wrehe, Jeffrey. "'Thus Glory Does Fade': A History of Fort McPherson and Fort Hartsuff." Master's thesis, University of Nebraska at Kearney, 2008.

Wunder, John R. *Inferior Courts, Superior Justice: A History of the Justices of the Peace on the Northwest Frontier, 1853–1889*. Contributions in Legal Studies. Westport CT: Greenwood Press, 1979.

Wyeth, Nathaniel Jarvis. *The Correspondence and Journals of Captain Nathaniel J. Wyeth, 1831–6*. Eugene OR: University Press, 1899. The Journals of Captain Nathaniel J. Wyeth's Expeditions to the Oregon Country, 1831– 36 (Fairfield WA: Ye Galleon Press, 1997). https://user.xmission.com/ ~drudy/mtman/html/wyeth1.html.

Yost, Nellie Irene Snyder. *The Call of the Range: The Story of the Nebraska Stock Growers Association*. Denver: Sage Books, 1966.

Young, F. G., ed. "Diary of Rev. Jason Lee [1834]." *Quarterly of the Oregon Historical Society* 17 (1916). http://archive.org/details/jstor-20610036.

Zimmerman, Dwight Jon, and Dee Brown. *Saga of the Sioux: An Adaptation from Dee Brown's Bury My Heart at Wounded Knee*. 1st ed. New York: Henry Holt, 2011.

INDEX

Page numbers in italics indicate illustrations.

ers and, 181; horse thieves and, 25; protecting, 238

cattle rustlers, 153, 165, 166, 219, 231, 269; actions against, 224, 225; hanging, 25, 246; term, 26

cattle rustling, xx, 25, 142, 154, 161, 172, 177, 210, 211, 247

Caws, 46

Cedar Canyon, horse theft at, 77

Central Pacific Railroad, 73

Central Protective Association, 226

Chadron, xx, 7, 31, 32, 77, 150, 193; horse theft in, 180, 181, 182, 228–29; settlement of, 179–80, 228

Champion, Nate, 221

Cherokees, 155

Cherry County, 194, 243; African Americans in, 186

Cheyenne Agency, 123

Cheyenne Breakout, 238

Cheyenne County, xix, 2, 96, 146, 181, 187, 218; crimes in, 178, 179; horse theft in, 144–45, 171, 177–79, 206, 231; lands in, 1; population of, 145; vagrancy cases in, 189

Cheyenne County District Court, 177, 191

Cheyenne Depot, 124

Cheyenne River Agency, 120, 124

Cheyennes, xvii, 36, 39, 45, 58, 60, 76, 79, 105, 125, 130, 131; attacks by, 61–62, 72; Crows and, 40; death of, 40, 61, 71; depredations by, 97; emigrant trains and, 46; horse economy and, 33; horse herds of, 83; horse theft and, 28, 35, 37, 59, 65, 70, 75, 81, 82, 85, 110, 134, 142, 147, 278; horse worship and, 17; Julesburg siege and, 97; Lakota Sioux and, 118; law enforcement and, 129; Little Bighorn and, 119; livestock and, 62–63; Pawnees and, 45; Platte Valley War and, 81; removal of, 68, 69, 113, 137; restrictions on, 140; truce with, 99; war on, 70; withdrawal of, 61. *See also* Northern Cheyennes

Cheyenne War, 58

Chicago, Burlington, and Quincy Railroad Company, 179

Chicago and Northwestern Railroad, 179

Chief of Many Buffalo, 34, 35

Chilton, Robert, 44, 45, 47, 52

Chimney Rock, xix, 5, 44, 53

Chivington, John, 68, 69, 70, 71

Church, Wally, 180

Citizens State Bank, 183

civil cases, 105, 213, 214, 217

civilization, 23, 270, 274

Clark, Charles M., 67

Clark, William P., 134

Clayton, Robert E. Lee, 258–59

Cody, Buffalo Bill, 23, 83, 88–89, 101, 102, 134, 152, 237, 239, 271, 280; Burke accusation and, 89; horse theft and, 229; Wild West and, 169–70

Coe, J., 203

Colfer, John, 173

Colorado War, 68

Comanches, 30, 32, 47, 125; horse theft and, 16, 219; horse wealth and, 16, 18–19; Kiowas and, 37

Commentaries (Blackstone), 210

commodities, 20, 22, 26, 198, 227, 253

Comstock, William, 194

Conquering Bear, 56

The Contested Plains (West), 63

Cook, Harold, 191, 246–47

Cook, Jack, 246

Cook, James, 22, 191, 246–47, 248

Cooper, Gary, 258

Corbin, Captain, 253

Costner, Kevin, 263–64

Cottonwood Canyon, 67–68

Cottonwood Pass, 89

Cottonwood Post, 67, 69, 70, 72, 76, 88, 89, 97, 171

Cottonwood Springs, 67, 68, 69

Council Bluffs, 45–46

coup counting, 111–12, 272

Court House Rock, 48

Cowboy Bebop (movie), 265

cowboys, 13, 22, 188, 266, 272; masculinity of, 192; underemployed, 272

Crabbe, Buster, 258

Crawford, xix, 7, 32, 179, 191; horse theft in, 181, 182

Crawford, Ernst, 126, 127

Crawford, Joe, 190

Crazy Horse, 101, 106, 116, 121, 137, 241; defeat of, 118; murder of, 172; surrender of, 129

crime rates, 143, 166, 177, 180, 228, 250; horse-stealing, 174

crimes, xiii, xx, xxi, 213, 218, 225, 232, 254, 279; horse-related, 174, 270; justice for, 106; non-violent, 177; preventing, 228, 269; property, 143, 167, 173, 175, 178, 180, 217, 250–51, 268, 269; urban, 215; violent, 209

Walker, Major, 106
War Department, 92, 95, 116, 138, 139; decision-making by, 43; horse theft and, 96–97
Ware, Eugene, 87, 90, 97, 98
War of the Mormon Cow, 55–64
Waseca County Horse Thief Society, 226
Watson, Benjamin, 180
Wayne, John, 267, 271
wealth: acquiring, xiv, 212; sources of, 113; transfer of, 105
Welch, James, 264
Wesselgarter, Peter, 183, 247
Wessels, Henry, 107, 140
West, Elliot, 63
The Westerner (movie), 258, 265
Western Horse and Cattle Insurance Company (WHCIC), 199, 200
Western movies, xiv, 257–58, 267; horse thieves and, 265–66; Japanese anime, 265
Western Nebraska, 3, 233; conflict in, 65; forts/battles around, 68, 68
Western Nebraska Stock Growers Association (WNSGA), 219, 223, 224
Western Nebraska Tourism Coalition, 2
Western Nebraska Travel Coalition, 3, 7, 26
Western Nebraskian, 24, 85, 238, 247
Wharton, Henry A., 44, 45, 46, 52, 60, 61
WHCIC. *See* Western Horse and Cattle Insurance Company
Whetstone Agency, 74, 111
Whisky-Peet, 23, 25
Whistler, murder of, 36, 101–2, 103, 105, 138, 139, 140
White, Jerry, 245
White, Walter (*Breaking Bad*), 265
Whitehead, Thomas, 189
White Man's Dog, 264
White River, 6, 7, 30, 74, 78, 193
Whitman, Walt, 170
Wichitas, 32
Wilcox, John, 72

"Wild West, Rocky Mountain, and Prairie Exhibition," 169
Wilkinson, Boyd, 196
Williams, Joseph, 46
Wilson, Hooky, 166
Wilson, James A., 180
Wilson, W. A., 166
Winnebagos, 84
Winners of the West, 275
Winship, Oscar F., 58
winter counts, 30, 31, 33, 34, 34
Witcher, E., 190
WNSGA. *See* Western Nebraska Stock Growers Association
Wolf Creek, 115
Women's Dress, 137
Wood, Charles O., 79, 148
Wood, John W., 181
Wood, Reuben, 94
Wood, William, 123
Wooden Leg, xix, 29, 33, 34, 35, 36, 37, 39, 74, 118, 119–20; audiences of, 276; horse theft and, 278; medicine making by, 40
Woodward, George, 95
Wounded Knee, 124
Wyeth, Nathaniel Jarvis, 42
Wyoming Stock Growers Association (WSGA), 189, 220–22, 227

Yankton, 58, 123
Yankton Agency, 123
Yeamans, Horace, 23
Yeast, Frank, 158
Yeast, Nancy, 159
Yeast, Perry A., 155, 163, 165, 166, 222; arrest of, 157; butchering by, 156; indictment of, 158–59; reputation of, 161
Yellow Hand, 81
Yellow Kidney, 264
Yost, Nellie Snyder, 155, 159, 232; on horse thieves, 269; vigilantism and, 231

Zweifel, John, 187

CPSIA information can be obtained
at www.ICGtesting.com
Printed in the USA
LVHW092036190920
666557LV00005B/46

9 781496 205148